BIOLOGICAL BASES OF SENSATION SEEKING, IMPULSIVITY, AND ANXIETY

BIOLOGICAL BASES OF SENSATION SEEKING, IMPULSIVITY, AND ANXIETY

Edited by

MARVIN ZUCKERMAN
University of Delaware

 LAWRENCE ERLBAUM ASSOCIATES, PUBLISHERS
1983   Hillsdale, New Jersey   London

Lawrence Erlbaum Associates, Inc. Publishers
365 Broadway
Hillsdale, New Jersey 07642

Library of Congress Cataloging in Publication Data

Biological bases of sensation seeking, impulsivity and
anxiety.

Bibliography: p.
Includes index.
1. Senses and sensation. 2. Impulse. 3. Anxiety.
4. Psychobiology. I. Zuckerman, Marvin. [DNLM:
1. Arousal—Physiology. 2. Sensation—Physiology.
3. Impulsive behavior. 4. Anxiety. 5. Psychophysiology.
WL 103 B6157]

BF233.B53 1983   155.2'34   82-21137
ISBN 0-89859-255-0

Printed in the United States of America
10 9 8 7 6 5 4 3 2 1

Contents

Preface

The study of personality and specific personality traits in a truly biosocial context has suffered from the biases of the broader field of psychology. It is disheartening to observe how even recent textbooks on personality use Sheldon's somatotype theory as *the* representative of biological approaches to personality and ignore or give the briefest mention to Eysenck's (1967, 1981) theory, which rests on a broad base of empirical research developed over the last 30 years.

What is the basis of this antagonism to biological explanation? If you push them to the philosophical wall, most psychologists are basically monists, that is, they believe that thinking is a reflection of physical events in the brain. Learning, whether of expectancies or conditioned responses, is represented and stored in the brain in some kind of neurochemical arrangement. The arguments against biological theorizing (Bandura, 1977; Skinner, 1953) have been pragmatic rather than epistemological. It is said that our knowledge of the neural events that immediately precede behavior are largely unknown, therefore it is useless to conjecture about such events. Studies using brain stimulation have yielded some insights into the effect of neural events on general aspects of behavior. But we do not have to know what the specific neural pathway is for a reinforced response to appreciate the fact that certain tracts in the brain are crucial for that type of learning and that certain neurochemicals determine the functioning status of these tracts. Stein (Chapter 5) and Gray et al.'s (Chapter 6) represent the possibilities for identifying such neural systems and their neurotransmitters and for demonstrating the dependence of reinforced behavior on these systems.

The study of abnormal behavior and personality have been closely linked after Freud showed that many abnormal manifestations were not qualitatively different from normal ones and that some symptoms were an expression of broader personality trends. It is therefore ironic that at a time when psychiatry is becoming more biological, personality psychology is turning to purely social explanations for behavior. Drug treatments for psychotic disorders have generally proven to be more powerful influences on the symptoms of those disorders than psychological treatments, and it is beginning to appear that this may be true for some neurotic disorders such as agoraphobia as well. How long will it be before personality disorders are shown to be partly controllable by drugs?

The idea that personality disorders represent extreme manifestations of temperament types based on body "humors" goes back to the Greeks in the 5th century B.C. Although the idea of humors affecting human temperament or its manifestations ("the persona") is not new, the discovery of the central bioamines and their regulating enzymes and the dramatic behavioral effects of changes in the balance of these biochemicals has pointed the way toward a new understanding of normal variations in personality, as well as the pathological extremes of psychoses. This book focuses on three dimensions of personality: impulsivity, sensation seeking, and anxiety.

All of the contributors to the volume except Stein have addressed the problem of the place of impulsivity and/or sensation seeking in the basic dimensions of personality revealed by factor analyses. All of these contributors have also discussed the relation of impulsivity and sensation seeking to the dimensions of anxiety and neuroticism. The opening chapter by Eysenck deals with the evidence that these dimensions of personality are in some part genetically encoded. Eysenck's analysis is based on biometric studies of humans. Schalling's chapter also contains some biometric data on the genetics of impulsivity and sensation seeking. My chapter (2) carries this into the realm of other species (mostly rodents) in reviewing the evidence for the inheritance of an animal analogue of sensation-seeking behavior in reactions to a novel environment (the open field).

The development of impulsivity and sensation-seeking scales is discussed in Chapters 1, 2, 3, and 4 by Eysenck, Zuckerman, Barratt, and Schalling, respectively. All of these investigators have not settled for the "quick and dirty" method of scale construction but have evolved their tests over the years, constantly seeking to improve their reliability and validity in order to assess the personality constructs on which the scales are based. Behavioral and experiential correlates of their scales are described by Zuckerman, Barratt, and Schalling.

Psychophysiological correlates of sensation seeking and impulsivity are discussed by Barratt (Chapter 3) and myself (Chapter 2). These chapters include studies of orienting and defensive reflexes and augmenting of the averaged evoked potential. The idea of individual differences in an "optimal level of stimulation" continues to furnish an intermediate level of explanation, although the value of the idea of an "optimal level of arousal" has been questioned.

Barratt (Chapter 3), Schalling (Chapter 4), and Zuckerman (Chapter 2) have speculated about the role of the central monoamine systems in the traits of impulsivity and sensation seeking. Chapter 5 by Stein presents a psychopharmacological analysis of the mechanisms of a nonspecific reward system. Some of the contributors, including myself, believe that these mechanisms are an essential part of the inherited basis for the personality dimensions discussed in this book. Although Stein's analysis is based on experimental studies of rats, the limbic systems involved are also a part of the human nervous system and are presumed to play a basic role in human motivations and emotions. In fact, the major impetus for the remarkable growth of the science of psychopharmacology has been the advances in biological psychiatry and the use of psychotropic drugs in the treatment of human behavior disorders. We must also acknowledge the debt owed to nonscientists who personally experimented with various illegal drugs in the 1960s and thereby piqued the curiosity of psychopharmacologists in the mechanisms of these drugs, Stein focuses primarily on the mechanisms for reward, but he has discussed his model for anxiety elsewhere (most recently, in Stein, 1980).

Chapter 6 by Gray et al. concentrates more on the pharmacological mechanisms of anxiety and presents a challenge to Stein's view of the chemistry of reward. In addition, Gray provides a model linking the neurophysiology of reward and anxiety to human dimensions of personality. The controversy between Gray and Stein is pursued in my comments on Gray's chapter. This kind of scientific confrontation of two diametrically opposed theories is often a useful stimulus for the advancement of knowledge in an area of science. It is to be hoped that other scientists will enter this arena and resolve some of the issues raised in the debate.

Chapter 7 by Zuckerman, Ballenger, and Post presents the results of a recent study of bioamine and enzyme correlates of the three dimensions of personality described in this volume. This is the first study of such breadth in normal humans using cerebrospinal fluid, plasma, and urinary metabolites of the nonoamines and enzymes that regulate them. The results provide an initial test of some of the models presented in this book.

Chapter 8 is my attempt to summarize the data and theories presented in this volume. Other editors of books will appreciate the problems in summing up such a collection of work. It would have been preferable to have a book written in a collaborative fashion with each author addressing a common set of issues from his or her own viewpoint. But like most edited volumes, this one grew in a less coordinated fashion with some potential contributors dropping out because they could not meet the deadlines for completion of the work. This book actually grew out of a symposium at the Eastern Psychological Association meeting held in Philadelphia in 1979. But only Gray, Stein, and I are the publishing survivors from that symposium. Fortunately, the other distinguished contributors volunteered to describe their own work in this area. I believe that the resulting volume provides a reasonably current view of the biological bases of these personality dimensions.

This book should be of value to all students of personality in advanced undergraduate or graduate classes as well as their teachers. Although the focus on impulsivity, sensation seeking, and anxiety traits is too narrow to provide the only sourcebook for a course in personality, it presents an application of a biosocial approach that points the way for the future. Eysenck published a pioneering work entitled *The Biological Bases of Personality* in 1967. I predict that before long he will be revising this classic, and I further predict that the other contributors to our volume will be writing their own versions of the theme in the near future. We cannot hope to agree on our particular versions of this broad theme, but our disagreements may sharpen the issues for future research and theory.

REFERENCES

Bandura, A. *Social learning theory.* Englewood Cliffs, N.J.: Prentice-Hall, 1977.

Eysenck, H. J. *The biological basis of personality.* Springfield, Ill.: Thomas, 1967.

Eysenck, H. J. General features of the model. In H. J. Eysenck (Ed.), *A model for personality.* Springfield, IL: Springer-Verlag, 1981.

Skinner, B. F. *Science and human behavior.* New York: Macmillan, 1953.

Marvin Zuckerman
University of Delaware

BIOLOGICAL BASES OF SENSATION SEEKING, IMPULSIVITY, AND ANXIETY

1 A Biometrical-Genetical Analysis of Impulsive and Sensation Seeking Behavior

H. J. Eysenck
University of London

INTRODUCTION

The title of this chapter contains two terms that may require some preliminary discussion. The first is *biometrical-genetical analysis;* the other is *impulsive behavior.* The first term requires discussion because there have been considerable changes in the methods of genetic analysis used by professional workers in this field, although these have not been widely recognized by psychologists; a well-known article by Jinks and Fulker (1970) is probably the first introduction to these modern methods to be found in the psychological literature. Some understanding of this new methodology, which has completely replaced the traditional intraclass correlational methods of twin research, is essential for anyone who is interested in the more recent work on genetic and environmental determinants of behavior—not only because of the methodology itself, but largely because the older methods did not in fact pose or answer the kinds of questions that modern genetics is interested in. It might be true to say that much of the criticism that has been leveled at psychological twin research in the past has been justified, at least in part, because of the statistical but nongenetical way the problem was put and the answers derived. Thus, some knowledge of the more recent methods is necessary in order to discover precisely what the problem is, let alone what the answer might be.

The notion of impulsive behavior, or *impulsivity,* and of sensation seeking as personality traits requires discussion because traits acquire scientific standing and meaning only in terms of wider theories; in particular, the trait approach requires some form of hierarchical analysis (Eysenck & Eysenck,

1

1969). Thus, impulsivity has been suggested to form part of a higher order concept (extraversion), together with sociability, sensation seeking, and other traits (Eysenck, 1970); hence, it is a subordinate concept, ranking below extraversion on this scale. But impulsivity itself is not a unitary trait; it can be analyzed into four relatively separate subtraits (Eysenck & Eysenck, 1977). The same is true of sensation seeking (Zuckerman, 1974). We do not enter the debate about the usefulness of trait theory here (Eysenck & Eysenck, 1980), but instead try to relate the hierarchical structure of personality, with special reference to impulsivity and sensation seeking, to the genetic framework of the biometrical-genetical analysis of behavior, in the hope of being able to clarify the problems arising in the hierarchical structure by reference to genetic factors.

The point made here is a relatively simple one. For example, we decide that impulsivity and sociability go to make up a superfactor of extraversion because these two traits are found to covary in some relevant sample of the population (Eysenck & Eysenck, 1963; Sparrow & Ross, 1964); similarly, we decide that impulsivity itself can be broken up into four subfactors because we find that the matrix of intercorrelations defining impulsivity shows a particular pattern requiring four (interpretable) factors for reconstitution. It is clearly possible to look at the genetic determination of these factors; that is what psychologists have always tried to do, although not very efficiently. But we can also look at the contribution of genetic and environmental factors to the *covariances* emerging from the analysis; in other words, we can show to what extent the relationships between factors are determined by genetic factors (Eaves & Eysenck, 1975). This is the essentially novel contribution that the biometrical-genetical method of analysis can make to this field, and there can be little doubt that this new information is of considerable importance for an understanding of personality.

NEW METHODS OF GENETICAL ANALYSIS

As has been explained, there is a rather outmoded "classical" approach to the estimation of heritability using correlations between relatives, in particular twins, and culminating in the estimation of various ratios describing the relative importance of genetic and environmental influences on trait variation. This approach has led to ratios such as the H of Holzinger (1929), the E of Neel and Schull (1954), and the HR of Nichols (1965). This approach concentrates essentially on heritability and makes estimates of heritability based on so many unverified assumptions that their genetic meaning must remain very doubtful.

By contrast, the biometrical-genetical approach was initiated by Fisher (1918) and extended and applied by Mather and Jinks (1971); the previously mentioned paper by Jinks and Fulker (1970) has applied this approach to the analysis of human behavior. Essentially, this approach goes beyond simple estimates of heritability to an assessment of the kinds of gene action and mating system operating in the population ("genetic architecture"). From this point of view, therefore, estimates of heritability are of relatively limited importance; what is of interest is a partitioning of the total phenotypic variance into a number of genetic, environmental, and interaction factors determining their relative contribution to the total variance.

The most fundamental formula in this connection analyzes the phenotypic variance into the sum of genotypic and environmental variance: $V(P) = V(G) + V(E)$. In other words, the total phenotypic variance is the sum of the genotypic and the environmental variance. When our analysis is based on twins, the analysis of variance partitions total trait variation into two sources: that between pairs and that within. To the extent that pairs resemble each other, the mean square between (B) will be greater than that within (W), the ratio (B − W / B + W) being a measure of this resemblance known as the intraclass correlation. It is to these mean squares that we equate our genetic and environmental components $V(G)$ and $V(E)$.

However, because people are typically raised in families, the environmental part of the model must be elaborated, replacing E with *two* components. One reflects the effects of home background together with shared or common experiences; the other reflects experiences that typically differ for children even though they are reared together. These two sources of variance are commonly referred to as between-family environmental variance, or common environment (CE), and within-family environmental variance, or specific environment (SE). Thus, the total phenotypic variance is now equal to $V(G) + V(CE) + V(SE)$.

Heritability itself is best understood in terms of the components of variance that enter into it: $h^2 = \frac{V(G)}{V(P)}$. The genetic variance can be divided into four main components: $V(A)$, which is the additive genetic variance; $V(D)$, which is the nonadditive genetic variance due to dominance at the same gene loci; $V(EP)$, which is the nonadditive genetic variance due to interaction between different gene loci, called epistasis; and $V(AM)$, which is the genetic variance due to assortative mating (i.e., the increment to the total variance attributable to the degree of genetic resemblance between mates on the trait in question). This gives us a formula for the genetic variance of $V(G) = V(A) + V(D) + V(EP) + V(AM)$.

The nongenetic variance is composed of the following factors: $V(E)$, which is the additive environmental variance that is independent of the genotype; $V(GE)$, which is variance due to interaction (i.e., nonadditive effects) of genotypes and environments; $Cov(GE)$, which is the covariance of genotypes and environments, also sometimes known as correlated environments; and $V(e)$ for the error variance due to unreliability of measurements, which is traditionally mixed in with the environmental variance, although strictly speaking the formula should be rewritten to exclude this and deal with the genetic and environmental variance of the "true" score alone.

It can be seen that the general formula for phenotypic variance embraces a large number of terms and that a numerical estimate of the importance of these various terms is of much greater interest and importance than a simple estimate of the heritability. In fact, we have two heritabilities, the so-called narrow heritability (h^2_N), which is the proportion of additive genetic variance: $h^2_N = \frac{V(A)}{V(P)}$, and heritability in the broad sense (h^2), which is $\frac{V(G)}{V(P)}$ (i.e., the proportion of the total phenotypic variance that the genetic variance is). There are many other complexities attending the concept of heritability. Thus, some estimates of heritability in the broad sense include Cov(GE) in the numerator; this is done either on the assumption that the covariance is due to the genotype and/or that a particular method of estimating h^2 does not permit separation of V(G) and Cov (GE).

When we come to relating empirical data from twin studies, from familial studies, from adoption studies, from inbreeding depression, or whatever they may be to the model, we find that usually the data do not allow us to estimate all the variables in the equation. Some can be directly estimated such as assortative mating, which may be estimated by measuring the correlation between spouses on a given trait. Others may be estimated directly from social happenings, which in effect constitute a genetic experiment; thus, it is possible to estimate the importance of dominance in inbreeding depression (i.e., the lowering in scores obtained from the offspring of relatives such as cousin marriages.) Mostly, however, what is done is to conduct an analysis starting out with a very simple assumption such as all the phenotypic variances are due to between-family environmental factors (usually denoted E_2); when this is found to give a very poor fit to the data, a second variable is brought in such as the additive genetic variance (usually denoted D_R).[1] If the combination of D_R and E_2 still gives a poor fit, we may go on to introduce the within-family environmental variance (E_1) and so forth. In this way we can show that certain variables, which would be very difficult to test directly (e.g., interaction effects), are not required because a simple analysis using D_R and E_1, for example, adequately represents the empirical data.

---

[1] In terms of the nomenclature used by the Birmingham school of biometric genetics (Mather & Jinks, 1971), V(G) is equivalent to $\frac{1}{2}D_R$. The reason for calling additive variation $\frac{1}{2}D_R$ is because D refers to the variance of additive *differences* between homozygous forms in a two-allele system and the subscript R indicates that mating is at random. The coefficient, $\frac{1}{2}$, arises because only half the maximum variation from homozygous combination can arise in a random mating population.

A detailed description of the method, applied to the genetic analysis of intelligence and proceeding at a rather elementary level, is given by Fulker and Eysenck (Eysenck, 1979); the book by Mather and Jinks (1971) or their more recent, shorter introduction to biometric genetics (1977) will probably be essential for a thorough understanding of the logic, the statistics, and the methodology involved. In this section, I have only been able to introduce the concepts used and have attempted to describe the way in which the analysis proceeds; an attempt is made later at dealing with the substantive data to take this discussion further. At this point, we should merely note that the methods of biometrical-genetical analysis are not restricted to *genetic* variables. They attempt to analyze the phenotypic variation that is measured by the psychologist, whether with reference to abilities, traits, attitudes, or whatnot, into *all* the components that must theoretically be distinguished, including environmental as well as genetic components and paying particular attention to interaction, where they appear to play a part. In this inclusiveness, they differ decisively from the usual run of sociological and social psychological attempts to demonstrate the relevance or importance of environmental variance, which invariably exclude consideration of genetic factors, thus rendering the analysis impossible to interpret. We are now ready to turn to a brief discussion of the hierarchical model of impulsivity, which we then subject to our biometrical-genetical analysis.

THE HIERARCHICAL NATURE OF IMPULSIVITY

One of the central problems in personality research has been the question of whether higher order factors such as extraversion can be regarded in any meaningful sense as *unitary* or whether there are several independent factors such as "sociability" and "impulsivity," which should not be combined in the same artificial manner. Carrigan (1960) concluded her survey of the literature by saying that: "The unidimensionality of extraversion/introversion has not been conclusively demonstrated [p. 335]." She further pointed out that several joint analyses of the Guilford and Cattell questionnaires show that at least *two* independent factors are required to account for the intercorrelations between the extraversion-impulsivity variables. She suggested that these two factors might correspond to the European conception of extraversion, with its emphasis on impulsivity and weak superego controls, and the American conception, with its emphasis on sociability and ease in interpersonal relations.

As already mentioned, the quite sizeable correlations between sociability and impulsivity reported by Eysenck and Eysenck (1963) and Sparrow and Ross (1964) make untenable the view that the factors and questions are *in-*

dependent, and later work by Eysenck and Eysenck (1969) emphasizes this point. Furthermore, Eysenck and Eysenck (1967) have shown that the correlations of extraversion items (whether sociability or impulsivity) with subjects' reactions on a physiological test devised on theoretical grounds were proportional to their loadings on the extraversion factor. The recognition that extraversion is a unitary factor in behavior is self-vindicated by prediction from a psychological theory as much as by a correlation between primary factors (Eysenck, 1967).

The whole concept of "undimensionality" put forward by Carrigan (1960) seems somewhat unrealistic. Extraversion-introversion has always been conceived of as a *higher order factor* in the factor analytic sense (i.e., as being composed of a number of correlated primary factors); unidimensionality suggests a matrix of item intercorrelation of rank order, which is clearly counter to the hypothesis in question. Such unidimensionality is hardly ever found in matrices of intercorrelations between items in the psychological field, and from this point of view we must question even the unidimensionality of such concepts as sociability and impulsivity. Eysenck (1956) has demonstrated that the supposedly unifactorial "social shyness" factor of Guilford could actually be factored into two independent factors representing unsociability (i.e., a preference for not being sociable) and social anxiety (i.e., a fear of being with people). Similarly, impulsivity can be shown to be made up of several correlated factors, rather than being unidimensional.

A relevant experiment has been reported by Eysenck and Eysenck (1977). Sets of items often included in impulsivity scales were administered to three different populations, together totaling over 2000 male and female subjects. The outcome of the factor analyses of the intercorrelations between items for these various groups is detailed in the paper referred to. The first factor to emerge was called *impulsivity in the narrow sense* (Imp_N). Typical high loading items on this factor are: Do you often buy things on impulse? Do you generally do and say things without stopping to think? Are you an impulsive person? Do you often do things on the spur of the moment? Do you get extremely impatient if you are kept waiting by someone who is late?

The second factor was called *risk-taking* and included questions like the following: Do you quite enjoy taking risks? Would life with no danger in it be too dull for you? Would you do almost anything for a dare? Do you often long for excitement?

The third factor was labeled *nonplanning;* questions typical of this factor are the following: Do you like planning things carefully well ahead of time? When buying things, do you usually bother about the guarantee? Would you agree that planning things ahead takes the fun out of life? When you go on a trip, do you like to plan route and timetables carefully?

The fourth factor was labeled *liveliness,* and some typical questions included the following: Do you usually make up your mind quickly? Are you slow and unhurried in the way you move? Do you prefer to "sleep on it" before making decisions? Can you put your thoughts into words quickly?

We thus obtain a picture that gives a *hierarchical* representation of the ordering of the items into primary and higher order factors. This picture is oversimplified in several ways. In the first place, even the four factors at the bottom of the picture are hardly "unidimensional" in the sense in which the term is used by Carrigan (1960); if we factor analyze a large number of items falling under any of the four categories here, we would almost certainly be able to show that the matrix of intercorrelations was not of rank one, that each factor in turn could be subdivided into smaller subfactors, and so on ad infinitum. There would presumably be little interest in doing this, but the possibility has to be borne in mind.

At the other end, it cannot be assumed that extraversion is the only superfactor that is involved with impulsivity; there are other superfactors such as neuroticism and psychoticism (Eysenck & Eysenck, 1969, 1976), and the possibility must be recognized that these may play some part in determining impulsive behavior. Furthermore, it is possible that these other superfactors show different correlations with the four subfactors of impulsivity. Eysenck and Eysenck (1963) already found that impulsivity had a moderate positive correlation with neuroticism, while sociability had a moderate negative correlation with neuroticism. The first detailed study to look at the intercorrelations between the four impulsivity subfactors and the P, E, and N superfactors is the one reported by Eysenck and Eysenck (1978). The main results are as follows. Impulsivity (Imp_N) is closely related to P and N (positively) and to L (negatively). (The L scale was originally designed as a lie or dissimulation scale, but it also seems to measure conformity in social relations.) Eysenck and Eysenck (1978) report: "Impulsiveness in its narrow form is apparently a somewhat pathological trait which is essentially unrelated to E in its pure form."

Risk-taking shows a clear relationship (positive) with extraversion and an almost equally clear one with P. It is doubtful if there is any relationship with N or L, as figures differ for different samples. Nonplanning is related positively to P and negatively to N; of the two semipathological groups, it appears that pseudoneurotics plan, whereas pseudopsychotics do not. This is perhaps what one would have expected on a priori grounds and in view of what is known about their pathological components. There is no obvious relationship with E or with L.

Liveliness clearly correlates with E (positively) and with N (negatively). It does not seem to relate at all with P or L. Again, these results are not surprising in the light of previous work and common sense. Clearly, the system of relationships between "primary" and higher order factors is complex.

There also seem to be some relationships between some of the aspects of impulsivity (particularly, perhaps, risk-taking) and venturesomeness or sensation seeking (Zuckerman, 1974). Zuckerman's factor, too, breaks up into four subfactors, but just looking at general impulsivity and general venturesomeness Eysenck and Eysenck (1978) have found correlations between these two concepts of .41 for males and .32 for females. Both venturesomeness and impulsivity correlated positively with psychoticism and extraversion, but although venturesomeness correlated negatively with neuroticism, impulsivity correlated positively with it.

We now have a rough picture of the hierarchical position of the different aspects of impulsivity within a more general system of personality description and its relationship with sociability, venturesomeness, and various higher order factors. We must now turn to look at the genetic links between these various concepts, insofar as they have been elucidated in recent research.

IMPULSIVITY AND SOCIABILITY

In the first of a series of studies reporting on the inheritance of personality traits, Eaves and Eysenck (1975) reported on a genetic analysis of extraversion, with particular reference to the composition of this type of construct in terms of impulsivity and sociability. The analysis was based on the response of 837 pairs of adult volunteer twins to an 80-item personality inventory. Of these items, 13 formed a scale of sociability, and 9 were items to provide a measure of impulsivity. The relevant items are given in Table 1.1. Twins were diagnosed for zygosity, and a sample of dizygotic twins of unlike sex was included in the study because it provides a critical test of sex limitation. Raw scores of the twins were standardized on both sociability and impulsivity by dividing the scores by the corresponding within-group standard errors. The inheritance of E was studied by analyzing the mean squares derived from the subjects' total scores on the two standardized tests. Certain assumptions were made to enable the analysis to proceed; these are outlined in the article and are, in part, testable.

Resting upon the six assumptions made, a model was developed for the *mean squares* for pairs of monozygotic (MZ) and dizygotic (DZ) twins in terms of an additive genetic component (D_R) and a within-family environmental component (E_1). The analysis showed that this model gave an excellent fit to the data; clearly both D_R and E_1 are highly significant components of the variation in extraversion. In this, E is similar to other personality traits that have been subjected to similar analyses (Eaves & Eysenck, 1977); unlike intelligence, nonadditive genetic components like assortative mating and dominance play little if any part in the genesis of personality, and neither does E_2, the between-family environmental variance.

TABLE 1.1
Personality Inventory Items Referring to Sociability and
Impulsiveness Included in the Genetic Analysis

Item	Key
18. Do you suddenly feel shy when you want to talk to an attractive stranger?	-S
23. Generally, do you prefer reading to meeting people?	-S
27. Do you like going out a lot?	+S
30. Do you prefer to have few but special friends?	-S
36. Can you usually let yourself go and enjoy yourself a lot at a gay party?	+S
40. Do other people think of you as being very lively?	+S
44. Are you mostly quiet when you are with other people?	-S
48. If there is something you want to know about, would you rather look it up in a book than talk to someone about it?	-S -S
56. Do you hate being with a crowd who play jokes on one another?	-S
66. Do you like talking to people so much that you never miss a chance of talking to a stranger?	+S
69. Would you be unhappy if you could not see lots of people most of the time?	+S
75. Do you find it hard to really enjoy yourself at a lively party?	-S
77. Can you easily get some life into a rather dull party?	+S
1. Do you often long for excitement?	+I
4. Are you usually carefree?	+I
8. Do you stop and think things over before doing anything?	-I
12. Do you generally say things quickly without stopping to think?	+I
16. Would you do almost anything for a dare?	+I
20. Do you often do things on the spur of the moment?	+I
33. When people shout at you, do you shout back?	+I
59. Do you like doing things in which you have to act quickly?	+I
62. Are you slow and unhurried in the way you move?	-I

Note: S denotes an item scored for sociability, I for impulsiveness; + indicates that
"yes" scored 1, and - indicates that "no" scored 1 for scale under construction.

Inasmuch as all the genetic variation is additive, there is no need to distinguish between "broad" and "narrow" heritability. When corrected for the unreliability of the scales, this heritability turned out to be .57; in other words, some 57% of the "true" variation in extraversion may be attributed to genetic causes. If the genetic model is in fact appropriate, it should enable us to predict the correlations between other degrees of relatives for extraversion. For parents and offspring, for example, we would expect a correlation of $\frac{1}{2}h^2 = .21$. Such data as are available suggest that the observed correlation is somewhat lower but not significantly so. Such a difference, if it turned out to be significant, might be attributed to the interaction of the genotypic difference between individuals with an overall difference between the environments of parents and offspring or to the fact that our estimate of the heritability is somewhat biased by undetected common environmental effects. A common environmental effect that accounted for about 10–15% of the total variance might explain the disparity and is more likely than not to be undetected in the twin study.

We must now turn to the analysis of the discrimination scores between sociability and impulsivity. Here, too, the simple model can be shown to work, D_R and E_1 leaving no significant residual. This means that the discrimination between sociability and impulsivity is justified in genetic terms. Apparently not all the genetic factors contributing to variation in sociability and impulsivity contribute equally and consistently to both, and the heritability of the interaction, shorn of the unreliability, amounts to .72. The data suggest that the positive covariation of sociability and impulsivity has both a genetic and environmental basis. It is possible to estimate separately the genetic and environmental components of the variation and covariation of sociability and impulsivity, and this was the next step in the analysis. Estimates for the *reliable* variance, which is due to genetic causes, are .61 for sociability and .60 for impulsivity. This finding is in agreement with that of Claridge, Cauter, and Hume (1973), who also report apparent genetic components of variation for both scales. There is no evidence for nonadditive genetic variation, and no evidence for common environmental effects.

We can now turn to the covariance of sociability and impulsivity, which also has both a genetic and environmental basis. The extent to which the two traits may be regarded as sharing common genetic and environmental factors is represented by the genetic and environmental correlations r_{D_R} and r_{E_1}, respectively:

$$r_{D_R} = D_{RS,I} / (D_{RS} \cdot D_{RI})^{1/2}$$
$$= .42$$
$$r_{E_1} = E_{1S,I} / (E_{1S} \cdot E_{1I})^{1/2}$$
$$= .32$$

Variation due to unreliability contributes to E_1 but not to D_R so we might expect the observed environmental correlation to be less than the genetic correlation. These correlations are a little less, though not considerably less, than the phenotypic correlation of .468 reported for sociability and impulsivity by Eysenck and Eysenck (1969).

If we may assume that the unreliability components of sociability and impulsivity are uncorrelated, it is possible to correct the estimate of r_{E_1} for unreliability; when this is done, r_{E_1} is .66. This indicates that the unitary nature of extraversion is clearly evident in the environmental determinants of the trait, even though the genetic correlation between sociability and impulsivity is rather less. As Eaves (1973) had suggested on the basis of a multivariate genetic analysis of monozygotic twins: "The apparently unitary nature of extraversion at the phenotypic level could be due to environmental rather than to genetical influences [p. 280]." However, such a finding needs clarification. As Eaves and Eysenck (1975) point out:

It does not necessarily support the view that extraversion is an "environmental mold" trait, to use the conception of Cattell, that is, a trait which reflects the structure of environmental influences inherent in the environment itself. We may obtain exactly the same picture because the organism, by virtue of the integration of its nervous system, *imposes* a unitary structure on externally unstructured environmental influences contributing to the development of behaviour [p. 110].

We may conclude that about 60% of the total reliable variation for sociability, impulsivity, and extraversion is due to hereditary causes. Both genetic and environmental factors contribute to the covariation of sociability and impulsivity, with the genetic correlation between the two factors being .42 and the environmental correlation being .65 after correction for unreliability. Combining sociability and impulsivity scores by addition to provide a measure of extraversion provides the most powerful single means of discriminating between individuals with respect to the genetic and environmental determinants of their responses to the sociability and impulsivity items of the questionnaire. The interaction between subjects and tests has a significant genetic component, so there is some justification for regarding sociability and impulsivity as distinguishable genetically. The fact that some 60% of the "reliable" variation is genetically determined does not, of course, suggest which genes are involved nor what may or may not be done to modify the trait. It does, however, suggest that the segregation and recombination of alleles may be a primary cause of variation in the dimensions of personality under discussion.

THE GENETICS OF DIFFERENT TYPES OF IMPULSIVITY

As pointed out earlier, Eysenck and Eysenck (1977) have suggested that impulsivity is capable of resolution into four correlated primary factors (impulsivity in the narrow sense, nonplanning, risk-taking, and liveliness). Of interest now is the psychogenetic study of these four factors and their interrelations. Eaves, Martin, & Eysenck (1977) conducted an experiment with 588 pairs of twins, of whom 75 were unlike sex pairs and the rest were divided between male and female MZ and DZ twins of like sex. All were circulated with a 52-item impulsivity questionnaire, of which 40 were selected as best representing the four component factors of impulsivity. Examples of these items have already been given.

The fundamental data for the analysis were the mean squares and mean products between and within pairs, computed for the four variables for each of the four like-sex twin groups separately. For the male–female pairs, the mean vector corresponding to the overall sex difference was also extracted from the intrapair variation. For each of the five twin groups, the linear age regression was partialed out of the variation and covariation between pairs. The age correction thus excludes from the variation between pairs any general linear trend with age but does not extract any interaction between age differences or genetic or environmental differences. Eaves and Eysenck (1976) have shown that such interactions may be detected in principle if they have a systematic component; otherwise they will remain confounded with the main effects of the genetic and environmental influences but do not constitute a major problem for the interpretation of individual differences.

The model adopted in this study (Eaves, Martin, & Eysenck, 1977) was the one found suitable in the Eaves and Eysenck (1975) study (i.e., one involving primarily the additive effects of many genes and the effects of environmental influences that were largely specific to individuals rather than common to families). The consistency over sexes of particular estimates in this study and the ability of the model to encompass data on unlike-sex pairs without additional parameters suggested that the causes of variation in extraversion and its components did not depend substantially on sex. The model assumes that the phenotypic variation for the four impulsivity traits may be related to a fairly simple model invoking a single factor common to the four variables (impulsivity in the broad sense) and components specific to each of the variables. Thus, by combining the simple causal model for impulsivity advanced by Eaves and Eysenck (1975) with the simple factorial model proposed by Eysenck and Eysenck (1977), it was proposed to discover whether the factorial unity of impulsivity applies with equal force to the genetic and environmental determinants of the traits.

The methodology used was an adaptation of that proposed in several papers by Jöreskog (1973), and the approach is described more fully by Martin and Eaves (1977). Details of this approach are contained in the original paper by Eaves, Martin, and Eysenck (1977) and need not be discussed at length in this chapter.

When the model was fitted, it turned out to give a relatively poor fit, although the departure from the model was barely significant ($p = .097$). Several modifications of the model were tried, without giving any very great improvement. Finally, by a process of tentative model fitting to the data on sexes separately, but leaving out the unlike-sex pairs, an indication was found that, although the factor loadings seem fairly consistent over sexes, the values obtained for the specific variances, especially the specific genetic variances, differed quite markedly between males and females. This suggested that the genetic determinants of trait-specific variation were different in the two sexes. If this were the case, one might expect the common factors to contribute to the covariation of male–female pairs, but it might also be expected that specific genetic variances would take different values in males and females and make no contribution to the covariance of unlike-sex twins. Thus, a final model was fitted, which differed from the initial model only in that specific genetic variances were fitted, which depended on sex, with the further specification that these were genetically quite distinct in the two sexes. This amounts to saying that the genetic component of the trait-specific variation can be best approximated by a model that assumes quite different genes are expressed in males from those expressed in females.

This model gives a very good fit to the data and, accordingly, was adopted. The maximum likelihood estimates for parameters of the final model allowing for the apparent effect of sex-limitation on specific genetic variation are given in Table 1.2. It can be seen that the estimate of the genetic-specific variance for the risk-taking factor is zero for males. This ac-

TABLE 1.2
Maximum-likelihood Estimates for Parameters of the Final Model
Allowing for the Inherent Effects of Sex-Limitation on the Specific
Genetical Variation in Impulsivity Sub-Scales

	Factor loadings		Specific standard deviations		
			Genetical		Environmental
Trait	Genetical	Environmental	Female	Male	
IMPN	0.161	0.142	0.188	0.180	0.181
	(0.012)*	(0.010)	(0.021)	(0.030)	(0.009)
RISK	0.158	0.140	0.189	0.189	0.200
	(0.012)	(0.010)	(0.022)	(28.658)	(0.009)
NONP	0.118	0.105	0.143	0.123	0.149
	(0.009)	(0.008)	(0.017)	(0.025)	(0.007)
LIVE	0.127	0.113	0.245	0.284	0.274
	(0.013)	(0.011)	(0.027)	(0.037)	(0.011)

*Estimated standard errors given in parentheses.

counts for the very large standard error of the estimate and suggests either that there is truly no specific genetic variance for this aspect of impulsivity in males or that in this one instance an alternative explanation of individual differences is warranted. However, because the overall fit of the multi-variate genotype-environment model is good, it would not be expedient to explain away such a specific anomaly, which could have arisen by chance. It seems likely that on repetition of the experiment this value would have to be revised upward.

The data show that the results are consistent with the view that the covariance structure of impulsivity is due to a single underlying factor that is affected jointly by genetic and environmental effects. The fact that the genetic and environmental loadings are proportional to one another demonstrates, in effect, that the ratio of variation due to common genetic factors to that due to the common environmental factor is consistent over all variables. Thus, there is a common factor, which may be called impulsivity in the broad sense, whose heritability is a simple function of the ratio, b, of the genetic and environmental loadings, given that the model fits. The fact that b differs significantly from zero indicates that the genetic loadings are jointly significant and justifies attempts to estimate the proportion of the common factor variance that is due to genetic factors.

We are now in a position to discover the heritability of the specific variance, corrected for measurement errors, for males and females separately. For impulsivity in the narrow sense the heritability is .57 for males and .60 for females. For risk-taking the values are .00 and .54; as already explained, the value for males is almost certainly in error and would probably be raised substantially if the experiment were repeated on a different sample. For nonplanning the values are .88 and .91, respectively, and for liveliness they are .55 and .48. In every case, rather more than half of the measurable specific environmental variation within families seems to be attributable to errors of measurement, and as Eaves, Last, Martin, & Jinks (1977) say: "In the case of the non-planning factor, we conclude that virtually all the detectable specific environmental variation is due to sampling errors in the scores [p. 36]."

Table 1.3 gives a summary of the relative contributions of common and specific genetic and environmental effects of the total variation in each of the components of impulsivity. In this table, error variation has not been deducted from the contribution of specific environmental factors, thus inflating these effects as compared with the genetic effects. Many other summary statistics can of course be derived from the estimates in Table 1.3, in-

TABLE 1.3
Summary of the Relative Contributions of Common and
Specific Genetical and Environmental Effects to the Total
Variation in Each of the Components of Impulsiveness

Sex	Trait	Proportion due to genetical effects			Proportion due to environmental effects		
		Common	Specific	Total	Common	Specific*	Total
Female	IMPN	0.155	0.211	0.366	0.241	0.392	0.633
	RISK	0.139	0.218	0.357	0.199	0.444	0.643
	NONP	0.138	0.219	0.357	0.203	0.440	0.643
	LIVE	0.064	0.101	0.165	0.238	0.596	0.835
Male	IMPN	0.158	0.245	0.404	0.197	0.399	0.596
	RISK	0.173	0.000	0.173	0.272	0.554	0.827
	NONP	0.146	0.231	0.377	0.158	0.465	0.623
	LIVE	0.059	0.094	0.153	0.296	0.551	0.847

*Error variation has not been deducted from the contribution of specific environmental factors.

cluding traditional heritability estimates for the individual variables. Adding together the contributions from the genetic and environmental common factor yields the familiar communality estimate for each variable. Adding the genetic contributions due to common and specific variance for each variable in turn, we have the usual heritability estimate applicable to each variable as it would be derived in any equivalent univariate analysis of the individual scales.

Eaves, Martin, and Eysenck (1977) make a particular point in their conclusion that:

> The specific application presented here should not be allowed to obscure the generality of our approach. Given adequate family groupings and sufficiently strong psychological expectations, it is possible to formulate and test a psychogenetical model for individual differences which embodies both the causal and psychological components of any theory of individual differences. . . . Even within the scope of our simple example we have seen some of the flexibiliy of the method because we have been able to decide between a model which allows for sex-limitation of the expression of the gene loci responsible for specific variation and one which assumes that the same specific gene effects operate in both sexes. We have been able to show that the genetical loadings can be regarded as constant multiples of the environmental loadings, and that the contribution of the common factors to trait covariation is consistent over sexes. . . . Providing the investigator possesses the ingenuity to write the appropriate model and collect the right data, the possibilities for the causal analysis of trait covariation in quantitative genetical terms seem extensive [p. 196].

THE GENETICS OF DIFFERENT TYPES
OF SENSATION SEEKING

The concept of *sensation seeking* can be broken down into four subscales (Zuckerman, 1974), and the concept as a whole has been found to relate both to extraversion and psychoticism (Eysenck & Eysenck, 1978). Because of the established strong heritability of these dimensions of personality and because of the relation between sensation seeking and physiological variables (Neary & Zuckerman, 1976; Zuckerman, Murtaugh, & Siegel, 1974), as well as the existence of biochemical correlations with level of gonadal hormones and level of platelet monoamine-oxidase (Murphy, Belmaker, Buchsbaum, Martin, Ciaranello, & Wyatt, 1977), it seems likely that genetic factors are involved in the establishment of individual differences in sensation seeking. Genetic studies of sensation seeking and physiological and biochemical correlates have given positive results (Buchsbaum, 1974; Nies, Robinson, Lamborn, & Lampert, 1973).

Fulker, Eysenck, and Zuckerman (1980) have carried out an analysis of the responses of 422 pairs of adult volunteer twins to the sensation-seeking questionnaires, with scores on each of the four subscales being based on answers to 10 questions. There are four subscales in the questionnaire, each measuring a different aspect of sensation seeking: Disinhibition (DIS), Thrill and Adventure Seeking (TAS), Experience Seeking (ES), and Boredom Susceptibility (BS). Composition of the twin sample to whom the questionnaires were given was very much the same as in the studies already described in previous sections. Systematic age and sex effects were observed and controlled where necessary in the analysis.

A simple D_R and E_1 model was fitted to the total score mean squares, and the highly significant estimate of both D_R and E_1 combined with the non-significant residual chi-square indicates an excellent fit for the simple model. It seemed likely, therefore, that the assumptions underlying this model were not seriously in error and that variation for sensation seeking is under the control of a predominantly additive gene action. In spite of the large sex differences in mean score, variation in both men and women would appear to be controlled by the same genetic system. It is interesting to note that here, as is so often the case in connection with personality variables, shared environmental influences seem to play no part in defining individual differences in sensation seeking.

The proportional variation that is heritable is 58%; this figure is quite high for a personality variable and indicates a substantial constitutional component in sensation seeking. The remaining variation, 42% due to E_1, might also in part be constitutional, although we are not able to tell. Consequently, 58% sets the lower limit for the importance of constitutional factors. When unreliability variance is taken into account, heritability of sensation seeking is increased to 69%; thus, *about 70% of reliable variance of the underlying trait appears to be genetic in origin,* a high figure that approaches that for tests of cognitive abilities.

Next, Fulker et al. (1980) proceeded to investigate the contribution of the four scales separately by means of subject × subscale interaction. The assumption is that if the four scales contribute unequally toward the subject's total score, this form of interaction will be present. In other words, the same total optimal level of sensation might be achieved in a variety of ways. Analysis suggested that the genes controlling subscale interaction are acting very differently in the two sexes, thus necessitating a more complex analysis than had at first been attempted. The evidence suggests that *subscale profiles are largely under the control of different genes in the two sexes.* The alternative explanation, that the same genes are in control but express themselves differently in the two sexes, seems unlikely for reasons discussed by Fulker et al. (1980). In any case, whichever interpretation is correct, there is an important constitutional difference determining the subscale profiles of men and women.

Next, the authors turn to an analysis of covariation of the four sensation-seeking subscales. Applying the underlying assumptions of the simple D_R, E_1 univariate models to the multivariate ones, the genetic covariance parameters define components of pleiotropy with precise biometric expectations, with the covariances defining the extent to which the same genes underly more than one trait. Fitting the model produced significant additive and environmental covariation. The major part of the genetic covariation, about 60%, is due to a general factor loading positively on all four subscales, and the remainder is due to a bipolar factor representing the interaction of additive variation with sex.

The authors do not, as they might have, calculate the contributions to the variance of the four subscales of genetic and environmental determinants, once the general sensation-seeking factor had been eliminated. This makes it impossible to compare this study with the preceding one, which analyzed out these components for the different types of impulsive behavior. For the purpose of this chapter, Tables 1.4 and 1.5 have been calculated to provide this information. Table 1.4 gives the maximum likelihood estimates for

TABLE 1.4
Maximum-Likelihood Estimates for Parameters of the Final
Model Allowing for the Inherent Effects of Sex-Limitation of the
Specific Genetical Variation in Sensation Seeking Subscales

| | Factor loadings | | Specific standard deviations | | |
| | | | Genetical | | Environmental |
	Genetical	Environmental	Female	Male	
DIS	.175	.248	.236	.311	.000
	(.030)*	(.011)	(.022)	(.034)	(.157)
TAS	.212	.048	.253	.262	.260
	(.024)	(.015)	(.026)	(.044)	(.009)
ES	.264	.046	.676	.089	.161
	(.025)	(.011)	(.083)	(.089)	(.006)
BS	.104	.095	.195	.233	.194
	(.023)	(.012)	(.018)	(.031)	(.007)

*Eliminated standard errors given in parenthesis

parameters of the final model allowing for the inherent effects of sex limitation on the specific genetic variation, and Table 1.5 gives a summary of the relative contributions of common and specific genetic and environmental effects to the total variation in each of the components of sensation seeking. It should be noted that in this case, unlike that of impulsivity, genetic, and environmental loadings were not constrained to be a simple ratio of each other because this model gave a substantially poorer fit than one not retaining this proportionality.

It can be seen that the total (i.e., common + specific) genetic variance for the four subscales is quite high, both for men and women. Furthermore, the genetic contribution is proportionate for the two sexes: ES has the highest

TABLE 1.5
Summary of the Relative Contributions of Common and Specific
Genetical and Environmental Effects to the Total Variation in
each of the Components of Sensation-Seeking

		Proportion due to genetical effects			Proportion due to environmental effects		
		Common	Specific	Total	Common	Specific*	Total
Female	DIS	.147	.266	.413	.588	.000	.588
	TAS	.180	.258	.438	.018	.544	.562
	ES	.528	.043	.571	.032	.396	.428
	BS	.076	.268	.344	.126	.529	.655
Male	DIS	.123	.386	.509	.492	.000	.492
	TAS	.177	.271	.448	.018	.534	.552
	ES	.519	.059	.578	.032	.389	.421
	BS	.068	.343	.411	.113	.475	.588

*Error variation has not been deducted from the contribution of specific environmental factors.

and BS has the lowest genetic contribution. ES also has the highest and BS the lowest genetic contribution the common variance. Clearly, the different aspects of sensation seeking do not cohere very well, with BS hardly seeming to belong genetically to the same superfactor. The total genetic variance for the sensation-seeking subscores is somewhat higher than that for the impulsivity subscores, but not too much importance should be attributed to these differences in the absence of replication. What cannot be doubted in that genetic factors play an important part in the genesis of both sets of four subscores, a part underestimated in the figures given in Table 1.3 and 1.5 because no correction has been made for unreliability of the scores. On any reasonable correction, genetic variance would be well in excess of .50 for all the scores.

P, E, N, L, AND THE IMPULSIVITY
AND SENSATION SEEKING FACTORS

In the preceding sections we have looked at the genetic determination of impulsivity and sociability as component factors of extraversion and at the genetic and environmental determinants of the four separate impulsivity factors. In this section we take up the question of the relationship between these four impulsivity factors and the higher order personality factors of P, E, N, and L. We also look at the four subfactors that make up Zuckerman's sensation-seeking scale and inquire about their relationship to both the impulsivity factors and the superfactors (Martin, Eaves, & Fulker, 1979).

As pointed out in the previous section, Zuckerman's sensation-seeking scale has been broken down into four subfactors called Disinhibition (Dis), Thrill and Adventure Seeking (TAS), Experience Seeking (ES), and Boredom Susceptibility (BS); the genetic and environmental covariance between these four factors has been explored by Fulker et al. (1980). There is good reason to believe that some of the subscales of the sensation-seeking questionnaire would have common variance with E, and possibly some of the other superfactors in the Eysenck model.

The analysis of the data was based on 430 pairs of twins, ranging in age from 16–73 with a mean of 31. An angular transformation was applied to the raw scores for each factor to improve the additive properties of the scales. Between- and within-mean products matrices were corrected for linear regression in age, which leads to a reduction of their degree of freedom by one. The within mean product matrix for DZ opposite-sex pairs was corrected for the mean difference between males and females, thus reducing its degrees of freedom by one also.

As before, a simple model was used for the sources of variation in the data, invoking only individual environmental experiences (E_1) and additive gene action (D_R). This model was fitted to females and males separately for each of the variables in the study, giving an adequate explanation in all cases except ES in males, and only in that case and L for both cases did a model incorporating the between-families environmental component (E_2) give a marginally better fit.

As a first step preceding the fitting of models of covariation, the observed correlations (age corrected) for males and females were calculated (see Table 1.6). With some exceptions, the correlations are remarkably consis-

TABLE 1.6
Observed Phenotypic Correlations between Traits[a]

	1	2	3	4	5	6	7	8	9	10	11	12
IMPN	100	41	36	30	34	36	20	-23	31	19	15	27
RISK	36	100	37	24	28	29	00	-13	38	46	21	31
NONP	40	43	100	23	33	17	-09	-14	23	23	31	20
LIVE	18	21	13	100	03	42	-23	-07	17	19	14	12
P	24	34	31	00	100	07	09	-29	25	11	20	24
E	20	27	07	34	-04	100	-21	-08	26	17	08	16
N	33	08	-01	-22	06	-14	100	-07	10	-14	-03	01
L	-15	-07	-09	00	-25	-04	-13	100	-25	-17	-27	-13
DIS	17	37	20	11	30	29	10	-26	100	26	42	44
TAS	-02	42	16	08	09	16	-24	-05	23	100	39	18
ES	05	27	35	02	30	12	-10	-10	36	27	100	23
BS	17	33	29	12	29	10	06	-01	41	04	22	100

[a]Females, Upper Triangle (620d.f.); Males, Lower Triangle (214 d.f.). Decimal Points Omitted.

tent between the sexes, which leads one to believe that the same factor structures could be fitted in males and females. The intercorrelations between P, E, N, and L are low except for the consistent negative correlation between P and L, which has been noted in other studies (e.g., Martin & Eysenck, 1976).

When tested, the simple E_1, D_R model was found to fit rather poorly. A likely cause of failure, suggested by previous analyses, was that for some of the characters under study the genetic control of variation might differ in males and females. It has already been pointed out in regard to the impulsivity data that, although the genetic covariation could be explained by the same common factor in both sexes, the specific genetic variation was controlled by different genes in males and females. Fulker et al. (1980) found a similar phenomenon in their analysis of the sensation-seeking data, where subscore profiles showed a different pattern of inheritance in males and females. When this new model was tested, it showed a great improvement on the first model, but still a rather poor fit. Several other models were tried, but none achieved an acceptable level of significance. This is not an infrequent finding when working with maximum likelihood factor analysis and analysis of covariance structures, the trouble being that the test of the model used is very sensitive and may fail for all sorts of trivial reasons not related to the hypothesis under test. Martin et al. (1979) give a discussion of this point, which is too technical to be included here.

If we decide to accept the final model provisionally, we can see in Table 1.7 the maximum likelihood estimates for parameters of this superfactor model, allowing for the apparent effect of sex limitation on the specific genetic variation. Table 1.8 then shows the percentage contribution of individual environment (E_1) and additive genetic (D_R) factor and specific components to total variation for each character in females. These percentages are much the same in males except in the specific genetic contributions for risk (0%), nonplanning (2%), liveliness (24%), and disinhibition (18%).

Clearly, most of the E_1 variance is specific to each variable; because E_1 variance is specific by nature, it is not surprising to find that this is an unimportant source of covariation. Such covariation as exists is more likely to be explained by the four genetic superfactors. The sum of components due to genetic factors and specific genes for any one variable is the heritability for that variable, and most of these are rather low. Nevertheless, for all variables except RISK over half the variation is due to common factors.

Martin et al. (1979) sum up their conclusions as follows:

> The genetical P factor accounts for much of the covariation with nonplanning, while the E factor loads heavily on disinhibition and boredom susceptibility. The N factor appears to account for little of the genetical covariation between variables. L, or social desirability, appears to be genetically related (inversely) to thrill and adventure seeking and experience seeking [p. 209].

TABLE 1.7
Maximum-Likelihood Estimates for Parameters of the Super-Factor Model Allowing for the Apparent Effects of Sex-Limitation on Specific Genetical Variation

| | Factor Loadings | | | | | | | | Specific Standard Deviations | | |
| | Environmental | | | | Genetical | | | | Environmental | Genetical | |
	I	II	III	IV	I	II	III	IV		Female	Male
IMPN	.113	.093	.198	.043	.088	.055	.064	.052	.000	.130	.153
RISK	.218	.053	.008	-.113	.045	.102	.016	.050	.079	.150	.000
NONP	.068	.007	.039	-.014	.113	.075	-.060	.049	.157	.120	.043
LIVE	.066	.110	.052	.015	-.021	.123	-.122	.019	.266	.180	.255
P	.046	–	–	–	.152	–	–	–	.118	–	–
E	–	.249	–	–	–	.177	–	–	.000	–	–
N	–	–	.056	–	–	–	.243	–	.197	–	–
L	–	–	–	-.027	–	–	–	-.138	.189	–	–
DIS	.156	.020	-.079	.147	.041	.227	.122	.113	.058	.152	.204
TAS	.123	.027	-.024	-.057	-.027	.078	-.110	.213	.242	.170	.138
ES	.041	-.015	-.029	.021	.074	.104	-.044	.177	.161	.139	.169
BS	.078	-.005	-.001	.030	.090	.143	.028	.017	.190	.172	.194

TABLE 1.8

Percentage Contributions of Individual Environmental (E_1) and Additive Genetic (D_R) Factor and Specific Components to Total Variation for each Character in Females

	Individual Environments (E_1)						Additive Genes (½ DR)					Total Expected Variance
	I	II	III	IV	Specific	(Error)ᵃ	I(P)	II(E)	III(N)	IV(L)	Specific	
IMPN	16	11	49	2	0	(26)	5	2	3	2	10	0.0797
RISK	54	3	0	15	7	(28)	1	6	0	1	13	0.0884
NONP	9	0	3	0	49	(41)	13	6	4	2	14	0.0504
LIVE	4	10	2	0	58	(34)	0	6	6	0	14	0.1218
P	8	–	–	–	50	(36)	42	–	–	–	–	0.0274
E	–	80	–	–	0	(15)	–	20	–	–	–	0.0775
N	–	–	4	–	54	(15)	–	–	42	–	–	0.0715
L	–	–	–	2	78	(26)	–	–	–	20	–	0.0458
DIS	23	0	6	20	3	(23)	1	24	7	6	10	0.1079
TAS	12	1	0	3	47	(20)	0	2	5	18	12	0.1248
ES	3	0	1	1	41	(39)	4	8	2	25	15	0.0634
BS	8	0	0	1	50	(34)	6	14	1	0	20	0.0727

ᵃ Expected measurement error is calculated as ¼n.

Because the raw data were subjected to an angular transformation, each variable has an expected measurement error variance equal to $\frac{1}{4}n$ (where the scale has n items), provided all items are of equal difficulty. These expected measurement errors, expressed as a percentage of the expected total variation for each variable, are shown in Table 1.8 under the column marked "error"; clearly, error accounts for a substantial part of the specific E_1 variation in many cases. Correction of "heritabilities" for this source of measurement error would increase the heritability of the reliable variance, substantially in some cases.

One way to judge the satisfactory nature or otherwise of the result is to calculate residual phenotypic correlation matrices for males and females. This was done by Martin et al., (1979) and most of the deviations were found to be respectably small. Of the larger deviations, many if not most were found to involve the L factor, suggesting that the authors had not satisfactorily incorporated this variable in their factor structure, possibly due to the fact that the high P-L correlation was not taken into account in the model, which forces these two factors into orthogonality. This may account for some of the unsatisfactory features of the model, if not most of them.

This study indicates most clearly the considerable degree of over-simplification noticeable in earlier models. Clearly, the subfactors of impulsivity and sensation seeking behave differently in relation to the super-factors from each other and have to be analyzed separately. Furthermore, whereas some show direct links with E, others show stronger links with P, or L, or N, and some show links with more than one superfactor. It cannot be said that all the necessary data, which enable us to give a satisfactory picture of these relationships, are in as yet. In any case, replication of this work is urgently needed. However, as Martin et al. (1979) state:

> Whatever the substantive findings of this paper, the work illustrates the value of the method in allowing us to combine the testing of structural psychological hypotheses with a variety of genetical and environmental models of covariation. The scientific advantage of this approach over the all too common practice of "look and see" cannot be overemphasized [p. 209].

SUMMARY AND CONCLUSIONS

It may be useful in this final section to discuss, in simple, nontechnical language, the major findings of the various studies that have been summarized and to try and interpret these findings. It has been found that for superfactors like P, E, N, and L, just as for primary factors like impulsivity, sensation seeking, and so on, and for subfactors like the four different types of impulsivity or the four different types of sensation seeking, a relatively simple model invoking nothing but additive genetic variation (D_R) and specific environmental factors (E_1) is sufficient to account for the observed data with considerable accuracy. There is no evidence of common environment (E_2), so that environmental variation, insofar as it exerts an influence at all, is within family and not between family. This absence of E_2 eliminates a host of social influences as likely determinants of individual differences in personality, and in particular it seems to rule out the type of influence usually adduced by psychoanalysts and psychiatrists as exerting a powerful influence on personality (viz. familial influences, determination by the mother figure, etc.). This is a very important conclusion indeed.

Next we note that the contribution of genetic factors, when we are dealing only with the "true" variance (i.e., variance purged of errors of measurement), is very high, reaching about the same level as the additive genetic variance in intelligence testing. Thus, genetic factors are of considerable importance in determining individual differences in personality, a conclusion directly counter to that held for many years by most personality theorists.

What of E_1? Fulker (1981) raises the interesting possibility that much of E_1, after correction for unreliability, might also have a constitutional basis. This argument may be summarized as follows. He points out that this suggestion might at first appear illogical because, although genetic factors must clearly originate at a constitutional level, environmental influences necessarily arise externally to the organism. However, as Fulker (1981) goes on to state:

> The effect of the environment may still be to modify the individual's constitution, especially if acting at an early developmental period, perhaps even before birth. Accidental factors affecting neural and hormonal balance during pregnancy, for example would most likely appear in our model as E_1 effects, rather than in those associated with E_2. The effects of illness may similarly result in constitutional differences and be reflected in E_1 variation [p. 89].

The transfusional syndrome in identical twins might be taken as a particularly good and prominent example of such constitutional but nongenetic influences that would emerge in analysis as E_1. Thus, it is important to note that although E_1 influences are environmental, they are not necessarily under the control of society, thus restricting even more the possibility of influencing differences in personality between people by direct social action, schooling, and so forth. This general conclusion is supported by the fact that in the analyses undertaken, the factor loadings are constrained so that the genetic loadings are a simple scalar function of the environmental loadings, an assumption that has usually found support in the analyses. This finding cannot but support Fulker's hypothesis.

The next major finding relates to the importance of sex differences, particularly as they relate to the subfactors of impulsivity and sensation seeking. There is of course no reason to expect that phenotypic behavior in humans should be determined by identical genes for males and females, and the evidence suggests that for many of the variables considered in this chapter sex limitation is an important factor and should always be taken into consideration as a possibility. This makes all the more important the inclusion of unlike-sex DZ twins in analyses of this kind, a practice hitherto shunned by most experimenters for reasons that have never been clearly explicated.

The studies summarized in this chapter have shown little evidence of assortative mating (excepting spouse correlations for sensation seeking), dominance, or other nonadditive sources of genetic variation. There has also been little evidence of genotype-environment interaction (G × E) and genotype-environment covariation (CovGE). It has often been suggested that such interaction or covariation makes impossible a worthwhile analysis of individual differences in human populations (Feldman & Levontin, 1975; Layzer, 1974; Moran, 1973). Eaves, Last, Martin, and Jinks (1977) have elaborated a comprehensive framework of theory and method in which these and other contributions to individual differences can be critically assessed, and the failure of such interaction to contribute in any marked degree to our analyses of sources of variation suggests that this criticism is at best premature and requires empirical support before being taken too seriously.

Finally, it should be stated explicitly that the results reported in this chapter are preliminary, not final. Twin studies require very large numbers in order to reduce fiduciary limits to reasonable proportion. They also require relatively unselected populations, and they are subject to obvious limitations. Clearly, replications of the studies summarized here are urgently required, using larger samples, better selected groups, and in particular longer and more reliable measuring instruments. Other methods of study are needed to supplement twin studies, such as familial relationships, studies of adopted children, and so on; until these are done and the results reported in the literature, it would be premature to make too many claims for the data reported here. Although the numbers of twin pairs involved, ranging from over 400 to over 800 in different studies, may seem large in comparison with previous investigations, it must be remembered that these samples have to be split into five groups for analysis (male and female MZ twins, male and female DZ like-sex twins, and DZ unlike-sex twins). Thus, the numbers are reduced, particularly when it is borne in mind that nearly always twice as many females as males come forward for testing, with the disproportion often being even larger than that.

What needs emphasis, equal to the recognition of inadequacies of past work, is the importance of the method used for the solution of hitherto very intractable problems in the analysis of personality differences and their causation. It is not too much to say that methods used in the past have been quite unsatisfactory and insufficient to give meaningful results or to enable us to write a proper specification equation detailing in principle with all the sources of variation—genetic, environmental, and interactional—which determine differences in human behavior. The possibility for doing that now exists, and there can be no excuse for repetitions of the earlier, unsatisfactory kinds of investigations that leave the topic pretty well where it was found, rather than advancing it to a higher plane.

ACKNOWLEDGMENTS

I am indepted to Dr. D. Fulker for a critical reading of this chapter and for reanalyzing some of his data to make the discussion in the section on the genetics of different types of sensation seeking comparable with that in the section on the genetics of different types of impulsivity.

REFERENCES

Buchsbaum, M. S. Average evoked response and stimulus intensity in identical and fraternal twins. *Physiological Psychology,* 1974, *2,* 365–370.

Carrigan, P. M. Extraversion–introversion as a dimension of personality: A reappraisal. *Psychological Bulletin,* 1960, *57,* 329–360.

Claridge, G., Cauter, S., & Hume, W. I. *Personality differences and biological variations: A study of twins.* New York: Pergamon Press, 1973.

Eaves, L. J. The structure of genotypic and environmental covariation for personality: An analysis of the PEN. *British Journal of Social and Clinical Psychology,* 1973, *12,* 275–282.

Eaves, L., & Eysenck, H. J. The nature of extraversion: A genetical analysis. *Journal of Personality and Social Psychology,* 1975, *32,* 102–112.

Eaves, L. J., & Eysenck, H. J. Genotype × age interaction for neuroticism. *Behavior Genetics,* 1976, *6,* 359–362.

Eaves, L. J., & Eysenck, H. J. A genotype-environmental model for psychoticism. *Advances in Behavior Research and Therapy,* 1977, *1,* 5–26.

Eaves, L. J., Last, K., Martin, N. G., & Jinks, J. L. A progressive approach to non-additivity and genotype-environmental covariance in the analysis of human differences. *British Journal of Mathematical and Statistical Psychology,* 1977, *30,* 185–197.

Eaves, L. J. Martin, N. G., & Eysenck, S. B. G. An application of the analysis of covariance structure to the psychological study of impulsiveness. *British Journal of Mathematical and Statistical Psychology,* 1977, *30,* 185–197.

Eysenck, H. J. The questionnaire measurement of neuroticism and extraversion. *Rivista di Psicologica,* 1956, *50,* 113–140.

Eysenck, H. J. *The biological basis of personality.* Springfield, Ill.: Thomas, 1967.

Eysenck, H. J. *The structure of human personality.* London: Methuen, 1970.

Eysenck, H. J. *The structure and measurement of intelligence.* New York: Springer-Verlag, 1979.

Eysenck, H. J., & Eysenck, S. B. G. On the unitary nature of extraversion. *Acta Psychologica,* 1967, *26,* 383–390.

Eysenck, H. J., & Eysenck, S. B. G. *Personality structure and measurement.* London: Routledge & Kegan Paul, 1969.

Eysenck, H. J., & Eysenck, S. B. G. *Psychoticism as a dimension of personality.* London: Hodder & Stoughton, 1976.

Eysenck, S. B. G., & Eysenck, H. J. On the dual nature of extraversion. *British Journal of Social and Clinical Psychology,* 1963, *2,* 46–55.

Eysenck, S. B. G., & Eysenck, H. J. The place of impulsiveness in a dimensional system of personality description. *British Journal of Social and Clinical Psychology,* 1977, *16,* 57–68.

Eysenck, S. B. G., & Eysenck, H. J. Impulsiveness and venturesomeness: Their position in a dimensional system of personality description. *Psychological Reports,* 1978, *43,* 1247–1255.

Feldman, H. W., & Levontin, R. C. The heritability hang-up. *Science,* 1975, *190,* 1163–1168.

Fisher, R. A. The correlation between relatives on the supposition of Mendelian inheritance. *Transactions of the Royal Society* (Edinburgh), 1918, *52,* 399–433.

Fulker, D. W. The genetic and environmental architecture of psychoticism, extraversion and neuroticism. In H. J. Eysenck (Ed.), *A Model for personality.* New York: Springer, 1981.

Fulker, D. W., Eysenck, S. B. G., & Zuckerman, M. A genetic and environmental analysis of sensation seeking. *Journal of Research in Personality,* 1980, *14,* 261–281.

Holzinger, K. J. The relative effect of nature and nurture influences on twin differences. *Journal of Educational Psychology,* 1929, *20,* 245–248.

Jinks, J. L., & Fulker, D. W. Comparison of the biometrical genetical, MAVA, and classical approaches to the analysis of human behavior. *Psychological Bulletin,* 1970, *73,* 311–349.

Jöreskog, K. J. Analysis of covariance structures. In P. R. Krishnaiah (Ed.), *Multivariate analysis III.* New York: Academic Press, 1973.

Layzer, D. Heritability analysis of IQ scores: Science or numerology. *Science,* 1974, *183,* 1259–1266.

Martin, N. G., & Eaves, L. J. The genetical analysis of covariance structure. *Heredity,* 1977, *38,* 77–95.

Martin, N. G., Eaves, L. J., & Fulker, D. W. The genetical relationship of impulsiveness and sensation seeking to Eysenck's personality dimensions. *Acta Med Gemellol,* 1979, *28,* 197–210.

Martin, N. G., & Eysenck, H. J. Genetic Factors in sexual behavior. In Eysenck, H. J. (Ed.), *Sex and personality.* London: Open Books.

Mather, K., & Jinks, J. L. *Biometrical genetics.* London: Chapman & Hall, 1971.

Mather, K., & Jinks, J. L. *Introduction to biometrical genetics.* London: Chapman & Hall, 1977.

Moran, P. A. P. A note on heritability and the correlation between relatives. *Annals of Human Genetics,* 1973, *37,* 217.

Murphy, D. L., Belmaker, R. W., Buchsbaum, M., Martin, N. F., Ciaranello, R., & Wyatt, R. J. Biogenic amino-related enzymes and personality variations in normals. *Psychological Medicine,* 1977, *7,* 149–157.

Neary, R. S., & Zuckerman, M. Sensation seeking, trait and state anxiety, and the electrodermal orienting reflex. *Psychophysiology,* 1976, *13,* 205–211.

Neel, J. V., & Schull, W. J. *Human heredity.* Chicago: University of Chicago Press, 1954.

Nichols, R. C. The National Merit Twin Study. In S. G. Vandenberg (Ed.), *Methods and goals in human behavior genetics.* New York: Academic Press, 1965.

Nies, A., Robinson, D. S., Lamborn, K. R., & Lampert, R. P. Genetic control of platelet and plasma monoamine oxidase activity. *Archives of General Psychiatry,* 1973, *28,* 834–838.

Sparrow, N. H., & Ross, J. The dual nature of extraversion: A replication. *Australian Journal of Psychology,* 1964, *16,* 214–218.

Zuckerman, M. The sensation seeking motive. In B. Maher (Ed.), *Progress in experimental personality research* (Vol. 7). New York: Academic Press, 1974.

Zuckerman, M., Murtaugh, T., & Siegel, J. Sensation seeking and cortical augmenting-reducing. *Psychophysiology,* 1974, *11,* 535–542.

COMMENTS ON CHAPTER 1
Marvin Zuckerman

It is fitting to begin this book with a chapter on the genetics of two of the traits of interest. When we try to separate cause and effect in biological–behavioral relationships, the demonstration of genetic influence in both biological and behavioral traits is a convincing argument for the priority of the biological over the environmental. We must also remember that all biological differences do not orginate in the genes. As Eysenck points out, accidental factors during pregnancy, effects of postnatal illness, nutrition, and other such factors are attributed to the environmental portion of the variance. Although the organic factors may originate in the pre- or postnatal environments, they are nevertheless biological, nonsocial factors.

The methods of genetic analysis (e.g., selective breeding) available for other species of animals cannot be applied to humans; therefore, we must rely on biometric approaches like twin or adopted child comparisons. Eysenck presents the most sophisticated biometric model now available. Despite the sophistication of this approach and the relatively large numbers of twins involved in these studies, we must recognize that the entire approach has been questioned by critics. Their argument usually runs as follows:

1. The study of identical (monozygotic, MZ) and fraternal (dizygotic, DZ) twins reared together confounds the genetic and environmental influences. Only the similarity of identical twins separated at birth and randomly assigned for adoption can reveal the degree of similarity or difference in a trait due to heredity.

2. One cannot make the assumption that the social environments are equally similar for MZ and DZ twins because MZ twins are more likely to be dressed and treated alike due to their greater similarity of appearance. If the social environment exerts an influence, it is more likely to be similar for MZ than for DZ twins.

3. Even if one accepted the assumptions of the method, hereditary and environmental factors are always interactive so that one cannot assign a proportion to either the claim that a trait is some percentage heredity and some percentage environment.

There are other criticisms of the approach, but these are the main ones other than the more recent "guilt-by-association" criticism of the entire methodology because of the data distortions of Burt. This is an unwarranted attack on the scientific reputations of others in the field. One could just as well point to Lysenko, who fabricated data to prove that genes could be altered by environment, as evidence of the untrustworthiness of all who espouse an environmental approach.

But let us examine the three reasonable objections to the twin methodology. When we look closely we find some basic assumptions behind them. Regarding the confounding of environmental and genetic factors in MZ twins raised together, it is assumed that a common rearing environment enhances personality similarities between those sharing such an environment. It is further assumed that to the degree that two siblings are treated alike they will be alike. These are all reasonable assumptions, but as scientists we must not confuse assumptions with data. Shields (1962) compared MZ twins raised together with MZ twins raised separately. Contrary to the environmental hypothesis, twins raised in a common environment were not more, but *less alike* on extraversion and neuroticism. This is not an isolated finding, nor is it limited to specific traits like extraversion. Farber (1981) collected all the recorded cases of separated MZ twins and had judges make global ratings of similarity in personality. Her twin sample was divided into groups on the basis of the degree of separation of the twins. Farber (1981) reports that the sets of twins most separated were the most similar in personality: "As a group, the more time MZ twins spend with no contact with each other the more similar they become [p. 249]." This astounding finding was especially true for lack of contact during the preschool years, the ages during which psychodynamic theorists assume that personality is shaped. One explanation for these findings is the phenomenon of *twinship*. MZ twins (and possibly DZs as well) influence each other in their development and sometimes tend to take complimentary roles. For instance, if one is dominant, the other develops a less dominant personality. Whatever the explanation, it is clear that the use of MZ twins raised together in research on personality may underestimate, rather than overestimate, the role of heredity in shaping personality.

The second assumption of the critics of twin comparisons is borne out in a large twin study by Loehlin and Nichols (1976). Through questionnaires given to the parents of twins they determined that MZ twins were more likely to have been dressed alike and treated alike by the parents and were more likely to have shared more time together than DZ twins. However the next assumption, that these similarities or differences in shared experience of twins and parental treatment of them affect their similarity in personality, is called into question by the Loehlin and Nichols data. Correlations between measures of differential early experience and measures of twin resemblance were quite low (median correlations .06 for MZ and .07 for DZ twins). A comparison of the impact of home environment (actively imposed or more permissive) also showed no relationship to personality similarity. The results demonstrate that the greater shared early experience of MZs cannot account for their greater similarity in personality than DZs.

The most conclusive study on the common environment hypothesis is being done on identical twins separated at birth or very closely thereafter. Bouchard (1981) has recently presented data on 24 pairs of such twins. Although the study is not yet completed (26 or more pairs remain to be run), the preliminary data show correlations on cognitive *and* personality traits between identical twins reared apart that are as high as, and for some traits higher than, the correlations for identical twins reared in the same homes.

Eysenck's results for impulsivity and sensation-seeking traits show the absence of E_2 (between family differences in environment). He notes that what differences exist do so within families. Inasmuch as the Loehlin and Nichols data show little effect of such differential treatment or twins within families, one must wonder how the environment does affect personality. Apart from Fulker's (1981) ideas that much of E_1 differences may represent some constitutional (biological) factors, it is possible that the major environmental influences on twins, or any other children, come from peers rather than parents. Although this suggestion may sound strange to psychoanalytic theorists, parents and developmental psychologists have observed the greater propensity of school-age children to model their behavior and adopt values and attitudes from peers as much or even more than from parents. Whatever the influence environment has on twins, it may stem from their different experiences with peers. Peers, of course, may react to the differences in behavior of the two twins. If one twin is more sociable, for instance, peers will respond to and reinforce the greater sociability of the one twin and thus enlarge the difference between them over time.

Apart from peer influences, developing children are undoubtedly influenced by adults unrelated to them (e.g., teachers, employers, etc.) who provide important modeling influences. Over the years I have noticed a significant tendency of some of my own male graduate students to grow beards after working with me for a couple of years. Although it is too early to judge if this superficial modeling is related to the tendency to pursue a research, as opposed to a primarily clinical, career after graduation, I would hope that they did acquire more than a preference for hirsuteness from their professor.

Apart from modeling influences from the social environment, other fortuitous events and complications can affect personality and vocational development. Freud was diverted from a promising research career in neurology by the antisemitic barriers to his academic advancement and by his understandable need to earn an income in private practice in order to marry the woman he desired. The temporary influence of various older and, for a time, respected models such as Breuer also led him into psychoanalysis.

But why are separated twins so alike in personality if their environments are different? The problem here is with the older behaviorist view of environment as an active force that somehow acts on a passive organism (a tabula rasa) to shape it. As Bandura (1977) says: "Though the *potential environment* is identical for all animals, the *actual environment* depends upon their behavior. . . . What we have here is a two-way regulatory system in which the organism appears either as an object or an agent of control, depending upon which side of the reciprocal process one chooses to examine [p. 196]."

Farber (1981) views separated twins as engaged in this kind of influence over their environments unhampered by the need to adapt to the major influence in their lives, their own twin: "Perhaps identical twins reared apart in effect 'seduce' their environment into acting in accord with their needs, and what they cannot seduce into similarity, they tend to experience in roughly similar ways anyway [p. 259]."

The final criticism is the difficulty, if not impossibility, of examining proportions of variance due to heredity or environment because of a failure to consider the interaction between the two. This criticism is more appropriately applied to older methods of estimating heritability from correlational models. The analysis of variance design does allow for examination of interaction and, as Eysenck notes, there is little evidence for genotype-environment interaction and genotype-environment covariation in these data.

We see that many of the criticisms of the twin method are based on a priori assumptions about environmental influences on personality, assumptions that do not stand up well in face of actual data. Developmental studies in general have failed to yield much evidence of strong relationships between early environmental influences (from parents) and later personality development. These negative results are probably more comprehensible to parents than to psychoanalysts who have been too busy in their own prolonged training to try to influence their own children. Siblings are different from the beginning and develop into what they will be in spite of our best efforts to shape their behavior. From their peers, and from the world at large, they select what they want.

Eysenck has attempted to order personality traits in a hierarchical model with the three superfactors (E, N, and P) as supraordinate, with traits such as sociability, impulsivity, and sensation seeking on the next level, and with subdivisions of these traits on a third level. As he points out, the pattern is not a neat one with each of the traits on the second level representing a subdivision of a single supraordinate trait. Sensation seeking, for instance, is related to both E and P and is unrelated to N. Impulsivity (narrow) is related to P and N but not to E.

Part of the problem is that Eysenck has worked from the top down, that is, from the broader traits to the narrower traits. Had he first developed narrower traits, as Cattell did, and derived the broader traits from the narrower ones using second order factor analysis, there would be a more coherent hierarchical pattern because the first order factors might have fit more neatly into the higher order factors. However, factor analyses of Cattell's factors have revealed essentially the same broad factors defined by Eysenck (see Eysenck, 1981, for a discussion of this issue).

It is conceivable that the narrower traits might be more heritable because they are closer to the genotype that shapes the particular biological mechanisms underlying behavior. Farber (1981), noting the remarkable similarity in the specific nervous habits, mannerisms, emotional tone, and styles of expression of separated MZ twins, writes: "It appears that the clearest signs of genetic determination may occur in traits closer to neurobiological functioning-arousal, sensory patterning, tempo, units of movement, and so forth [p. 254]."

The 58% uncorrected heritability figure for sensation seeking is about the same as that reported by Jinks and Fulker (1970), 54% for the supertrait of neuroticism, but it is somewhat higher than the 42% for psychoticism (Eaves & Eysenck, 1977). Inasmuch as sensation seeking is related to E and P but not to N, it appears that sensation seeking has a higher genetic determination than the superordinate traits of which it is a component. Although the lower figure for P might be explained in terms of the lower reliability of the scale, the E scale is certainly as reliable as the sensation-seeking scale, and corrections for their reliability raise them about the same: E to 57% and SS to 70%.

Eysenck presents data that disputes this hypothesis of greater heritability for the narrower traits. The corrected (for reliability) heritabilities of the narrower traits of sociability and impulsivity (.61 and .60) are only slightly, and certainly insignificantly, higher than the .57 corrected heritability for the supertrait of extraversion (composed of both of the narrow trait measures).

Other data supporting Eysenck's position can be found in the large twin study by Loehlin and Nichols (1976). These investigators employed scales measuring the broad traits of neuroticism and extraversion using the items of the California Psychological Inventory (CPI). Intraclass correlations of identical and fraternal twins on these scales yield heritabilities that are about the same as those obtained from the medians of the 27 CPI scales measuring narrower traits. It would seem, therefore, that the heritabilities of broad traits are no greater or less than those of narrower traits measured by questionnaires. But the possibility remains that some traits, whether broad or narrow, are more closely aligned with specific biological variables that are more direct expressions of the genotypes.

But the overall analysis of E, N, P, impulsivity, and sensation seeking scales in this chapter also bears on this question of what is heritable. Referring to Table 1.8, we see that the P and N scales contribute heavily to the genetic portion of factors I and III. However, on factor II the major contribution of the E scales is to the environmental variance of the factor, whereas the major portion of the variance in the Dis and BS sensation seeking scales is found in the genetic component of the factor. This could be interpreted to mean that the E scale assesses more of the phenotype, whereas the SS-Dis scale is closer to the genotype of this factor.

It is clear that we can go only so far with a straight biometric analysis of the psychological traits. Ultimately, we must analyze the biological traits together with the correlated psychological traits assessed in the same twins. There has been only one study of this type that I know of. One of the correlates of sensation-seeking trait is the relation between the amplitude of the cortical average evoked potential and stimulus intensity (see Chapter 2). The slope of this relationship is measured for each individual. A range of slopes from negative (reducing) to positive (augmenting) is typically found, and the slope measure has been related to a variety of phenomena including disposition to hypomania and psychopathy as well as sensation seeking trait. Slope measures, based on the evoked potential-light intensity relationship, showed a substantial genetic contribution in a twin study (Buchsbaum, 1974), the augmenting measure correlating .71 for MZ twins and .09 for DZs. The essentially zero correlation for DZ twins is genetically impossible but may represent a sampling error. The number of twins involved in this study was not large enough to yield completely reliable results, and the actual correlation may be closer to the .30 figure more commonly found for fraternal twins on personality trait measures. Buchsbaum took the 18 MZ pairs more alike and 18 MZ pairs least alike on the slope measure and correlated the Sensation Seeking Scale (SSS) scores of twins within each of these groups. The correlation of SSS scores for those twins most similar on the psychophysiological measure was .68; the correlation for those least alike on the evoked potential slope was .08. There is a strong inference that the genetic similarity on the psychological trait depended on the similarity on the psychophysiological trait. One could take this kind of analysis a step further. If we knew, for instance, that the psychophysiological phenomenon depended on a particular neurotransmitter that could be measured, we could analyze the similarity in slope of the evoked potential in MZ twins as a function of the bioamine.

In the chapters that follow, we see what kinds of psychophysiological and biochemical measures have been related to impulsivity and sensation seeking. The genetic work of Eysenck, Fulker, and Eaves has certainly shown that at least 50% of the variance in these traits is genetically determined. But because it is difficult to see how genes would directly determine personality traits, we must consider the intermediate biological traits that may link the genes to consistent patterns of behavior.

At the Eastern Psychological Association conference, where we held the symposium that provided the initial core of this book, Kamin (1979) gave a somewhat one-sided view of the nature–nurture problem in intelligence. His conclusion was that genes have no role in the determination of general intellectual ability. At dinner we were discussing this paper, and Larry Stein wondered aloud if Kamin thought that the only difference between the intelligence of a fly and a human was their social environments. Someone else suggested that it might be a dietary factor; flies tend to eat a lot of garbage. At the extremes of the genetic versus social environment arguments we do find a lot of garbage suppressing intellectual development.

REFERENCES

Bandura, A. *Social learning theory.* Englewood Cliffs, N.J.: Prentice-Hall 1977.

Bouchard, T. J., Jr. *The Minnesota study of twins reared apart: Description and preliminary findings.* Paper presented at 89th convention of the American Psychological Association, Los Angeles, August 1981.

Buchsbaum, M. S. Average evoked response and stimulus intensity in identical and fraternal twins. *Physiological Psychology,* 1974, *2,* 365–370.

Eaves, L. J., & Eysenck, H. J. The nature of extraversion: A genetical analysis. *Journal of Personality and Social Psychology,* 1975, *32,* 102–112.

Eaves, L. J., & Eysenck, H. J. A genotype-environmental model for psychoticism. *Advances in Behavior Research and Therapy,* 1977, *7,* 5–26.

Eysenck, H. J. General features of the model. In H. J. Eysenck (Ed.), *A model for personality.* New York: Springer-Verlag, 1981.

Farber, S. L. *Identical twins reared apart.* New York: Basic Books, 1981.

Fulker, D. W. The genetic and environmental architecture of psychoticism, extraversion and neuroticism. In H. J. Eysenck, (Ed.), *A model for personality.* New York: Springer, 1981.

Jinks, J. L., & Fulker, D. W. Comparison of the biometrical genetical MAVA and the classical approaches to the analysis of human behavior. *Psychological Bulletin,* 1970, *73,* 311–349.

Kamin, L. J. *Psychology as social science: The Jensen affair, ten years later.* Presidential address at the 50th meeting of the Eastern Psychological Association, Philadelphia, April 1979.

Loehlin, J. C., & Nichols, R. C. *Heredity, environment, and personality.* Austin: University of Texas Press, 1976.

Shields, J. *Monozygotic twins.* Oxford: Oxford University Press, 1962.

2 A Biological Theory of Sensation Seeking

Marvin Zuckerman
University of Delaware

SOCIOBIOLOGICAL SPECULATIONS

The strong genetic influence in the sensation seeking trait has been discussed by Eysenck in the first chapter of this book. If the biological basis for a human trait is genetically encoded, the trait must have been evolving for some time in the mammalian ancestry of humans and should be apparent in some forms of behavior in currently existent species other than humans, particularly the nonhuman primates. Sociobiology (Wilson, 1975) has an unfortunate tendency to generalize about traits within a species and across species, making it vulnerable to charges of anthropomorphism or "zoomorphism" (attributing traits of other species to humans). One way to demonstrate that similar behavior in humans and other species has evolved from a common genotype is to show that the same biological characteristics underlie the behavior in both humans and other species.

The most current definition of sensation seeking as a human trait (Zuckerman, 1979a) is: "a trait defined by the need for varied, novel, and complex sensations and experiences and the willingness to take physical and social risks for the sake of such experiences [p. 10]."

Whether they "need" to or not, species other than humans do show spontaneous variation in instrumental behavior (Glanzer, 1953; Tolman, 1925), prefer stimuli of some complexity to simpler stimuli (Sackett, 1972), and approach and investigate novel stimuli in spite of their initial fears of such stimuli (Suomi & Harlow, 1976).

Play, as a form of behavior not directly tied to imperative biological needs, has evolved to a particular prominence in the extended developmental period of primates (Bruner, 1976). Van Lawick-Goodall (1976) has described the risky tree play of young chimpanzees, and Jones (1976) has noted the similarity of rough-and-tumble play in young chimpanzees and human children (particularly males).

Exploration, approaching novel stimuli, and risky play have both adaptive and nonadaptive consequences. Exploring territory and registering and storing impressions may be advantageous to a roving animal. But too much curiosity may indeed "kill the cat," or the primate, and falling from trees may certainly damage any beast. Evolution has probably worked to build into the organism an "optimal level" of this trait, which differs both between and within species.

Variation is a rule of nature, and within a species we generally find a certain range of biological and behavioral traits. The survival of species that live and move in groups is enhanced by having some members who are adventurous and others who are more cautious and orderly. The biological value of a Columbus to the species is incalculable, but for every Columbus there must be more cautious types who stay at home and keep the books, make the star charts, codify the laws, and plant the crops.

Ellison (1977) describes rats who need the security of their burrows and spend little time in foraging or social interactions and contrasts them with those who explore the limits of their territory and spend much of their time in social behavior. He has shown the dependence of this trait on biochemical factors, which are discussed later in this chapter.

Pavlov (1927/1960) contrasted two types of dogs: one an active, socially active extravert, but too easily dearoused by monotonous conditioned stimuli, and the other a more nervous, socially timid type who tirelessly salivated to the sound of a metronome. Pavlov explained these behavioral differences in terms of hypothetical types of nervous systems.

Examples such as these suggest that variations in basic human temperaments of the types defined by the ancient Greeks (e.g., sanguine and phlegmatic) probably have evolved in other species.

Physical anthropologists suggest that hominids evolved when primates abandoned the protection of the forests and began to roam on the open plains of Africa. The shift from pure vegetarianism to hunting of animal food put a premium on the trait of adventurousness, particularly in the hunting of large animals in competition with other predators. Aggressiveness was also a necessary trait in competition between bands for territory, and a more graded kind of aggressiveness became involved in the dominance hierarchies characteristic of the human species. Both adventurousness and social dominance are traits highly associated with sensation seeking (Zuckerman, 1979a). Aggressiveness tends to show a relation with at least one type of sensation seeking (Disinhibition).

If there were no high sensation seekers in these bands of early hominids, the group would remain confined within a limited territory and eventually would exhaust the food resources and starve. Conversely, if they were all high sensation seekers,they would probably take too many chances and be killed by wild animals or, moving too incautiously into territories of other bands, would be beaten and eaten.

There is another vital adaptive function that is, after all, the whole point of evolution: mating. Human sensation seekers have a predilection to seek and enjoy sexual experience with a greater variety of partners than low sensation seekers. Harlow, Dodsworth, and Harlow (1965) demonstrated how early social isolation of monkeys creates severe deficits in sexual and maternal behavior in adult life. As with many sexually dysfunctional humans, the problem of these monkeys was not that they were not aroused but that they were too aroused by the complex social stimulation of an interested sexual object. There is an optimal level of arousal for proficient sexual behavior, and love does *not* always find a way.

Many species (e.g., lions, many monkeys, and apes) avoid incestuous relations and seek mates outside of the immediate family band. More formalized incest taboos in humans demand that males seek mates outside of the prescribed social group. Avoidance of sexual relations with close relatives makes sound biological sense because it avoids the adverse genetic consequences of inbreeding. However, the individual who is fearful of approaching strangers, or is generally unsocial, is at a biological disadvantage given the demands of exogamous mating. Low sensation seeking in combination with incest taboos may result in unproductive celibacy.

Inasmuch as polygamy was probably more prevalent in early pre-history than monogamy, the need of the sensation seeker for a variety of sexual partners would also confer a reproductive advantage. In animal bands where there is competition for mating, it has been observed that a minority of the males father a majority of the progeny. These "big daddys" are usually the more dominant and aggressive types.

Sociobiology is great intellectual fun, but like psychoanalysis it is basically unverifiable when limited to post hoc types of retrospective interpretation. Let us see how far we can go beyond "primal horde" fantasies to find the biological traits that link sensation seeking to a common genotype in humans *and* other species.

A MODEL FOR COMPARATIVE STUDY OF A TRAIT

Table 2.1 shoes a model for study of a trait at the human and animal level. The link between the two levels of study is biochemical and psychophysiological correlates of the behavior, which are considered relevant to the construct in humans and animals. I use this model as an outline

TABLE 2.1
A Model for Comparative Study of a Trait

	BEHAVIORAL	GENETIC	CORRELATIVE BIOLOGICAL	EXPERIMENTAL BIOLOGICAL
HUMANS	Trait tests Experience reports Preferences Observations	Biometric: Twins, adopted children		Drug experiments, treatments

ANIMALS	Observations:
	Natural behavior
	Experimental
	  situations
		Selective
		  breeding
		Cross-fostering
			Biochemical
			Psychophysio-
			logical
				Drugs
				Surgery
				Brain stimulation
				Autopsy

for discussing the research on the trait of sensation seeking.

First, we must define what we believe to be self-report and behavioral definitions of the phenotype in humans and animals. Inasmuch as systematic observation of large numbers of humans in natural settings is difficult, the more common approach is to assess the trait by self-report questionnaires and ratings on the trait by peers or other observers. These ratings are often summaries of general tendencies and therefore are subject to conceptual distortions of actual behavior. One of the first tests of the accuracy of our early conceptualization of the trait is whether the components of our measure (items in the test or ratings), usually selected on a theoretical or rational basis, actually show the structure that we have postulated. This phase is called content validity. After the scales have been defined, further tests of their internal reliability are conducted, and cross-cultural studies may be used to show the generality of the factor structure.

Because our scales and ratings are often not specific about actual responses or use general trait terms, it is useful to ask people about their life experience in areas that we consider relevant to the construct. Preferences may be useful data and may provide a behavioral definition for the trait. Preferences for designs, tones, or foods, for instance, may be related to broader traits.

Observations of behavior in natural settings or in controlled experiments, where variables may be manipulated, are considered the most powerful methods of study. However, observation of humans introduces factors such as experimenter demand, self-consciousness produced by being observed, and the experimenter bias in the selection of what is observed as well as in the observations themselves. Behavior in laboratory situations often turns out to be situation-specific and of little value for the study of broad personality trends.

With animals we must observe because we cannot ask them anything. We must decide on the units of observation, which may range from a bar-press response to a complex social action such as dominance or aggression behaviors. Narrowly defined behaviors might be too unlike the "natural" behavior of animals and therefore may tell us little about such behavior. Broadly defined behaviors may be too unreliable to judge or occur too infrequently for systematic study. Perhaps the best compromise is to study complex behaviors that are partially controlled in their expression so as to yield reliable measures. An example could be a measure of dominance based upon which animal gets food, a mate, or the order of passage through a passageway to the goal. Activity in the open field is another example. Preferences of animals for various kinds of stimuli can also be tested because behavioral response defines the preference.

Genetic studies in humans of the type described by Eysenck in the first chapter are based on biometric analyses of the trait measures in persons of different degrees of genetic relatedness. The study of the similarity of adoptive children to biological and foster parents is an even better way of separating heriditary and environmental influences.

In animals there is the advantage of control of the breeding selection and cross-fostering. Considerations of expense and time (of the breeding-generational cycle) prohibit using primates rather than lower forms such as rodents.

Correlative biological approaches can be used to investigate whether the behavioral traits in humans and animals have common relationships with biological variables measurable in both species. Here again we have more opportunity with animals because we can measure chemicals in the brain and record electrical reactions in subcortical brain structures. In humans we are generally limited to biochemical indices from blood, urine, or cerebrospinal fluid, and our recordings must be made from the peripheral surface of the body such as the scalp and the palms.

In the past it has been possible to do some limited drug experiments in humans, but these experiments are becoming increasingly difficult. Certainly, we cannot give potentially harmful drugs, such as neurotoxins, to human subjects. The placebo-controlled study of drugs given for therapeutic reasons to persons suffering from psychiatric disorders may furnish some knowledge about the basis of normal traits in brain biochemistry, but selective factors in who gets the drug, the heterogeneity of the population, and the unknown role of the disorder itself make this a limited experimental approach.

Using animals, we may administer drugs directly into the brain as well as peripherally. We may stimulate any part of the brain as well as record from it, or we may make stimulation contingent upon the animal's own response. We may destroy or block response in selected brain areas and observe the effects on behavior. Finally, we may autopsy the animal after behavioral observations have been made and measure relevant chemicals in specific brain structures.

In testing a biological model, more relevant research must be done on humans, but more precisely controlled research is only possible in animals. Pursued simultaneously on both phylogenic levels, we may come closer to discovering the biological basis for temperament than by uncoordinated study at both levels. Such coordinated research is presently quite rare. By showing the convergences for the trait of sensation seeking, it is hoped that the programs of this type will be undertaken and underwritten.

PHENOMENAL DEFINITION
OF SENSATION SEEKING

Humans

Test definition.   Research on sensation seeking in humans has centered around the Sensation Seeking Scales (SSS) as the central definition of the general trait and its specific factors. The first published version of the SSS (form II, Zuckerman, Kolin, Price, & Zoob, 1964) contained a General scale based on the principal factor derived from factor analyses of a variety of rationally derived items. This General scale was carried over into form IV of the SSS (Zuckerman, 1971), which also included four new scales derived from further factor analyses. These factor scales included:

1. *Thrill and Adventure Seeking (TAS):* items reflecting a desire to engage in physical activities involving elements of speed, danger, novelty, and defiance of gravity (e.g., parachuting, scuba-diving).

2. *Experience Seeking (ES):* items reflecting seeking of novel experiences through travel, music, art, and a spontaneous, nonconforming life style with similarly inclined persons.

3. *Disinhibition (Dis):* items describing the need to seek release in uninhibited social activities with or without the aid of alcohol.

4. *Boredom Susceptibility (BS):* items reflecting an aversion to repetitive experience, routine work, or predictable people with a reaction of restless discontent when unavoidably exposed to such experience.

With the possible exception of the last scale (BS), all of the scales showed good factor, internal, and retest reliabilities. Moderate intercorrelations between the scales suggested that they were all related aspects of a broad factor.

Form V (Zuckerman, Eysenck, & Eysenck, 1978) was constructed to balance the representation of the four factors in the items yielding a total score to replace the General scale. The factor structure of the test was replicated in an English sample, and 10 items representing each factor in samples of males and females in England and America were put together in a 40-item scale. The factor structure has been further replicated in a study by Feij, Orlebeke, Gazendam, and van Zuilen (1979) using a Dutch translation of the SSS.

Experience. Using self-report drug histories administered to college students and noncollege samples of adults and drug abusers, significant relationships have been found between the SS scales and extent of drug use, particularly marijuana, hashish, amphetamines, and psychodelic drugs (Brill, Crumpton, & Grayson, 1971; Carrol & Zuckerman, 1977; Feij et al., 1979; Kaestner, Rosen, & Appel, 1977; Khavari, Humes, & Mabry, 1977; Kilpatrick, Sutker, & Smith, 1976; Murtaugh, 1971; Platt, 1975; Segal, 1976; Zuckerman, 1972; Zuckerman, Bone, Neary, Mangelsdorff, & Brustman, 1972). Drug experience typically correlates with all four of the SS scales, not just the ES scale, which contains items reflecting a willingness to try drugs. Segal (1976) actually removed drug-related items and found the correlations unchanged. In studies relating a variety of personality variables to drug-use reports, it is clear that the SSS measures the trait most highly related to drug use and accounts for most of the personality variance in drug use.

Cigarette smoking has also been related to sensation seeking (Feij et al., 1979; Zuckerman, 1972; Zuckerman & Neeb, 1980; Zuckerman et al., 1972), although the relationships with extent of cigarette smoking are not strongly linear and in women appear to be curvilinear with the heaviest smokers as low as nonsmokers in sensation seeking (Zuckerman & Neeb, 1980).

Alcohol use tends to be more highly related to the Disinhibition subscale in college students, although it does show significant relationships with some of the other scales (Schwarz, Burkhart, & Green, 1978; Zuckerman et al., 1972).

Sex experience in college students (Zuckerman et al., 1972; Zuckerman, Tushup, & Finner, 1976) and sexual responsiveness, arousability, and frequency in samples of young married women (Fisher, 1973) are related to the broad sensation-seeking trait measured by the SS scales.

A different kind of risk-taking is reflected in driving habits. A large-scale survey found a linear and very strong relationship between all of the SS scales and the speeds at which the respondents reportedly drove on highways having 55 m.p.h. speed limits (Zuckerman & Neeb, 1980).

Preferences. High sensation seekers prefer more complex designs than lows in experiments where they are asked to rate designs (Looft &

Baranowski, 1971; Zuckerman et al., 1972). They also prefer either complex classical or jazz music to bland popular music of the Muzak variety (Zuckerman & Hopkins, 1965). Given a choice between mundane and novel similes, the high sensation seekers tend to choose the novel ones (Bone, Cowling, & Belcher, 1974; Farley, 1971).

Observations. High sensation seekers volunteer for a variety of types of unusual experiments or activities including experiments in sensory deprivation, hypnosis, drug effects and activities (Zuckerman, 1978), and activities such as encounter groups (Stanton, 1976), alpha training, sensitivity groups, gambling instruction (Zuckerman, 1974), and training in transcendental meditation (Myers & Eisner, 1974). They also engage in novel and risky sports like parachute jumping (Hymbaugh & Garrett, 1974) and scuba diving (Heyman & Rose, 1979). The activities cover a wide range from minimal stimulation (sensory deprivation, meditation) to intense stimulation and arousal (encounter groups, gambling, scuba diving). What they all have in common is exposure to some kind of relatively novel experience. However, volunteering and actual performance are two different matters.

In sensory deprivation or any monotonous confinement situation, high sensation seekers get measurably more restless compared to lows (Zuckerman, Persky, Hopkins, Murtaugh, Basu, & Shilling, 1966) and may seek visual stimulation (Lambert & Levy, 1972) or the opportunity to move around freely (Hocking & Robertson, 1969). Similarly, the high sensation seekers who volunteer for meditation training tend to quit early, do not practice, and make poor meditators (Myers & Eisner, 1974).

However, in situations where they may interact socially, such as unstructured discussion groups (Ozeran, 1973) or confinement with another person (Zuckerman, Persky, Link, & Basu, 1968), high sensation seekers function well and enjoy themselves, whereas the lows show high arousal, withdrawal, and report dysphoric feelings.

The high sensation seekers who volunteer for gambling experiments or training tend to bet more in some of the games (Zuckerman & Kuhlman, 1978) at higher odds (Waters & Kirk, 1968) than do the lows.

Sensation seeking predicts how long novice scuba divers will stay under water and how deep they will go on their first free dive (Heyman & Rose, 1980). The SSS scores are relatively high in members of volunteer salvage scuba divers and volunteer firefighter groups, which take even greater chances than sports divers (Bacon, 1974, data published in Zuckerman, 1978). The Thrill and Adventure Seeking subscale was predictive of how far female subjects would go in looking over an exposed parapet 16 stories high. It also predicted fear reactions in this and other phobic situations, such as exposure to a snake or darkness (Mellstrom, Cicala, & Zuckerman,

1976). Low sensation seekers were observed to be more fearful in these experimental situations.

The behavior and internal reactions of high and low sensation seekers in risky situations have been used to develop a model for risk-taking (Zuckerman, 1979b). High sensation seekers generally appraise risk as less than do lows, but even given equal appraisal of risk, the highs anticipate more positive arousal, whereas the lows anticipate more fear or anxiety. The balance between states of fear and sensation seeking as risk increases predicts whether a person will enter into the activities or not participate in them (Zuckerman, 1976).

Animals

A prime candidate for an analogue of human sensation seeking in animals, particularly rodents, is behavior in the open field or arena. McClearn (1959) investigated the exploratory behavior of six strains of mice in four types of apparatus including the open-field, arena, hole-in-the-wall, and barrier situations. The strains differed significantly in all of these situations, and the rank order of the strain medians was highly consistent from one situation to another. McClearn (1959) states: "The situational generality of the behavior suggests that a fundamental mouse 'personality' dimension is being measured [p. 66]." However, McClearn did not demonstrate consistency of transsituational behavior in individuals within species so that conclusions about a mouse "personality" are not warranted from the data presented.

Royce (1977) has studied open-field behavior and summarized the results of his research and that of other investigators. Three first order factors consistently appear in factor analyses of behavior in the open field:

1. Latency to move, activity, and penetration to the center of the field are the primary indices of a factor that Royce calls "motor discharge," which corresponds to the construct of exploratory tendency. This behavior could be analogous to the sensation seeking trait in humans or to the *thrill and adventure seeking* type in particular. Royce regards the impulsive, active behavior in this situation as a mode of autonomic discharge through the motor system as opposed to the type embodied in the next factor.

2. Defecation in the open field constitutes an index of autonomic balance or internal discharge of autonomic tension. The analogue at the human level would presumably be the *fearfulness* or *anxiety* trait.

3. Urination in the open field is regarded by Royce as an index of territorial marking. Egan, Royce, and Poley (1972) found a positive relationship between this type of open-field behavior and behavioral indices of aggression and social dominance in mice so that *aggressiveness* or *social*

dominance might be a human analogue of this behavior.

A problem is posed by the nonindependence of these factors. Poley and Royce (1976) found that these three third order factors form a fourth order factor, including all three, which Royce calls *emotional stability*. The nonindependence of activity and defecation factors is also seen in a selective breeding study by Broadhurst (1967). This investigator bred emotionally reactive and nonreactive strains of rats using defecation scores in the open field as an index of "reactivity." The nonreactive strain had higher activity scores, whereas the reactives had lower scores. Because the rats were bred for reactivity, not exploration, the resultant difference in activity shows the linkage between the two behavioral traits.

Whimbey and Denenberg (1967) have shown that the relationship between exploration (activity) and emotional reactivity (defecation) depends on the novelty of the open-field situation. On the first day the rat was exposed to the open field there was a positive correlation between activity and defecation, but on subsequent days the correlation was negative. It appears that activity and defecation become independent factors only after the animal has habituated to the open field. The meaning of activity in terms of exploration or autonomic arousal varies with experience in the open field. When the animal is first exposed to the field, activity reflects autonomic arousal. On the next several exposures, "freezing" or inactivity is the primary response to autonomic arousal, and activity indicates low internal arousal. Later, as autonomic arousal decreases with habituation, the two response patterns may be independent.

There is an analogue of these relationships in self-reported states of sensation seeking (positive arousal) and anxiety in humans. Zuckerman (1976), reporting the results of Neary (1975), showed that sensation and anxiety states are uncorrelated on neutral occasions (e.g., group testing in a classroom) but correlate negatively in high stress situations (e.g., participation in a drug experiment). Similarly, although there is little or no correlation between sensation seeking and anxiety traits, one type of SS trait (thrill and adventure seeking) predicted fear responses in three phobic type situations (Mellstrom et al., 1976).

The open field involves putting the animal in a novel situation. As rodents are nocturnal burrow-inhabiting creatures, they have a certain amount of "built-in" agoraphobia and photophobia. Another method used in the study of fearfulness consists of suddenly presenting the animal with a novel stimulus. Suomi and Harlow (1976) have shown how novel stimuli, particularly those that move and emit noise, elicit fear and flight in monkeys. Approach, investigation, play, and aggressive responses to the stimulus only emerge after some habituation and maturation have occurred. Two studies (Hall, Rappaport, Hopkins, & Griffin, 1970; Lukas & Siegel,

1977) have used such fright-provoking stimuli with cats in order to study the relation of behavior to augmenting of the cortical evoked potential, a correlate of human sensation seeking. Their results are discussed in a later section.

Ethology constitutes another approach to the study of behavior, consisting of the observation of animals making responses that are typical for their species in their natural environments. This method is probably better for studying "personality" differences in animals because it samples the animal's natural behavior over time and is more representative of traits than is behavior in contrived experimental situations.

Ellison (1977) provides a good example of this kind of observation in his studies of the effects of biochemical lesioning on behavior. He constructed a room-sized arena containing burrows for the rats, a "behavior arena" where animals could interact, activity wheels and toys, ramps leading to a water tower, climbing structures, and a feeding area that could be reached only by going through a tube large enough for only one rat at a time to enter. Behavioral measures in the natural environment included: time spent in burrows, time spent in the behavior arena area, activity in the activity wheel, fighting, mounting, and order of precedence through the tube to the feeding area (a measure of dominance). Because human sensation seeking is related to exploration of the novel, high sociability, and social dominance, such natural social behaviors in rats might constitute another analogue for human behavior. Ellison's linkage of rat behaviors to central bioamines provides experimental tests for hypotheses being developed for human sensation seeking and is discussed at the end of this chapter.

Redmond, Murphy, and Baulu (1979) have observed natural behavior in rhesus monkeys, relating it to levels of platelet monoamine oxidase, which is another biological correlate of human sensation seeking. Behaviors noted in monkeys included: time alone, social contact, foraging, moving, inactivity, sleep or rest, playing, giving or receiving grooming, self-grooming, dominant-agonistic behavior, and submissive behavior or receiving aggression. Each behavioral category was defined in terms of the characteristic expressions of the species. For instance, according to Redmond et al., (1979) play behavior included: "running, bouncing, or jumping with no detectable purpose; social may include chasing, wrestling, or pulling [p. 89]."

Approach or avoidance reactions to stimuli may be used to test preferences for complexity or other attributes of stimuli. Sackett (1972) tested monkeys' responses to stimuli projected onto a screen in an adjoining cage. The stimuli varied in complexity from very simple to complex. He measured latency to enter the cage, duration of motor activity in the cage, and investigation of the stimulus on the screen. Ferally reared monkeys and those reared in captivity with their natural mothers or peers showed a preference (greater exploration time) for the more complex stimuli.

Monkeys raised in isolation for 6 months or more with inanimate "mothers" preferred stimuli of intermediate complexity. Monkeys raised in isolation from 9 to 12 months showed no preference or preferred the simplest pattern.

Because preference for complex stimuli has been shown to be a characteristic of human sensation seekers, these animal results suggest that early environments that restrict social stimulation could play a role in producing low sensation-seeking individuals. One limitation of this conclusion is that social isolation also produces some deprivation of sensory variation. One wonders what the result would be if stimuli of varying complexity were projected into the animals' cages when they were in the early developmental phases.

GENETIC STUDIES

Eysenck has described the genetic studies of sensation seeking in humans in Chapter 1 of this volume, so in this section I focus on studies of animal analogues of the trait.

Using six strains of mice, McClearn (1959) found consistent rankings of exploratory behavior in strains across six situations. When he crossed the strains that were highest and lowest on exploration, the resultant strain was intermediate in exploratory activity, supporting a polygenic model rather than a single-locus model for the trait.

In a further study, McClearn (1959) and De Fries (1973) used an intermediate strain, developed from a cross between a high and low exploratory strain, and selectively bred high and low activity mice for 18 generations. A clear response to selection was observed, with the differences between the two selected strains increasing with each generation.

Royce, Holmes, and Poley (1975) did a genetic analysis of diallel cross-matings, starting with six inbred strains of mice tested in 10 situations. The motor discharge factor, identified by latency and activity measures in the open field and straightaway situations, showed a significant genetic variation in both sexes mostly accounted for by additive genetic effects, but with some partial dominance.

Broadhurst (1967) selectively bred rats for the emotional reactivity factor measured by defecation in the open field. Selection achieved maximal divergence of the two strains by 8 generations of selection, and the divergence was maintained through 20 generations even though selection was suspended after the 15th generation. The selection for emotional reactivity also produced a correlated difference in ambulation (exploration) scores. The emotionally nonreactive rats showed *more* activity in the open field.

In the study by Royce et al. (1975), using the diallel cross-mating design, genetic variation was difficult to specify for the autonomic balance and territoriality factors. Females were lower (less emotionally reactive) on the former as well as on territoriality.

In both humans and rodents, factors of exploration (sensation seeking in the human, movement in the open field in rodents) and emotional arousal (measured by psychophysiological, behavior-rating, and test data in humans and by defecation in the open field in rodents) have been identified. Both factors in both species have been shown to be heritable, and a polygenic model of inheritance seems most applicable for both. Although the two factors seem to be relatively independent at the trait level in humans, they do interact during *states* of high arousal (Zuckerman 1976, 1979b). The two behavioral factors in rodents are clearly not independent, and breeding for one of them seems to affect the other.

CORRELATIVE BIOLOGICAL STUDIES

Orienting Reflex

The orienting reflex (OR) is defined by physiological and behavioral reactions in response to stimuli of moderate intensity. Pavlov (1927/1960), who first used the term, regarded this alerting, attentional reaction to a novel stimulus as an analogue of human "curiosity." If the stimulus is repeated within a reasonably close interval, the strength of the OR tends to diminish and may even disappear (although evoked potentials show that the stimulus is still having some impact on the central nervous system).

Stimuli of stronger intensity may elicit a defensive response (DR), which can be differentiated from ORs on some measures. Heart rate, for instance, tends to show a beat-by-beat deceleration (OR) immediately following a moderate intensity stimulus and an acceleration (DR) following a more intense stimulus. In animals, the OR is often followed by investigative, approach responses, whereas the DR typically precedes "freezing" or flight reactions. On the assumption that high sensation seekers have a stronger curiosity or willingness to investigate novel stimuli, it was postulated that they would have a stronger OR than low sensation seekers.

This prediction was confirmed in two experiments by Neary and Zuckerman (1976), which selected subjects from the extremes of the distribution of scores on the General SSS. High sensation seekers had stronger electrodermal ORs to novel visual and auditory stimuli than lows, but the differences between these groups tended to disappear rapidly on repetition of the stimulus. No difference was found between the two groups on basal skin-conductance levels or on habituation rates of response. Actually, most of the habituation of the high sensation-seeking group occurred on the second presentation of the stimulus, and habituation is measured from the second stimulus on.

Feij et al. (1979) replicated the Neary and Zuckerman results using a Dutch translation of the SSS and measuring skin-conductance response to auditory stimuli. They found a significant correlation between the General SSS and the amplitude of the skin-conductance response to the first presentation of the tone. However, only one of the subscales, Thrill and Adventure Seeking (TAS), correlated with the first OR. Feij et al. also used heart rate so that they could distinguish ORs and DRs in response to the tones. They used an 80 db tone, which is on the border between intensities that elicit ORs and those that generally provoke DRs on first presentation. On the first three trials the subjects with high scores on the Disinhibition SS subscale tended to react with heart-rate decelerations (ORs), whereas the low scorers usually reacted with heart-rate accelerations (DRs). Feij et al. (1979) concluded that: "These results provide evidence that the TAS dimension is related to the strength of reactions to novel stimulation whereas the Dis dimension bears upon reactivity to intensity aspects, or, in other words, to protective inhibition." The relation of Dis to the stimulus-intensity aspect of stimulation is amplified later in the discussion of the cortical evoked potential. In a further analysis of the results in the Neary and Zuckerman (1976) study, Neary (1975) also found that the electrodermal ORs to novel stimuli correlated only with the TAS subscale.

Further evidence of a relationship between the OR, DR, and sensation seeking is found in a study by Cox (1977). Cox compared responses to moderate (60 db) and intense (110 db) tones by male subjects scoring at the extremes on the General scale of the SSS. Although not able to replicate the skin-conductance results of Neary and Zuckerman, Cox showed that high sensation seekers gave stronger heart and respiratory rate ORs (deceleration) to the moderate intensity in contrast to the heart-rate DRs (acceleration) produced by low sensation seekers reacting to both the moderate and intense tones. Ridgeway and Hare (1981) found the same result contrasting the heart-rate responses of high and low disinhibitors to the first presentation of a moderate intensity tone.

Table 2.2 shows some of the other correlates of the OR in human subjects. Young subjects tend to have stronger ORs than older subjects (Shmavonian, Miller, & Cohen, 1968). Persons with strong ORs tend to be more alert and interested in the phenomena to which they are reacting, but persons in a high state of anxiety and arousal are distractible and tend to give weak ORs. The OR can be considered a measure of focused attention that is at maximal strength at levels of intermediate arousal.

It is this relation to focused attention that probably mediates the superior conditioning and paired associate learning accompanying strong ORs (Maltzman & Raskin, 1965). Kish (1967) and Kish and Ball (1968) found

TABLE 2.2
Correlates of the Orienting Reflex (OR)

	SS	Age	Associated States	Performance	Psychopathology
Strong OR	High	younger Ss	alert, interested moderate arousal	good conditioning & paired associate learning	schizophrenics, active types psychopaths in response to intense stimuli
Weak OR	Low	older Ss	distracted or disinterested high *or* low arousal	poor conditioning & learning	anxiety neurotics schizophrenics, inactive types

that relatively high sensation seekers among alcoholics and schizophrenics tended to be better at serial anticipation learning than lows, although Kish (personal communication) could not replicate these results in college students.

In clinical populations, anxiety neurotics and schizophrenics, who are behaviorally inactive, tend to give weak ORs and in some cases do not give any ORs at all (Venables, 1975). Schizophrenics of the inactive type also score low in sensation seeking (Kish, 1970). However, schizophrenics who are more active often give strong ORs. Psychopaths tend to give strong ORs to stimuli that would normally elicit DRs (Hare, 1975), a characteristic which Feij et al. (1979) found in high sensation seekers.

Average Evoked Potential

The average evoked potential (AEP) is a signal evoked from the brain by external stimuli. The stimulus is presented a number of times. Averaging the time-locked half second EEG signals yields a characteristic response in a complex wave form. The particular wave form is reliable for an individual, and identical twins show a remarkable similarity in the wave form (Buchsbaum, 1974).

Buchsbaum and Silverman (1968) developed the method of measuring the magnitudes of the AEP in response to different intensities of a stimulus; this function is expressed as the slope of the stimulus intensity versus the AEP amplitude relationship. The high positive end of the distribution of slope measurements is called *augmenting,* and a negative slope is called *reducing.* Reliable individual measures are found at all points in the distribution of slopes. Most often, the difference between augmenters and reducers is produced by their different responses to high intensities of stimulation. At these high intensities, the augmenter shows additional increase in magnitude of the AEP, and the reducer shows an inhibition of response relative to responses to stimuli of lesser intensity.

Buchsbaum and Silverman (1968) developed this method as a more direct measure than that used by Petrie (1967) of the construct he developed. Petrie used the kinesthetic figural aftereffect (KFA) method, involving judgments of the width of a wooden block before and after tactile stimulation. Although the two methods are low to moderately correlated and show a similar relationship to pain tolerance, they differ in other types of relationships to personality and psychopathology. Some of this difference may stem from the fact that the KFA method uses low intensity somatosensory stimulation, whereas the AEP measure is produced primarily by what happens at high intensities of stimulation. Because augmenting–reducing is a construct based on brain events and because the KFA method has low reilability for an individual difference measure, it is eminently sensible to use the more direct and reliable AEP method rather than the KFA. This discussion refers entirely to the AEP-defined augmenting–reducing.

Augmenting of the AEP has been related to the SSS in five studies: Buchsbaum (1971); Coursey, Buchsbaum, and Frankel (1975); Lukas (1981); von Knorring (1980); and Zuckerman, Murtaugh, and Siegel (1974). In both the von Knorring and Zuckerman et al. studies, where the SSS form IV containing the subscales was used, the Disinhibition subscale was most highly related to augmenting, and high disinhibitors showed augmenting of the AEP, whereas lows usually exhibited the reducing pattern. The General scale was also related to augmenting in all the studies except the one by Zuckerman et al. (1974).

Table 2.3 shows some of the other correlates of AEP augmenting–reducing in humans and animals (cats). Sex differences have been found in humans with more females showing augmenting and more males exhibiting

TABLE 2.3
Correlates of AEP Augmenting-Reducing

AEP	NORMALS (HUMANS)	PATIENTS (HUMANS)	BEHAVIOR (CATS)
Augmenting	High SSS Age drop F > M Low endorphins	Manics & their well-relatives Delinquents Heroin users Alcoholics Process schiz. Low MAO	Exploratory Active Aggressive Social Reactive to novel stim.
Reducing	Low SSS Age rise M > F High endorphins	Stimulant users Reactive schiz. Insomiacs High MAO	Socially avoidant Unreactive to novel Si

reducing (Buchsbaum, Henkin, & Christiansen, 1974; Buchsbaum & Pfefferbaum, 1971). This direction of the sex difference is not consistent with the fact that males score higher than females on the SSS, particularly on the Disinhibition scale, which is the strongest correlate of augmenting. However, sex differences on augmenting were not found in Israel (Gershon & Buchsbaum, 1977), and the direction of the sex differences was reversed in an American sample of delinquents in which the male delinquents showed greater augmenting than either control males and females or delinquent females (Silverman, Buchsbaum, & Stierlin, 1973). Younger subjects tend to be augmenters, whereas older ones tend to be reducers (Buchsbaum et al., 1974). This age difference is consistent with the decline in scores on the SSS as a function of age (Zuckerman et al., 1978; Zuckerman & Neeb, 1980).

Sensation seeking and augmenting were related to sleep efficiency by Coursey et al. (1975). Sleep inefficient subjects, or insomniacs, tended to have low sensation seeking scores and to be reducers. Feij et al. (1979) found that high sensation seekers reported needing less sleep than low sensation seekers.

The manic seems to need little sleep, but the depressive often reports sleep disturbances, either insomnia or early awakening. Augmenting has been found to be characteristic of the bipolar manic-depressives, even when they are not in the manic state (Buchsbaum, Landau, Murphy, & Goodwin, 1973; Buchsbaum, Post, & Bunney, 1977; Gershon & Buchsbaum, 1977). However, reducing is not characteristic of all unipolar depressive disorders; the males tend to be reducers, and the females are more often augmenters (Buchsbaum et al., 1973).

The relation of augmenting to the bipolar affective disorder is similar to that found between sensation seeking and mania. The SSS consistently correlates with the Hypomania scale of the MMPI but not with the Depression scale (Zuckerman, 1979a). A group of former manic-depressive patients scored higher on the SSS than matched controls, but a group of unipolar depressives did not differ from controls (Zuckerman & Neeb, 1979).

Schizophrenics tend to be reducers (Davis, Buchsbaum, van Kammen, & Bunney, 1979; Landau, Buchsbaum, Carpenter, Strauss, & Sacks, 1975), which is consistent with the finding of low sensation seeking scores in hospitalized schizophrenic patients (Brownfield, 1966; Kish, 1970; Tumilty & Daitzman, 1977). However, Zuckerman and Neeb (1979) found that persons reporting a history of schizophrenia, but not currently hospitalized, do not score higher than matched controls on the SSS. The reducing function may be related to behavioral inactivity in schizophrenia. Kish (1970) found that the most behaviorally inactive patients were the ones who scored lowest on the SSS. Both inactivity and low sensation seeking may serve a protective function against painful overstimulation.

Augmenting seems to represent the prevalent pattern in a broad spectrum of psychopathic types of males including alcoholics (Buchsbaum & Ludwig, 1980; Coger, Dymonds, Serafetinides, Lowenstam, & Pearson, 1976; von Knorring, 1976) and delinquents (Silverman et al., 1973). This is consistent with the findings relating the SSS to psychopathy in college students (Zuckerman et al., 1972) and groups of incarcerated criminals (Blackburn, 1978; Emmons & Webb, 1974). Sensation seeking has also been found to be high in drug abusers, both polydrug-user types (Kilpatrick et al., 1976) and young heroin users (Platt, 1975). Despite the absent or weak association between sensation seeking and relative preference for stimulant or depressant drugs (Carrol & Zuckerman, 1977), Murtaugh (1979) found a relation between the AEP patterns and drug histories. Drug abusers who had a relatively preponderant history of depressant drug use tended to be augmenters, whereas those who primarily used stimulants (amphetamine and cocaine) tended to be reducers. Because alcohol and opiates tend to produce a reducing pattern and amphetamines tend to produce an augmenting pattern, it seems that the drugs preferred are those that serve a homeostatic function (i.e., return the extreme types closer to an intermediate level of stimulus regulation). If all drug abusers tend to be high sensation seekers, then those who are also augmenters need some protection against stimulus overload, whereas those who are reducers need high levels of arousal to process the stimuli they seek. Young alcoholics and heroin users do not usually use their respective drugs as sleeping potions; they use them to stay "cool" while engaging in a variety of social, antisocial, and sensual sensation-seeking activities.

Studies of the relationship between the augmenting–reducing dimension and behavior of cats showed that augmenting cats were rated by observers as more exploratory, active, aggressive, and emotionally responsive to novel stimuli than were reducing cats. These behavioral data from another species are consistent with the trait correlates of sensation seeking in humans (Zuckerman, 1979a) and the association between mania and sensation seeking discussed previously.

The drug lithium is used as a treatment for bipolar affective disorders. Behaviorally, it prevents the manic episodes or reduces their severity and, in many cases, also reduces the depressive swings of the cycle as well. Biochemically, lithium seems to reduce activity in brain neurons by replacing sodium in the neuron and stabilizing the potassium-sodium ion balance. It also tends to deplete the supplies of catecholamines in the neurons. In view of these effects, it is interesting to find that lithium tends to change augmenting patterns to reducing patterns in bipolar disorders (Buchsbaum, Goodwin, Murphy, & Borge, 1971). Manic-depressives who are augmenters before lithium treatment tend to show a more clinical response to lithium than do reducers (Baron, Gershon, Rudy, Jonas, & Buchsbaum, 1975; Buchsbaum et al., 1971).

Monoamine Oxidase

Monoamine oxidase (MAO) is an enzyme that is contained in the mitochondria of neurons in the brain as well as in other tissues. In the brain, MAO serves the function of degrading the monoamine neurotransmitters. MAO is an essential factor in determining the levels of these neurotransmitters available for transmission across the synapse. Generally speaking, MAO in conjunction with other biochemical factors determines the sensitivity of the neural systems it regulates. High levels of MAO would be expected to reduce sensitivity; low levels, by allowing high levels of neurotransmitters to accumulate in the neurons, would increase sensitivity. The highest levels of MAO are found in the limbic brain systems, which have important functions in the regulation of appetites, pleasure, pain, sensitivity to reward and punishment, and emotional and motivational states in general. As a regulator of these systems, MAO is obviously an important enzyme to study in humans. The problem, as with other brain chemicals, is how to obtain an index of the chemical in an intact, living person. In the 1970s, the method of studying MAO levels in blood platelets was developed. The MAO-B type found in these platelets is of the same type as is found in primate brain. Much of the behavioral and biochemical evidence indicates the likelihood of a relationship between platelet MAO and brain MAO.

As Tables 2.3 and 2.4 indicate, a negative relationship has been found between platelet MAO and augmenting of the AEP in individuals with affective disorders or "normals" with those tendencies (Buchsbaum et al., 1973; Haier, Buchsbaum, Murphy, Gottesman, & Coursey, 1980), but no relationship between MAO and AEP has been found in normals free from tendencies toward affective disorder. These findings suggest that the limits of arousability (augmenting–reducing) in persons with affective disorders may be controlled by internal biochemical regulators. As is shown later, there is ample evidence that MAO and the monoamines it regulates are implicated in these disorders.

Platelet MAO levels constitute a highly reliable biological trait of individuals with high retest reliabilities for periods of up to 10 weeks (Murphy, Wright, Buchsbaum, Nichols, Costa, & Wyatt, 1976). Levels are not affected by extreme changes in activity and mood, such as those accompanying the shift from depression to mania, or from either of these clinical states to a normal one in the bipolar affective disorders (Murphy & Weiss, 1972).

Two studies conducted on normal subjects in America have found significant *negative* correlations between platelet MAO and the SSS (Murphy, Belmaker, Buchsbaum, Martin, Ciaranello, & Wyatt, 1977; Schooler, Zahn, Murphy, & Buchsbaum, 1978). The General SS scale yielded the most consistent findings with significant correlations in both male samples and one of the two female samples.

The negative correlation between sensation seeking and MAO means that high sensation seekers tend to have low MAO levels and low sensation seekers tend to have high MAO levels. As is shown later, this is consistent with other correlates of MAO in that low MAO is related to activity, sociability, and mania, whereas the reverse is true for high MAO.

Table 2.4 summarizes the other correlates of MAO. Females have higher MAO levels than males at all ages (Murphy, Wright, Buchsbaum, Nichols, Costa, & Wyatt, 1976), a fact which is consistent with the higher SS Total

TABLE 2.4
Correlates of MAO (Monoamine Oxidase)

	NORMALS (HUMANS)	PATIENTS (HUMANS)	HIGH RISK (HUMANS)	BEHAVIOR (MONKEYS)
LOW MAO	High SSS Younger Ss Males	Manics & their well-relatives Chronic para- noid schiz. Alcoholics AEP augmenters	Socially active Criminal Drug use Psy. contacts	Play (M) Receive grooming (F) Social (M) Dominant- aggressive-sexual (M)
HIGH MAO	Low SSS Older Ss Females	AEP reducers	Low social activity	Alone (M&F) Rest and sleep (M&F) Self-groom (M)

scale scores of males at all ages (Zuckerman et al., 1978). Although an earlier study by Robinson, Davis, Nies, Ravaris, and Sylvester (1971) had shown an increase in MAO with age (consistent with the fall in SSS scores with age), the Murphy et al. (1976) study failed to confirm this MAO finding.

Coursey, Buchsbaum, and Murphy (1979) examined the characteristics of college students whose MAO levels were in the upper or lower deciles of the distribution of MAO values. A prominent difference between low and high MAO subjects was found in the time spent in social activities. Low MAO males and females spent more time in social activities than did high MAO subjects of both sexes. The low MAO males smoked more cigarettes and used more drugs than the high MAO types. The high and low MAO males also differed in convictions for criminal offenses, with the lows having more convictions. These latter findings point to a connection between MAO and sensation seeking in psychopathic behavior and drug abuse. There were also signs of a link with affective disorders in that more low MAO subjects than highs reported suicide attempts in their families and psychiatric contacts for themselves.

Among actual clinical groups, low MAO levels have been found in manic-depressive disorders (Murphy & Weiss, 1972), but neither high nor low levels were found in unipolar depressive disorders (Wyatt & Murphy, 1976). It should be recalled that sensation seeking has been found to be elevated in persons with histories of bipolar affective disorders but not in those with unipolar disorders (Zuckerman & Neeb, 1979); therefore, there is consistency in these common clinical correlates of MAO and sensation seeking. Low MAO levels are also found in chronic schizophrenics but not in acute schizophrenics (Murphy, Belmaker, & Wyatt, 1974; Wyatt & Murphy, 1976). The finding of low MAO levels in chronic schizophrenics is inconsistent with the finding of low sensation seeking scores in chronic schizophrenics (Kish, 1970). However, it seems to be the paranoid types who have the low MAO levels (Potkin, Cannon, Murphy, & Wyatt, 1978; Schildkraut, Herzog, Orsulak, Edelman, Shein, & Frazier, 1976) in contrast to the inactive catatonic types who are lowest in sensation seeking (Kish, 1970).

Low MAO levels have also been found among chronic alcoholics (Major & Murphy, 1978; Sullivan, Cavenar, Maltbie, Lester, & Zung, 1979) and chronic marijuana users (Stillman, Wyatt, Murphy, & Rauscher, 1978).

MAO-inhibiting drugs have been used in the treatment of depression because of their ability to provide a long-lasting activation effect, particularly in the behaviorally retarded type of depression. The effect of these drugs is presumed to be through their reduction of MAO in the brain, thereby allowing norepinephrine to build up in the neurons. Tricyclic antidepressants have the same end result through actions other than MAO inhibition. The action of these drugs is consistent with the catecholamine theory of depression (Schildkraut, 1965), which suggests that an excess of brain catecholamines might produce the overactivity seen in mania and a deficiency of these brain amines might affect the constriction of activity, interest, and motivation seen in depression. MAO-inhibiting drugs may precipitate mania when given to a bipolar affective patient in the depressed phase. MAO inhibitors can also produce some unwanted behavioral effects including transient maniclike behavior, euphoria, aggressiveness, hallucinations, and paranoid episodes in other types of patients and normals (Murphy, 1977b). Amphetamine, which also acts through the release of norepinephrine, often produces similar effects, although the energizing effects and euphoria are more characteristic of prehabituated users, and the aggressive hallucinatory and paranoid effects are more characteristic of addicted, chronic users.

All of these clinical and drug findings suggest that the negative correlations of MAO with sensation seeking are possible indicators of correlations between the behavioral trait and levels of catecholamines in the brain. This hypothesis is elaborated later in the theoretical section of this chapter.

Endorphins

The discovery of endogenous morphinelike peptides, or endorphins, in the brain (Hughes, 1975; Terenius & Wahlström, 1975) occurred only recently in the mid-1970s. The endorphins seem to serve the direct function of protection against pain or excessive stimulation and, like exogenous morphine, they may dampen mood and behavior in general. Because AEP reducing has also been postulated to serve the function of protection against excessive or intense stimulation, one would hypothesize a relationship between endorphins and reducing of the AEP. This relationship has been demonstrated by von Knorring, Almay, Johansson, and Terenius (1979) in a group of patients with chronic pain syndromes. Augmenters have significantly *lower* levels of endorphins (obtained from cerebrospinal fluid) than reducers.

Inasmuch as von Knorring and his colleagues had already found a relationship between augmenting–reducing and their Swedish translation of the SSS, they proceeded to compare SSS scores of patients with high and low levels of endorphins (Johansson, Almay, von Knorring, Terenius, & Astrom, 1979). The patients with *low* levels of endorphins were significantly higher on all of the SS scales than those with high endorphin levels. Significant negative correlations were found between endorphins and the Disinhibition ($r = -.39$) and Boredom Susceptibility ($r = -.54$) subscales. Table 2.5 shows some of the correlates of endorphin levels.

TABLE 2.5
Correlates of Endorphins

	SSS	HUMAN PATIENTS
Low Endorphins	High	Pain Sensitivity Organic Pain Pts. AEP Augmenting
High Endorphins	Low	Neuroticism Psychogenic Pain Pts. Schizophrenia ? AEP Reducing

No significant correlation was found between endorphins and age, and no sex difference in endorphins was found in the Johansson et al. study. Endorphins were not related to the Extraversion scale from the Eysenck Personality Inventory (Eysenck & Eysenck, 1964) but correlated positively and significantly with the Neuroticism scale ($r = +.38$). Patients with high levels of endorphins had higher Neuroticism scores than those with low levels of endorphins.

Studies have shown that naloxone, an opiate antagonist, produces hypersensitivity to pain in humans (Buchsbaum, Davis, & Bunney, 1977) and animals (Frederickson, Burgis, & Edwards, 1977) although some studies have failed to confirm these results. Endorphins have been directly related to pain perception (von Knorring, Almay, Johansson, & Terenius, 1978). Patients with organic pain syndromes had lower levels of endorphins than patients with psychogenic pain syndromes (Johansson et al., 1979).

Terenius, Wahlström, Lindström, and Widerlöv (1976) reported increased levels of endorphins in the cerebrospinal fluid of chronic schizophrenics. This was followed by the exciting discovery that low doses of naloxone reduced schizophrenics' auditory hallucinations. Studies by Bloom, Segal, Ling, and Guillemin (1976) and Jacquet and Marks (1976) showed that intracerebral administration of endorphins produced rigidity in rats similar to catatonic symptoms in schizophrenia. These kinds of findings led Volavka, Davis, and Ehrlich (1979) to propose a theory linking endorphin findings to the dopamine hypothesis of schizophrenia. They suggest that an endorphin excess exists in schizophrenia, which results in a supersensitivity of dopamine receptors. A phenomenon frequently noted in chronic schizophrenics is their apparent insensitivity to pain. Davis et al. (1979) showed that this insensitivity could be reversed by the administration of naltrexone. The study also linked the endorphins to the AEP: The pain insensitivity in schizophrenics was related to smaller somatosensory evoked potentials (EPs) to painful stimuli. The schizophrenics who were treated with naltrexone showed both increased pain sensitivity and increased EP amplitudes at higher stimulus intensities. Naltrexone tended to eliminate the reducing characteristic of schizophrenic AEPs and changed them in the augmenting direction.

Chronic schizophrenics are generally low in sensation seeking, as discussed previously, and the lowered sensation seeking is directly related to the amount of retardation of behavioral activity. Could endorphins be the mediator of the link between chronic schizophrenic inactivity, apathy, and low sensation seeking?

Gonadal Hormones

Investigation of the role of sex hormones in sensation seeking was undertaken because of consistent findings of sex differences on the test-measured trait (Zuckerman, 1979a). Although not discounting the likelihood of a cultural-learning basis for the sex differences, we decided to see if the differences found in every country investigated thus far might also have a biological basis. Sex differentiation in structure (size, muscle distribution, etc.) in our species is likely to have been associated with evolved differences between the sexes in temperament. Natural selection would have favored a higher level of a sensation seeking trait in males than in females considering the speculations on the characteristics of early hominid ancestors discussed in the first part of this chapter. Although anatomy is certainly *not* destiny, there is a conservative force in evolution that maintains differences past the point where they are functionally adaptive, provided they are not nonadaptive. The falling birthrate in women who are electing careers (presumably the higher sensation seekers) in preference to the role of housewife is an illustration of a selective factor which, if maintained over a long period of time, might result in lower sensation-seeking trait in the population.

Until recently, most of the studies on gonadal hormones have assayed the hormones from plasma. Such measures are subject to diurnal and other fluctuations and do not tell us about the production rate or the availability of the gonadal steroids at receptor sites in the brain. But if pooled samples taken at the same time of day are used, one can obtain a reasonably reliable trait measure for individuals.

It is important to note that although androgens usually predominate over estrogens in adult males, with the opposite true for adult females, some estrogen is present in males and some testosterone is present in females. In males, estrogen is produced by the conversion of androsteredione and testosterone to estrone and estradiol, and by direct testicular and adrenal secretion. In females, androgens are produced by the adrenal cortex and the follicle cells of the ovary and are converted to estrone and estradiol as in males.

Daitzman, Zuckerman, Sammelwitz, and Ganjam (1978) studied the relationship between sensation seeking and total androgens in two samples of males, and between sensation seeking and total estrogens in one of these samples. In both of these male samples androgens correlated positively and significantly with the Disinhibition subscale of the SSS, and these correlations remained significant even when controlled for the subjects' heights, weights, ages, and recencies of orgasm. Estrogens also correlated significantly with the Disinhibition scale, as well as the General scale, in the second sample of males. In a very small sample of females, similar correlations were found.

This study was followed by one in which Daitzman and Zuckerman (1980) selected male subjects from the extreme ranges of scores on the Disinhibition subscale and did specific assays for testosterone, 17B-estradiol, estrone, and progesterone. Males scoring high on the Disinhibition scale had significantly higher levels of testosterone, estradiol, and estrone than low scorers on the scale. The differences on progesterone were not significant. Thus, three studies have shown a relationship between the Disinhibition type of sensation seeking and androgens in males, and two studies have shown a relationship between Disinhibition and estrogens.

Most of the work on correlates of the gonadal hormones in humans has focused on testosterone, therefore Table 2.6 is confined to correlates of

TABLE 2.6
Correlates of Testosterone

	SSS, SEX, AGE	BEHAVIORAL TRAITS
HIGH TESTOSTERONE	High SSS M > F Younger males	Aggressive Sociable Dominant Active
LOW TESTOSTERONE	Low SSS Older Females	Low sexual arousal Neurotic-introversion Unsociable, submissive inactive

this hormone. The study of Daitzman and Zuckerman (1980) used a variety of trait measures other than the SSS in their study of gonadal hormone correlates. They found that measures of extraversion, sociability, self-acceptance, dominance, and activity correlated positively with testosterone. Measures of neuroticism and introversion correlated negatively with this hormone in males. Testosterone also correlated positively with variety of sexual experience and permissive sexual attitudes.

Many of these correlates of testosterone in human males have analogues in animal research. Animals high in testosterone tend to mate more often and to dominate both territory and females in species where such dominance hierarchies are prominent. Although the relationship of testosterone in the normal range to sexual activity has not been clearly shown, there is ample evidence that the absence, or very low levels, of testosterone in the male is accompanied by difficulties in physical sexual arousal and a reduction in desire and fantasies (Bremer, 1959; Stürup, 1968). Testosterone also seems to mediate arousability in females. Although testosterone does have some influence in sexual arousability, it does not seem to influence object choice in humans. Rose (1975) has reviewed the literature on male homosexuality and concluded that there are no differences in testosterone between homosexual and heterosexual males. However, it was estrogen (estradiol) that was related to homosexual experience in the Daitzman and Zuckerman (1980) study. Injection of estrogen into castrated male rats usually elicits a lowered threshold for the female "presenting" response in these males. Actually, research is lacking on the role of estrogen in human male homosexuality.

Aggressiveness is a frequent correlate of testosterone in many species of animals. Domestic male animals are often castrated to reduce their aggression and unmanageability. Human research has not revealed a clear correlation between aggressiveness (or hostility) and testosterone in the normal range, but some samples of prisoners who committed particularly aggressive crimes show high levels of testosterone in contrast to other prisoners (Rose, 1975, 1978). It is interesting that aggressiveness, as a measured trait, tends to correlate primarily with Disinhibition, the scale most consistently correlated with testosterone (Zuckerman, 1979a).

In the Daitzman and Zuckerman (1980) study, low levels of testosterone were related to neuroticism. There is no evidence of testosterone insufficiency in clinical neurosis, but it is known that prolonged stress can lower testosterone levels. Psychotic and psychopathic traits were related to estrogen in males. Here again most of the clinical research has focused on testosterone levels in males.

Gonadal hormone levels decline with age. Testosterone declines constantly in the male (Harman, 1978) from the 20s on. It is possible that this decline in gonadal hormones has some relationship to the lower SSS scores seen in older persons.

One obvious effect of declining gonadal hormones is the reduction of activity in general and sexual activity in particular. But gonadal hormones also have an influence on MAO (Redmond, Murphy, Baulu, Zeegler, & Lake, 1975). In animal studies, MAO levels increase in castrated animals and seem to vary inversely with seasonal hormone levels. There is also the possibility that gonadal hormones have directly sensitizing effects on the primary reward areas that lie close to sexual arousal areas in the limbic system.

A BIOLOGICAL THEORY OF SENSATION SEEKING

The data thus far show a genetic basis for sensation seeking in humans and for analogous behaviors in animals. Common biological correlates, including a "strong" nervous system (augmenting of the AEP at high intensities of stimulation), levels of MAO, endorphins, and gonadal hormones provide the biological links between behavior in humans and animals. Drug treatments, which alter levels of the endogenous biochemicals and change behavior in predictable ways, provide some experimental tests of the hypothesis that such chemicals control sensation-seeking behavior rather than that the behavior alters biochemistry. Human behavior disorders, such as mania, depression, sociopathy, and schizophrenia, have provided another area where extreme forms of sensation seeking or sensation avoidance have been related to endogenous biochemicals and psychophysiological traits.

At what point is it appropriate to construct a theory or model that attempts to integrate findings such as the ones presented in this chapter? Caution would argue that we wait until all the evidence is provided (whenever that may be). The debate between Stein and Gray over the role of the neurotransmitter norepinephrine, and the behavior system that it serves, is a good example of the unsettled state of the field. Impulsivity would argue that the controversies will never be resolved until we present our hypotheses in the framework of an organized theory so that research can be appropriately designed to test the essential questions. As Gertrude Stein was said to have asked on her deathbed: "What is the answer?" (Silence) "In that case, what is the question?" To this we might add: "Is the question meaningful?"

The first theory of sensation seeking (Zuckerman, 1969) was simply an extension of general *optimal level of arousal* theories, such as those of Hebb (1955) and Lindsley (1957, 1961), to explain individual differences in the trait. If the reticulo-cortical system serves a homeostatic function in the regulation of stimulation and brain arousal, then individual differences must depend on sensitivities of the system or the balance of excitation and inhibition in the system. Persons with high optimal levels of arousal seek high levels of stimulation in order to maintain central arousal at high levels where they feel best and function most efficiently (Zuckerman, 1969). Variety or change in stimulation is sought in order to avoid the habituation produced by repetition. Eysenck (1967) formulated a similar theory to explain the traits of extraversion.

Problems have developed with this theory, which make it difficult to support. First, there are the findings that sensation seekers who use drugs typically use those that depress central nervous system function (alcohol, barbituates, heroin) as well as those that increase arousal (amphetamine and cocaine). Second, the endogenous biochemicals found to be related to sensation seeking (MAO and endorphins) are found in highest concentrations in subcortical structures of the limbic system. Third, the types of phenomena associated with sensation seeking (e.g., sexuality, strong positive emotional responses and appetites) are also based on systems in these limbic structures. Fourth, and most important, is the failure of a well-controlled experiment (Carrol, Zuckerman, & Vogel, 1982) to confirm hypotheses derived from an optimal level of arousal theory.

Carrol et al. (1982) selected high and low sensation seekers from the extremes of the distribution of scores on the SSS and gave them on different occasions a placebo, a CNS depressant (diazepam), and a CNS stimulant (D-amphetamine). A number of affect scales were used to test subjective feelings, and several performance tests were used to test behavioral efficiency. If the optimal level of arousal theory is correct, the high sensation seekers should feel and function better after taking amphetamine, and the low sensation seekers should have been happiest and achieved their best scores after taking diazepam. At the beginning of an experiment most subjects were somewhat aroused, as judged from elevated pulse and blood pressure. Amphetamine tended to maintain this high level of arousal over the period of the experiment, whereas diazepam, or just confinement and habituation (placebo), tended to lower arousal. Both groups felt and functioned best in the condition where high arousal was maintained by amphetamine. The interactions between the sensation seeking trait and drugs, predicted from the optimal level of arousal theory, were not found.

But even before this critical experiment, I was revising the biological model for sensation seeking to accomodate the MAO findings (Zuckerman 1979b). Figure 2.1 shows the revised model that moves the basic site of sensation seeking from the reticulo-cortical system to the limbic reward system, which includes the parts of the septum, medial forebrain-bundle and lateral hypothalamus. These areas yield high rates of self-stimulation in rats (Olds & Milner, 1954). Berlyne (1967) suggested that this system might mediate response to stimuli with moderate "arousal potential." Schneirla (1959) and Gray (1973) hypothesized that this system governed the general tendency to approach rather than withdraw from stimuli. Gray makes this system the basis for the trait of "impulsivity" (see Chapter 6, this volume).

The limbic reward and punishment systems can stimulate the reticular activating system through collaterals; the punishment system (orbital frontal cortex-septo-hippocampal) probably exerts its major arousal effect in this manner. But this kind of arousal more often leads to either a paralysis of behavior or withdrawal, associated with the emotion of fear, rather than the approach behavior associated with positive affective arousal. Routtenberg (1968) suggested that the reward system constitutes a "second arousal system," which may directly activate the cortex and dampen the other arousal system. He suggests that the strength of the orienting reflex (OR) stems from the sensitivity of the second arousal system. This suggestion is in accord with our findings that sensation seeking is positively related, and anxiety is negatively related, to the amplitude of the OR to a novel stimulus. These findings are not congruent with Gray's assumption that the OR is produced by sensitivity of the punishment or anxiety system.

If we assume that the sensitivity of the reward system produces alertness and interest in novel stimuli associated with strong ORs, the next question concerns the basis of the sensitivity of this system. The data showing low MAO levels in high sensation seekers and high MAO levels in low sensation seekers point to the monoamines regulated and metabolized by MAO as the possible basis of the trait. Stein's (1978) theory (see also Chapter 5, this volume) suggests that norepinephrine and dopamine mediate two components of the reward mechanism: Dopamine controls the readiness to explore and approach novel stimuli; norepinephrine regulates the sensitivity to, or expectation of, positive reinforcement. This theory makes the data relating sociability, activity, and impulsivity in humans and animals to *low MAO levels* comprehensible, assuming that low levels of MAO in the neurons of the reward system allow the accumulation of high levels of norepinephrine and dopamine. In other words, a negative relationship between brain MAO and catecholamines is postulated.

A BIOLOGICAL MODEL
FOR SENSATION SEEKING

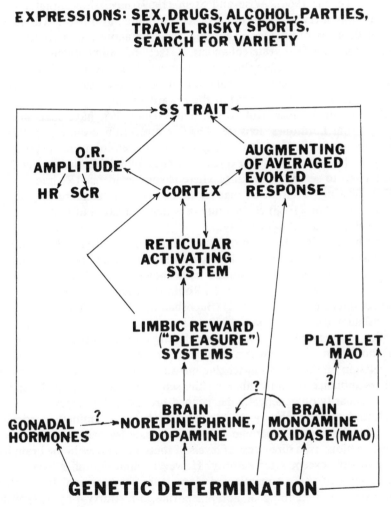

FIG. 2.1 A biological model for sensation seeking. (From Zuckerman, 1979a. Reprinted by permission.)

Human studies of manic-depressive psychosis and drugs that control or exacerbate it (i.e., switch depression into mania) support this theory. MAO-inhibiting drugs as well as amphetamine and cocaine, which have the effect of increasing available norepinephrine, produce increases in activity in animals and euphoria in people. Administration of α-methyl-O-tyrosine, an inhibitor of tyrosine hydroxylase, which is involved in the biosynthesis of the catecholamines, results in a blocking of the euphoric effect of amphetamine in humans (Jönsson, Ånggård, & Gunne, 1971) and markedly reduces the hyperactivity effects of amphetamine in animals (Weissman, Koe, & Tenen, 1966). Wise and Stein (1969) have shown that the self-stimulation of reward areas in the brain is inhibited by 6-hydroxydopamine, which depletes brain norepinephrine. This antagonist of norepinephrine also eliminates the rate-enhancing effect of amphetamine on self-stimulation. These studies show that the rewarding effects of chemical (amphetamine) or electric stimulation depend on the availability of catecholamines in the neurons of the reward system.

Broverman, Klaiber, Kobayashi, and Vogel (1968) have suggested that the gonadal hormones activate behavior and brain arousability through their antagonistic effects on MAO, thereby increasing norepinephrine activity. If this is true it would explain why both gonadal hormones and MAO are related to sensation seeking. There is some evidence (Redmond et al., 1975) showing variation of platelet MAO with the menstrual cycle, and Broverman et al. (1968) cite a study in which castration of male rats raised the level of brain MAO activity.

The heritability of the sensation-seeking trait (see Eysenck, Chapter 1, this volume) must depend on the heritability of the biological systems that govern it. Small-scale twin studies have shown substantial heritability for platelet MAO (Murphy, 1973; Nies, Robinson, Lamborn, & Lampert, 1973) and for augmenting of the AEP (Buchsbaum, 1974). Data from a study by Buchsbaum (in Zuckerman, 1979a) show that identical twins who have similar augmenting AEP slopes have highly correlated scores on the SSS, but those twins who show less resemblance on the AEP measure show little correlation on the sensation-seeking measure. These data tend to show that the resemblance of individuals on the sensation-seeking trait depends on their similarity on genetically determined brain characteristics.

Central to this theory is the idea that brain amines, particularly norepinephrine and dopamine, are the substrate for sensation seeking. In work on humans, a direct test of levels of these substances in the brain itself is impossible except after autopsy. However, clinical studies have utilized metabolites of the monoamines derived from cerebrospinal fluid, blood, and urine. A metabolite of norepinephrine, 3-methoxy-4-hydroxyphenyl-glycol (MHPG), obtained from urine, is estimated to be derived in some part from brain norepinephrine rather than peripheral norepinephrine. Unlike platelet MAO, which tends to be a rather stable biological trait measure, MHPG shows marked intraindividual state variations as a function of diurnal rhythms, diet, activity, stress, and clinical phase and recovery in the bipolar affective disorders. The variations due to diet, activity, and mood have been found in patients but not in normal controls. As so many factors can affect the immediate level of MHPG, one might be pessimistic about demonstrating the direct relationship between MHPG and sensation seeking, which the theory dictates. However, such a relationship has been found in a small sample of 10 normals whose urine was obtained during a stressful and a nonstressful period (Buchsbaum, Muscettola, & Goodwin, 1981). In both conditions, significant positive correlations were found between MHPG and the General SSS. However, no significant correlations were found in the patient group consisting of 12 affective disorders. These preliminary findings suggest that metabolites of brain norepinephrine are related to sensation seeking (see Chapter 7, this volume).

This theory of sensation seeking was published (Zuckerman 1979a, 1979b) only months before the findings relating endorphins to sensation seeking were reported in a personal communication from von Knorring. Although I had speculated (Zuckerman, 1979a) on the role of endorphins in sensation seeking, based on Stein's (1978) idea of their role in the reward system, I guessed wrong about the direction of the relationship. Here is one of the "substantial penalties" for premature theory. There was no place for endorphins in the system shown in Fig. 2.1. The findings that endorphins relate negatively to sensation seeking requires both replication and some readjustment in the theory.

The opioid peptides seem to be concentrated in pathways that overlap those of the catecholamines, particularly dopamine. Similar to the effects of opiates found outside of the body, the endorphins have pain reduction and euphoric effects. Goldstein (1978) has speculated that different endorphins may account for these two separate effects. It may be that the euphoric effect explains the initial attraction of sensation seekers to these drugs, whereas the pain-reduction effect explains the addiction. The fact that high sensation seekers are low in the endogenous opiates may explain why they are so sensitized to the exogenous opiates. These drugs feed a starvation that they were born with. The low sensation seekers, who are already high in endorphins, do not need any additional sedation of the type produced by depressant drugs or alcohol. Their high endorphin levels may explain why they are less interested and active, have a less reactive OR, and an effective reducing type of cortex.

Both MAO and the endorphins seem to be high in low sensation seekers, and both are related to reducing the AEP. We need to know more about the relationships between the endorphins, MAO, and the monoamine neurotransmitters. There is much to be learned in a study that assesses all of these measures in the same subjects.

Experimental studies of animals in the open-field situation and social behavior in laboratory environments similar to their natural habitats are also needed. Earlier in this chapter, I described the ethological methods used by Ellison (1977) to study the effects of depletion of brain-norepinephrine and serotonin. Using selective monoamine toxins, 6-hydroxydopamine for norepinephrine and 5, 6 dihydroxy-tryptamine for serotonin, injected into the ventricles of the brain, he studied the effects of the depletion of one or both of these neurotransmitters.

Rats that were depleted of both neurotransmitters were underresponsive to positive gustatory reinforcers and overresponsive to negative reinforcers. They were helpless in the open-field test, huddling close to the walls and showing no exploration. Low norepinephrine animals locomoted in the open field but showed fewer observation responses (rearing up) and, in the author's words, seemed "inattentive." Serotonin-depleted rats locomoted less than controls, reared more, stayed near the walls, and "appeared to be frightened anxious animals."

In their more familiar environments, the low serotonin rats, who were assumed to be higher in norepinephrine, were "aroused and exploratory," active, and more willing to approach humans. Ellison (1977) describes these animals as in a: "state appropriate for a vigilant animal out foraging in the environment and . . . involved in a type of positive affect related to goal-directed approach arousal [p. 1043]." If he is right in assuming an inverse relationship between serotonin and norepinephrine, then a kind of sensation-seeking approach behavior in their normal environments seems to be characteristic of high norepinephine animals. The fearful behavior of these animals in the novel situation of the open field is not consistent with a sensation-seeking norepinephrine relationship, but the double-depleted animals were even more fearful, suggesting that serotonin also plays a role in open-field behavior and sensation seeking.

According to Ellison (1977) the norepinephrine-depleted rat is a good model for low sensation seeking: "for it tends to remain in its burrow and is lethargic and it gradually becomes the underdog in social interactions [p. 1042]." The low human sensation seeker is also reluctant to leave secure environments and tends to show a submissive trait in social interactions.

Animal experiments such as this may be more appropriate for the study of the animal analogue of sensation seeking than the self-stimulation studies of Stein or the learning studies of Gray because they examine the effect of alterations in brain chemistry on behavior that is more natural for the species. The animal data lend credibility to the sociobiological speculation that temperament has evolved in humans from their mammalian antecedents. These studies further advance the status of our behavioral science by supplying the biological mechanisms that underlie the variations in both human and animal behavior.

REFERENCES

Bacon, V. *Sensation seeking levels for members of high risk volunteer organizations.* Unpublished manuscript, 1974.

Baron, M., Gershon, E.S., Rudy, V., Jonas, W.Z., & Buchsbaum, M.S. Lithium response in depression as predicted by unipolar/bipolar illness, average evoked response and COMT and family history. *Archives of General Psychiatry,* 1975, *32,* 1107-1111.

Berlyne, D. E. Arousal and reinforcement. In D. Levine (Ed.), *Nebraska Symposium on Motivation* (Vol. 15). Lincoln: University of Nebraska Press, 1967.

Blackburn, R. Electrodermal and cardiovascular correlates of psychopathy. In R. D. Hare & D. Schalling (Eds.), *Psychopathic behavior: Approaches to research.* New York: Wiley, 1978.

Bloom, F., Segal, D., Ling, N., & Gullemin, R. Profound behavioral effects in rats suggest new etiological factors in mental illness. *Science,* 1976, *194,* 630-632.

Bone, R. N., Cowling, L. W., & Belcher, M. M. *Sensation seeking and the Similes Preference Inventory.* Personal Communication, 1974.

Bremer, J. *Asexualization: A follow-up study of 244 cases.* New York: Macmillan, 1959.

Brill, N. Q., Crumpton, E., & Grayson, H. M. Personality factors in marijuana use. *Archives of General Psychiatry,* 1971, *24,* 163-165.

Broadhurst, P. L. The biometrical analyses of behavioural inheritance. *Science Progress, Oxford,* 1967, *55,* 123-139.

Broverman, D. M., Klaiber, E. L., Kobayashi, Y., & Vogel, W. Roles of activation and inhibition in sex differences in cognitive abilities. *Psychological Review,* 1968, *75,* 23-50.

Brownfield, C. A. Optimal stimulation levels of normal and disturbed subjects in sensory deprivation. *Psychologia,* 1966, *9,* 27-38.

Bruner, J. S. Nature and uses of immaturity. In J. S. Bruner, A. Jolly, & K. Sylva (Eds.), *Play: Its role in development and evolution.* New York: Basic Books, 1976.

Buchsbaum, M. S. Neural events and the psychophysical law. *Science,* 1971, *172,* 502.

Buchsbaum, M. S. Average evoked response and stimulus intensity in identical and fraternal twins. *Physiological Psychology,* 1974, *2,* 365-370.

Buchsbaum, M. S., Davis, G. C., & Bunney, W. E. Jr. Naloxone alteration of pain perception and somatosensory evoked potentials in normal subjects. *Nature,* 1977, *270,* 620-622.

Buchsbaum, M. S., Goodwin, F. K., Murphy, D., & Borge, G. AER in affective disorders. *American Journal of Psychiatry,* 1971, *128,* 19-25.

Buchsbaum, M. S., Henkin, R. I., & Christiansen, R. L. Age and sex differences in averaged evoked responses in a normal population with observations on patients with gonadal dysgenesis. *Electroencephalography and Clinical Neurophysiology,* 1974, *37,* 137-144.

Buchsbaum, M. S., Landau, S., Murphy, D., & Goodwin, F. Average evoked response in bipolar and unipolar affective disorders: Relationships to sex, age of onset, and monoamine oxidase. *Biological Psychiatry,* 1973, *7,* 199-212.

Buchsbaum, M. S., & Ludwig, A. M. Effects of sensory input and alcohol administration on visual evoked potentials in normal subjects and alcoholics. In H. Begleiter (Ed.), *Biological effects of alcohol.* New York: Plenum Press, 1980.

Buchsbaum, M. S., Muscettola, G., & Goodwin, F. K. Urinary MHPG, stress response, personality factors and somatosensory evoked potentials in normal subjects and patients with affective disorders. *Neuropsychobiology,* 1981, *7,* 212-224.

Buchsbaum, M. S., & Pfefferbaum, A. Individual differences in stimulus-intensity response. *Psychophysiology,* 1971, *8,* 600-611.

Buchsbaum, M. S., Post, R. M., & Bunney, W. E., Jr. AER in a rapidly cycling manic-depressive patient. *Biological Psychiatry,* 1977, *12,* 83-99.

Buchsbaum, M. S., & Silverman, J. Stimulus intensity control and the cortical evoked response. *Psychosomatic Medicine*, 1968, *30*, 12–22.

Carrol, E. N., & Zuckerman, M. Psychopathology and sensation seeking in 'downers,' 'speeders,' and 'trippers': A study of the relationship between personality and drug choice. *International Journal of Addictions*, 1977, *12*, 591–601.

Carrol, E. N., Zuckerman, M., & Vogel, W. H. A test of the optimal level of arousal theory of sensation seeking. *Journal of Personality and Social Psychology*, 1982, *42*, 572–575.

Coger, R. W., Dymond, A. M., Serafetinides, E. A., Lowenstam, I., & Pearson, D. Alcoholism: Averaged visual evoked response amplitude-intensity slope and symmetry in withdrawal. *Biological Psychiatry*, 1976, *11*, 435–443.

Coursey, R. D., Buchsbaum, M. S., & Frankel, B. L. Personality measures and evoked responses in chronic insomniacs. *Journal of Abnormal Psychology*, 1975, *84*, 239–249.

Coursey, R. D., Buchsbaum, M. S., & Murphy, D. L. Platelet MAO activity and evoked potentials in the identification of subjects biologically at risk for psychiatric disorders. *British Journal of Psychiatry*, 1979, *134*, 372–381.

Cox, D. N. *Psychophysiological correlates of sensation seeking and socialization during reduced stimulation.* Unpublished doctoral dissertation, University of British Columbia, 1977.

Daitzman, R. J., & Zuckerman, M. Disinhibitory sensation seeking personality, and gonadal hormones. *Personality and Individual Differences*, 1980, *1*, 103–110.

Daitzman, R. J., Zuckerman, M., Sammelwitz, P. H., & Ganjam, V. Sensation seeking and gonadal hormones. *Journal of Biosocial Science*, 1978, *10*, 401–408.

Davis, G. C., Buchsbaum, M. S., van Kammen, D. P., & Bunney, W. E., Jr. Analgesia to pain stimuli in schizophrenics reversed by naltrexone. *Psychiatry Research*, 1979, *1*, 61–69.

Egan, O., Royce, J. R., & Poley, W. Evidence for a territorial marking factor of mouse emotionality. *Psychonomic Science*, 1972, *27*, 272–274.

Ellison, G. D. Animal models of psychopathology: The low-norepinephrine and low-serotonin rats. *American Psychologist*, 1977, *32*, 1036–1045.

Emmons, T. D., & Webb, W. W. Subjective correlates of emotional responsivity and stimulation seeking on psychopaths, normals, and acting-out neurotics. *Journal of Consulting and Clinical Psychology*, 1974, *42*, 620–625.

Eysenck, H. J., & Eysenck, S. B. G. *Eysenck Personality Inventory.* San Diego: Educational and Industrial Testing Service, 1964.

Eysenck, H. J. *The biological basis of personality.* Springfield, Ill.: Thomas, 1967.

Farley, F. H. Measures of individual differences in stimulation seeking and the tendency toward variety. *Journal of Consulting and Clinical Psychology*, 1971, *37*, 394–396.

Feij, J. A., Orlebeke, A., Gazendam, A., & van Zuilen, R. *Sensation seeking: Measurement and psychophysiological correlates.* Paper presented at International Conference on Temperament, Need for Stimulation and Activity, Warsaw, Poland, September 1979.

Fisher, S. *The female orgasm.* New York: Basic Books, 1973.

Frederickson, R. C. A., Burgis, V., & Edwards, J. D. Hyperalgesia induced by naloxone follows diurnal rhythm in responsivity to painful stimuli. *Science*, 1977, *198*, 756.

Gershon, E. S., & Buchsbaum, M. S. A genetic study of average evoked response: Augmentation/reduction in affective disorders. In C. Shagass, S. Gershon, & A. J. Friedhoff (Eds.), *Psychopathology and brain dysfunction.* New York: Raven Press, 1977.

Glanzer, M. Stimulus satiation: An exploration of spontaneous alteration and related phenomena. *Psychological Review*, 1953, *60*, 257–268.

Goldstein, A. Opiate receptors and opioid peptides: A ten-year overview. In M. A. Lipton, A. DiMascio, & K. F. Killam (Eds.), *Psychopharmacology: A generation of progress.* New York: Raven Press, 1978.

Gray, J. A. Causal theories of personality and how to test them. In J. R. Royce (Ed.), *Multivariate analysis and psychological theory.* New York: Academic Press, 1973.

Haier, R. J., Buchsbaum, M. S., Murphy, D. L., Gottesman, I. I., & Coursey, R. D. Psychiatric vulnerability, monoamine oxidase, and the average evoked potential. *Archives of General Psychiatry*, 1980, *37*, 340–345.

Hall, R. A., Rappaport, M., Hopkins, H. K., & Griffin, R. B. Evoked response and behavior in cats. *Science*, 1970, *170*, 998–1000.

Hare, R. D. Psychophysiological studies of psychopathy. In D. C. Fowles (Ed.), *Clinical applications of psychophysiology*. New York: Columbia University Press, 1975.

Harlow, H. F., Dodsworth, R. O., & Harlow, M. K. Toward social isolation in monkeys. *Proceedings of the National Academy of Sciences*, 1965, *54*, 90–97.

Harman, S. M. Clinical aspects of aging of the male reproductive system. In E. L. Schneider (Ed.), *The aging reproductive system* (Aging, Vol. 4). New York: Raven Press, 1978.

Hebb, D. O. Drives and the CNS (conceptual nervous system). *Psychological Review*, 1955, *62*, 243–254.

Heyman, S. R., & Rose, K. G. *Psychological variables affecting SCUBA performance*. In C. H. Nadeau, W. R. Halliwell, K. M. Newell, & G. C. Roberts (Eds.), *Psychology of motor behavior and sport*. Champaign, Ill.: Human Kinetics Press, 1980.

Hocking, J., & Robertson, M. The Sensation-Seeking Scale as a predictor of need for stimulation during sensory restriction. *Journal of Consulting and Clinical Psychology*, 1969, *33*, 367–369.

Hughes, J. Isolation of an endogenous compound from the brain with pharmacological properties similar to morphine. *Brain Research*, 1975, *88*, 295–308.

Hymbaugh, K., & Garrett, J. Sensation seeking among skydivers. *Perceptual and Motor Skills*, 1974, *38*, 118.

Jacquet, Y. F., & Marks, N. The C-fragment of beta-lipotropin: An endogenous neuroleptic or antipsychotogen. *Science*, 1976, *194*, 632–634.

Johansson, F., Almay, B. G. L., von Knorring, L., Terenius, L., & Astrom. Personality traits in chronic pain patients related to endorphin levels in cerebrospinal fluid. *Psychiatry Research*, 1979, *1*, 231–239.

Jones, N. B. Rough-and-tumble play among nursery school children. In A. Jolly & K. Sylva (Eds.), *Play: Its role in development and evolution*. New York: Basic Books, 1976.

Jönsson, L. E., Aṅggård, E., & Gunne, L. M. Blockade of intravenous amphetamine euphoria in man. *Clinical Pharmacology and Therapeutics*, 1971, *12*, 889–896.

Kaestner, E., Rosen, L., & Appel, P. Patterns of drug abuse: Relationships with ethnicity, sensation seeking and anxiety. *Journal of Consulting and Clinical Psychology*, 1977, *45*, 462–468.

Khavari, K. A., Humes, M., & Mabry, E. Personality correlates of hallucinogen use. *Journal of Abnormal Psychology*, 1977, *86*, 172–178.

Kilpatrick, D. G., Sutker, P. B., & Smith, A. D. Deviant drug and alcohol use: The role of anxiety, sensation seeking and other personality variables. In M. Zuckerman & C. D. Spielberger (Eds.), *Emotions and anxiety: New concepts, methods and applications*. Hillsdale, N.J.: Lawrence Erlbaum Associates, 1976.

Kish, G. B. *Stimulus seeking and learning*. Unpublished manuscript, 1967.

Kish, G. B. Reduced cognitive innovation and stimulus-seeking in chronic schizophrenia. *Journal of Clinical Psychology*, 1970, *26*, 170–174.

Kish, G. B., & Ball, M. E. *Effects of individual differences in stimulus seeking upon learning rate in schizophrenia*. Unpublished manuscript, 1968.

Lambert, W., & Levy, L. H. Sensation-seeking and short term sensory isolation. *Journal of Personality and Social Psychology*, 1972, *24*, 46–52.

Landau, S. G., Buchsbaum, M. S., Carpenter, W., Strauss, J., & Sacks, M. Schizophrenia and stimulus intensity control. *Archives of General Psychiatry*, 1975, *32*, 1239–1245.

Lindsley, D. B. Psychophysiology and motivation. In M. R. Jones (Ed.), *Nebraska Symposium on Motivation*. Lincoln: University of Nebraska Press, 1957.

Lindsley, D. B. Common factors in sensory deprivation, sensory distortion, and sensory overload. In P. Solomon et al. (Eds.), *Sensory deprivation.* Cambridge, Mass.: Harvard University Press, 1961.

Looft, W. R., & Baranowski, M. D. An analysis of five measures of sensation seeking and preference for complexity. *Journal of General Psychology,* 1971, *85,* 307-313.

Lukas, J. H. *Human augmenting-reducing and sensation seeking.* Paper presented at meeting of the Society for Psychophysiological Research. Washington, D.C., October 1981.

Lukas, J. H., & Siegel, J. Cortical mechanisms that augment or reduce evoked potentials in cats. *Science,* 1977, *196,* 73-75.

Major, L. F., & Murphy, D. L. Platelet and plasma amine oxidase activity in alcoholic individuals. *British Journal of Psychiatry,* 1978, *132,* 548-554.

Maltzman, I., & Raskin, D. C. Effects of individual differences in the orienting reflex on conditioning and complex processes. *Journal of Experimental Research in Personality,* 1965, *1,* 1-16.

McClearn, G. E. Genetics of mouse behavior in novel situations. *Journal of Comparative and Physiological Psychology,* 1959, *52,* 62-67.

McClearn, G. E., & De Fries, J. C. *Introduction to behavioral genetics.* San Francisco, Calif.: Freeman, 1973.

Mellstrom, M., Cicala, G. A., & Zuckerman, M. General versus specific trait anxiety measures in the prediction of fear of snakes, heights, and darkness. *Journal of Consulting and Clinical Psychology,* 1976, *44,* 83-91.

Milstein, V., Small, J. G., Small, I. F., & Sharpley, P. Evoked potential augmenting and reducing in psychiatric patients. *EEG Clinical Neurophysiology,* 1975, *38,* 522. (Abstract)

Murphy, D. L. Technical strategies for the study of catecholamines in man. In E. Usdin & S. Snyder (Eds.), *Frontiers in catecholamine research.* Oxford: Pergamon Press, 1973.

Murphy D. L. Animal models for mania. In I. Hanin & E. Usdin (Eds.), *Animal models in psychiatry and neurology.* New York: Pergamon Press, 1977. (a)

Murphy, D. L. The behavioral toxicity of monoamine oxidase-inhibitory anti-depressants. In *Advances in pharmacology and chemotherapy.* New York: Academic Press, 1977, *14,* 71-105. (b)

Murphy, D. L., Belmaker, R. H., Buchsbaum, M. S., Martin, N. F., Ciaranello, R., & Wyatt, R. J. Biogenic amine related enzymes and personality variations in normals. *Psychological Medicine,* 1977, *7,* 149-157.

Murphy, D. L., Belmaker, R. H., & Wyatt, R. J. Monoamine oxidase in schizophrenic and other behavioral disorders. *Journal of Psychiatric Research,* 1974, *11,* 221-247.

Murphy, D. L., & Weiss, R. Reduced monoamine oxidase activity in blood platelets from bipolar depressed patients. *American Journal of Psychiatry,* 1972, *128,* 1351-1357.

Murphy, D. L., Wright, C., Buchsbaum, M. S., Nichols, A., Costa, J. L., & Wyatt, R. J. Platelet and plasma amine oxidase activity in 680 normals: Sex and age differences and stability over time. *Biochemical Medicine,* 1976, *16,* 254-265.

Murtaugh, T. L. *Perceptual isolation, drug addition and adaptation phenomena.* Unpublished master's thesis, Temple University, 1971.

Murtaugh, T. L. *Neurophysiological factors in the choice of abused substances.* Unpublished doctoral dissertation, University of Delaware, 1979.

Myers, T. I., & Eisner, E. J. *An experimental evaluation of the effects of karate and meditation* (Report No. 42800 [p-391X-1-29]). Washington, D.C.: The American Institutes for Research, October 1974.

Neary, R. S. *The development and validation of a state measure of sensation seeking.* Unpublished doctoral dissertation, University of Delaware, 1975.

Neary, R. S., & Zuckerman, M. Sensation seeking, trait and state anxiety, and the electrodermal orienting reflex. *Psychophysiology,* 1976, *12,* 205-211.

Nies, A., Robinson, D. S., Lamborn, K. R., & Lampert, R. P. Genetic control of platelet and plasma monoamine oxidase activity. *Archives of General Psychiatry,* 1973, *28,* 834–838.

Olds, J., & Milner, P. Positive reinforcement produced by electrical stimulation of septal area and other regions of rat brain. *Journal of Comparative and Physiological Psychology,* 1954, *47,* 419–427.

Ozeran, B. J. *Sensation-seeking as a predictor of leadership in leaderless, task oriented groups.* Unpublished master's thesis, University of Hawaii, 1973.

Pavlov, I. P. *Conditioned reflexes: An investigation of the physiological activity of the cerebral cortex* (G. V. Anrep, Ed. and trans.). New York: Dover Publications, 1960. (Originally published, 1927.)

Petrie, A. *Individuality in pain and suffering.* Chicago: University of Chicago Press, 1967.

Platt, J. J. "Addiction proneness" and personality in heroin addicts. *Journal of Abnormal Psychology,* 1975, *84,* 303–306.

Poley, W., & Royce, J. R. Factors of mouse emotionality at the second order, third order, and fourth order. *Multivariate Behavioral Research,* 1976, *11,* 63–76.

Potkin, S. G., Cannon, H. E., Murphy, D. L., & Wyatt, R. J. Are paranoid schizophrenics biologically different from other schizophrenics? *New England Journal of Medicine,* 1978, *298,* 61–66.

Redmond, D. E., Jr., Murphy, D. L., & Baulu, J. Platelet monoamine oxidase activity correlates with social affiliative and agonistic behaviors in normal rhesus monkeys. *Psychosomatic Medicine,* 1979, *41,* 87–100.

Redmond, D. E., Murphy, D. L., Baulu, J., Ziegler, M. G., & Lake, C. R. Menstrual cycle and ovarian hormone effects on plasma and platelet monoamine oxidase (MAO) and plasma dopamine-beta-hydroxylase (DBH) activities in the rhesus monkey. *Psychosomatic Medicine,* 1975, *37,* 417–428.

Ridgeway, D., & Hare, R. D. Sensation seeking and psychophysiological responses to auditory stimulation. *Psychophysiology,* 1981, *18,* 613–618.

Robinson, D. S., Davis, J. M., Nies, A., Ravaris, C. L., & Sylvester, D. Relation of sex and aging to monoamine oxidase activity of human brain, plasma, and platelets. *Archives of General Psychiatry,* 1971, *24,* 536–539.

Rose, R. M. Testosterone, aggression, and homosexuality: A review of the literature and implications for future research. In E. M. Sachar (Ed.), *Topics of endocrinology.* New York: Grune & Stratton, 1975.

Rose, R. M. Neuroendocrine correlates of sexual and aggressive behavior in humans. In M. A. Lipton, A. DiMascio, & K. F. Killam (Eds.), *Psychopharmacology: A generation of progress.* New York: Raven Press, 1978.

Routtenberg, A. The two-arousal hypothesis: Reticular formation and limbic system. *Psychological Review,* 1968, *75,* 51–81.

Royce, J. R. On the construct validity of open-field measures. *Psychological Bulletin,* 1977, *84,* 1098–1106.

Royce, J. R., Holmes, T. M., & Poley, W. Behavior genetic analysis of mouse emotionality. III. The diallel analysis. *Behavior Genetics,* 1975, *5,* 351–372.

Sackett, G. P. Exploratory behavior of rhesus monkeys as a function of rearing experiences and sex. *Developmental Psychology,* 1972, *6,* 260–270.

Schildkraut, J. J. The catecholamine hypothesis of affective disorders: A review of supporting evidence. *American Journal of Psychiatry,* 1965, *122,* 509–522.

Schildkraut, J. J, Herzog, J. M., Orsulak, P. J., Edelman, S. E., Shein, H. M., & Frazier, S. H. Reduced platelet monoamine oxidase activity in a subgroup of schizophrenic patients. *American Journal of Psychiatry,* 1976, *133,* 438–439.

Schneirla, T. C. An evolutionary and developmental theory of biphasic processes underlying approach and withdrawal. In M. R. Jones (Ed.), *Nebraska Symposium on Motivation.*

Lincoln: University of Nebraska Press, 1959.

Schooler, C., Zahn, T. P., Murphy, D. L., & Buchsbaum, M. S. Psychological correlates of monoamine oxidase in normals. *Journal of Nervous and Mental Diseases,* 1978, *166,* 177–186.

Schwarz, R. M., Burkhart, B. R., & Green, B. Turning on or turning off: Sensation seeking or tension reduction as motivational determinants of alcohol use. *Journal of Consulting and Clinical Psychology,* 1978, *46,* 1144–1145.

Shmavonian, B. M., Miller, L. H., & Cohen, S. I. Differences among age and sex groups in electrodermal conditioning. *Psychophysiology,* 1968, *5,* 119–131.

Segal, B. Personality factors related to drug and alcohol use. In D. J. Lettieri (Ed.), *Predicting adolescent drug abuse: A review of issues, methods and correlates* (Publication Ms. ADM 77-299). Washington, D.C.: Department of Health, Education and Welfare, 1976.

Silverman, J., Buchsbaum, M. S., & Stierlin, H. Sex differences in perceptual differentiation and stimulus intensity control. *Journal of Personality and Social Psychology,* 1973, *25,* 309–318.

Stanton, H. E. Hypnosis and encounter group volunteers: A validational study of the sensation seeking scale. *Journal of Consulting and Clinical Psychology,* 1976, *44,* 692.

Stein, L. Reward transmitters: Catecholamines and opioid peptides. In M. A. Lipton, A. DiMascio, & K. F. Killam (Eds.), *Psychopharmacology: A generation of progress.* New York: Raven Press, 1978.

Stillman, R. C., Wyatt, R. J., Murphy, D. L., & Rauscher, F. D. Low platelet monoamine oxidase activity and chronic marijuana use. *Life Sciences,* 1978, *23,* 1577–1582.

Stürup, G. K. Treatment of sexual offenders in Herstedvester Denmark: The rapists. *Acta Psychiatrica Scandinavica,* 1968, Suppl., *204,* 1–63.

Sullivan, J. L., Cavenar, J. O., Jr., Maltbie, A. A., Lester, P., & Zung, W. W. K. Familial biochemical and clinical correlates of alcoholics with low platelet monoamine oxidase activity. *Biological Psychiatry,* 1979, *14,* 385.

Suomi, S. J., & Harlow, H. F. The facts and functions of fear. In M. Zuckerman & C. D. Spielberger (Eds.), *Emotions and anxiety: New concepts, methods, and applications.* Hillsdale, N.J.: Lawrence Erlbaum Associates, 1976.

Terenius, L., & Wahlström, A. Morphine-like ligand for opiate receptors in human CSF. *Life Sciences,* 1975, *16,* 1759–1764.

Terenius, L., & Wahlström, A., Lindström, L., & Widerlöv, F. Increased CSF levels of endorphins in chronic psychosis. *Neuroscience Letters,* 1976, *3,* 157–162.

Tolman, E. C. Purpose and cognition: The determiners of animal learning. *Psychological Review,* 1925, *32,* 285–297.

Tumilty, T. N., & Daitzman, R. *Locus of control and sensation seeking among schizophrenics: Extensions and replication.* Unpublished manuscript, 1977.

van Lawick-Goodall, J. Chimpanzee locomotor play. In J. S. Bruner, A. Jolly, & K. Sylva (Eds.), *Play: Its role in development and evolution.* New York: Basic Books, 1976.

Venables, P. H. A psychophysiological approach to research in schizophrenia. In D. C. Fowles (Ed.), *Clinical applications of psychophysiology.* New York: Columbia University Press, 1975.

Volavka, J., Davis, L. G., & Ehrlich, Y. H. Endorphins, dopamine, and schizophrenia. *Schizophrenia Bulletin,* 1979, *5,* 227–239.

von Knorring, L. Visual averaged evoked responses in patients suffering from alcoholism. *Neuropsychobiology,* 1976, *2,* 233–238.

von Knorring, L. Visual evoked responses and platelet monoamine oxidase in patients suffering from alcohol. New York: Plenum Press, 1980.

von Knorring, L., Almay, B. G. L., Johansson, F., & Terenius, L. Pain perception and endorphin levels in cerebrospinal fluid. *Pain,* 1978, *5,* 359–365.

von Knorring, L., Almay, B. G. L., Johansson, F. and Terenius, L. Endorphins in CSF of chronic pain patients in relation to augmenting–reducing response in visual averaged evoked response. *Neuropsychobiology,* 1979, *5,* 322–326.

Waters, L. K., & Kirk, W. E. Stimulus-seeking motivation and risk taking behavior in a gambling situation. *Education and Psychological Measurement,* 1968, *28,* 549–550.

Weissman, A., Koe, B. K., & Tenen, S. S. Antiamphetamine effects following inhibition of tyrosine hydroxylase. *The Journal of Pharmacology and Experimental Therapeutics,* 1966, *151,* 339–351.

Whimbey, A. E., & Denenberg, V. H. Two independent behavioral dimensions in open field performance. *Journal of Comparative and Physiological Psychology,* 1967, *63,* 500–504.

Wilson, E. O. *Sociobiology.* Cambridge, Mass.: Harvard University Press, 1975.

Wise, C. D., & Stein, L. Facilitation of brain self-stimulation by central administration of norepinephrine. *Science,* 1969, *163,* 299.

Wyatt, R. J., & Murphy, D. L. Low platelet monoamine oxidase activity and schizophrenia. *Schizophrenia Bulletin,* 1976, *2,* 77–89.

Zuckerman, M. Theoretical formulations: I. In J. P. Zubek (Ed.), *Sensory deprivation: Fifteen years of research.* New York: Appleton-Century-Crofts, 1969.

Zuckerman, M. Dimensions of sensation seeking. *Journal of Consulting and Clinical Psychology,* 1971, *36,* 45–52.

Zuckerman, M. Drug usage as one manifestation of a "sensation seeking" trait. In W. Keup (Ed.), *Drug abuse: Current concepts and research.* Springfield, Ill.: Thomas, 1972.

Zuckerman, M. The sensation seeking motive. IN B. A. Maher (Ed.), *Progress in experimental personality research* (Vol. 7). New York: Academic Press, 1974.

Zuckerman, M. Sensation seeking and anxiety, traits and states, as determinants of behavior in novel situations. In I. Sarason & C. D. Spielberger (Eds.), *Stress and anxiety* (Vol. 3). Washington, D.C.: Hemisphere, 1976.

Zuckerman, M. Sensation seeking. In H. London & J. Exner, Jr. (Eds.), *Dimensions of personality.* New York: Wiley, 1978.

Zuckerman, M. *Sensation seeking: Beyond the optimal level of arousal.* Hillsdale, N.J.: Lawrence Erlbaum Associates, 1979. (a)

Zuckerman, M. Sensation seeking and risk taking. In C. E. Izard (Ed.), *Emotions in personality and psychopathology.* New York: Plenum Press, 1979. (b)

Zuckerman, M., Bone, R. N., Neary, R., Mangelsdorff, D., & Brustman, B. What is the sensation seeker? Personality trait and experience correlates of the Sensation Seeking Scales. *Journal of Consulting and Clinical Psychology,* 1972, *39,* 308–321.

Zuckerman, M., Eysenck, S. B. G., & Eysenck, H. J. Sensation seeking in England and America: Cross-cultural, age and sex comparisons. *Journal of Consulting and Clinical Psychology,* 1978, *46,* 139–149.

Zuckerman, M., & Hopkins, T. R. Unpublished manuscript, 1965.

Zuckerman, M., Kolin, E. A., Price, L., & Zoob, I. Development of a Sensation-Seeking Scale. *Journal of Consulting Psychology,* 1964, *28,* 477–482.

Zuckerman, M., & Kuhlman, D. M. *Sensation seeking and risk taking in response to hypothetical situations.* Paper presented at the meeting of the International Association of Applied Psychology, Munich, Germany, August 1978.

Zuckerman, M., Murtaugh, T. M., & Siegel, J. Sensation seeking and cortical augmenting-reducing. *Psychophysiology,* 1974, *11,* 535–542.

Zuckerman, M., & Neeb, M. Sensation seeking and psychopathology. *Psychiatry Research,* 1979, *1,* 255–274.

Zuckerman, M., & Neeb, M. Demographic influences in sensation seeking and expressions of sensation seeking in religion, smoking, and driving habits. *Personality and Individual Differences,* 1980, *1,* 197–206.

Zuckerman, M., Persky, H., Hopkins, T. R., Murtaugh, T., Basu, G. K., & Shilling, M. Comparison of stress effects of perceptual and social isolation. *Archives of General Psychiatry,* 1966, *14,* 356–365.

Zuckerman, M., Persky, H., Link, K. E., & Basu, G. K. Responses to confinement: An investigation of sensory deprivation, social isolation, movement, and set factors. *Perceptual and Motor Skills,* 1968, *27,* 319–334.

Zuckerman, M., Tushup, R., & Finner, S. Sexual attitudes and experience: Attitude and personality correlates and changes produced by a course in sexuality. *Journal of Consulting and Clinical Psychology,* 1976, *44,* 7–19.

3 Impulsivity: Cognitive, Behavioral, and Psychophysiological Correlates

Ernest S. Barratt
Jim H. Patton
*Department of Psychiatry
and Behavioral Sciences,
The University of Texas Medical Branch*

INTRODUCTION AND OVERVIEW

Impulsivity is an elusive and controversial concept among personality theorists, yet a concept that is widely used by clinicians and laypeople alike. The purpose of this chapter is to review the applied use of this concept (e.g., as a symptom in clinical syndromes), to review theoretical problems related to defining it, and to suggest an operational definition of impulsivity within a general system theory model. We relate data (cognitive, behavioral, and psychophysiological) from our laboratory to this definition. We also discuss the hypothetical role of brain functioning within an impulsive system and the relationship of other selected personality dimensions to this system.

The scope of this chapter reflects not only some of the main problems with which we have grappled since the last major review of our research (Barratt, 1972), but also our attempts to integrate recently acquired data and some of our earlier conceptualizations of impulsivity. In attempting to resolve these problems, we have adopted a systems theory model for organizing our research results. This model complements our multivariate approach for studying personality variables. The need at the conceptual level for a system approach to defining impulsivity became obvious to us as we tried to clarify the relationship of brain functioning to behavior while defining several personality dimensions. For example, what brain processes relate to both anxiety and impulsivity? Or, more specifically, what brain-behavior relationships characterize impulsivity? To avoid circularity in defining personality dimensions in terms of brain-behavior relationships, the definitions have to be at least one level of abstraction higher than the first order relationships. It appeared to us that much of the confusion in the literature about defining impulsivity stemmed from this circularity problem and from attempts to categorize the data that formed the bases for the definitions. The main goal of our research has been to arrive at a definition of impulsivity that will at least recognize the circularity problem and at the same time help bridge the gap between the laboratory study of concept and its applied clinical uses in approaching everyday life problems.

In many ways our methodological approach to the study of personality as currently conceived parallels that outlined by Fiske (1971). His guidelines for conceptualizing a variable encompass our approach rather well. At the juncture within Fiske's methodological process where naturalistic and experimental observations come together to help define a personality concept, we have imposed (as noted earlier) a general system theory model. The use of this model (after Ashby, 1960) is discussed in more detail in a subsequent section.

The reason we have placed so much emphasis on our methodological approach relates to what we feel is a major problem in defining impulsivity. That is, the self-awareness or conscious awareness of impulsivity is difficult to cope with in research. The conscious experiences of cognitive processes are private events. It is much easier, therefore, to ignore them and study only overt behavior. Cognition is not behavior, however. Further, to deny that cognition does not relate to behavior or does not have a significant place in an "impulsive system" (or an anxious system) does not appear realistic to us. Because we conclude from our research that impulsivity includes both cognitive and motor components, our model had to include both cognitive and behavioral measurements. Modern psychophysiology is helping to make less private brain processes that are related to cognitive processes (Donchin, 1979). We have directed much of our research efforts toward the psychophysiological correlates of cognition in order to test our hypothesis that impulsivity has both cognitive and motor components.

IMPULSIVITY: CLINICAL SIGNIFICANCE

Impulsivity is often included as part of the symptom pattern of a wide range of psychopathological, learning, and social disorders. Some typical examples of the use of this personality dimension are presented within this broader context in this section. The purpose of this brief clinical review is twofold: (1) to emphasize the importance of clarifying the definition and measurement of impulsivity in order to better understand the broader syndrome or disorders that include it as a symptom; (2) to note the confusion between cognitive and behavioral aspects of impulsivity in clinical applications.

Impulsivity has often been implicated, either implicitly or explicitly, as part of the hyperactive child syndrome and related disorders. Cantwell (1975) lists impulsivity as one of the four cardinal symptoms of the hyperactive child syndrome: "Impulsivity is shown by such behaviors as jumping into the deep end of a swimming pool without knowing how to swim, running into the street in front of cars, climbing out on too high rooftops and ledges, and blurting out tactless statements [p. 6]." In discussing the "syndrome issue" in hyperactivity, Ross and Ross (1976) state: "Hyperactivity becomes a cause for concern when it is clearly inappropriate, when the child is unable to inhibit his activity despite considerable pressure to do so, when he often appears to be capable of only one speed of response in situations where he is clearly motivated to exhibit other response speeds, and if the hyperactivity is accompanied by related behavioral or physiological symptoms [pp. 6–7]." The research findings of Shaffer, McNamara, and Pincus (1975) "suggest that two of the most important features of the so called hyperactivity syndrome—that is overactivity and impulsivity—are also components of a more frequently recognized conduct disorder syndrome [pp. 299–300]." Douglas (1972) argues: "A core of symptoms involving inability to sustain attention and to control impulsivity can account for most of the symptoms found in the hyperactive group [p. 259]." It is clear that within the context of the hyperactive child syndrome, the concept of "impulsivity" includes social responsibility, risk-taking, and speed of response.

Tangential to the consideration of impulsivity as a symptom in hyperactivity and conduct disorders among children, impulsivity has also been related to dyslexia and other childhood learning disorders. For example, the Kagan Matching Familiar Figures Test (Kagan, 1966), which purportedly measures impulsivity, has been used extensively in research on dyslexia and minimal brain disorders. This test is discussed in the next section.

Impulsivity has often been listed as a personality characteristic in psychopathy. Cleckley (1964) includes impulsivity as part of this syndrome in his widely quoted definition. In DSM II (American Psychiatric Association, 1968), the antisocial personality is characterized in part as impulsive. In DSM III (American Psychiatric Association, 1978), impulsivity is listed as part of several disorders (e.g, borderline personality organization) and also is the basis for a separate section entitled *Disorders of impulse control not elsewhere classified;* this section includes pathological gambling, kleptomania, pyromania, intermittent explosive disorders, and isolated explosive disorders.

Another group of disorders that involves impulsivity as a symptom is episodic behavioral disorders as discussed by Monroe (1970) and Maletzky (1974). Monroe (1970) notes that one purpose in writing *Episodic Behavior Disorders* was: "to establish a systematic nosology of patients manifesting impulsivity, acting out, or other intermittent behavioral disorders [p. vii]." He approaches this task by integrating both psychophysiological and psychodynamic concepts into a hierarchical model. In discussing the hierarchical levels of episodic dyscontrol, Monroe (1970) draws a distinction between impulse dyscontrol and instinctual dyscontrol as follows:

> Acts of impulse dyscontrol are characterized by abrupt, explosive dimensions of primitive affects, usually rage and aggression, characterized by overt homicidal, suicidal, or sexually aggressive behavior. At the purely phenomenological level, there is little difference between the act of impulse dyscontrol and the act of instinct dyscontrol, except for the likelihood that the former is more explosive. What does differentiate impulsive acts from acts of instinct dyscontrol is that the impulsive act is preceded by a period of varying duration in which there is mounting tension with debate and indecisiveness about whether the urge should be obeyed or whether controls should be maintained. Finally, this tension becomes unbearable and overpowering. At this point, the explosive act occurs [pp. 38–59].

It is clear that there are both cognitive and behavioral components in Monroe's definition of impulsivity.

Many other examples of the relationships of impulsivity to violent and aggressive behavior (e.g, Eleftheriou & Scott, 1971; Kolb, 1972) and to other clinical syndromes could be presented. It is obvious that the range of the applied clinical uses of the concept of impulsivity is multidimensional and involves both cognitive and motor components. An important practical question, which underlies all impulsivity research, is whether or not there are common underlying dimensions in the various impulse control pathologies.

TECHNIQUES FOR MEASURING IMPULSIVITY

If the clinical use of impulsivity is confusing, the range of techniques for measuring it is even more confusing. Impulsivity has been measured by a broad spectrum of techniques. We have compared many of these techniques in our research and find that they often are not even intercorrelated significantly, even though they all purport to measure impulsivity. Some of the techniques were developed on the basis of the definition of impulsivity within a more comprehensive personality theory. Others were developed as part of omnibus personality test batteries, usually defined on the bases of factor analyses or other multivariate techniques. Still others were developed out of a more restricted interest in impulsivity per se (or a closely related personality construct). The purposes of this section are to provide examples of the range of measurements of impulsivity, to give some of the rationale for these measurements, and to examine the results of our research in comparing selected measures of impulsivity.

Two examples of impulsivity measures developed on the basis of more comprehensive personality theories are the Id, Ego, Superego (IES) Test

(Dombrose & Slobin, 1958) and Plutchik's (1974) Monroe Test. The development of the IES Test was based on psychoanalytic theory. It was designed to measure impulse strength (I), ego strength (E), and superego strength (S). Of particular interest is the relationship of I to S because this ratio is primarily related to the expression of impulsive behavior. The developers of the IES Test (Dombrose & Slobin, 1958) note:

> The I score indicates the degree of acceptance of impulses as part of the self. . . . A high I score signifies the realization of considerable impulse needs within one's own psychological self. A low I score indicates a minimizing, rejecting or denying of impulses, an unawareness of these forces from within. . . . The ΣS score indicates superego pressures or demands. . . . Pathological personality trends are revealed by low I or high ΣS scores. The individual who must deny his sexual or aggressive urges, as does the paranoid, is forced into distorting not only the reality of himself, but also that of the outer world [pp. 350-351].

As this test was developed within the framework of psychoanalysis, one would expect the emphasis to be on cognitive functions.

Using Monroe's (1970) analysis of episodic behavioral disorders as a starting point, Plutchik (1974) developed the Monroe Scale. This scale, which is heavily weighted with impulsivity items, contains 18 items that are answered as never, rarely, sometimes, or often. Some typical impulsivity items on the scale are: (1) *I have acted on a whim or an impulse;* (16) *I have had the impulse to kill myself.* An a priori analysis of the items on this scale indicates that both anxiety and impulsivity are being measured by many of the items. For example, item 11, *I have become so angry that I smashed things,* would probably be loaded in a factor analysis of items on both an anxiety (or anger) and an impulsivity dimension. This test, then, although containing impulsivity items, probably measures a third order combination of several personality dimensions in line with Monroe's theory.

In an attempt to study personality correlates of underachievement, Kipnis (1971) developed an impulsivity scale containing biographical items. The goal of his research was to search for ways of helping students who underachieve because of impulsivity. After 10 years of research, Kipnis (1971) noted in the preface to this book that: "I am impressed with the wide range of social behaviors in which we may detect the influence of variations an impulsiveness [p. x]." Kipnis' Impulsiveness Scale correlated with other measures loaded with impulsivity items as follows: .41 with the Extraversion Scale of the Maudsley Personality Inventory; .45 with the Socialization Scale of the MMPI: and , in two separate studies, .29 and .53 respectively with the Pd Scale of the Minnesota Multiphasic Personality Inventory (MMPI). The Kipnis Scale significantly correlated (.66) with psychiatrists' diagnoses of psychopathic personalities among incoming psychiatric patients at the Bethesda Naval Hospital. Kipnis (1971) summarized his findings relating impulsivity to achievement as follows:

The findings were consistent with the view that impulsive and restless persons would be less attracted to vocations that require day-to-day persistence and study, as represented by courses in the physical sciences and mathematics. At a more general level, the findings were also supportive of a view proposed by Super and Holland that people search for environments and vocations that permit them to satisfy and express their personalities. At both Temple and Delaware, non-impulsive students sought what Holland would term an intellectual or scientific environment, whereas more impulsive students were attracted to business careers. The findings further revealed that more impulsive students who entered the field of science did not find it to their liking. Less satisfaction was expressed by impulsive than non-impulsive students over their choice of science as an academic major [p. 96].

Kipnis' research further emphasizes the importance of the question of whether or not there are common bases for a wide range of impulsive behaviors that have been documented socially and clinically. This issue is addressed briefly again in the next section of this paper.

Projective tests have often been used to measure impulsivity. The Thematic Apperception Test (TAT) (Murray, 1943), the Holtzman Inkblot Technique (Holtzman, 1961; Holtzman, Thorp, Swartz, & Herron, 1961), and the Rorschach Inkblot Test (Holtzman, 1950; Rorschach, 1942) along with many others have been used extensively to measure strength of impulses and impulse control or impulsivity. Although not universally so, the responses to projective tests were often interpreted within a psychoanalytic personality model. Two examples can be presented to indicate the use of projective tests in measuring impulsivity.

Purcell (1965) used the TAT to "examine certain disturbances of the impulse-control balance as they are manifested in TAT productions [p. 548]." He tested six hypotheses related to antisocial behavior within the context of three different facets of impulse-control balance: the impulse system, the external control system, and the internal control system. One hypothesis that he (Purcell, 1965) tested was:

Among antisocial individuals, themes of external punishment are more likely to serve as justification for aggression than among non-antisocial individuals. This hypothesis is derived from Redl and Wineman's detailed account of the 'delinquent ego.' By this is meant the ego whose every effort is bent toward obtaining guilt-free and anxiety-free enjoyment of delinquent impulsivity [p. 549].

Purcell found that antisocial subjects differ from nonantisocial subjects in quantity and quality of fantasy aggressions, the former producing not only a larger number of fantasy aggressions but also finding it less necessary to obscure or minimize the hostile impulse. The superego measure of anticipated internal punishments was found to be of far greater significance in inhibiting antisocial behavior than fear of retaliatory punishment (Purcell, 1965).

Megargee (1970) in a study of "overcontrolled" and "undercontrolled" delinquents used a wide range of psychometric tests, a standard interview, and several projective tests (TAT and the Holtzman Inkblot Technique) in a search for a psychological profile of differences between the two groups. Overcontrol and undercontrol obviously relate to impulse control or impulsivity. In this study, overcontrol and undercontrol were defined in terms of the crimes committed by male delinquents. The psychological techniques were used as predictor variables. In summarizing his research, Megargee (1970) raised the important problem of face validity in measuring personality dimensions, especially impulsivity:

> Within the psychological test data, the more obvious the instrument, the more likely it is that a defensive attitude could alter the results. This is consistent with the fact that the most obvious tests, the P-F (Rosenweig's Picture Frustration Test), the TAT and the hostility scale of the HIT (Holtzman Inkblot Test) failed to show the predictive patterns, but the less easily distorted measures such as the empirically derived CPI Self-Control Scale and the Movement-Color Index of the HIT did show the hypothesized patterns [p. 116].

Both Megargee's and Purcell's studies emphasize different cognitive aspects of impulsivity; in addition, Megargee raises the important question of the face validity of these techniques. This reinforces the question raised earlier: How well can impulsive individuals assess their own impulsive state?

Another technique purported to measure impulsivity involves perceptual-motor tasks such as the Porteus Maze Q measure (Porteus, 1965) and the Trails A and B tasks (Lezak, 1976). Both techniques require "planning ahead" and have been used in many studies as measures of impulsivity. Jacobson (personal communication) used the Porteus Q measure along with the Barratt Impulsiveness Scale (BIS) (Barratt, 1959) as measures of impulsivity in a study of adult alcoholism. The BIS and Q measures did not correlate significantly with each other. Both scales discriminated at a low level between those who remained in treatment and those who dropped out. This is another example of lack of a significant relationship between scales that purport to measure impulsivity.

One of the most widely used techniques that claims to measure impulsivity is Kagan's Matching Familiar Figures (MFF) Test (Kagan, 1966). This test has three forms that were developed for preschool and school-age children, adolescents, and adults, respectively. The test involves choosing one of six to eight "response" figures that is most like a standard figure. The standard figures are relatively complex; the response figures are all very similar to the standard figure, but only one response figure is exactly like the standard. Scores consist of the mean time (latency to first response) on all items and the number of errors. Kagan and his colleagues state that fast, inaccurate scores measure impulsivity, whereas slower, accurate scores indicate a reflective tempo. This test has been criticized both on theoretical and conceptual bases (Becker, Bender, & Morrison, 1978; Block & Harrington, 1974) and on the basis of scoring procedures and other psychometric features (Ault, Michaell, & Hartman, 1976). The MFF Test has been used extensively with preschool and school-age children in studies ostensibly relating impulsivity–reflection to academic achievement and school adjustment. There have been several excellent reviews of the test (e.g., Messer, 1976).

Self-report questionnaires have been by far the most commonly used technique for measuring impulsivity among adolescents and adults. Some of these scales have also been modified for use with children. The number of questionnaire-type scales that have been developed to measure impulsivity are extensive. As noted earlier, some scales have been developed as part of more global measures of personality dimensions or traits, but a few have been developed specifically to measure impulsivity.

Typical multitrait or multidimensional personality questionnaires that include impulsivity subscales are: the Thurstone Temperament Schedule (Thurstone, 1951, 1953); the Guilford Zimmerman Temperament Survey (Guilford & Zimmerman, 1949); Sixteen Personality Factor Questionnaire (16 PF) (Cattell, Saunders, & Stize, 1957); the Omnibus Personality Inventory (Heist & Yonge, 1962); and the Personality Research Form (Jackson, 1967). These are but a few of the many multitrait scales that could be listed. The development of these scales, the meaning of each subscale score, and which scales are the true measures of selected personality traits have been debated extensively in the literature. For example, Guilford (1975) traced the development of the so-called Guilford items and discussed some of the disagreements among himself, Cattell, and Eysenck over the "true" definition of the personality dimensions. In contrast to Guilford's and Cattell's multiple personality factors, the Eysencks (Eysenck, 1958; Eysenck & Eysenck, 1969) proposed essentially a two factor theory of personality: Factor E (extraversion) and Factor N (neuroticism). The E factor is heavily loaded with impulsivity items in line with their theoretical position that impulsivity is part of extraversion. They have more recently added a psychotism (P) dimension (Eysenck, 1978; Eysenck & Eysenck, 1976) to their theory and have developed a separate impulsivity scale (Eysenck & Eysenck, 1977, 1978).

Guilford has been critical of Eysenck's research:

As for his [Eysenck's] Factor E, I am forced to conclude that it is not a factor at all, but a kind of "shotgun wedding" of R (Rhathymia) and S (sociability). It should be noted the average of a number of samples of correlations of R and S is actually .11 for men and .23 for women (when R is scored for Rhathymia at the high end, as Esyenck would have it). On the other hand, R correlates with T (thoughtfulness) with an average of .37 for men and .31 for women. Average correlations betwen S and A (Ascendance) are .64 and .58 for men and women respectively. To complete the picture, the average correlations between R and A are .00 and −07. All these correlations account for the pairings of SA and RT, in disagreement with the affiliation forced by Eysenck [p. 809].

The Eysencks (1977; see also, Eysenck, 1977; Guilford, 1977) replied to Guilford:

> Guilford's conclusion is somewhat at odds with demonstrations by S. B. G. Eysenck and H. J. Eysenck (1963), replicated by Sparrow and Ross (1964), that sets of impulsiveness items and sets of sociability items correlate together quite well ($R = 0.47$); this would seem to contradict the notion of a shotgun wedding. The position is complicated by the fact that impulsiveness also tends to correlate positively with neuroticism (N), while sociability correlates negatively with N; in addition, Guilford's sociability factor is by no means univocal, but breaks down into two quite independent parts (Eysenck, 1956) correlating respectively with R and with neuroticism [p. 57].

The Eysencks, in earlier work prior to their postulating a separate impulsivity dimension as part of their personality theory, suggested that the Barratt Impulsiveness Scale was really a measure of their Factor E. (This is discussed in the next section.)

This discussion about the "true" factors could be extended ad nauseam. There have been studies aimed at reconciling the differences among these questionnaire measures of personality (e.g., Sells, Demaree, & Will, 1971). The Eysencks have also included sensation-seeking items from Zuckerman's Sensation Seeking Scale (Zuckerman, 1974) in their impulsivity studies. It appears to us that many of these analyses and related debates suffer from lack of external criterion measures and biosocial measures other than questionnaire scales. We have tried to break the circular nature of these debates by including a broad range of neuropsychological and psychophysiological measures in our research on impulsivity. It should be noted that the Eysencks have also done this in their research and that there is a great similarity, generally, between their results and ours.

Over the past 7 years, we have studied the interrelationships of a large number of these impulsivity measures. This has been done primarily as part of our research on the Barratt Impulsiveness Scale (BIS) (Barratt, 1959). In an effort to measure impulsivity better and to develop a scale that was less loaded with anxiety items, the BIS has gone through nine revisions since the original 1959 scale was constructed. Starting with Form 7A, the format of the BIS was changed to allow four levels of response to each item (rarely or never, occasionally, often, or usually), and the number of items were reduced from 85 to 48. Forms 7A, 7B, and 8 differ in the weights for the 48 items and in clusters of items keyed for different subscales. For example, BIS 7B has five subscales: sensory stimulation, motor impulsivity, interpersonal behavior, self-assessment of impulsivity, and risk-taking. At this point, we feel that more research is necessary to make the subtests reliable and meaningful. However, the total scores from the various forms of the BIS significantly intercorrelate and are reliable. For example, the total scores on BIS 7B and BIS 8 correlate .83 ($n = 240$) with each other. Because, for reasons indicated later in this chapter, we are primarily interested in the total scores, any of the later forms of the BIS are adequate for our research purposes when we use a psychometric scale to measure impulsivity.

From our research interrelating the BIS with other measures of impulsivity, two general conclusions are obvious: (1) most questionnaire measures of impulsivity are significantly intercorrelated (usually at an average to high level); (2) the questionnaire measures usually have low order and often insignificant correlations with the nonquestionnaire measures of impulsivity. As evidence for the first conclusion, in addition to our earlier reported results (Barratt, 1972), the BIS has been significantly correlated with the Thorndike Impulsiveness Scale (.70, $N = 114$), the Impulse Expression Subscale of the Omnibus Personality Inventory (.50, $N = 156$), the Disinhibition Subscale of the Zuckerman Sensation Seeking Scale (.47, $N = 42$), the Order Subscale ($-.50$, $N = 120$), the Change Subscale (.44 = 120) of the Edwards Personal Preference Inventory, and the Eysenck E Scale (.68, $N = 212$). In contrast, the BIS correlated .33 ($N = 120$) with Porteus Maze Q Score, $-.26$ ($N = 47$) with the MFFT Latency Score, $-.08$ ($N = 47$) with the MFFT Error Score, .34 ($N = 29$) with the IES S Score. Saunders, Repucci, and Sarata (1973) also reported that the MFFT did not correlate significantly with either the BIS or the Hirschfield (1965) Impulsiveness Scale, although the latter two scales correlated significantly with each other. In our research, the BIS did correlated significantly with Trails B ($-.51$, $N = 98$) and with the logical Memory Subscale of the Wechsler Memory Test, Form I (.54, $N = 35$); these two techniques are nonquestionnaire psychometric measures.

This brief survey indicates that all techniques that purport to measure impulsivity are not measuring the same variable or construct. This conclusion appears to be based on more than differences in techniques. As noted earlier, part of the problem possibly stems from cognitive versus motor emphases in measuring and defining impulsivity. Once again we return to the question: How capable are subjects of assessing their own impulsive acts? It is possible that people are more aware of anxiety or other affective-type personality traits because these traits are "feeling" dimensions. One *feels* anxious, but one *does not feel* impulsive. Thus, when asked to assess impulsivity via a questionnaire, its impact may be difficult to evaluate. In an informal "game," one of us (ESB) has often asked acquaintances or patients, "Are you anxious?" followed by "Are you impulsive?" The response to "Are you anxious?" is usually readily forthcoming, whereas the answer to "Are you impulsive?" results in a pause during which the responder appears to be evaluating past behaviors.

It appears to us that analyses involving the intercorrelations of tests that purport to measure anxiety and impulsivity result in semantic quibblings and attempts "to lift oneself up by one's bootstraps." Only by including external criterion measures and biosocial measures systematically in the conceptual arguments will one be able to break the circular nature of the debates typified by the Guilford–Eysenck exchange discussed earlier. Further, those doing impulsivity research should be cognizant of the range of measurement techniques employed to measure impulsivity if these measurement problems are to be resolved.

IMPULSIVITY, ANXIETY, AND SOCIALIZATION

Although the main thrust of our research has been aimed at defining and measuring impulsivity, we have a secondary research interest in anxiety because of its orthogonal relationship to impulsivity. Further, when we started to use a systems model to integrate our data, we became interested in the socialization personality dimension. Our research has never attempted to encompass a study of all personality dimensions. We have related the BIS and selected anxiety scales to a broad range of personality-questionnaire measures to reach a better understanding of the relationship between impulsivity and anxiety. In this section, we briefly present our understanding of the interrelationships between the impulsivity , anxiety, and socialization personality dimensions. In the next section, the bases for our theoretical position on these dimensions become more obvious. The main reason for including this section is to clarify what appears to be some misunderstanding about our position on the relationship of anxiety to impulsivity (Eysenck & Eysenck, 1969).

As we stated earlier (Barratt, 1972), our position is that anxiety and impulsivity are orthogonal dimensions. For example, the BIS and the State-Trait Anxiety Inventory (STAI) measure orthogonal dimensions. We took this position because in our research using the BIS with either the Manifest Anxiety Scale (Taylor, 1953) or the STAI (Speilberger, Gorsuch, & Lushene, 1970), the latter scales consistently loaded on a factor orthogonal to the BIS in factor analyses.

The Eysencks (Eysenck & Eysenck, 1969) took exception to our claim. In one of our earlier studies (Barratt, 1965a), we published data in which subscales of the BIS loaded at a moderate level on an anxiety factor. The Eysencks (1969) interpreted these data as follows:

> The BIS, it may be concluded, is not a true measure of impulsiveness, but rather is a general E Scale misnamed; it may, however, be admitted that the scale is deficient in sociability items, so that some degree of correlation with N might be expected. . . . Barratt's results, therefore, fit in perfectly with our own, provided we are willing to regard his BIS as a measure of the E factor with sociability items removed. As such, his studies give valuable support to our own experiments [p. 149].

It is not our aim to dispute the Eysenck's interpretation but rather, to clarify our current theoretical position. It should be noted, however, that much of our earlier research involved male subjects. In our more recent research aimed at the etiology of impulsivity and anxiety (started in 1977), we have been studying both male and female subjects and now realize that we cannot generalize all of our earlier findings to females. We have in our more recent research started to include both male and female subjects regularly in our research. In a factor analysis of selected personality questionnaires administered to freshman medical students (1977–1978 and 1978–1979 entering students at UTMB), differences in male and female factor profiles indicate part of the bases for the limitations of generalizing our earlier results to females.

In this factor analysis, we included: the 14 subscales of the Omnibus Personality Inventory; the BIS-7B total score; STAI state and trait anxiety; Eysenck's E, N, and L scales; the CPI socialization subscale; and the L, F, Pd, Ma, and Si subscales of the MMPI. The factor analysis for the male medical students (Table 3.1) indicated that impulsivity, anxiety, and socialization are orthogonal factors as measured by the BIS-7B, STAI, and CPI socialization subscale (Gough, 1956) respectively. Among the males, Eysenck's E scale had a higher loading on the socialization factor than on the impulsivity factor.

In the factor analysis of the female medical students, R matrix (Table 3.2), anxiety was defined as a separate factor, but impulsivity and socialization were a combined factor. Thus, anxiety and impulsivity as defined by the STAI and BIS are orthogonal for both male and female subjects, but socialization appears to relate differently to impulsivity among male and female subjects.

In the next section, where we define impulsivity within a systems theory model, we again refer to this factor analysis. Our current position is that the problem of defining impulsivity is on shaky grounds if the definition is restricted to questionnaire-personality measures. In both the Eysencks' and our own research, two divergent personality dimensions have been postulated and in many ways these dimensions are similar. We have not extended our research to include psychoticism as have the Eysencks (Eysencks & Eysenck, 1976), but we would postulate the same P dimension as did the Eysencks if we were to study psychoticism. Further, the results of the Eysencks' research program in relating nonquestionnaire measures of cognition and behavior to E and N parallel our results where common experiments have been done (e.g., Barratt, 1971) as the Eysencks have noted.

The Eysencks (Eysenck & Eysenck, 1977) also draw a distinction between impulsivity in the broad sense (Imp_B), which is comprised of four subfactors, and a narrower impulsivity dimension (Imp_N). Imp_B correlates with E and P, whereas Imp_N correlates with N and P.

As noted earlier, it appears to us that the main disagreement about these personality dimensions will have to be resolved by research using nonques-

TABLE 3.1
Varimax Rotated Factor Pattern
Male Medical Students (N = 261)

			I	II	III	IV	V	VI	VII
						FACTORS			
1.	Thinking Introversion	OPI	.29	.08	-.67	-.42	.13	.02	-.19
2.	Theoretical Orientation	OPI	.64	.13	-.55	.07	.12	-.13	-.21
3.	Estheticism	OPI	.27	.18	-.26	-.76	.12	.06	.09
4.	Complexity	OPI	-.09	.49	-.60	-.24	.09	-.15	-.05
5.	Autonomy	OPI	-.00	-.08	-.85	.11	-.20	-.07	-.11
6.	Religious Orientation	OPI	.21	.22	-.54	.57	.01	-.01	.10
7.	Social Extraversion	OPI	.11	.18	-.04	-.07	.04	-.18	-.88
8.	Impulse Expression	OPI	-.08	.80	-.13	.11	-.23	.09	-.15
9.	Personality Integration	OPI	.23	-.39	-.15	.19	.16	-.42	-.62
10.	Anxiety Level	OPI	.18	-.20	-.13	.18	-.00	-.67	-.43
11.	Altruism	OPI	.01	-.19	-.38	-.35	.23	-.19	-.61
12.	Practical Outlook	OPI	.04	.07	.87	.27	-.06	.09	.10
13.	Masculinity – Feminity	OPI	.15	.05	.16	.79	.00	-.16	.05
14.	Response Bias	OPI	.58	-.26	-.11	-.04	.22	-.21	-.46
15.	BIS-7 Total		.09	.74	.02	-.00	-.27	-.10	-.24
16.	STAI-State Anxiety		-.14	-.01	.05	-.03	.04	.83	.04
17.	STAI-Trait Anxiety		-.10	-.09	.03	-.01	-.10	.84	.22
18.	Eysenck – E Factor		-.08	.45	.02	.11	-.15	-.06	-.73
19.	Eysenck – N Factor		-.14	.25	.12	-.14	-.29	.66	.34
20.	Eysenck – L Scale		.29	-.05	.07	-.15	.74	-.09	.15
21.	MMPI – L		-.06	-.23	-.05	.03	.84	-.07	-.16
22.	MMPI – F		-.31	.44	-.22	.27	.21	.15	.39
23.	MMPI – Pd		-.56	.16	-.05	-.01	-.07	.28	.14
24.	MMPI – Ma		-.32	.53	.08	-.15	.11	.23	-.09
25.	MMPI – Si		-.05	-.11	.29	.12	.05	.35	.59
26.	CPI Socialization		.29	.25	-.07	.03	-.01	-.13	-.81

tionnaire measures within a broader context. Most of the grand attempts (e.g., Sells et al., 1971) to resolve these debates at the questionnaire or item level of measurement have not added much to our understanding of personality theory.

TOWARD A DEFINITION OF IMPULSIVITY

From the perspectives of clinical usage, measurement techniques, and its relationship to other selected personality dimensions, impulsivity is at least a third order dimension. It includes the second and first order dimensions of speed of response, risk-taking, acting without thinking, and inability to plan ahead. Throughout the preceding sections, we have suggested that impulsivity is part of a more inclusive class of action-oriented personality predispositions that includes extraversion, sensation seeking, and, in

TABLE 3.2
Varimax Rotated Factor Pattern
Female Medical Students (N = 94)

			I	II	III	IV	V	VI	VII
						FACTORS			
1.	Thinking Introversion	OPI	.08	-.11	.84	-.00	-.01	.26	.06
2.	Theoretical Orientation	OPI	-.08	-.03	.68	.10	-.15	.05	.54
3.	Estheticism	OPI	.15	-.24	.74	.12	.26	-.12	-.03
4.	Complexity	OPI	.21	-.31	.59	-.19	.23	.39	.05
5.	Autonomy	OPI	.09	-.14	.13	.29	.18	.79	.17
6.	Religious Orientation	OPI	.18	-.13	.09	.03	.07	.21	.86
7.	Social Extraversion	OPI	-.31	-.78	.04	.05	-.09	.18	-.16
8.	Impulse Expression	OPI	.20	-.59	.24	.35	.49	.01	.19
9.	Personality Integration	OPI	-.64	-.07	-.29	-.29	-.53	.10	-.19
10.	Anxiety Level	OPI	-.78	.09	-.28	-.09	-.32	.12	-.09
11.	Altruism	OPI	-.23	-.35	-.06	-.23	-.34	.38	-.51
12.	Practical Outlook	OPI	.01	-.13	-.57	.11	.05	-.70	-.02
13.	Masculinity – Feminity	OPI	-.54	.29	-.42	-.12	-.26	-.13	.37
14.	Response Bias	OPI	-.43	-.00	.24	-.15	-.56	-.29	-.17
15.	BIS-7 Total		.15	-.71	.08	.14	.05	-.11	-.04
16.	STAI-State Anxiety		.68	.26	-.05	-.19	-.06	.16	-.01
17.	STAI-Trait Anxiety		.87	.11	-.03	.07	-.04	.02	.08
18.	Eysenck – E Factor		-.11	-.88	.03	-.04	.11	.11	.06
19.	Eysenck – N Factor		.81	.07	.18	.23	.10	-.00	.19
20.	Eysenck – L Scale		-.15	.07	-.11	-.77	-.10	-.26	-.08
21.	MMPI – L		-.06	.07	.06	-.86	.01	.09	-.01
22.	MMPI – F		.30	.04	.23	-.22	.59	.27	.31
23.	MMPI – Pd		.10	.11	-.04	.22	.64	.02	-.05
24.	MMPI – Ma		-.19	-.19	.17	-.22	.69	-.03	-.05
25.	MMPI – Si		.53	.50	-.16	.14	.02	.11	-.04
26.	CPI Socialization		-.21	-.79	.18	.01	-.11	.03	.10

general, lack of "inhibitory" behavioral controls. Further, this action-oriented class of behaviors is orthogonal to another class of personality dimensions that includes selected affective symptoms and anxiety (moods and feelings). Let us examine this argument further.

The range of definitions of impulsivity in the literature would encompass one or more of the foregoing subdimensions of the more inclusive action-oriented dimension. Buss and Plomin (1975), for example, include impulsivity as one of the four basic temperaments in their theory. They define impulsivity as "the tendency to respond quickly rather than inhibiting the response [p. 8]." Further, they "assume two main components: (1) resisting versus giving in to urges, impulses, or motivational states; and, (2) responding immediately and impetuously to a stimulus versus lying back and planning before making a move [p. 8]." Other definitions corroborating our position could be given. Two studies, which may be less well known, can be cited as typical examples.

Cabiles (1976) studied impulsivity and depression as predictor variables in suicide. He defined impulsivity within a psychoanalytic viewpoint as follows:

> Impulsiveness can be described in terms of swiftly executed actions. In the impulsive individual, primary process thinking and urges predominate and secondary thought processes are inadequately developed. . . . Impulsiveness is considered to be both a general response to conscious activity and a discharge reaction for tensions. It can be considered as an enduring personality trait or style . . . [p. 13].

Wangeman (1976) measured impulsivity as both a state and trait dimension, similar to Spielberger's emphasis on state-anxiety measures. Wangeman related state-trait impulsivity to anxiety under stress conditions. After reviewing the rationale related to measuring impulsivity, Wangeman (1976) noted:

> The [Wangeman] thesis therefore employs and measures impulsivity in the broader sense, as a characteristic style of cognitive appraisal and motor functioning which is reflected in behaviors marked by quick and prompt reaction to stimulus events.
>
> The following behavioral tendencies noted by Kagan and Barratt as characteristic of their dimensions of "conceptual tempo and impulsiveness," are accepted as applicable to impulsivity as employed within the thesis investigation—acting without thinking or adequate reflection, reacting quickly to first impressions or on the spur of the moment, taking risks and chances, getting things done sooner rather than later, experiencing difficulty in concentrating, restlessness, and distractability [p. 71]

In much of our research to date we have operationally defined impulsivity in terms of self-report questionnaires. We have studied it in relation to anxiety (Barratt, 1972) and have attempted to relate these two personality dimensions to a wide range of laboratory and everyday life behaviors. In designing our experiments, we have used a wide range of conceptual models including:

1. Intraindividual variability of psychophysiological and behavioral measures (Barratt, 1963, 1964).

2. Risk-taking and a limbic system model (Barratt, 1965b).

3. A mathematical latency model of reaction time data (Barratt, 1966).

4. An operant model of response control (Barratt, 1968); four major modes of control were hypothesized:

(a) *Conditioned control:* Nonreinforcement and punishment of a response class result in the extinction and supression of this behavior under stimulus conditions similar to those that prevailed at the time of nonreinforcement or punishment.

(b) *Stimulus control:* Because conditioned control tends to be stimulus specific, behavior can be manipulated by varying stimulus conditions.

(c) *Motor control:* Conditioned control also tends to be response specific, which permits response differentation by nonreinforcement and/ or punishment contingent upon this form of response.

(d) *Motivational control:* Conditioned control may also be reinforcer specific. If this is so, conditioned control is lost when a change occurs in the motivational state that determines the efficiency of the reinforcer upon which the conditioned control is based.

Within this model, conditioned control is a prerequisite for stimulus, motor, and/or motivational control; therefore, conditioned control is the most basic type. An individual deficient in susceptibility to conditioned control will necessarily be deficient with respect to all types of control. We hypothesized that individual differences in impulsivity resulted from individual differences in one or more of these four main types of control. Because the "generalized" reinforcers believed to control most human behavior draw their potency from a wide variety of motivational states, we assumed in the intial uses of this model that impulsive behavior did not result from lack of motivational control. Therefore, we concentrated our research on conditioned, stimulus, and motor control. We designed experiments based on the following hypothetical relationships:

(a) Conditioned control should relate to short- and long-term memory and to the ability to learn rapidly and adjust quickly to new conditions.

(b) Stimulus control should be related to the ability to attend closely and to concentrate, and to differences in the ability to recognize subtle differences among objects or situations.

(c) Motor control should be related to coordination, motor skill, and to verbal articulation, enunciation, and fluency.

5. A motor set theory of impulsivity (Barratt, 1972).

In addition to the foregoing theoretical formulations, we tried other mini-system models and techniques. We used DRL, complex chained operant schedules, and the conditioned emotional response paradigm schedule in both our animal[1] and human level research. Many of these specific techniques are still being used in our research, especially our animal research. For example, our reaction time experiments with monkeys are designed using a chained operant schedule.

As we extended our research to more practical, everyday problems, we found the aforementioned models to be inadequate in bridging the gap between everyday life behavior and laboratory research. The response control model appeared to be most helpful in the more applied studies, but we

---

[1]Our animal research is not discussed in this chapter.

realized that our assumptions within this model about motivational states, even though characteristic of most operant research, were not valid for the study of impulsivity. As we reassessed our research, we realized that we had possibly been too technique oriented in our theorizing. Our theoretical orientations resulted in objective data, but it was difficult to use these data to define impulsivity as a personality dimension. Further, work from other laboratories using the BIS was obtaining mixed and often negative results (e.g., Cabiles, 1976; Edelberg, personal communication; Jacobson, personal communication). The psychopathy research of Hare and Cox (1978) was, to us, illustrative of the problem:

> Desocialization, impulsivity, rebelliousness, and socially deviant attitudes, are capable of defining a personality type that is related to the clinical conception of psychopathy. Although the DPI (Jackson & Messick's Differential Personality Inventory) hasn't been used yet in psychophysiological studies, it may prove to be quite useful especially with noncriminal populations.
>
> From the clinical point of view, the dimensions of anxiety, impulsivity, and empathy should be of particular interest. In the study mentioned above, we administered the State Trait Anxiety Inventory (Spielberger et al.), the Hogan Empathy Scale, the Barratt Impulsivity Scale, and the Socialization Scale. For each of these scales three groups of inmates ($N = 20$ in each group) were formed (from the total pool of volunteers), representing those who scored in the lower, middle, and upper thirds of the distribution. The physiological correlates of each scale were then obtained. . . . Without going into any detail here, only the Socialization Scale showed any consistent and theoretically meaningful (insofar as the concept of psychopathy is concerned) relationship with the physiological measures obtained. We also looked at the physiological correlates of various combinations of personality scores, e.g., high impulsivity and low anxiety, but failed to find anything of significance. An approach of this sort is difficult, of course, since a very large number of subjects is needed in order to obtain a reasonable N for each of the combinations of personality scores involved. Another problem is the uncertainty of the meaningfulness of some self-report inventories used with prison inmates in general and psychopathic ones in particular [p. 16].

Recent research in our laboratory on the etiology of impulsivity and anxiety (Barratt, 1979; White, Barratt, & Adams, 1978) among delinquents, "normal" controls, and adolescent psychiatric patients produced conflicting results among tests that purport to measure impulsivity.

It appeared that there were four questions of both practical and theoretical significance that had to be addressed:

1. Why don't the nonquestionnaire measures of impulsivity correlate significantly (or at a practical level) with the questionnaire measures?
2. What role does the "sociability" dimension play in relationship to the impulsivity and anxiety dimensions?
3. How does one measure both the cognitive and behavioral components of impulsivity? Further, are there meaningful subdimensions of impulsivity and how independent are they?

4. Are there characteristics of impulsivity that are common to all of the impulse control disorders (e.g., the disorders as categorized in DSM III)?

As a result of the reassessment of our impulsivity research program and that from other laboratories, we adopted a general systems theory approach. We explored a number of system models in the literature including Miller et al.'s TOTE system (Miller, Galanter, & Pribram, 1960), Eysenck's and Monroe's hierarchical models, and Gray's two factor learning theory model. Although the TOTE model when combined into more complex strategy and tactic feedback models was close to what we wanted, it appeared difficult to us to include cognitive measures of motivations as part of this system. We dismissed the hierarchical models because of their lack of consideration of interaction effects. We felt that within a feedback model one could postulate hierarchies of higher and lower order functions, but the hierarchical approach did not sufficiently "tie-together" all of the measures that we used in our research. We felt that learning theory models were too restrictive in line with our earlier discussion, but we did want a model that would allow us to consider, for example, cortical inhibition and learning.

In our search for a model, we were heavily influenced by a number of authors writing in the general area of systems research (Ashby, 1960; Diamond, Balvin, & Diamond, 1963; Metzler, 1977; Sutherland, 1973; Szentagothai & Arbib, 1975; Weiss, 1973). Although some of these publications appeared after our initial attempts to use a systems approach (Barratt, 1975), the later publications simply reinforced our choice. We were well aware of the criticisms that are often aimed at the use of a systems approach in personality theory. However, we had been using multivariate approaches in our research since its inception and found this to be fruitful. The systems approach was just one step further toward integrating our laboratory data in relationship to practical problems. Possibly, "cause and effect" models were no longer appropriate. Weiss (1973) notes the need for less "simplisticism" and a broader "context" in research—the need for a regard for the ever changing "ecology of contexts":

> One of the didactic needs . . . is a sharp turn from the engrained thought patterns of linear "single cause–effect–chain" causality to the network causality of "system dynamics," which would render the need for a "context concept" not only more compelling, but almost self-evident [p. 124].

Although the systems concept has become more widely accepted during the 1970s, this approach is still not generally accepted in science (e.g., see Erickson, 1979). Possibly, the recent recognition of Prigogine's research will help make the systems approach more acceptable (Brent, 1978).

The basic model that we chose for classifying and interrelating our data was one outlined by Ashby (1960) and discussed relative to *Inhibition and*

Choice (Diamond et al., 1963). Although Ashby's use of this model was related to a more restricted problem than ours, we chose this model for several reasons. First, the four classes of variables within the model allow for the consideration of both cognitive and behavioral data. We consider the motivation box as including "experiential memory storage," long- and short-term. Second, this model includes the environment as part of a closed system. Because the environment can be generalized to include other individuals, this model allows measures of "social" dimensions to be included in the synthesis of experimental results. We cannot elaborate on our more detailed use of this model because of space limitations. The broad philosophical basis for our use of this model is related to our desire to retain the rigor of logical positivism and at the same time pursue the role of cognition in impulsivity (Barratt, 1975). The problem of inferring private events, as noted earlier, had to be broached. We feel that higher order personality dimensions like impulsivity and anxiety can only be adequately defined by interrelating data among the four classes of variables as postulated in a model similar to the Ashby model. Profiles interrelating measurements of variables within these four classes will define the impulsive state or anxious state of the system.

In the next section, we review some of our research within this systems context. Timing of processes within the system is crucial. This is true within a particular class of variables as well as among the four classes of variables. For example, within current cognitive research the time relationship of mental process is a major concern (McClelland, 1979; Posner, 1978). We speculate that there are individual differences in the timing of cognitive and behavioral processes that characterize differences in impulsivity. Thus, tempo of cognitive processes, tapping tempo, reaction time, time judgment experiments, and the concurrent recording of event-related potentials while the subjects perform these tasks characterize much of our current research efforts and provide the basic measurements that define an impulsive system.

We also think, as noted earlier, that impulsivity is part of a larger action-oriented class of variables that characterize a given state (or trait) of the total system. Likewise, we noted that we consider anxiety to be part of a separate state (or trait) condition of the system. Although we may measure many independent personality dimensions using questionnaires, it is difficult to conceive of these dimensions as being independent system wide. We feel that the Eysencks (1978) were correct in postulating two or three basic personality predispositions. In the following section on brain functions, we discuss this further. It is our position that the action-oriented and feeling-mood dimensions are related to two different, broad brain systems. Thus, the action-oriented dimension would include impulsivity, extraversion, sensation seeking, risk-taking, and "speed of response" behavioral measures. The feeling-mood dimension would include anxiety and other "feeling" dimensions. This is an important distinction both theoretically and practically. For example, consider the use of psychopharmacological agents. If one cannot isolate distinct neurochemical systems related to a broad range of personality dimensions, the clinical range of psychopharmacological effective agents may likewise be restricted, and the broader range of psychopathologies beyond the two basic dimensions would be best treated by "learning theory" based or mileau intervention.

We can make one last general observation about a systems approach to studying higher order personality dimensions. We have often obtained a low order relationship among variables that was not statistically significant but was almost significant. Or we may have actually obtained a significant relationship in one experiment but on replication failed to get a significant relationship, although the results were almost significant. We feel that the use of path analysis (or similar techniques, Asher, 1976) in interrelating different classes of variables within a system allows for more flexibility in integrating low order relationships into a meaningful theoretical explanation of higher order dimensions than do the more traditional linear cause and effect techniques. Several of our "timing" measures fall in this category. On the basis of a single experiment, we may have rejected selected results as statistically nonsignificant. Using the systems approach, we are more inclined to be cautious in rejecting the results of an experiment.

BEHAVIORAL, COGNITIVE, AND PSYCHOPHYSIOLOGICAL CORRELATES OF IMPULSIVITY

The purpose of this section is to review some of our more recent research data. Some of the data presented herein are being prepared for more detailed publication, and some are taken from project reports. However, the experiments are presented in enough detail to make the results meaningful within the general context of this chapter.

We do not include the results of our extensive item analyses of the BIS and other questionnaire measures in this section. In line with our data indicating the three (possibly four including Eysenck's P factor) major or inclusive personality dimensions mentioned earlier (i.e., action-oriented vs. feeling vs. socialization), we do not feel that these item analyses would add much to this section. Rather, we include only select examples of our research related to the basic characteristics of an impulsive system. These selected experiments primarily illustrate timing functions related to the cognitive and motor components of impulsivity.

As noted earlier, the concept of time and timing within our systems model is crucial in our definition of impulsivity. We have completed a series of experiments relating time judgments, rhythm, and reaction time to psychometric measures of impulsivity. Most definitions of impulsivity implicate both "quickness" of response and short-term rewards versus long-term rewards. We hypothesized that within the cognitive sphere, estimation of relatively brief time intervals as well as "perceived" time zone measurements involving broader periods of life span would relate to impulsivity. This research is briefly reviewed next.

Time judgment research has waxed and waned since 1857 (Zelkand & Sprug, 1974). There has been an increasing interest in the "time" dimension in psychological research in recent years including a renewed interest in time judgment research. As part of this research, time judgments have been related to psychopathology and personality traits including introversion–extraversion. The results of the latter research have not always been consistent (DuPreez, 1964, 1967; Eysenck, 1959). However, the differences in data could be attributed at least, in part, to differences in methodology (see Eysenck & Eysenck, 1969). The specific method used in obtaining judgments of time intervals is critical.

In our earlier research, which relates time judgments to impulsivity, we primarily used the production method with relatively long time intervals (1 to 4 minutes). The results of this research were consistent in indicating that high impulsive subjects underproduce time intervals, whereas low impulsive subjects would more likely overproduce time intervals. Also, high impulsive subjects were less accurate in these tasks than low impulsive subjects. Experientially, for the high impulsive subjects time appeared to pass more slowly.

In more recent time judgment research (Barratt, 1981), we have used a modification of the time judgment techniques of Carlson and Feinberg (1968). In this research, we have used a wide range of intervals ranging from 1 second to 120 seconds. The results essentially replicated those from our earlier time judgment studies. However, there was one major difference—the BIS did not relate significantly to time judgments involving intervals of 10 seconds or less. Interestingly, the Kagan MFFT did relate to these judgments. For example, in one study that included juvenile delinquents, adolescent psychiatric patients, and normal controls, the MFFT test was significantly correlated with the slopes of time perception curves for judging time intervals ranging from 1 to 10 seconds (Barratt, 1981). The more impulsive subjects were as measured by the MFFT, the more they underproduced the time intervals. The results of our time judgment studies in relationship to an action-oriented personality dimension, then, are consistent with those of Eysenck (1959) and Lynn (1961). Although the techniques used to measure impulsivity and time judgments have varied among these studies, the majority of the data indicates that time does appear to pass more slowly (experientially) for high impulsive subjects.

Further, our work indicates that impulsivity is negatively correlated with accuracy of time interval judgments.

In our research involving the perception of time zones, we modified techniques described by Cottle (1976). We were primarily interested in the relationship of impulsivity to future and past time perspectives. We asked the question: Do high impulsive subjects tend to be present, past, or future oriented? We related Cottle's Experiential Inventory to the BIS, Eysenck's E and N, and the Socialization subscale of the California Psychological Inventory (CPI). The Experiential Inventory gives an indication of where subjects anchor important life events within broad time zones. Impulsivity, anxiety, and E and N were not significantly correlated with the Experiential Inventory measure of time perspective among 153 medical students, but the CPI Socialization Subscale was significantly correlated (+.29) with the Experiential Inventory. We next related Cottle's Future Commitment Scale, which measures the degree to which people will predict the future, to the same personality inventories. The Eysenck E scale and the BIS were both significantly correlated (+.31 and +.27) with the Future Commitment Scale, but the CPI Socialization Scale was not. Thus, where individuals anchor important events in their life span appears to relate to socialization, whereas the willingness to predict the future relates more to impulsivity. It may be that this latter relationship reflects the risk-taking tendency among high impulsive subjects.

In our 1972 review, we (Barratt, 1972) noted that anxiety was related to "time estimation," but impulsivity was not. The task used in that research involved holding down a key for 2 to 4 seconds prior to making a response within a reaction time paradigm. We have replicated the 1972 results several times. That task, however, was different than the time judgment methods that we have more recently used. In the 1972 task, the subject was instructed to "hold a key down" following a light cue and then to release it "as quickly as possible" after the estimated interval. This is different than asking the subject to indicate verbally when a time interval has passed (using a voice-activated switch to record judged time intervals). The subject had a set for a "quick release" in the first experiment; thus, a reaction time set was confounded with the task of judging a time interval.

As noted earlier, time judgments have also been related to psychopathology. Depressed patients underproduce time intervals (Mezey & Cohen, 1961; Straus, 1947; Wyrick & Wyrick, 1977), and schizophrenics overproduce brief time intervals (1 to 5 seconds; Guertin & Rabin, 1960; Lhamon & Goldstone, 1956). Thus, the fact that impulsive subjects underproduce time intervals is not unique. The relative importance of time judgment patterns that characterize a schizophrenic, depressed, or impulsive system can only be known by using these measurements with broader combinations of multivariate data. Poor time judgments or time passing slowly does not cause impulsivity.

As we previously reported (Barratt, 1967, 1972), impulsivity is inversely related to mean reaction time. In reaction time experiments, the higher the information level of the cues to be processed, the more obvious is the negative effect of impulsivity on performance. In this research, anxiety and impulsivity usually interact, with the higher impulsive–lower anxiety (HILA) subjects having the slowest reaction times. We have recently completed a reaction time experiment in which we randomly varied the presentations of the S_1 – S_2 intervals of different durations. In this experiment, S_1 was an auditory "get ready" signal that was followed by another auditory signal (S_2), which cued the subject to release, as quickly as possible, a key they had depressed. The S_1 – S_2 intervals were 1000 ms, 600 ms, and 20 ms, in addition to a "no S_2" condition. The effects of impulsivity and anxiety on reaction time during the 1000 ms interval were similar to those reported by us earlier. At the 600 ms interval, these effects were less obvious, and at the 20 ms interval, the effects of impulsivity were reversed. At 1000 ms intervals, higher impulsive subjects, especially HILA subjects, responded more slowly than lower impulsive subjects. At the 20 ms interval, higher impulsive subjects responded more quickly than lower impulsive subjects. As we reported earlier (Barratt, 1972), a set (possibly motor set) appeared to be established among higher impulsive subjects, and it was difficult for them to change this set. Tangentially, when we first studied the relationship of impulsivity to reaction time, we hypothesized that higher impulsive subjects would have faster reaction times because they often "act on the spur of the moment." The data just cited suggest that our initial hypothesis may be correct for very brief S_1 – S_2 intervals. When there is sufficient time for a "set" to be established, the reaction times are slower for higher impulsive subjects.

In addition to time judgments and reaction time data, we have just finished a "rhythm" study[2]. The main purpose of the study was to relate the accuracy of tapping at a given rhythm to two different models of the timing of movement: a clock model and a rhythm model. Further, speed and accuracy of timing were related to several personality variables including impulsivity and anxiety. Impulsivity was significantly related to both magnitude of error and speed of response. Higher impulsive subjects made more errors under all conditions than did low impulsive subjects. In addition, high impulsive subjects tapped faster under all conditions. Anxiety was not consistently related to the rhythm measures.

In another experiment involving a "knob turning" task, subjects were asked to turn a knob as "quickly" as possible, as "slowly" as possible, and at a natural or comfortable speed. Impulsivity was positively related to the "fast" turning measurements but not to the natural or slow component of

---

[2]Mr. Gregg Olsson, a graduate student in the Department of Psychology, University of Texas, Austin, completed this study as part of his doctoral dissertation.

the task. Again, performing a task with less time-imposed constraint, the higher impulsivity subjects were faster.

In summary, during sequential tasks involving paced tapping to a given rhythm, high impulsive subjects made more errors and tapped faster. In reaction time tasks where they were given a warning signal followed by a response cue at an interval of 600 ms or more, the responded more slowly. In a reaction time task, in which the $S_1 - S_2$ interval was 20 ms, the higher impulsive subjects responded faster than lower impulsive subjects. In a cognitive task (judging time intervals), higher impulsive subjects under-produced time intervals and made errors of greater magnitude than did lower impulsive subjects. As noted earlier, higher impulsive subjects were also more variable in performing perceptual motor tasks (Barratt, 1972).

During the performance of many of these tasks, we obtained selected psychophysiological measurements. We have also obtained psychophysiological measures independent of performance (e.g., visual augmenting/reducing paradigm) and related these to impulsivity. We briefly review these data next.

Augmenting–reducing of visual evoked potentials is well established (Callaway, 1975). We have data indicating (Barratt, in press) that higher impulsive subjects tend to be augmenters, whereas lower impulsive subjects are reducers. We have also demonstrated that augmenting–reducing of visual stimuli is related to time perception (Barratt, in press). Further, our data reveal that augmenting–reducing differs among adolescent psychiatric patients, delinquents, and normal controls and that time judgments and conceptual tempo (as measured by the MFFT) also are significantly different among these same groups. Zuckerman, Murtaugh, and Siegel (1974) have shown a similar relationship between augmenting–reducing and sensation seeking.

We have not found consistent differences related to impulsivity in auditory evoked potentials recorded during performance of the reaction time tasks. We have found differences in contingent negative variation (CNV) related to impulsivity. For example, in the reaction time task discussed earlier in which the $S_1 - S_2$ intervals were varied randomly, higher impulsive subjects consistently either did not produce a measurable CNV or produced a very low CNV during the 600 ms and 1000 ms interval presentations. The lower impulsive subjects showed a very clear, well-developed CNV in all instances. In another experiment involving CNV in our laboratory, subjects were required to respond as liking or disliking two series of visually presented slides. In one series, the slides contained provocative pictures from *Playboy* and similar magazines; the other series contained slides of geometric designs. The higher impulsive subjects did not produce measurable CNVs to the geometric figures but did produce CNVs to the more "sensational" slides. The lower impulsive subjects produced

CNVs to both series of slides. These results emphasize the need to consider a taxonomy of environmental stimuli in personality research.

In a vigilance task, 46 medical students were required to attend to a screen for 30 minutes during which time 16 slides were presented at variable intervals. The slides were items from Thurstone's "hand" test; the subjects were required to press levers to indicate whether the slide depicted a left or right hand. In addition to being paid to participate, they received $1.00 for each slide correctly identified, a $5.00 bonus for getting 80% correct, and $10.00 bonus for getting 100% correct. Each slide was exposed for 100 ms. Heart rate, GSR, and respiration were recorded during the performance of this task as well as EEG from leads O_1 and O_2. These subjects were also administered the STAI, BIS, Eysencks E and N Scales, Kagan's MFFT (Adult From), the CPI Socialization Subscale, and the IES Test. Impulsivity and extraversion were significantly negatively correlated with accuracy of performance on this taks. The level of autonomic measures was negatively related to both impulsivity and extraversion. Further, the EEG was more activated (lee alpha and more LVF activity) for the introverts than for the extraverts. Thus, impulsivity was significantly related to vigilance, and the psychophysiological measures indicate a nonactivated nervous system for the "action-oriented" subjects. This finding is consistent with recent results reported by Gange, Geen, and Harkins (1979). The Kagan MFFT did not significantly relate to performance on this task. The STAI (State) was positively correlated with performance at a level that just failed to reach statistical significance.

In another time judgment experiment, 18 medical students were administered questionnaire measures of personality, responded to visual stimulation at three intensity levels to obtain augmenting–reducing measures, and gave urine samples before and after performing the time judgment tasks. The personality variables (impulsivity and anxiety) and evoked potential data were consistent with that reported earlier (i.e., high impulsive subjects were underproducers of time and were visual evoked potential augmenters). The urine samples were analyzed for epinephrine and norepinephine levels. Basal norepinephrine was significantly positively related to rate of time judgments, to Kagan's MFFT impulsivity score, and negatively related to the MFFT error score. Neither epinephrine nor norepinephrine was significantly correlated with the BIS or STAI in this study.

In these studies, impulsivity was defined by the BIS, Eysenck's E factor, or the MFFT. In line with our earlier discussion about the psychometric measures of impulsivity, we consider the use of these tests to be a general weakness in much of our research. Having made that observation, the research should be considered more suggestive than definitive. However, we have used the BIS and E scale in enough research in which the group differences on impulsivity and extraversion were in the direction predicted that we feel the question of the validity of the questionnaire measures may be less serious overall using a systems model than would be true for a linear cause–effect model. For example, in the previously mentioned study of juvenile delinquents, adolescent psychiatric patients, and "normal" controls, both the delinquents and patients scored higher on the BIS and MFFT, although the BIS differences were not statistically significant (Barratt, 1979). In the same study, however, the delinquents and patients scored significantly higher on the Delay Avoidance, Work Methods, Teacher Acceptance, and Education Acceptance subscales of the Brown–Holtzman Survey of Study Habits (Brown & Holtzman, 1967). The group differences on the latter scale were very significant. The items on the Brown–Holtzman Study Habits Inventory are possibly more comprehensible to most teenagers than are the BIS items. If one considers that impulsivity is part of an "action-oriented predisposition" within the systems model, the overall results of the psychophysiology, cognitive, and behavioral studies are consistent.

The BIS has been related to a wide range of measures as noted earlier. A few relationships not presented, but which give further insight into what the questionnaire is measuring, are its positive relationship with the Stroop Time Score ($r = +.55$; the Stroop Test is a measure of cognitive dissonance or cognitive "interference") and a positive relationship with alpha percentage in the EEG ($+.36$; this would suggest that impulsivity is related to low CNS arousal).

BRAIN FUNCTIONS AND IMPULSIVITY

The purpose of this section is to discuss possible brain systems that may be related to impulsivity. Although we discussed our use of the Ashby model earlier, several points need to be reiterated at the beginning of this section. First, our use of the "motivation" box differs from Ashby's use. For Ashby, it was a register of success and failure in trial and error behavior in an ultrastable system. For us, the box is more inclusive and contains "conscious experience" in general. We realize, as noted earlier, that conscious experiences are inferred from data in the other three boxes in the model. This is true of all cognitive research in that private events are inferential in nature. Even where psychophysiological measurements (e.g., P300 of event-related potentials) are time locked with the performance of a cognitive task, these measurements do not represent cognition itself (see Donchin, 1979, for an excellent discussion of this point). These basic concepts are often overlooked in cognitive research. For us, it is meaningful to have a class of variables that, although inferred, function in the system by providing explanations for changes in the combinations of measurements (profiles) in the other three boxes. Thus, in this section, we describe an impulsive system including cognitive characteristics. If people underproduce time intervals, we assume that their conceptual tempo (cognition) is faster than if they overproduce time intervals. The data that belong in the other three boxes of the model are relatively easier to categorize than are these cognitive data. We do not present a more detailed description of the model at this time, although it should be obvious that our model is more detailed than Fig. 3.1 depicts. If nothing else, the model as presented has heuristic value in integrating our data. What, then, are the characteristics of an impulsive system?

In general, research indicates that impulsivity involves impared cognition in "timed" tasks where it is necessary to ignore or overcome a "mental" set The psychophysiological data indicate, in part, that a lower arousal level (i.e., brain stem reticular arousal) is related to higher impulsivity. The higher impulsive subjects are visual-response augmenters compared to low impulsive subjects. Further, higher basal norepinephrine levels in urine appear to be related to higher levels of impulsivity. There is evidence to indicate that the arousal properties of stimuli have to be considered within the total system. It is not that high impulsive subjects cannot produce CNVs, for example, but that they produce CNVs to stimuli which to them have some positively cathected properties. When aroused, they produce CNVs like low impulsive subjects. In brief, we propose that action-oriented subjects (including high impulsive subjects) have a fast conceptual tempo and respond quickly (motor impulsivity) where a mental set is not well estab-

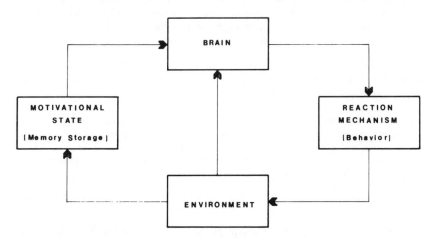

FIG. 3.1   Double feedback: Ashby's minimal requirement for an adaptive nervous system (adapted from Diamond et al., 1963, p. 108).

lished or where regulating speed of response is a requirement. We conjecture then, as noted earlier, that timing and time judgments are crucial to understanding impulsivity. Let us next consider some possible roles in the brain in this system.

Smith (1973) has proposed a homeokinetic feedback theory of physiological-behavioral integration to explain the timing properties of the brain related to perceptual-motor functioning:

> The homeokinetic feedback doctrine . . . . states that the brain functions as a central timing and synchronizing mechanism for the integration of organ-metabolic (including neurohormonal), exteroceptive, interoceptive, motion. The timing operations are feedback governed as delay circuits whose frequency characteristics are determined primarily by the length of the nerve circuits and response characteristics of particular motor, sensory, and biochemical mechanisms. Three main motor operations are integrated by the brain through such timed integration. The first is the guidance of articulated components of the skeletal motor system through exteroceptive feedback and space-organized feature detection measures of the cortex. The second is the timed control of receptor-efferent mechanisms, including the gamma efferent systems of muscles, that operate through space and time-synchronized feature detection neurons of the cerebellum, pons, and basal ganglia of the nervous system. The third consists of the limbic and autonomic systems that are differentiated for control of both generalized (sympathetic) and organ specific (parasympathetic) neural activities [pp. 24–26].

Time perception has also been theoretically related to reaction time performance in several recent models. For example, Ollman (1973) notes:

> A hypothetical process of covert time estimation figures important in some recently proposed reaction time models. The basic notion is that the subject uses some sensory event to initiate a subjective "deadline" and then makes either a "stimulus-controlled" or else a "guess" response according to whether a stimulus analysis is completed before or after the deadline terminates. The reaction time similarly is decided by whichever delay is smaller so the term "rate model" is also apt [p. 572].

Luce's (1973) discussion of the perception of time within the context of biological rhythms is also relevant here. In the discussion of subjective time sense, she (Luce, 1973) states:

> Time sense and rhythm develop before language. Before a baby speaks, he will drum on his crib and show a love of music and rhythm. . . . Surely young children show need of dance, poetry, marching and rhythmic repetitions. However, some of our earliest time measures are not like the heartbeat, but mark off stages of growth or other intervals [pp. 427–428].

Thus, the role of the brain in timing and making time judgments has been alluded to by others.

We propose that action-oriented predispositions and affect or mood dimensions involve two different brain systems. Action-oriented predispositions include impulsivity, sensation seeking, episodic dyscontrol, and risk-taking. The affective or "feeling" predispositions include anxiety and other "mood feeling" traits. We suggest further that socialization is a third personality dimension that relates primarily to input from the environmental facets of the system and is orthogonal or has a low order relationship with the other two clusters.

It is now our task to speculate beyond these more general observations about the mechanisms of the brain systems related to the action-oriented and mood dimensions as they affect timing and other indices of an impulsive system. The brain is certainly a very complex organ, and just as certainly it is very little understood. Several assumptions regarding the role of the brain in the function of the total system should be noted at this point. In the most simplistic terms, the function of the brain is to aid in a coordinated quest for physiological homeostasis (Ashby's ultrastable system). Teleologically, the purpose of this homeostasis, if we are to believe Darwin, is to provide for survival of the species. In agonistic confrontations, speed of response may be highly adaptive. However, in certain other situations, motor impulsivity should be avoided in order to preserve homeostasis.

Although the complexity of the nervous system possessed by any one organism depends largely on the demands placed on that organism by its environment, some basic functions are universal. Two such dimensions characteristic of the brain are its function in activity (e.g., as noted at a gross anatomical level in Smith's theory) and arousal. These are basic mechanisms that serve to modulate the response an organism makes to any environmental situation. These basic "phenomena" serve as the basis of an organism's interaction with its environment. Action is a continuum along which the organism is predisposed to act on the environment or to remain passive in response to it (a go–no go system). Arousal refers to the potential perceived gain or loss being faced by the organism as a result of action orientation (e.g., Ashby's success or failure in the motivation box). For impulsivity we see these are two important dimensions. These attributes of activation and arousal are well documented in the literature (Ax, 1953; Engel, 1960; Engel & Bickford, 1961; Engel & Moos, 1967; Lacy, 1959; Lacy, Bateman, & VanLehn, 1953; Pribram & McGuinness, 1975). Further, they fit well into Ashby's brain and behavior box. They also fit our interpretation of our data and are consistent with existing notions of personality structure (e.g., Eysenck, 1967). Duffy (1972) provides an excellent review of activation within the context of psychophysiology:

> An individual, i.e., organism as a whole, is sometimes excited, sometimes relaxed, and sometimes in one of a variety of intermediate conditions. Those obvious states suggested the concept of activation or arousal, which attempts to describe the physiology of these conditions and to consider their cause and effects.

> Activation refers not to the overt activity of the organism but to the release of energy into various internal physiological systems, in preparation for overt activity. The overt activity need never occur; if it does, activation is its constant internal accompaniment and sustainer [p. 578].

Of the models using activation and arousal as components, Pribram and McGuinness' model (1975) has been the most useful to us. It distinguishes three basic brain mechanisms: activation, arousal, and effort. Pribram and McGuinness go on to define and to relate these conceptual components to anatomy and neurochemistry. We return to their model after reviewing some specific information relevant to our data and the development of our thoughts regarding the function of these models within the brain box.

In general, we would consider the affective disorders to be more related to the general biochemical arousal pathways as we speculated in 1972. Although there were some indications of arousal being related to impulsivity in our data, it is difficult to relate it specifically to the differences in responses among high and low impulsive subjects when "mental sets" are part of the task requirements. Thus, fronto-limbic connections must be considered. Much of our future nonhuman primate research will be directed to studying these fronto-limbic connections using both anatomically and biochemically related techniques.

We feel that risk-taking, speed of response, poor perceptual-motor performance, time judgments, and behavioral timing within an impulsive system are related to selected limbic system input into the cortex. The limbic system structures include primarily the amygdala and hippocampal input through the anterior thalamic nucleus and via the cingulum bundle to the cingular cortex and orbital-frontal cortical areas. At the human level, cingulatomies and amygdalectomies have been successfully related to the surgical treatment of impulse disorders. Recent anatomical data from the squirrel monkey indicate that the limbic-anterior thalamic nucleus connections may be more complex than was previously indicated. It has been shown (Powell, 1973) that the amygdala, for example, has a direct input into the anterior thalamic nucleus as well as through the mammillary body. It is possible that a feedback loop including these limbic structures and the anterior thalamic nucleus has a gating function on the input into the cingulum bundle. Timing behaviors in monkeys have been shown to be related to the cingulum and prefrontal cortex (Niki & Watanabe, 1979). In brief, we postulate that the action-oriented class of personality predispositions relates at least in part to the control of cognitive and behavioral timing, which is controlled by these fronto-limbic connections. We do not feel that arousal per se or activation per se is sufficient to explain our data because the establishment of a "set" appears crucial in determining the role of impulsivity in cognitive and perceptual-motor tasks. This set, we feel, is also established as part of the function of the fronto-limbic system.

Milner (1977), in an exposition on reinforcement, drive, and motivation, has provided a relevant summary of brain activity related to brain functioning and set. Milner proposes an expectancy model[3] and relates it to

---

[3]See Donchin (1979) for a discussion of expectancy related to P300, CNV, and uncertainty.

neurophysiology in a way that is useful in conceptualizing our future research. Milner observes that cortical arousal has an inhibiting effect on investigatory responses. Lesions of frontal cortex and hippocampus disinhibit responding and habituation (similar to decreased levels of serotonin as discussed later). According to Milner, an important link in this network connecting the cortex and the motor system is the nucleus accumbens-neostriatal complex. This area is below the anterior cortex and receives projections from it. The accumbens projects to the pallidal region and serves, at least in part, as an inhibitory influence there. Damage to the neostriatum (caudate-putamen) produces release of involuntary motor behaviors that persist in the face of restraint and other stereotyped behaviors.

Milner believes that cortical activity representing engrams of past events, which represent uninteresting or nonproductive stimuli, may finally exert an inhibitory effect on motor approach behavior via the cortico-striatopallidal route. Cortical activity associated with engrams that have led to rewards (and thus activity of consumatory mechanisms) fail to inhibit the approach system. It would be difficult to say what mechanism correlates this disinhibition of motor approach behavior with previously reinforced ("stamped in") stimuli. Pribram and McGuinness (1975) believe the hippocampus plays an important part. It is parsimonious to speculate that it occurs by disinhibition of existing approach systems rather than to postulate a separate system. Milner hypothesizes that ascending nigrostriatal and mesolimbic dopamine (DA) neurons could block the striatal and accumbens (because DA is inhibitory in these loci) motor inhibitory effects and thus the cortex. Although much research needs to be done, we believe, as does Milner, that the frontal and cingulate cortex achieves its inhibitory input through the monoamine systems located in areas directly beneath it. In addition we believe, as does Milner (1977) and Crow (1977), that although the primary or original function of these systems might have once been food related, they now subserve additional, more encompassing approach and inhibitory functions. These systems are also highly important in the mechanism of association of previously neutral stimuli with innately determined stimuli (food, water, sex, etc.). Acquired drive, motivation, and response set vis-a-vis environmental stimuli perhaps play a most significant role in human personality predispositions such as impulsivity. Theories of learning such as Mowrer's (1960) two factor theory, Gray's (1971, 1972) use of two factor theory, and Solomon's (1977) opponent process theory of acquired motivation depend heavily on Pavlovian conditioning of previously neutral stimuli (CS) using innate or previously conditioned stimuli as UCSs. As Pavlov (1949) himself stated: "Involuntary action can become voluntary only with the aid of a second signal system [p. 337]." This represents the basic mechanism for the development of second order function (beyond primary reinforcement) in Ashby's motivation box. We agree with Milner in that this is one possible input point for relating cognitive function to behavior.

Existing knowledge of the functional neurochemistry of nervous transmission is developing at a fast pace. But, we are still a long way from being able to relate specific biochemical pathways to personality dimensions, normal or pathological (Kinsbourne, 1979). However, let us briefly review some of the functional interrelationships of these monoamine systems and proffer some possible biochemical bases for the "action-oriented" and arousal predispositions.

Nigrostriatal dopamine (DA) neurons possibly represent the motor excitation component of our activating system (action) (Crow, 1977). Dopamine neurons, which project to the nucleus accumbens, olfactory tubercle, and frontal cortex (meso-limbic DA system), have been implicated in cognitive-affective behavior and possibly in such disorders as schizophrenia (Stevens, 1979). However, relatively less is known about the function of the meso-limbic pathway than about the nigrostriatal pathway (e.g., its role in Parkinsonian disorders). Taken together these pathways may be necessary for maintaining oral approach behaviors, complex patterned behavior, and sensory attentional function (as viewed by Crow, 1977). Crow (1977) states: "Dopaminergic neurons may function as an 'activating mechanism' which mediates the organism's response to significant environmental stimuli [p. 164]." This system corresponds to Pribram and McGuinness' (1975) activation or "go" system. Randrup, Munkvad, Fog, and Ayhan (1975) review their own and other's work interrelating dopamine pathways and schizophrenia, manic depressive psychosis, and amphetamine induced psychosis. The fact that the dopamine antagonist (neuroleptics) has a potent "antimanic" (Randrup et al., 1975), antiactivating effect underscores the importance of dopamine vis-a-vis activation. In addition, depressed patients were quite consistently activated when given L-Dopa (precursor to DA). L-Dopa, however, had antidepressant effects in only a small proportion of the patients (Murphy & Redmond, 1975). So it is seen that DA activates depressives but does not alter their mood.

Another important amine to be recognized in our biochemical considerations of the brain box is the serotonergic (5-HT) system. This system is not as well-known as the other two monoamine systems. The function of the various serotonin pathways is still a matter of intense investigation. Much is known, however, concerning the overall effects of rises and falls in brain 5-HT, and some specific regional information is also available (Azmitia, 1978; Marczynski, 1976). The work of Jouvet (1969) on the role of 5-HT in sleep is well-known. Decreases in 5-HT produced by raphe lesion cause increased cortical arousal (EEG) (Marczynski, 1976). Electrical stimulation of the raphe blocks habituation, and several synthetic tryptamine-like derivative compounds (having serotonin-like effects) when administered to cats and rats produce blockade of hippocampal theta waves and raise the threshold for EEG desynchronizing in response to electrical stimulation of the brain stem reticular formation. Even while animals remain awake and responsive to stimuli (Marczynski, 1976), serotonin derivatives also block conditioned avoidance-escape response as do the major tranquilizers (dopamine blockers) (Marczynski, 1976). In general, however, as 5-HT is functionally elevated there is a decrease in sensitivity to environmental cues and decreased irritability and aggressiveness. As 5-HT is functionally reduced there is an increased sensitivity to pain, enhanced reactivity to normal stimuli, decreased freezing, increased performance in shuttle avoidance, and increased activity in open field and running wheel (Azmitia, 1978; Crow, 1977; Marczynski, 1976). Crow (1977) concludes: "These observations are consistent with the hypothesis that the 5-hydroxytryptamine system arising from the median raphe (B_8) nucleus exerts inhibitory influence on motor behavior and may mediate some of the behaviorally suppressive effects of aversive stimuli [p. 169]." Therefore, 5-HT could play an important role in modulating the overall framework within which the organism perceives incoming stimuli.

Serotonin corresponds to our arousal component. Pribram and McGuinness (1975) relate arousal, in their system, to amygdala function. The amygdala is often considered a basal ganglia structure, and Pribram and McGuinness (1975) note: "Brain structures similar in morphology, though different in their connections, control arousal and activation [p. 132]." We find that this conceptualization of DA-basal ganglia (striatum) control of activation and 5-HT-basal ganglia (amygdala) control of arousal fits our system. Crow's (1977) notions are also substantially consistent with those of Pribram and McGuinness.

The final member of the monoamine triad is norepinephrine (NE). This compound is the sister catecholamine to DA. Norepinephrine is just as diffuse in its action as DA is specific. Although it is difficult, if not impossible, to untie some of the shared influences of these two catecholamines (CAs), Crow stresses the importance of NE for reinforcement, confirming reaction, results of action signals, or satiety mechanisms. This is a long held view concerning the role of norepinephrine in reinforcement.

It is Crow's assertion that the major ascending CA systems may have evolved as controllers of ingestive related behaviors. He divides these pathways into three structure-function related areas. The first, involved with peripheral sensory reception (olfaction), serves to "activate" the organism toward a detected potential food source. This "incentive effect" function falls to dopamine. Food in the mouth stimulates gustatory receptors, and at this point the "confirming reaction" or "results of action" signal provides reinforcement signaling. This role falls to norepinephrine tracts from the locus coeruleus to the cerebellar cortex, cerebral cortex, and hippocampal areas. The third pathway serves a satiety function; it is thought to be responsive to food in the stomach. This pathway is the ventral NE pathway projecting ventro-rostrally (medial forebrain bundle). Crow (1977) states:

> It is suggested that the three ascending catecholamine systems may have their phylogenetic origins in relation to the three afferent-pathways concerned with food intake. In the course of evoluntionary development other afferent modalities have come to influence these systems but their functions with respect to behavior may have remained fundamentally the same [p. 165].

A rapidly expanding area of interest involves one of the monoamine degrading enzymes, monoamine oxidase (MAO). This enzyme inactivates DA, NE, and 5-HT. Aberrant MAO levels have either been found or postulated to exist in a number of clinical disease entities including alcoholism and schizophrenia (Wyatt, Potkin, & Murphy, 1979). Monoamine oxidase inhibitors are sometimes administered as a therapeutic technique in depressive disorders (Berger, 1977). These states contain components of mood and affective disorder as well as activation pathology. MAO levels are then critical to the function of the entire system. Levels of this enzyme are under genetic control and may be a primary disposing factor in pathology.

Crow's (1977) analysis was written after Pribram and McGuinness' (1975), and Crow does not mention Pribram and McGuinness' work. The degree of similarity between their conclusions regarding what amines are functioning at different loci in the control of different dispositions is remarkable. Pribram and McGuinness are more cognitively and wholistically oriented; however, NE in their system subserves the "effort" system. They conceptualize this system as modulator of the reciprocal input of activation and arousal. The focal point of this interaction, anatomically, is the hippocampus. This would correspond to Crow's locus coeruleus to cerebellar cortex, cerebral cortex, and hippocampus NE tract. Pribram and McGuinness (1975) state: "Hippocampal control over the organization of the relationship between arousal and activation leads to changes in central representations which may be conceived as changes of state, set, or 'attitude.' [p. 132]."

These notions of state, set, and "attitude" would fit into our various system boxes. State would be a condition of the total system (i.e., impulsivity). Attitude would certainly fit into our motivational state box. Set would be more difficult to place in one particular box because our data indicate that high impulsive subjects have difficulty with both cognitive (motivational state box) and motor (reaction mechanism box) sets.

It is at this point that our conception really begins to gel with Pribram and McGuinness'. It is precisely such attention to notions such as state, set, and attitude that we believe will be productive in our research. We noted earlier that high impulsive subjects seem to have lower cortical arousal. This is indicated by the facts that: (1) high impulsivity (BIS) correlates with increased percentage of time spent in alpha (EEG); (2) high impulsives tend to be cortical evoked potential augmenters; and (3) high impulsives produce normal CNV only when aroused by highly cathected stimuli. But low cortical arousal is not unique to impulsivity.

Those factors that interact with cortical arousal in our system (e.g., the role of behavioral set) may shed further light on what is unique to an impulsive system. But, in our view, many factors must be examined within a systems context before answers are forthcoming. We are not moving in the direction of reductionism as we believe it will not provide the answers we need.

FUTURE RESEARCH

At the human level, our impulsivity research will continue to involve measures of timing, time perception, and rhythm during cognitive and perceptual-motor performance. We will also continue to record event-related cortical potentials during the performance of these tasks. We feel that the orienting process and readiness potential in the CNV (Donchin, 1979) are important to study in relation to impulsivity. We will also be doing more research that includes females because we have evidence of sex differences in the influence of impulsivity in everyday life and performance of laboratory tasks.

At the lower animal level, we will continue to explore for brain correlates of impulsivity. This will involve a study of the comparison of the two different brain systems, which we propose are related to the action-oriented and mood dimensions, respectively.

ACKNOWLEDGMENTS

This research was supported by the Office of Naval Research, Washington, D.C.

REFERENCES

American Psychiatric Association. *Diagnostic and statistical manual of mental disorders* (2nd ed.). Washington, D.C.: American Psychiatric Association, 1968.
American Psychiatric Association. *Diagnostic and statistical manual of mental disorders* (3rd ed.). Washington, D.C.: American Psychiatric Association, 1978.
Ashby, W. *Design for a brain*. New York: Wiley, 1960.
Asher, H. Causal modeling. In E. Uslaner (Ed.), *Quantitative applications in the social sciences* (No. 3). Beverly Hills, Cal.: Sage Publications, 1976.

Ault, R., Michaell, C., & Hartman, D. Some methodological problems in reflection-impulsivity. *Child Development*, 1976, *47*, 227–231.

Ax, A. The physiological differentiation between fear and anger in humans. *Psychosomatic Medicine*, 1953, *15*, 433–442.

Azmitia, E. The serotonin-producing neurons of the midbrain dorsal raphe nuclei. In L. Iverson, S. Iverson, & S. Snyder (Eds.), *Handbook of psychopharmacology, Vol. 9: Chemical pathways in the brain*. New York: Plenum Press, 1978.

Barratt, E. Anxiety and impulsiveness related to psychomotor efficiency. *Perceptual and Motor Skills*, 1959, *9*, 191–198.

Barratt, E. Intraindividual variablity of performance: ANS and psychometric correlates. *Texas Reports on Biology and Medicine*, 1963, *21*, 496–504.

Barratt, E. *Intraindividual variability of performance: Parameters and subcortical correlates.* Annual report submitted to the Office of Naval Research, Washington, D.C., 1964.

Barratt, E. Factor analysis of some psychometric measures of impulsiveness and anxiety. *Psychological Reports*, 1965, *16*, 547–544. (a)

Barratt, E. *Psychophysiological correlates of impulsiveness and risk taking: Cross sectional and longitudinal correlates.* Annual report submitted to the Office of Naval Research, Washington, D.C., 1965. (b)

Barratt, E. *Psychophysiological correlates of impulsiveness and risk taking: Cross sectional and longitudinal studies.* Annual report submitted to the Office of Naval Research, Washington, D.C., 1966.

Barratt, E. Perceptual-motor performance related to impulsiveness and anxiety. *Perceptual and Motor Skills*, 1967, *25*, 485–492.

Barratt, E. *Psychophysiological correlates of impulsiveness and risk taking: Cross sectional and longitudinal studies.* Annual report submitted to the Office of Naval Research, Washington, D.C., 1968.

Barratt, E. Psychophysiological correlates of classical differential eyelid conditioning among subjects selected on the basis of impulsiveness and anxiety. *Biological Psychiatry*, 1971, *3*, 339–346.

Barratt, E. Anxiety and impulsiveness: Toward a neuropsychological model. In C. Spielberger (Ed.), *Current trends in theory and research* (Vol. 1). New York: Academic Press, 1972.

Barratt, E. *Brain-behavior relationships: A general systems theory model.* Paper presented at the annual meeting of the Association of Children with Learning Disorders, Dallas, Texas, 1975.

Barratt, E. *Multivariate diagnostic assessment of juvenile delinquents.* Final report submitted to Criminal Justice Division, Office of the Governor of the State of Texas, Austin, 1979.

Barratt, E. Time perception and cortical evoked potentials among male juvenile delinquents, adolescent psychiatric patients, and normal controls. In K. Roberts, R. Hays, & L. Soloway (Eds.), *Violence and the violent individual*. New York: Spectrum Publishers, 1981.

Becker, L., Bender, N., & Morrison, G. Measuring impulsivity–reflection: A critical review. *Journal of Learning Disabilities*, 1978, *10*, 626–632.

Berger, P. Antidepressant medications and the treatment of depressions. In J. Barchas, P. Berger, R. Ciaranello, & G. Elliot (Eds.), *Psychopharmacology: From theory to practice*. New York: Oxford University Press, 1977.

Block, J., & Harrington, D. Some misgivings about the matching familiar figures test as a measure of reflective impulsivity. *Developmental Psychology*, 1974, *10*, 611–632.

Brent, S. Prigonine's model for self-organization in non-equilibrium systems. *Human Development*, 1978, *21*, 374–387.

Brown, W., & Holtzman, W. *Manual for the survey of study habits and attitudes*. New York: Psychological Corporation, 1967.

Buss, A., & Plomin, R. *A temperament theory of personality development*. New York: Wiley, 1975.

Cabiles, P. Impulsivity and depression as factors in suicidal males. *Dissertation Abstracts International,* 1976, 76–23, 714.

Callaway, E. *Brain electrical potentials and individual psychological differences.* New York: Grune & Stratton, 1975.

Cantwell, D. *The hyperactive child.* New York: Spectrum Publications, 1975.

Carlson, V., & Feinberg, I. Individual variations in time judgment and the concept of an internal clock. *Journal of Experimental Psychology,* 1968, *77,* 631–640.

Cattell, R., Saunders, D., & Stize, E. *Handbook for the Sixteen Personality Factor Questionnaire.* Champaign, Ill.: Institute for Personality and Ability Testing, 1957.

Cleckley, H. *The mask of sanity.* St. Louis: Mosby, 1964.

Cottle, T. *Perceiving time.* New York: Wiley, 1976.

Crow, T. Neurotransmitter-related pathways: The structure and function of central monoamine neurons. In A. Davidson (Ed.), *Biochemical correlates of brain structure and function.* New York: Academic Press, 1977.

Diamond, S., Balvin, R., & Diamond, F. *Inhibition and choice.* New York: Harper & Row, 1963.

Dombrose, L., & Slobin, M. The I.E.S. test. *Perceptual and Motor Skills,* 1958, *8,* 437–399. (Monograph Supplement 3)

Donchin, E. Event related brain potentials: A tool in the study of human information processing. In H. Begleiter(Ed.), *Evoked brain potentials and behavior.* New York: Plenum Press, 1979.

Douglas, V. Stop, look, and listen: The problem of sustained attention and impulse control in hyperactive and normal children. *Canadian Journal of Behavioral Science,* 1972, *4,* 259–282.

Duffy, E. Activation. In N. Greenfield & R. Sternbach (Eds.), *Handbook of psychophysiology.* New York: Holt, Rinehart, & Winston, 1972.

DuPreez, P. Judgment of time and aspects of personality. *Journal of Abnormal and Social Psychology,* 1964, *69,* 228–233.

DuPreez, P. Field dependence and accuracy of comparison of time intervals. *Perceptual and Motor Skills,* 1967, *24,* 467–472.

Eleftheriou, B., & Scott, J. *The physiology of aggression and defeat.* New York: Plenum Press, 1971.

Engel, B. Stimulus–response and individual-response specificity. *Archives of General Psychiatry,* 1960, *2,* 305–313.

Engel, B., & Bickford, A. Response-specificity: Stimulus–response and individual-response specificity in essential hypertensives. *Archives of General Psychiatry,* 1961, *5,* 478–489.

Engel, B., & Moos, R. The generality of specificity. *Archives of General Psychiatry,* 1967, *16,* 574–581.

Erickson, R. Society for general systems research at twenty-five: What agenda for our second quarter-century? *Behavioral Science,* 1979, *24,* 225–237.

Eysenck, H. A short questionnaire for the measurement of two dimensions of personality. *Journal of Applied Psychology,* 1958, *42,* 14–17.

Eysenck, H. Personality and the estimation of time. *Perceptual and Motor Skills,* 1959, *9,* 405–406.

Eysenck, H. *The biological basis of personality.* Springfield, Ill.: Thomas, 1967.

Eysenck, H. Personality and factor analysis: A reply to Guilford. *Psychological Bulletin,* 1977, *84,* 405–411.

Eysenck, H. Superfactors, P, E, and N in a comprehensive factor space. *Multivariate Behavioral Research,* 1978, *13,* 475–481.

Eysenck, H., & Eysenck, S. *Personality structure and measurement.* San Diego, Cal.: Knopp, 1969.

Eysenck, H., & Eysenck, S. *Psychoticism as a dimension of personality.* London: Hodder & Stoughton, 1976.

Eysenck, S., & Eysenck, H. The place of impulsiveness in a dimensional system of personality description. *British Journal of Social and Clinical Psychology*, 1977, *16*, 57–68.

Eysenck, S., & Eysenck H. Impulsiveness and venturesomeness: Their position in a dimensional system of personality description. *Psychological Reports*, 1978, *43*, 1247–1255.

Fiske, D. *Measuring the concepts of personality*. Chicago: Aldine, 1971.

Gange, J., Geen, R., & Harkins, S. Autonomic differences between extraverts and introverts during vigilance. *Psychophysiology*, 1979, *16*, 392–397.

Gough, H. *California Psychological Inventory* (Manual). Palo Alto, Cal.: Consulting Psychologists Press, 1956.

Gray, J. *The psychology of fear and stress*. London: Weidenfeld & Nicholson, 1971.

Gray, J. The structure of emotions and the limbic system. In *Ciba Foundation Symposium, 8* (New Series). New York: Elsevier, 1972, *87*–130.

Guertin, W., & Rabin, A. Misperception of time in schizophrenia. *Psychological Reports*, 1960, *7*, 57–58.

Guilford, J. Factors and factors of personality. *Psychological Bulletin*, 1975, *82*, 802–814.

Guilford, J. Will the real factor of extraversion–introversion please stand up? A reply to Eysenck. *Psychological Bulletin*, 1977, *84*, 412–416.

Guilford, J., & Zimmerman, W. *The Guilford–Zimmerman Temperament Survey* (Manual). Beverly Hills, Cal.: Sheridan Supply Co., 1949.

Hare, R. D., & Cox, D. N. Clinical and empirical conceptions of psychopathy and the selection of subjects to research. In R. D. Hare, & D. N. Schalling (Eds.), *Psychopathic behavior: Approaches to research*. Chichester: Wiley, 1978.

Heist, P., & Yonge, G. *Omnibus Personality Inventory* (Manual). New York: Psychological Corporation, 1962.

Hirschfield, P. Response set in impulsive children. *Journal of Genetic Psychology*, 1965, *107*, 117–126.

Holtzman, W. Validation studies of the Rorschach Test: Impulsiveness in the normal superior adult. *Journal of Clinical Psychology*, 1950, *6*, 348–351.

Holtzman, W. *Holtzman Inkblot Technique guide*. New York: Psychological Corporation, 1961.

Holtzman, W., Thorp, J., Swartz, J., & Herron, E. *Inkblot perception and personality: Holtzman Inkblot Technique*. Austin: University of Texas Press, 1961.

Iverson, L., Iverson, S., & Snyder, S. (Editors) *Handbook of psychopharmacology, Vol. 9: Chemical pathways in the brain*. New York: Plenum Press, 1978.

Jackson, D. *Personality research form manual*. Goshen, N.Y.: Research Psychologists' Press, 1967.

Jouvet, M. Biogenic amines and the states of sleep. *Science*, 1969, *163*, 32–44.

Kagan, J. Reflection–impulsivity: The generality and dynamics of conceptual tempo. *Journal of Abnormal Psychology*, 1966, *1*, 17–24.

Kinsbourne, M. Mapping a behavioral cerebral space. *The International Neuropsychological Society Bulletin*, 1979, September, 6–9.

Kipnis, D. *Character structure and impulsiveness*. New York: Academic Press, 1971.

Kolb, L. Violence and aggression: An overview. In J. Fawcett (Ed.), *Dynamics of violence*. Chicago: American Medical Association, 1972.

Lacy, J. Psychophysiological approaches to the evaluation of psychotherapeutic processes and outcome. In E. Rubenstein, & M. Parloff (Eds.), *Research in psychotherapy* (Vol. 1). Washington, D.C.: National Publishing Co., 1959.

Lacy, J., Bateman, D., & VanLehn, R. Autonomic response specificity: An experimental study. *Psychosomatic Medicine*, 1953, *15*, 8–21.

Lezak, M. *Neuropsychological Assessment*. New York: Oxford University Press, 1976.

Lhamon, W., & Goldstone, S. The time sense: Estimation of one second duratioby schizophrenic patients. *Archives of Neurology and Psychiatry,* 1956, *76,* 625–629.

Luce, G. Biological rhythms. In R. Ornstein (Ed.), *The nature of human consciousness.* New York: Viking Press, 1973.

Lynn, R. Introversion–extroversion (MPI) differences in judgments of time. *Journal of Abnormal Psychology,* 1961, *63,* 457–458.

Maletzky, B. Episodic dyscontrol: A controlled replication. *Diseases of the Nervous System,* 1974, *35,* 175–179.

Marczynski, T. Serotonin and the central nervous system. In C. Hockman & D. Bieger (Eds.), *Chemical transmission in the mammalian central nervous system.* Baltimore: University Park Press, 1976.

McClelland, J. On the time relations of mental processes: An examination of systems of processes in cascade. *Psychological Review,* 1979, *86,* 287–330.

Megargee, E. Undercontrolled and overcontrolled personality types in extreme antisocial aggression. In E. Megaree & J. Hockanson (Eds.), *The dynamics of aggression.* New York: Harper & Row, 1970.

Messer, S. Reflection–impulsivity: A review. *Psychological Bulletin,* 1976, *83,* 1026–1052.

Metzler, J. *Systems neuroscience.* New York: Academic Press, 1977.

Mezey, A., & Cohen, S. The effect of depressive illness on time judgment and time experience. *Journal of Neurology, Neurosurgery, and Psychiatry,* 1961, *24,* 269–270.

Miller, G., Galanter, E., & Pribram, K. *Plans and the structure of behavior.* New York: Henry Holt, 1960.

Milner, P. Theories of reinforcement, drive, and motivation. In L. Iverson, S., Iverson, & S. Snyder (Eds.), *Handbook of psychopharmacology, Vol. 7: Principles of behavioral pharmacology.* New York: Plenum Press, 1977.

Monroe, R. *Episodic behavioral disorders.* Cambridge, Mass.: Harvard University Press, 1970.

Mowrer, O. *Learning and behavior.* New York: Wiley, 1960.

Murphy, D. L., & Redmond, D. The catecholamines: Possible role in affect, mood, and emotional behavior in man and animals. In A. Friedhoff (Ed.), *Catecholamines and behavior II: Neuropsychopharmacology.* New York: Plenum, 1975.

Murray, H. *Thematic Apperception Test Manual.* Cambridge, Mass.: Harvard University Press, 1943.

Niki, H., & Watanabe, M. Prefrontal and cingulate unit activity during timing behavior in the monkey. *Brain Research,* 1979, *171,* 213–224.

Ollman, R. Simple reactions with random countermanding of the "go" signal. In S. Kornblum (Ed.), *Attention and performance IV.* New York: Academic Press, 1973.

Pavlov, I. P. *Wednesdays,* 1949, *1,* 337. *Pavlov's Clinical Wednesdays:* Minutes and stenographic records of the physiological discussion. Moscow, Leningrad: Akad, Nauk, USSR, 1949.

Plutchik, R. *Research strategies for the study of human violence.* Paper presented at the fifth annual Cerebral Function Symposium, Coronodo, Cal., 1974.

Porteus, S. *Porteus Maze Tests: Fifty years application.* Palo Alto, Calf.: Pacific Books, 1965.

Posner, M. *Chronometric explorations of mind.* Hillsdale, N.J.: Lawrence Erlbaum Associates, 1978.

Powell, E. Limbic projections to the thalamus. *Experimental Brain Research,* 1973, *73,* 394–401.

Pribram, K., & McGuinness, D. Arousal, activation, and effort in the control of attention. *Psychological Review,* 1975, *82,* 16–149.

Purcell, K. The Thematic Apperception Test and antisocial behavior. In B. Murstein (Ed.), *Handbook of projective techniques.* New York: Basic Books, 1965.

Randrup, A., Munkvad, I., Fog, R., & Ayhan, I. Catecholamines in activation, stereotypy, and level of mood. In A. Friedhoff (Ed.), *Catecholamines and behavior, Vol. 1: Basic neurobiology.* New York: Plenum Press, 1975.

Rorschach, H. *Psychodiagnostics.* New York: Grune & Stratton, 1942.

Ross, D., & Ross, S. *Hyperactivity: Research, theory, action.* New York: Wiley, 1976.

Saunders, J., Repucci, N., & Sarata, B. An examination of impulsivity as a trait characterizing delinquent youth. *American Journal of Orthopsychiatry,* 1973, *43,* 789-795.

Sells, S., Demaree, R., & Will, D. Dimensions of personality: II separate factor structures in Guilford and Cattell trait markers. *Multivariate Behavioral Research,* 1971, *6,* 136-165.

Shaffer, D., McNamara, N., & Pincus, J. Controlled observations on patterns of activity, attention, and impulsivity in brain damaged and psychiatrically disturbed boys. In S. Chess & A. Thomas (Eds.), *Annual progress in child psychiatry and child development.* New York: Brunner Mazel, 1975.

Smith, K. Physiological and sensory feedback of the motor system: Neural metabolic integration for energy regulation in behavior. In J. Maser (Ed.), *Efferent organization and the integration of behavior.* New York: Academic Press, 1973.

Solomon, R. An opponent process theory of motivation: The affective dynamics of drug addiction. In J. Maser & M. Seligman (Eds.), *Psychopathology: Experimental models.* San Francisco: Freeman, 1977.

Spielberger, C., Gorsuch, R., & Lushene, R. *Manual for the State-Trait Anxiety Inventory.* Palo Alto, Cal.: Consulting Psychologists Press, 1970.

Stevens, J. Schizophrenia and dopamine regulation in the limbic system. *Trends in Neurosciences,* 1979, *2,* 102-105.

Straus, E. Disorders of personal time in depressive states. *Southern Medical Journal,* 1947, *40,* 254-258.

Sutherland, J. *A general systems philosophy for the social and behavioral sciences.* New York: George Braziller, 1973.

Szentagothai, J., & Arbib, M. *Conceptual models of neural organization.* Cambridge, Mass.: MIT Press, 1975.

Taylor, J. A personality scale of manifest anxiety. *Journal of Abnormal and Social Psychology,* 1953, *48,* 285-290.

Thurstone, L. The dimensions of temperament. *Psychometrica,* 1951, *16,* 11-20.

Thurstone, L. *Examiner's manual for the Thurstone Temperament Schedule.* Chicago: Science Research Associates, 1953.

Wangeman, J. *Coping with stress: Impulsivity trait-state reactions under stressful and nonstressful conditions.* Unpublished master's thesis, University of Melbourne, Melbourne, Australia, 1976.

Weiss, P. *The science of life.* Mt. Krisco, N.Y.: Futura Publishing Co., 1973.

White, J., Barratt, E., & Adams, P. The hyperactive child in adolescence. *Journal of the American Academy of Child Psychiatry,* 1978, *18,* 154-169.

Wyatt, R., Potkin, S., & Murphy, D. Platelet monoamine oxidase activity in schizophrenia: A review of the data. *American Journal of General Psychiatry,* 1979, *136,* 377-385.

Wyrick, L. A., & Wyrick, L. A. Time experiences during depression. *Archives of General Psychiatry,* 1977, *34,* 1441-1443.

Zelkind, I., & Sprug, J. *Time research: 1172 studies.* Metuchen, N.J.: Scarecrow Press, 1974.

Zuckerman, M. The sensation seeking motive. In B. Maher (Ed.), *Progress in experimental personality research* (Vol. 7). New York: Academic Press, 1974.

Zuckerman, M., Murtaugh, T., & Siegel, J. Sensation seeking and cortical augmenting-reducing. *Psychophysiology,* 1974, *11,* 535-542.

Barratt has been committed to a behavioral–biological approach to the trait of impulsivity for 2 decades. His work is characterized by careful analysis of the behavioral aspects of impulsivity, laboratory definition of these aspects, and further definition of the brain mechanisms in psychophysiological studies. As one can see in the latter part of the chapter, he is beginning to theorize about the wiring in the "black-box" (actually four "boxes" in Fig. 3.1), which mediates the behavioral and psychophysiological responses. But he stops short of forming specific hypotheses about what differentiates an impulsive from a nonimpulsive personality.

In the first part of the chapter, Barratt and Patton attempt to define the trait of impulsivity, as measured by the BIS scale, in terms of the factors of impulsivity, sociability, and anxiety. Although the broad measure of impulsivity is clearly orthogonal to the dimension of anxiety, it is related to sociability in the females but not in the males. Eysenck and Eysenck (1977) found correlations of .34 for women and .20 for men between their total impulsivity and sociability scores. The correlations are both significant for the large samples used, and they support the Eysencks' idea that impulsivity and sociability are both components of the broader trait of extraversion. But the magnitude of the relationship between impulsivity and sociability falls short of a clear refutation of Guilford's (1975) claim that these are distinct first order factors.

Barratt and Patton include sensation seeking and extraversion together with impulsivity in a class of action-oriented personality predispositions. They report a correlation of .47 between the SSS and DIS scale, and one of

.68 between BIS and extraversion. Sensation seeking and impulsivity, as measured by BIS, do have in common their orthogonality to the anxiety-neuroticism dimension, their correlation with extraversion (although the SSS correlates much lower with E), and most significantly their correlation with augmenting of the cortical evoked potential. But Barratt has focused on his total score and does not report on correlations of other measures with his subscales. Table 3.3 shows the correlations between Eysenck's impulsivity subscales and the SSS subscales taken from Table 1.6 in Eysenck's chapter. These data show that the SS scales are related to some aspects of broad impulsivity but not to others. Specifically, sensation seeking is related more to the risk-taking and nonplanning aspects and less to the narrow (N) impulsivity and liveliness aspects. Both impulsivity N and liveliness scales contain items suggesting a tempo or speed of reaction factor, but the items in the impulsivity N scale suggest a lack of control over impulses (*Do you often get into a jam because you do things without thinking?*), whereas those in the liveliness scale suggest fast speed of cognitive processes without the problem in impulse control (*Do you usually make up your mind quickly?*). The impulsivity N scale correlates positively, but the liveliness scale correlates negatively with neuroticism.

TABLE 3.3
Correlations[a] between Eysenck's Impulsivity Subscales
and Sensation Seeking Subscales (from Table 1.3)

	Dis		TAS		ES		BS	
	F[b]	M[c]	F	M	F	M	F	M
Imp N	31*	17	19*	-02	15	05	27*	17
Risk	38*	37*	46*	42*	21*	27*	31*	33*
Non P	23*	20	23*	16	31*	35*	30*	29*
Liveliness	17*	11	19*	08	14	02	12	12

[a] Decimals omitted
[b] Females (F) n - 621
[c] Males (M) n = 215
*p < .0001

Barratt and Patton have focused their behavioral research on the tempo aspects of the impulsivity construct including such subjects as time judgment, reaction time, and speed of rhythmic movements with more positive results with the latter two dimensions. I would not expect sensation seeking to correlate with these kinds of response style traits. Sensation seeking does correlate with perceptual and cognitive styles, with the preference for complexity and ambiguity, as well as with risk-taking proclivities (Zuckerman, 1979a). It is possible to favor arousing stimuli and situations and to enter into risky situations without being impulsive in the precipitous sense. Some sensation seekers lack impulse control and, in the words of Oscar Wilde, "can resist everything but temptation," but others choose their activities after due consideration of risks and benefits. They tend to underestimate the risks relative to low sensation seekers and tend to value the hedonic sensory reinforcements more than the lows. This distinction between sensory-cognitive mechanisms, related to sensation seeking, and response mechanisms, related to impulsivity, may have some relevance to the underlying biological mechanisms. The first suggests different information processing and reward mechanisms; the second a failure of inhibition mechanisms.

Of the four sensation-seeking subscales, Disinhibition is most like Barratt's conception of impulsivity. The Dis scale is also the one most related to augmenting of the evoked potential, a common biological correlate of the BIS and SSS. The Dis scale is the one most related to psychopathy (Zuckerman, 1978), a diagnostic construct more like Eysenck's narrow impulsivity and Barratt's behavioral dimension.

One of the most interesting psychophysiological results reported by Barratt and Patton is the finding that whereas low impulsives produce CNVs to both geometric figures and *Playboy* nudes, high impulsives show a cortical response only to the erotic stimuli. My original theory of sensation seeking suggested that certain stimuli are preferred by high sensation seekers because of their greater arousal potential and the higher optimal level of arousal of the sensation seeker. Barratt and Patton's data support this idea as a basis for impulsivity. But work with the orienting reflex (OR) (Neary & Zuckerman, 1976) shows that the OR of high sensation seekers is *greater* than that of lows in response to simple geometric stimuli as long as they are novel (first presentation of the stimulus). In other words, it is not a failure of physiological reactivity that distinguishes high from low sensation seekers, nor is it a difference in basal or tonic levels of cortical arousal.

Barratt and Patton suggest that high impulsive subjects are underaroused, but the basis for this assertion is questionable. Percentage of time in alpha is not necessarily an index of *low* arousal except in relation to beta activity. Ordinarily, alpha represents an intermediate, optimal level of arousal. The fact that the impulsives are augmenters does not mean that their tonic level of arousal is low. The fact that high impulsives only produce CNV when aroused by interesting stimuli suggests that they are selectively arousable, not that they are underaroused in general. Barratt and Patton do not make an adequate distinction between arousal and arousability, a common failing in this field.

But Barratt and Patton's model does not depend exclusively on the construct of arousal (or arousability). Even when arousal is held constant, their data suggest that impulsivity depends on a "conceptual tempo" factor related to limbic, anterior-thalamic, cingulum, and orbital-frontal cortex processing of information. The limbic structures involved are those relating to memory with the hippocampus as the primary subcortical nucleus involved in the information processing. This system closely resembles the one described by Gray (1972, 1982, & Chapter 6, this volume). Gray hypothesizes that activity in this system underlies differences in the trait of anxiety, expressed in "sensitivity" to signals of punishment and nonreward (frustration) and inhibition of punished and nonrewarded behavior. Extrapolating from this formulation we would conclude that impulsivity is related to a weakness in this "Behavioral Inhibition System" (Gray's term). This would make impulsivity the converse of anxiety, returning to an older view that psychopathy (of the primary kind) is simply the opposite of anxiety and that impulsive psychopaths suffer from a weakness in the mechanisms that mediate anticipatory anxiety. It should be noted, however, that Gray has conceptualized anxiety and impulsivity as two independent or orthogonal personality dimensions. But in his most recent formulation, Gray (1982) suggests that there may be two kinds of impulsivity: one associated with high neuroticism (N) and the other with low N, primary psychopathy, stable extraversion, and sensation seeking. Presumably, Barratt's type of impulsivity would be of the latter (low N) type. But this model runs aground on the observed orthogonality of Barratt's measure of impulsivity and my measure of sensation seeking to the test-measured trait of anxiety. According to Gray's idea, there should be a negative correlation between these traits and anxiety. The difficulties here are probably related to our common failure to understand the interactions between the reward and punishment systems in the brain and the phenomenal expressions in personality traits of impulsivity and sensation seeking.

The failure of an optimal level of arousal hypothesis in the Carrol, Zuckerman, & Vogel, 1982), experiment as well as the findings of a relationship between MAO and sensation feeling, led to a new hypothesis concerning the biological basis of sensation seeking. This hypothesis involves neurotransmission within the limbic system. Barratt and Patton also seem to be turning to psychopharmacology as an explanation for personality differences. They suggest that dopamine neurons represent the excitation phase of motor activity, whereas serotonin (5-HT) neurons exert an inhibitory influence on the arousal process. Norepinephrine neurons are thought to be involved in the appraisal and reinforcement process. The theory is quite similar to the one presented by Stein (Chapter 5). It has been suggested that dopamine and norepinephrine are the neurotransmitters involved in sensation-seeking behavior (Zuckerman, 1979b). Inasmuch as Barratt and Patton's model of impulsivity stresses the lack of motor inhibition, the balance between dopamine and serotonin would seem to furnish a possible basis for impulsivity as a personality trait. But, at this point, Barratt and Patton stop short of making specific hypotheses relating structure and physiology to behavior. Instead they quote Kinsbourne on the dangers of reductionism.

The spectre of reductionism is usually conjured up as a justification of the lack of interest in adjacent fields. Clearly, this does not apply to Barratt who has been most active at the border of biology and behavior. No science has ever been reduced to another, but the most interesting and fruitful developments usually happen at the border areas. Where would the field of neurophysiology be without neurochemistry, and where would neurochemistry be without molecular biology? Where will psychology be without neurophysiology? It is a sign of maturity in a science when it looks to the more molecular science for insights into its more complex phenomena. The phenomena always have emergent properties that are best studied at more molar levels. But fundamental understanding at the theoretical level must be parsimonious, which means we must try simpler explanations before we move up to more complex and hypothetical ones.

Incidentally, anyone who feels that the field of psychopharmacology is simple, relative to psychology, has not read the literature in this area. The same stories of unreplicable results, individual variation, effects of irrelevant variables, the state versus trait problem, and errors of measurement plague the biologist as well as the psychologist.

But this does not mean that we should confine ourselves to strictly behavioral models as suggested in the quote. When my clinical students head off into the real world to deal with real patients I urge them that if they cannot do research they should at least read the literature. I would give the same advice to nonclinical behavioral researchers regarding developments in neurophysiology relevant to their fields. At least read the literature and consider the implications for your explanations of behavior.

REFERENCES

Carrol, E. N., Zuckerman, M., & Vogel, W. H. A test of the optimal level of arousal theory of sensation seeking. *Journal of Personality and Social Psychology,* 1982, *42,* 572-575.

Eysenck, S. B. G., & Eysenck, H. J. The place of impulsiveness in a dimensional system of personality description. *British Journal of Social and Clinical Psychology,* 1977, *16,* 57-68.

Gray, J. A. The psychophysiological nature of introversion–extraversion: A modification of Eysenck's theory. In V. D. Nebylitsyn & J. A. Gray (Eds.), *Biological bases of individual behavior.* New York: Academic Press, 1972.

Gray, J. A. *The neuropsychology of anxiety: An inquiry into the functions of the septo-hypocampal system.* New York: Oxford University Press, 1982.

Guilford, J. P. Factors and factors of personality. *Psychological Bulletin,* 1975, *82,* 802-814.

Neary, R. S., & Zuckerman, M. Sensation seeking, trait and state anxiety, and the electrodermal orienting reflex. *Psychophysiology,* 1976, *13,* 205-211.

Zuckerman, M. Sensation seeking and psychopathy. In R. D. Hare & D. Schalling (Eds.), *Psychopathic behavior: Approaches to research.* New York: Wiley, 1978.

Zuckerman, M. Sensation seeking and risk taking. In C. E. Izard (Ed.), *Emotions in personality and psychopathology.* New York: Plenum Press, 1979.(a)

Zuckerman, M. *Sensation seeking: Beyond the optimal level of arousal.* Hillsdale, N.J.: Lawrence Erlbaum Associates, 1979.(b)

4 Impulsive Cognitive Style and Inability to Tolerate Boredom: Psychobiological Studies of Temperamental Vulnerability

Daisy Schalling
Gunnar Edman
Marie Åsberg
Department of Psychiatry,
Karolinska Hospital
and Department of Psychology,
University of Stockholm, Sweden

INTRODUCTION

The explosive development of neurobiology in recent years has brought about a fresh interest in biological aspects of personality and methodology for studying biological bases of temperament (Prentky, 1979). This chapter reviews our research on two related personality factors—impulsivity and inability to tolerate boredom (monotony avoidance)—as measured by personality inventory scales. It deals with these factors' relations to other personality dimensions and their neuropsychological and biochemical correlates. Some speculations about possible underlying psychobiological processes are ventured. Inasmuch as the personality trait model has been under attack in the last decades, especially by social learning theorists who have been influential in the United States, we have chosen to include a short presentation of a clinically oriented trait research tradition, which has been "alive and well" (Epstein, 1977) all the time, especially in Europe. However, trait measures are now increasingly included in experimental and clinical studies in the United States, as well as in Europe. Interactionist research has contributed to the elucidation of the merits and limits of the trait approach, emphasizing the distinction between the trait model and the trait measurement model (Magnusson, 1980). The trait researchers have

123

become more aware of the necesssity of taking into consideration situational parameters (Schalling, 1977).

In psychiatry there is a very old tradition of regarding at least some aspects of personality as determined by relatively stable dispositions or personality dimensions, interpreted as mediating factors between various kinds of biological vulnerability and psychopathology (Haier, Buchsbaum, Murphy, Gottesman, & Coursey, 1980; Meehl, 1962; Millon & Millon, 1974; Zubin & Spring, 1977). The basic idea of Hippocrates, that body fluids are important for mood and behavior, has received support from present-day neurochemistry. Advances in biochemical measurement techniques have made possible the exploration of monoaminergic transmitter mechanisms in the central nervous system. The turnover of the cerebral transmitter amines serotonin, dopamine, and noradrenaline have been intensively researched by analysis of their metabolites in the cerebrospinal fluid (CSF) in various psychiatric illnesses. A study on healthy volunteers by Sedvall, Fyrö, Gullberg, Nybäck, Wiesel, and Wode-Helgodt (1980) showed that those who had a family disposition for schizophrenia tended to have high values of the serotonin metabolite (5-HIAA) and the dopamine metabolite (HVA), whereas those with a family disposition for psychotic depression tended to have low values. This study thus provides some support for the concept of biological vulnerability for certain types of psychiatric illness related to the turnover of neurochemical substances. There is much evidence that these monoamines are functioning as neuromodulators in the central nervous system and are involved in the control of basic neuropsychological pressures like attenuation of sensory input, attention, and sensitivity to pain (Ungerstedt, 1979). These neuropsychological processes are also postulated to underly individual differences in the broad temperamental factors to be described later. Thus, the biochemical monoamine research is of great potential importance for personality models.

The four temperament types proposed by Hipprocrates have been taken up by many psychologists. For example, Wundt pointed out that the four categories could be looked upon as joint effects of two independent continuous dimensions: "strength and emotions" and "speed of change" (Fig. 4.1). This fruitful idea has been made the basis of the personality system by Eysenck (1967, 1980), with "strength" being identified with the superfactor of neuroticism (instability, emotionality) and changeability with extraversion. A third factor, psychoticism, has been added to the system, covering suspiciousness, hostility, cruelty, and odd behavior. These variables measured by inventory scales are viewed as orthogonal second order factors. A series of studies has supported the assumptions of an important genetic influence in which from one half to two thirds of the variance is accounted for by genetic factors (Fulker, 1980).

Extreme positions in the Eysenckian superfactors are assumed to make

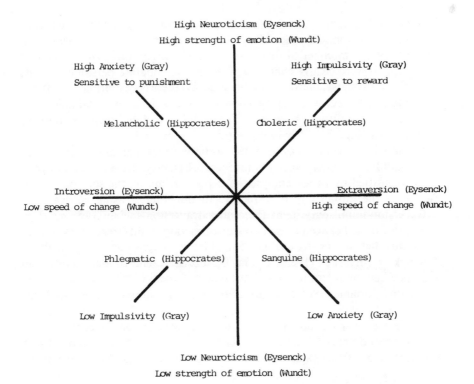

High Neuroticism (Eysenck)
High strength of emotion (Wundt)

High Anxiety (Gray)
Sensitive to punishment

High Impulsivity (Gray)
Sensitive to reward

Melancholic (Hippocrates)

Choleric (Hippocrates)

Introversion (Eysenck)
Low speed of change (Wundt)

Extraversion (Eysenck)
High speed of change (Wundt)

Phlegmatic (Hippocrates)

Sanguine (Hippocrates)

Low Impulsivity (Gray)

Low Anxiety (Gray)

Low Neuroticism (Eysenck)
Low strength of emotion (Wundt)

FIG. 4.1   Impulsive cognitive style and the inability to tolerate boredom.

the individual more vulnerable to certain psychiatric illnesses: for high N, neurotic disturbances (if combined with high E, a disturbance of the hysteric type; if combined with low E, a "dysthymic" neurosis, that is, depressive, obsessive, and anxiety states) and for high P, psychotic illness. Similar ideas have been proposed by many earlier psychiatric writers, for example, Bleuler and Kretschmer (for a review, see Eysenck & Eysenck, 1969) who also believed that extreme positions on certain personality traits are 'patoplastic'' (i.e., contribute to the form of psychopathology, if such occurs).

IMPULSIVITY AND THE DUAL NATURE
OF EXTRAVERSION

In the model preferred by Eysenck, extraversion is defined as a broad super-factor ("type"). There is much evidence that extraversion is not a homogeneous dimension. As defined by Eysenck, extraversion covers two tendencies, which on a common-sense basis are not closely related, namely a preference for company (sociability) and a tendency to act impulsively, "on the spur of the moment" (impulsivity). Interestingly, these two aspects of extraversion were clearly conceptualized as two separate personality traits by the Swedish psychiatrist and personality theorist Sjöbring (1973). In Sjöbring's terminology, extraversion-sociability is called *stability,* and extraversion-impulsivity is called *solidity.* High sociability corresponds to low stability; high impulsivity corresponds to low solidity.

In the extraversion scales included in the Eysenck Personality Inventory (EPI) and Eysenck Personality Questionnaire (EPQ), there are a number of items identified by factor analyses as either loading on the sociability trait factor or the impulsivity trait factor. In our studies using subscales of extraversion-impulsivity items (E_i) and extraversion-sociability items (E_s), the correlations between these two subscales vary in different types of subjects, but they are mostly around .50, which is in agreement with results of Eysenck and Eysenck (1963). E_i and E_s subscales tend to load in different factors when the factor analyses have included the Sjöbring impulsivity and sociability variables (Solidity and Stability). An example is given in Table 4.1.

There are several problems with a unitary extraversion concept (i.e., using the second order factor scores). The first refers to the correlations with the other main Eysenckian factors. E_i tends to have high positive correla-

TABLE 4.1
Rotated Factor Loadings of Personality Inventory Scales
in a Group of Students (n = 133)

| Variable | Factor | | | | h^2 |
	I	II	III	IV	
N (EPI)	-.11	-.90	-.05	.15	.85
V (MNT)	-.44	.78	.11	.03	.83
E_i (EPI)	-.83	.19	-.06	-.27	.79
Sol (MNT)	.70	.06	.38	.28	.71
E_s (EPI)	-.13	.30	-.19	-.79	.77
Stab (MNT)	.35	.11	-.06	.79	.77
Lie (EPI)	.22	.25	.75	.00	.67
SD (MCSD)	.03	-.09	.89	.08	.80
Proportion of total variance	.33	.23	.12	.09	.77

From Schalling (1975). The variables are:
From the Eysenck Personality Inventory (EPI): Neuroticism (N), Extraversion-Impulsivity (E_i), Extraversion-Sociability (E_s) and Lie. From the Marke-Nyman Temperament schedule (MNT): Validity (V), Solidity (Sol) and Stability (Stab).
In addition, a short version of Marlow-Crowne Social Desirability scale was included (SD).

tions with N, whereas E_s tends to have negative correlations with N. When the P factor items were included in the Eysenck studies, it became evident that some E_i items tended to load highly in the P factor as well (Eysenck & Eysenck, 1977). This was the reason for a change in the content of the extraversion scale from EPI to EPQ. The EPQ E scale appears to have fewer pure E_i items, some of which are found in the P scale instead. In this way the relative independence of the dimensions was preserved.

A second problem is that the Eysenckian assumption of a tendency to lower cortical arousal in extraverts seems to be more readily found in high impulsive than in high sociable subjects. For example, the predictions of lower conditionability as well as greater attenuation of input (e.g., pain stimuli) are borne out more often for impulsivity than for sociability (see Schalling, 1976, 1977). In a study by Eysenck and Levey (1972), conditionability was significantly related to the impulsivity subscale but not to sociability. Further, the solidity and E_i scales have been significantly associated with pain tolerance, with more impulsive subjects having higher pain thresholds and pain tolerance levels (Schalling, 1971; Schalling, Rissler, & Edman, 1970). Further, cigarette smoking has been consistently associated with high impulsivity (Schalling, 1977). In all cases, sociability scales failed to show these relations.

Finally, impulsivity and sociability measures are sometimes clearly dissociated. For example, delinquents were significantly more impulsive as compared to matched controls, but significantly less sociable in a study by Schalling and Holmberg (1970). Summing up, when research is focused on the biological basis of temperament, it appears more fruitful to concentrate on measures of impulsivity.

IMPULSIVITY AND ANXIETY

As already noted, impulsivity tends to correlate positively with N. However, in studies on psychiatric patients, we found that impulsivity was related especially to some components of anxiety proneness such as panic feelings in acute situations, vegetative symptoms ("somatic anxiety"), and self-reported muscular tension. Much lower relations, which in many studies were in the opposite direction, have been obtained with another type of anxiety disposition, including insecurity, worrying, anticipating stressful events, and difficulty in relaxing after such events (cognitive-social anxiety, "psychic anxiety"). On the basis of studies both on psychiatric patients and normal subjects (reviewed by Schalling, 1978; Schalling, Cronholm, & Åsberg, 1975), we have concluded that inventory measures of different aspects of impulsivity and anxiety proneness can explain a large amoung of interindividual differences in psychobiological research. These two dimensions have also been focused upon in the long-term research project by Barratt and his collaborators (Barratt, 1972).

Our choice of anxiety proneness and impulsivity as main dimensions is in agreement with the model presented by Gray (1970, 1973). On the basis of animal experimentation, using drugs which selectively influence systems underlying passive and active avoidance behavior and sensitivity to reward and punishment, he tried to establish cross-species generalizations. His analyses led him to regard N as a dimension of increasing sensitivity to signals of both reward and punishment, and E as a dimension of increasing sensitivity to reward and decreasing sensitivity to signals of punishments. Later, Gray (1973) stated that the "major links of causal influence" are probably not along the E and N axes but rather along the diagonals (Fig. 4.1), that is, anxiety and impulsivity (Gray, 1973). His experiments indicate that high anxiety depends on activity in the orbito-frontal septo-hippocampal "stop-system," and high impulsivity depends on high activity in the "approach system" (medial forebrain and lateral hypothalamus). Impulsive individuals are thus assumed to have a more reactive "go system" and to be more sensitive to promise of reward but less sensitive to threat of punishment than less impulsive individuals (Fig. 4.1).

Personality and Biological Vulnerability

Theoretical efforts to build bridges between animal brain research, biochemical and neuropsychological processes in humans, and human behavioral dispositions may serve to identify those personality variables that have a biological basis. Such variables should have some stability over time and manifest themselves in different situational contexts. If they are also associated with psychopathology, they may be indicators of temperamental vulnerability that are more easily available than the biochemical variables. There is evidence for the importance of impulsivity in psychopathy (Arieti, 1963; Cleckley, 1976; Hare, 1980; Schalling, 1978) and in at least some types of hyperactivity syndromes (Cantwell, 1975; Loney, 1981). Sensation-seeking scores have been associated with manic-depressive illness (Zuckerman & Neeb, 1979). Further, impulsivity is one of the most prominent symptoms in frontal lobe lesions (Luria, 1966).

THE CONSTRUCT OF IMPULSIVITY

In view of our consistent psychophysiological and neuropsychological findings with the Solidity scale and the E_i subscale, we decided to construct a new scale for impulsivity (partly because the item content of the Solidity scale constructed in the 1950s had become old-fashioned). As a preparation for the scale-construction work, we first made a survey of clinical and psychometric studies and analyzed the various clinical and common-sense meanings of impulsivity. The earlier clinical experience of one of the authors (DS) when working with patients with frontal lobe lesions influenced the construction of the variable. The lack of foresight, the inability to stick to plans and intentions, and the carefree, haphazard way of living characterizing many of these patients gave good illustrations of everyday life manifestations of impulsive style. One clinical description of impulsivity that comes close to our conception is that of the psychoanalyst Shapiro (1965), who defines impulsive style as a tendency to act on the spur of the moment, without planning and without a clear sense of decision or wish, as if "the regular executive apparatuses or generally operative modes of functioning are bypassed or broken through [p. 135]."

We made a series of item analyses of Solidity and other impulsivity scales (e.g., Guilford's Rhathymia and Reflectiveness scales) and an early version of the Barratt scale and classified the contents (for details, see Wredenmark, 1973). The analyses resulted in the following three clusters of content: (1) acting on the spur of the moment, "impulsively," without previous planning or experience of intention; (2) rapid decision making, without consideration of alternative action, preference for speed rather than carefulness; (3) carefreeness, "rhathymia," taking each day as it comes. Among the Solidity scale items corresponding to these content clusters are: Do you more often make up your mind quickly rather than working out a decision slowly and carefully? Would you describe yourself as a rather happy-go-lucky person who is not always careful and methodical? Do you often sleep on a problem before making a decision? (false) Do you follow the inspiration of the moment and start things which you will later find difficult to manage?

The work resulted in the construction of a new Impulsiveness scale with 20 items. In further developments, 10 items were selected to form a short scale with a 4-point scoring system (Table 4.2).

INABILITY TO TOLERATE BOREDOM: A SEPARATE CONCEPT?

In our analyses of the Solidity scale we discovered that it also includes another type of item concerned with thrill seeking and difficulty in tolerating boredom such as: When you get bored, do you like to do something exciting? Do you prefer change and excitement to security and peace? Do you lightheartedly make provocative statements because you like to shock people? This item content is similar to that of the Sensation Seeking Scales (SSS) of Zuckerman (1971, 1979). We had earlier translated the

TABLE 4.2
KSP Impulsiveness and Monotony Avoidance Items

Impulsiveness items

I have a tendency to act on the spur of the moment without really thinking ahead.
When I have to make a decision, I "sleep on it" before I decide. (F).
I usually get so excited over new ideas and suggestions that I forget to check if there
  are any disadvantages.
I often throw myself too hastily into things.
I am a very particular person. (F)
I think it is quite right to describe me as a person who takes things as they come.
I usually "talk before I think".
When I'm about to make a decision I usually make it quickly.
I take life easy.
I consider myself an impulsive person.

Monotony avoidance items

I am always keen on trying out things that are all new.
I like leading a quiet and organized life. (F).
I prefer people who come up with exciting and unexpected activities.
I have an unusually great need for change.
I try to get to places where things really happen.
I almost always have a desire for more action.
In a way I like to do routine jobs. (F).
I like doing things just for the thrill of it.
To be on the move, travelling, change and excitement – that's the kind of life I like.
When listening to the radio, I want it really loud, so that I can feel "turned on".

SSS into Swedish but found them difficult to administer because there seems to be too much emphasis on extravagant activities and dangerous sports like parachuting, which appear far-fetched to our patients. Further, there was in the SSS form translated (IV) a forced-choice format that is difficult to translate correctly, keeping relations between alternatives. A content analysis of the Solidity items resulted in two clusters related to sensation seeking: (1) need for change and novelty, avoiding routine; (2) seeking thrill and strong stimuli, preferring unusual activities and people.

Items from the SSS, Solidity, and other scales covering these contents were collected and subjected to item analyses. We avoided more unusual and deviant contents, which should make the scale less appropriate for use with psychiatric patients and older subjects. The resulting scale was denoted *Monotony avoidance,* thus emphasizing what is avoided or not tolerated, rather than what is wanted or needed. We assumed that a difficulty tolerating boredom may express itself not only in preference for wild parties, sexual debauches, or drug use (referred to in SSS items) but also in hard work and efforts. A relationship between sensation seeking and achievement strivings has been reported (Blankstein, Darte, & Donaldson, 1976). A preliminary scale with 20 items was tested on various groups and was finally developed into a 10-item scale (Table 4.2) corresponding in format to the impulsiveness scale (details are given in Wredenmark, 1973).

IMPULSIVENESS
AND MONOTONY AVOIDANCE SCALES

The influence of age.   We are currently giving these scales (together with other scales in the Karolinska Scales of Personality (KSP) inventory) both to psychiatric patients and normal, healthy subjects from whom we collect various biological data (measures of monoamine metabolites in cerebrospinal fluid, neuroendocrine, and psychophysiological measures) in a long-term joint project at the Department of Psychiatry of the Karolinska Hospital. The influence of age has been tested on a random sample of about 200 men (in collaboration with Bergman & Schalling, 1980). As seen from Table 4.3, there were no marked differences between age groups in Impulsiveness but there was a decreasing trend with advancing age for

TABLE 4.3
Means and Standard Deviations in KSP Impulsiveness and Monotony
Avoidance Scales in a Random Sample of 196 Men,
Stratified According to Age. (Bergman & Schalling, 1980)

	20 − 29 (n = 38)		30 − 39 (n = 38)		40 − 49 (n = 39)		50 − 59 (n = 40)		60 − 65 (n = 39)		20 − 65 (n = 194)	
	M	SD	M	SD	M	SD	M	SD	M	SD	M	SD
Impulsiveness	23.2	3.4	22.6	3.7	22.1	3.9	21.9	3.7	22.6	4.8	22.5	3.9
Monotony avoidance	25.1	3.6	25.4	3.1	22.7	3.4	21.0	3.9	21.5	2.9	23.1	3.8

scores in Monotony avoidance. There was a significant correlation with age ($r = -.44$) for the latter scale. Test-retest correlation obtained under nonoptimal conditions on a group of alcoholic patients during a stay in a clinic and during a control examination 6 months later was .71 for Impulsiveness and .70 for Monotony avoidance.

The influence of genetic factors.   The two scales were included in a study of twins differing in degree of cardiovascular disease. The intrapair correlation for the 14 monozygotic twin pairs was for Impulsivity .74 ($p < .01$) and for Monotony avoidance .57 ($p < .05$). For dizygotic twins, the corresponding values were − .59 and .14 (Theorell, de Faire, Schalling, Adamson, & Askevold, 1979).

Relations with other scales.   Impulsiveness and Monotony avoidance have been included in a series of studies. The scales are positively correlated in all samples, mostly between .30 and .40. Both scales correlate with the EPI and EPQ extraversion scales, more highly with E_i than with E_s. This is true especially for Impulsiveness. Monotony avoidance, on the other hand, sometimes yields equally high or higher positive correlations with sociability scales. Correlations with Neuroticism are low and nonsignificant. In many samples, Monotony avoidance has been significantly positively correlated with P and negatively with lie and social desirability scales. The correlations with anxiety scales have been low in most studies. However, significant negative correlations have sometimes been obtained with the KSP Psychic Anxiety scale for both scales.

In a recent study of 100 male blood donors between 18 and 49 years of age, (mean age 33 years), a number of personality scales were given. They were taken from three inventories: the EPQ (Eysenck & Eysenck, 1975), the KSP (Schalling, Tobisson, Åsberg, Cronholm, & Edman, 1981), and the IVE inventory (Eysenck & Eysenck, 1978). In addition, some scales from the Rosén Socialization Subscales (Rosén & Schalling, 1974) were included. The scales are listed in Table 4.4. A principle component analysis with varimax rotation was performed. The number of factors to be extracted was equal to the number of eigen values exceeding 1.0. The analysis resulted in seven components, which explained 69% of the total variance. The loadings of the scales in the factors are shown in Table 4.5. The main loading for each scale is indicated in Table 4.4. The first two factors are anxiety factors. High loadings in the first, *Psychopathy related instability,* are found in Neuroticism, Somatic Anxiety, and Muscular Tension as well as scales related to deficient socialization. High loadings in factor II, *Cognitive-social anxiety,* are found in Psychic Anxiety, Psychasthenia, and Inhibition of Aggression, and some socialization subscales related to sensitivity to being evaluated. High loadings in factor III, *Nonconformity and indirect aggressiveness,* are found in Lie and Social Desirability as well as some of the aggression scales. Separate factors appear for the two impulsivity scales and the two sensation-seeking scales. These factors are denoted *Impulsivity* (VI) and *Inability to tolerate boredom* (IV). High loadings in a factor of *Social withdrawal* (V) are found in a schizoidia scale, Detachment, and in Empathy and Extraversion-sociability (reversed). Finally, Psychoticism and a hostility scale, guilt, have loadings in a separate factor denoted *Tough-mindedness, hostility* (VII).

MONOTONY AVOIDANCE, SENSATION SEEKING, TESTOSTERONE MEASURES, AND SELF-REPORTED LIFE STYLE

The correlations between Impulsiveness and Monotony avoidance, and Swedish translations of the Zuckerman Sensation Seeking Scales have been

TABLE 4.4
Personality Inventory Scales Included in a Study on 100 Blood Donors,
and Their Main Factor Loading (Schalling & Edman)

	I Psychopathy related instability	II Cognitive social anxiety	III Nonconformity and aggr.	IV Inability to tolerate boredom	V Social withdrawl	VI Impulsivity	VII Tough-mindedness hostility
The Eysenck Personality Questionnaire (EPQ)							
Neuroticism	+						
Extraversion impulsivity		−					
Extraversion sociability					−		
Psychoticism							+
Lie			−				
The Karolinska Scales of Personality (KSP)							
Somatic Anxiety	+						
Muscular Tension	+						
Psychic Anxiety		+					
Psychasthenia	+	+					
Inhibition of Aggression		+					
Impulsiveness						+	
Monotony avoidance				+			
Detachment					+		
Verbal Aggression (Buss, Aggr. modif)			+				
Irritability (Buss, Aggr. modif)			+				
Indirect Aggression (Buss, Aggr. modif)			+				
Suspicion (Buss, Host. modif)	+						
Guilt							−
The Rosen Socialization Subscales (RSS)							
Positive interpersonal experiences	−						
Conformity	−						
Evaluation anxiety		+					
Low self-regard		+					
Super ego strength	−						
Poise vs dysphoric mood	−						
The Impulsiveness-Venturesomeness Empathy Questionnaire (IVE)							
Impulsiveness						+	
Venturesomeness				+			
Empathy					−		

133

TABLE 4.5

Factor Loading in a Principal Components Analysis (Varimax Rotation) of Scores in Personality Inventory Scales in a Group of Blood Donors (n = 100) · (Schalling & Edman)

	Scale	I	II	III	IV	V	VI	VII	Communality
I	Socialization (CPI–KSP)	-.82	.03	-.37	-.10	.01	-.04	-.11	.84
	Neuroticism (EPQ)	.73	.29	.23	-.08	-.02	.11	.12	.69
	Positive interpers. exper. (RSS)	-.73	.05	-.26	-.10	.20	-.04	.04	.65
	Somatic Anxiety (KSP)	.65	.38	.32	-.10	.12	.14	.17	.74
	Poise vs dysphoric mood (RSS)	-.63	-.14	-.17	-.18	-.16	.02	.01	.51
	Super ego strength (RSS)	-.62	.05	-.01	-.04	.04	-.05	.10	.41
	Conformity (RSS)	-.59	-.08	-.12	-.13	-.03	-.12	.02	.41
	Muscular Tension (KSP)	.58	.35	.14	-.09	.15	.17	.13	.55
	Psychasthenia (KSP)	.50	.50	.27	-.18	.05	.17	.34	.73
	Suspicion (Buss-KSP)	.46	-.08	.08	.11	.26	.06	.41	.50
II	Extraversion-impulsivity (EPQ)	-.11	-.64	-.13	.35	-.16	.37	.18	.76
	Psychic Anxiety (KSP)	.46	.64	.15	-.17	.19	.08	.40	.88
	Inhibition of Aggression (KSP)	.15	.63	-.08	-.20	.03	.05	.19	.51
	Evaluation anxiety (RSS)	-.09	.60	.22	.03	.01	-.25	.12	.49
	Psychasthenia (KSP)	.50	.50	.27	-.18	.05	.11	.34	.73
	Low self-regard (RSS)	.00	.41	-.01	.21	.02	.01	.35	.34
III	Social Desirability (M–C–KSP)	-.16	-.08	-.75	.00	-.07	.08	-.09	.61
	Verbal Aggression (Buss–KSP)	.20	-.12	.64	.20	.03	.15	-.05	.53
	Irritability (Buss–KSP)	.43	.25	.62	-.01	.18	-.01	.09	.67
	Indirect Aggression (Buss–KSP)	.32	.25	.61	.00	-.05	.10	.02	.55
	Lie (EPQ)	-.24	-.03	-.50	-.05	.28	-.20	.27	.50
IV	Monotony avoidance (KSP)	.15	-.12	.05	.75	-.13	.24	.10	.69
	Venturesomeness (IVE)	.12	-.10	.10	.71	-.10	.05	-.15	.57
V	Detachment (KSP)	.14	.22	.09	-.05	.65	-.17	.04	.54
	Empathy (IVE)	.24	.41	.10	.16	-.64	-.07	.10	.68
	Extraversion-sociability (EPQ)	-.19	-.42	-.01	.28	-.57	.07	.16	.64
VI	Impulsiveness (KSP)	.10	-.08	.10	.12	-.13	.72	-.07	.58
	Impulsiveness (IVE)	.49	-.07	.13	.26	.01	.65	.10	.76
VII	Psychoticism (EPQ)	-.26	.19	-.10	-.16	-.07	-.20	.55	.49
	Guilt (Buss-KSP)	-.16	-.16	-.04	.00	.07	-.06	-.43	.25
		28	14	7	6	5	4	4	3

studied in a group of 40 students (Table 4.6). As expected Monotony avoidance but not Impulsiveness was positively correlated with the Sensation Seeking Scales, especially with General Sensation Seeking and Boredom Susceptibility. The Sensation Seeking Scales have been reported to be correlated with testosterone levels (Zuckerman, Buchsbaum, & Murphy, 1980). It is noteworthy that we have found the same trend for Monotony avoidance. Among juvenile delinquents, those with the highest urinary testosterone levels, calculated from several samplings, had significantly higher scores in Monotony avoidance. There were no significant differences in Impulsivenss (Mattsson, Schalling, Olweus, Löw, & Svensson, 1980). Other differences between our high and low testosterone delinquents included higher E and higher verbal aggression. The high testosterone subjects reported that they were often asked to be leaders in group activities and that they were the ones who protested if teachers were unfair to the group. This is noteworthy because in a recent investigation of the life style of subjects high and low in Monotony avoidance, the group with highest scores reported the very same tendencies—taking the lead in groups ($p<.10$) and protesting against unjustice ($p<.10$). In light of the findings by Zuckerman and Neeb (1979) on a relation between Sensation Seeking Scores and manic-depressive illness, it is also of interest that the high Monotony avoidance scorers reported having been in high mood for some period without apparent reason ($p<.05$). They were also more often

TABLE 4.6
Correlations between the Sensation Seeking Scales (SSS):
General SSS (Gen.), Thrill and Adventure Seeking (TAS), Experience
Seeking (ES), Disinhibition (Dis.), Boredom Susceptibility (BS),
and the EPQ Scales and the KSP Extraversion-Related Scales
Detachment (De), Impulsiveness (I) and Monotony Avoidance (M) in a
Group of 40 Students (Study 1)
(From Schalling, Åsberg, Oreland, Askanas, Pfannschmidt, Tiberg & Edman, 1981)

				SSS		
		Gen	TAS	ES	Dis	BS
EPQ	E	.11	.03	-.02	.22	.06
	P	.48**	.21	.67***	.30[+]	.49***
	N	.05	-.20	.29[+]	.18	.17
	Lie	-.14	.05	-.41**	-.25	-.42**
KSP	De	-.20	.07	-.22	-.23	.15
	I	.20	.05	.23	.13	.05
	M	.50***	.23	.31*	.41**	.51***

[+] $p<.10$
* $p<.05$
** $p<.01$
*** $p<.001$

smokers, had tried marijuana, and more often admitted to having hit someone in a sudden attack of violent temper ($p<.01$). In a study by Fowler, von Knorring, and Oreland (1980), mountaineers were found to have significantly higher scores in Monotony avoidance ($p<.01$), in Impulsiveness ($p<.05$), and also in one of the Sensation Seeking Scales (Thrill and Adventure Seeking) and General Sensation Seeking. Thus, the life style associated with high Monotony avoidance agrees very well with the findings of the Sensation Seeking Scales.

IMPULSIVITY: TRAIT AND STATE

From the definition of the impulsivity concept and the scale item contents it would be tempting to speculate that high scores would make an individual more prone to commit suicide in frustrating or stressful situations. However, in a study comparing former psychiatric patients who had made suicidal attempts with those who had not, the attempters were not higher in impulsiveness. Rather, they were higher in P and in hostility as estimated from the thematic content in TAT stories (Schalling, Åsberg, Träskman, Lublin, Rantzén, & Rydin, 1980). Maybe projective methods are more revealing of the way in which an individual handles suicidal and other impulses in acute situations, that is, they are better indicators of the *state of impulsivity*.

IMPULSIVE COGNITIVE STYLE
AND HEMISPHERIC DIFFERENCES:
A NEUROPSYCHOLOGICAL MODEL

The cognitive style of highly impulsive people is described as follows by Shapiro (1965) on the basis of clinical work and experience with projective methods: "The impulsive person's attention does not search actively and analytically, we may add that his attention is quite easily and completely captured; he sees what strikes him, and what strikes him is not only the starting point of a cognitive process, but also, substantially, it is its conclusion. In this sense, his cognition may be called passive [pp. 150–151]." Thus, the attention of more impulsive people may be caught more easily by what happens around them ("acting on the spur of the moment"), whereas less impulsive people with their greater involvement in processing of past events and future projects are less easily distracted.

Individuals' scores in an impulsivity variable may be related to the extent to which their cognition and acts are determined predominantly either by immediate, holistic processing of sensory input attending to physical properties (high impulsive) or predominantly by semantic categorization and analysis of input by stored content (memories) and by anticipation and comparison of outcomes of alternative possible action (low impulsive). These differing cognitive styles, which are assumed to characterize persons high and low in impulsivity, are strongly reminiscent of the modes of information processing considered to be associated with the right and left brain hemisphere functioning, respectively. Hemisphere differences in the processing of visuo-spatial versus language stimuli and in parallel versus serial processing are well established. However, there is also growing evidence suggesting that the right hemisphere is more involved in the preliminary holistic processing of input, whereas the left hemisphere is more involved in the processing of stimuli in terms of description systems already existing in the cognitive repertoire, such as dealing with linguistically coded material (Goldberg, Vaughan, & Gerstman, 1978; Levy, 1974). Short-term storage is assumed to proceed in the right hemisphere, whereas the semantic or abstract analysis, which is a prerequisite for a longer-term storage, is predominantly a left hemisphere function (Nebes, 1974). Kinsbourne (1973) has suggested that control of attention is dependent on the balance of reciprocal inhibition between the two hemispheres.

There is some evidence that predominance of the right or left hemisphere activation may be related to personality style. Using lateral eye movements as an indicator of immediate hemispheric activation following questions, Smokler and Shevrin (1979) found evidence of more right hemisphere activation in hysterical subjects than in subjects with an obsessive-compulsive style. Hysterical personality traits are closely related to the dimension of solidity (Sjöbring, 1973) and impulsivity (Shapiro, 1965). The cognitive style in highly impulsive individuals is consistent with assumptions of a lower involvement of left hemisphere processing (i.e., reduced efficiency in recording information in terms of linkage with verbal symbols and stored mental content).

One of the predictions that may be drawn from this model is that individuals who score highly on impulsivity scales will tend to rely less on semantic aspects in the processing of stimuli. This was indeed the case in a study of generalization of autonomic responses to word stimuli (Schalling, Levander, & Wredenmark, 1980). Such responses may generalize along two dimensions: phonetically (similarity of sound, e.g., *hat-cat*) or semantically (similarity of meaning, e.g., *cat-animal*). Students with high scores in the combined Impulsiveness and Monotony avoidance scales generalized significantly more along the phonetic dimension.

A study by Edman, Schalling, and Levander (1983) makes a contribution to the construct validity of the impulsivity concept. Young boys were tested twice with a highly reliable computerized reaction time test, which gave measures of mean choice reaction times and number of errors for a series of light stimuli. Scores in the impulsivity scale were consistently related to both measures. High impulsive boys were faster and more inaccurate.

IMPULSIVE STYLE AND CORTICAL AROUSAL

Another neuropsychological model (Eysenck, 1967) associates impulsive behavior with deficiencies in cortical and brain stem activating systems, leading to a proneness for low cortical arousal and difficulties in maintaining appropriate vigilance levels in monotonous situations (reviewed by Schalling, 1976, 1978). These activating systems are related to frontal lobe functioning (see, e.g., Luria, 1966). A marked increase in impulsivity has been described in patients with frontal lobe lesions (e.g., in the classical study by Rylander, 1939). More recent evidence suggests that lower vigilance after frontal lobe lesions (and in impulsive individuals?) may be an effect of interfering with the coeruleo-cortical noradrenergic fibers. These fibers enter the cortex at the frontal pole and innervate large areas of cortex (Morrison, Molliver, & Grzanna, 1979).

Both models that have been proposed for the neuropsychology of impulsivity have as yet insufficient bases in replicated empirical data. Like the neurochemical model for sensation seeking presented by Zuckerman (1979), they are intended to provide guidelines for designing studies aimed at testing various inferences that can be drawn from them.

RELATIONSHIPS AMONG IMPULSIVITY
AND SENSATION SEEKING SCALES,
AND BIOGENIC AMINES

The validity of the assumption that impulsivity and sensation seeking or monotony avoidance are useful as intervening variables between biological vulnerability and psychopathology would receive considerable support if they were shown to correlate with neurochemical measures. A group of such measures, which have attracted considerable interest during recent years, are estimates related to the turnover of biogenic amines (e.g., dopamine, noradrenaline, and serotonin). Although turnover and concentration of transmitter amines in the brain cannot be studied directly in humans, it is possible to get some information about them by studying their metabolites in the cerebrospinal fluid or the enzymes involved in their synthesis or degradation (e.g., monoamine oxidase, MAO). MAO activity can be measured in various peripheral tissues, including blood platelets which are readily accessible. To some extent the use of platelet MAO activity rests on the assumption that it reflects MAO activity in the brain, but this has not yet been proven. Although differences between certain categories of psychiatric patients and controls have been found both for platelet MAO activity (Murphy & Kalin, 1980) and spinal flued monoamine metabolites (Åsberg & Träskman, 1980; Goodwin, Webster, & Post, 1978), most studies show a very considerable overlap between normal and pathological groups. Thus, it appears that the biochemical variables may not be directly related to psychiatric illness as such, but rather to a constitutional vulnerability that may lead to illness or breakdown, provided some other factors (psychosocial or somatic) are present (Coursey, Buchsbaum, & Murphy, 1979; Zubin & Spring, 1977). The previously described study by Sedvall et al. (1980) supports this assumption.

In an attempt to explain the empirically observed associations between a low activity of the platelet enzyme, MAO, and an increased incidence of bipolar affective disorder and criminal and suicidal behavior, Buchsbaum and co-workers have initiated a series of studies of personality variables in relation to the enzyme (Buchsbaum, Coursey, & Murphy, 1976). Most of these personality studies have been performed by contrasting groups of college students with very high and very low platelet MAO activity. Personality has been assessed by means of a few inventories, mainly the Sensation Seeking Scales and the MMPI. Low MAO activities have been found to correlate with high scores on some of the Sensation Seeking Scales, but only in male subjects (Murphy, Belmaker, Buchsbaum, Martin, Ciaranello, & Wyatt, 1977; Schooler, Zahn, Murphy, & Buchsbaum, 1978). Further, low MAO activity has been associated with scores in the pathological direction on three MMPI scales—the Hypochondriasis Scale, the Hysteria Scale, and the Psychopathic Deviate Scale (Coursey et al., 1979). The Karolinska Scales of Personality (KSP) have been used in some recent studies of platelet MAO activity. Perris, Jacobsson, von Knorring, Oreland, Perris, and Ross (1980) studied 24 consecutively admitted patients (men and women) hospitalized for depressive illness and found significant negative correlations between Monotony Avoidance and platelet MAO activity (rank correlation $-.40$ using beta-phenylethylamine as substrate, $-.55$ with tryptamine as substrate in the enzyme assay). There was no association with Impulsiveness.

In a study from our group (Schalling, Åsberg, Oreland, Askanas, Pfannschmidt, Tiberg, & Edman, 1981), we obtained platelet MAO measures from a group of 20 male psychology students and 20 male law students (mean age 28). Blood samples were obtained by a single venipuncture in the morning, and platelet MAO activity was determined at the Department of Pharmacology in Umeå University by Professor Lars Oreland, using both beta-phenylethylamine and tryptamine as substrates. The MAO values were correlated to scores in Extraversion (E), Neuroticism (N), and Psy-choticism (P) from the EPQ, the Zuckerman SS Scales, IV, and the KSP scales (including the Impulsiveness and Monotony avoidance scales). The correlations between the MAO measures and the EPQ scores E, N, and P were all low and nonsignificant. Correlations between MAO and Impulsiveness (I) and Monotony avoidance (M) scores can be seen in Table 4.7. Both scales showed negative correlations with MAO. The correlations with M were significant for both substrates, whereas those for I were nonsignificant. However, when the group was subdivided into high and low

TABLE 4.7
Correlations between MAO Activity and Extraversion-Related Scales
(From Schalling, Åsberg, Oreland, Askanas, Pfannschmidt,
Tiberg, & Edman, 1981)

		Study 1 (n = 40)		Study 2 (n = 58)	
		MAO_{PEA}	MAO_{TRY}	MAO_{PEA}	MAO_{TRY}
EPQ	Extraversion (E)	-.08	-.07	-.09	-.11
KSP	Detachment	.09	.06	.15	.12
KSP	Impulsiveness (I)	-.14	-.06	-.23*	-.25*
IVE	Impulsiveness (Imp)	–	–	-.28*	-.32**
KSP	Monotony avoidance (M)	-.33*	-.30*	-.11	-.16
IVE	Venturesomeness (Vent)	–	–	.11	.06
SSS	General Sens Seeking	-.24	-.25	–	–
SSS	Thrill and Adv. Seeking	.02	.03	–	–
SSS	Experience Seeking	-.20	-.20	–	–
SSS	Disinhibition	-.24	-.26*	–	–
SSS	Boredom Susceptibility	-.07	-.11	–	–

*$p < .05$ (one-tailed test of significance)
**$p < .01$

MAO groups (27% of the sample in each group) and a middle group with moderate MAO levels, analysis of variance showed that there was a significant relation between MAO and I scores ($F = 6.79 < .01$). Both low and high MAO subjects had elevated Impulsiveness scores, most prominently for low MAO subjects. The correlations between MAO and the SSS were mostly negative, as expected, and significant only for Disinhibition.

In a second study, 58 male volunteers were recruited among blood donors to a hospital (23–42-years old, mean age 33 years). MAO was determined as in the earlier study. In addition to the KSP and EPQ scales, the subjects also filled in the IVE scales, in which two newly constructed scales for impulsivity and sensation seeking were included—the Impulsiveness Scale and the Venturesomeness Scale (Eysenck & Eysenck, 1978). The correlations with MAO are shown in Table 4.7. There were significant correlations between MAO and the two impulsivity scales, but none with Venturesomeness and Monotony avoidance. The low MAO subgroup had higher impulsivity scores, significant for the IVE Impulsiveness Scale. There were significant differences between the low, middle, and high MAO groups also on the item level for the Impulsiveness Scale (see Table 4.8).

Thus, our results in the younger student group are in line with the American studies in showing relations among self-reported inability to tolerate boredom sensation seeking, and low MAO levels. However, it appears from our two studies that impulsivity is also important. The United States studies do not seem to have included any scales specifically intended to measure impulsivity. The consistent findings—in different subject groups from different countries—of an association between aspects of impulsivity and sensation seeking and platelet MAO activity strongly support the hypothesis of a biological basis for these particular personality traits. It has been suggested, by Oreland (1980) among others, that low platelet MAO may reflect some constitutional weakness of monoamine systems in the brain. The suggestion was based on relations between MAO activity in the human brain and brain levels of serotonin and its metabolite 5-hydroxyindole acetic acid (5-HIAA) (Adolfsson, Gottfries, Oreland, Ross, Wilberg, & Winblad, 1978). It has received some support from the finding of positive correlations between platelet MAO activity and spinal fluid concentrations of the dopamine metabolite, homovanillic acid (HVA) and 5-HIAA in normal controls, but not in psychiatric patients (Oreland, Wilberg, Åsberg, Träskman, Sjöstrand, Thorén, Bertilsson, & Tybring, 1981).

Studies of the relationsip between spinal fluid monoamine metabolite concentrations and personality are in progress in our group, and pre-

TABLE 4.8
Impulsiveness Items Discriminating between Individuals with Low,
Mid or High MAO Activity
(From Schalling, Åsberg, Oreland, Askanas, Pfannschmidt,
Tiberg, & Edman, 1981)

Item (No refers to item number in the IVE scale)	Percent agreement responses			
	Low	Mid	High	p less than
18. Do you often get into a jam because you do things without thinking?	33	3	8	.01
21. Would you often like to get high (drinking liquor or smoking marijuana)?	16	0	0	.05
24. Are you an impulsive person?	83	47	33	.05
30. Do you often do things on the spur of the moment?	83	41	8	.01
36. Do you mostly speak before thinking things out?	75	44	8	.01
39. Do you often get involved in things you later wish you could get out of?	42	15	0	.05
42. Do you get so "carried away" by new and exciting ideas that you never think of possible snags?	58	26	17	.10

liminary findings suggest a negative relationship between the concentration of HVA and 5-HIAA and Monotony avoidance, and a negative relationship between the concentration of the noradrenaline metabolite MHPG and Impulsiveness.

ACKNOWLEDGMENTS

The research reported has been financially supported by grants from the Swedish Council for Research in the Humanities and Social Sciences and from the Swedish Medical Research Council.

REFERENCES

Adolfsson, R., Gottfries, C.-G., Oreland, L., Ross, B. E., Wilberg, Å., & Winblad, B. Monoamine oxidase activity and serotonergic turnover in the human brain. *Progress in Neuro-Psychopharmacology,* 1978, *2,* 225–230.

Arieti, S. Psychopathic personality: Some views on its psychopathology and psychodynamics. *Comprehensive Psychiatry,* 1963, *4,* 301–312.

Åsberg, M., & Träskman, L. Studies of CSF 5-HIAA in depression and suicidal behavior. In B. Haber (Ed.), *Serotonin—Current aspects of neurochemistry and function.* New York: Plenum Press, 1980.

Barratt, E. S. Anxiety and impulsiveness: Toward a neuropsychological model. In C. D. Spielberger (Ed.), *Anxiety: Current trends in theory and research* (Vol. 1). New York: Academic Press, 1972.

Bergman, H., & Schalling, D. The influence of age and sex on the KSP personality scales. Unpublished manuscript, 1980.

Blankstein, K. R., Darte, E., & Donaldson, P. A further correlate of sensation seeking. *Perceptual and Motor Skills,* 1976, *42,* 1251–1255.

Buchsbaum, M. S., Coursey, R. D., & Murphy, D. L. The biochemical high-risk paradigm: Behavioral and familiar correlates of low platelet monoamine oxidase activity. *Science,* 1976, *194,* 339–341.

Cantwell, D. *The hyperactive child.* New York: Spectrum, 1975.

Cleckley, H. M. *The mask of sanity* (5th ed.). St. Louis: Mosby, 1976.

Coursey, R. D., Buchsbaum, M. S., & Murphy, D. L. Platelet MAO activity and evoked potentials in the identification of subjects biologically at risk for psychiatric disorders. *British Journal of Psychiatry,* 1979, *134,* 372–381.

Edman, G., Schalling, D., & Levander, S. E. *Impulsivity, and speed and error in a reaction time task.* Acta Psychologica, 1983.

Epstein, S. Traits are alive and well. In D. Magnusson, & N. S. Endler (Eds.), *Personality at the crossroads. Current issues in interactional psychology.* Hillsdale, N.J.: Lawrence Erlbaum Associates, 1977.

Eysenck, H. J. *The biological bases of personality.* Springfield, Ill.: Thomas, 1967.

Eysenck, H. J. *A model for personality.* New York: Springer, 1980.

Eysenck, H. J., & Eysenck, S. B. G. *Personality structure and measurement.* London: Routledge & Kegan Paul, 1969.

Eysenck, H. J., & Eysenck, S. B. G. *Manual of the Eysenck Personality Questionnaire.* London: Hodder & Stoughton, 1975.

Eysenck, H. J., & Levey, A. Conditioning, introversion–extraversion and the strength of the nervous system. In V. D. Nebylitsyn, & J. A. Gray (Eds.), *Biological bases of individual behavior.* New York: Academic Press, 1972.

Eysenck, S. B. G., & Eysenck, H. J. On the dual nature of extraversion. *British Journal of Social and Clinical Psychology,* 1963, *2,* 46–55.

Eysenck, S. B. G., & Eysenck, H. J. The place of impulsiveness in a dimensional system of personality description. *British Journal of Social and Clinical Psychology,* 1977, *16,* 57–68.

Eysenck, S. B. G., & Eysenck, H. J. Impulsiveness and venturesomeness: Their position in a dimensional system of personality description. *Psychological Reports,* 1978, *43,* 1247–1255.

Fowler, C. J., von Knorring, L., & Oreland, L. Platelet monoamine oxidase activity in sensation seekers. *Psychiatry Research,* 1980, *3,* 273–279.

Fulker, D. W. The genetic and environmental architecture of psychoticism, extraversion and neuroticism. In H. J. Eysenck (Ed.), *A model for personality.* New York: Springer, 1980.

Goldberg, E., Vaughan, H. G., & Gerstman, L. J. Nonverbal descriptive systems and hemisphere asymmetry: Shape versus texture discrimination. *Brain and Language,* 1978, *5,* 249–257.

Goodwin, F. K., Webster, M. H., & Post, R. Cerebrospinal fluid amine metabolites in affective illness and schizophrenia: Clinical and pharmacological studies. In E. Usdin & A. J. Mandell (Eds.), *Biochemistry of mental disorders: New vistas.* New York: Dekker, 1978.

Gray, J. A. The psychophysiological basis of introversion–extraversion. *Behaviour Research and Therapy,* 1970, *8,* 249–266.

Gray, J. A. Casual theories of personality and how to test them. In J. R. Royce (Ed.), *Multivariate analysis and psychological theory.* New York: Academic Press, 1973.

Haier, R. J., Buchsbaum, M. S., Murphy, D. L., Gottesman, I. I., & Coursey, R. D. Psychiatric vulnerability, monoamine oxidase and the average evoked potential. *Archives of General Psychiatry,* 1980, *37,* 340–345.

Hare, R. D. A research scale for the assessment of psychopathy in criminal populations. *Personality and Individual Differences,* 1980, *1,* 111–119.

Kinsbourne, M. The control of attention by interaction between the cerebral hemispheres. In S. Kornblum (Ed.), *Attention and performance. IV.* Elsevier: North-Holland, 1973.

Levy, I. Psychobiological implications of bilateral asymmetry. In S. J. Dimond, & J. G. Beaumont (Eds.), *Hemisphere function in the human brain.* London: Elek Science, 1974.

Loney, J. Hyperkinesis comes of age: What do we know and where should we go?, manuscript, 1981.

Luria, A. R. *Higher cortical functions in man.* New York: Basic Books, 1966.

Magnusson, D. Personality in an interactional paradigm of research. *Zeitschrift fur Differentielle und Diagnostische Psychologie,* 1980, *1,* 17–34.

Mattsson, Å., Schalling, D., Olweus, D., Löw, H., & Svensson, J. Plasma testosterone, aggressive behavior, and personality dimensions in young male delinquents. *Journal of the American Academy of Child Psychiatry,* 1980, *19,* 476–490.

Meehl, P. Schizotaxia, schizotypy, and schizophrenia. *American Psychologist,* 1962, *17,* 827–838.

Millon, T., & Millon, R. *Abnormal behavior and personality.* Philadelphia: Saunders, 1974.

Morrison, J. H., Molliver, M. E., & Grzanna, R. Noradrenergic innervation of cerebral cortex: Widespread effects of local cortical lesions. *Sinec,* 1979, *205,* 313–316.

Murphy, D. L., Belmaker, R. H., Buchsbaum, M. S., Martin, N. F., Ciaranello, R., & Wyatt, R. J. Biogenic amine-related enzymes and personality variations in normals. *Psychological Medicine,* 1977, *7,* 149–157.

Murphy, D. L., & Kalin, N. H. Biological and behavioral consequences of alteration in monoamine oxidase activity. *Schizophrenia Bulletin,* 1980, *6,* 355–367.

Nebes, R. D. Hemispheric specialization in commissurotomized man. *Psychological Bulletin,* 1974, *81,* 1–14.

Oreland, L. Monoamine oxidase activity and affective illness. *Acta Psychiatrica Scandinavica,* 1980, *61,* (Suppl. 280), pp. 41–46.

Oreland, L., Wilberg, A., Asberg, M., Träskman, L., Sjöstrand, L., Thorén, P., Bertilsson, L., & Tybring, G. Platelet MAO activity and monoamine metabolites in cerebrospinal fluid in depressed and suicidal patients and in healthy controls. *Psychiatry Research,* 1981, *4,* 21–29.

Perris, C., Jacobson, L., von Knorring, L., Oreland, L., Perris, H., & Ross, S. B. Enzymes related to biogenic amine metabolism and personality characteristics in depressed patients. *Acta Psychiatrica Scandinavica,* 1980, *61,* 477–484.

Prentky, R. A. (Ed.). *The biological aspects of normal personality.* Lancaster: Press Lancaster House, 1979.

Rosén, A.-S., & Schalling, D. On the validity of the CPI Socialization scale: A multivariate approach. *Journal of Consulting and Clinical Psychology,* 1974, *42,* 757–765.

Rylander, G. *Personality changes after operations on the frontal lobes.* Cophenhagen: Munksgaard, 1939.

Schalling, D. Tolerance for experimentally induced pain as related to personality. *Scandinavian Journal of Psychology,* 1971, *12,* 271–281.

Schalling, D. *Psychopathic behaviour: Personality and neuropsychology.* Paper presented at the conference Psychopathic Behaviour, Les Arcs, 1975.

Schalling, D. Anxiety, pain, and coping. In I. G. Sarason & C. D. Spielberger (Eds.), *Stress and anxiety* (Vol. 3). Washington, D.C.: Hemisphere, 1976.

Schalling, D. The trait-situation interaction and the physiological correlates of behaviour. In D. Magnusson & N. S. Endler (Eds.), *Personality at the crossroads.* Current Issues in Interaction Psychology. Hillsdale, N.J.: Lawrence Erlbaum Associates, 1977.

Schalling, D. Psychopathy-related personality variables and the psychophysiology of socialization. In R. D. Hare & D. Schalling (Eds.), *Psychopathic behaviour: Approaches to research.* Chichester, England: Wiley, 1978.

Schalling, D., Cronholm, B., & Asberg, M. Components of state and trait anxiety as related to personality and arousal. In L. Levi (Ed.), *Emotions: Their parameters and measurement.* New York: Raven Press, 1975.

Schalling, D., Asberg, M., Oreland, L., Askanas, I., Pfannschmidt, W., Tiberg, B., & Edman, G. *Impulsivity and platelet MAO activity in two groups of normal male subjects.* Unpublished manuscript, 1981.

Schalling, D., Asberg, M., Tr¼askman, L., Lublin, H., Rantz*en, V., [Rydin, E. *Hostility, social support and suicidal behaviour—A follow up study of depressed patients.* Unpublished manuscript, 1980.

Schalling, D., & Holmberg, M. *Extraversion in criminals and the "dual nature" of extraversion* (Rept. No. 306). Stockholm: The University of Stockholm, Psychological Laboratories, 1970.

Schalling, D., Rissler, A., & Edman, C. *Pain tolerance, personality, and autonomic measures* (Rept. No. 304). Stockholm: The University of Stockholm, Psychological Laboratories, 1970.

Schalling, D., Tobisson, B., Asberg, M., Cronholm, B., & Edman, G. KSP. *Skalor för mätninig av angestbenägenhet och impulsivitet. [KSP. Scales for measuring anxiety-proneness and impulsivity.]* Manual in preparation, 1981.

Schalling, D., Levander, S. E., & Wredenmark, G. Generalization of conditioned SC responses to homonyms in impulsive subject. Manuscript, 1980.

Schooler, C., Zahn, T. P., Murphy, D. L., & Buchsbaum, M. S. Psychological correlates of monoamine oxidase activity in normals. *Journal of Nervous and Mental Disease,* 1978, *166,* 177–186.

Sedvall, G., Fyrö, B., Gullberg, B., Nybäck, H., Wiesel, F.-A., & Wode-Helgot, B. Relationships in healthy volunteers between concentrations of monoamine metabolites in cerebrospinal fluid and family history of psychiatric morbidity. *British Journal of Psychiatry*, 1980, *136*, 366–374.

Shapiro, D. *Neurotic styles*. New York: Basic Books, 1965.

Sjöbring, H. Personality structure and development. A model and its application. *Acta Psychiatrica*, 1973, Suppl. 244.

Smokler, I. A., & Shevrin, H. Cerebral lateralization and personality style. *Archives of General Psychiatry*, 1979, *36*, 949–954.

Theorell, T., de Faire, U., Schalling, d., Adamson, U., & Askevold, F. Personality traits and psychophysiological reactions to a stressful interview in twins with varying degrees of coronary heart disease. *Jouranl of Psychosomatic Research*, 1979, *23*, 89–99.

Ungerstedt, U. Central dopamine mechanisms and unconditioned behaviour. In A. S. Horn (Ed.), *Neurobiology of dopamine*. New York: Academic Press, 1979.

Wredenmark, G. *Vidareutveckling av skalor för att mäta extraversion-impulsivitet-monotofobi. [Development of scales for measuring extraversion-impulsivity-monotony avoidance]*. Unpublished thesis, 1973, Dept. of Psychology, University of Stockholm.

Zubin, J., & Spring, B. Vulnerability—A new view of schizophrenia. *Journal of Abnormal Psychology*, 1977, *86*, 103–126.

Zuckerman, M. Dimensions of sensation seeking. *Journal of Consulting and Clinical Psychology*, 1971, *36*, 45–52.

Zuckerman, M. *Sensation seeking: Beyond the optimal level of arousal*. Hillsdale, N.J.: Lawrence Erlbaum Associates, 1979.

Zuckerman, M., Buchsbaum, M. S., & Murphy, D. L. Sensation seeking and its biological correlates. *Psychological Bulletin*, 1980, *88*, 189–214.

Zuckerman, M., & Neeb, M. Sensation seeking and psychopathology. *Psychiatry Research*, 1979, *1*, 255–264.

Like others in this volume, Schalling, Edman, and Åsberg stated their chapter with an analysis of the primary dimensions of personality. They have argued that of the two correlated components of extraversion—sociability and impulsivity—impulsivity seems to have more of a biological basis as shown in conditionability and pain studies. But conditionability and pain measures are not simply biological because they involve voluntary response. Eysenck has shown an equal genetic contribution for both components of extraversion (see Chapter 1), but Buss and Ploman (1975) report moderate to strong heritability for sociability and weak or inconsistent evidence of heritability for impulsivity. Daitzman and Zuckerman (1980) reported that two measures of sociability correlated with testosterone at a higher level than measures of impulsivity. Disinhibitory sensation seeking was also strongly related to testosterone in this study, but sensation seeking is not the same as impulsivity. Sociability has also been shown to be a major behavioral correlate of MAO levels in both male and female monkeys (Redmond, Murphy, & Baulu, 1979) and humans (Coursey, Buchsbaum, & Murphy, 1979). Behavioral correlates of impulsivity (e.g., criminality and drug use) are also related to low levels of MAO in males. A more reasonable conclusion at this point is that both sociability and impulsivity have biological bases, which in some cases may be the same.

Like other investigators, Schalling has felt the need to develop her own impulsivity and sensation-seeking scales. The reasons for developing a nonforced-choice SS scale (monotony avoidance) are cogent. I am currently developing a nonforced-choice scale of sensation seeking for similar reasons. But the scales used by Schalling for impulsivity and monotony avoidance (sensation seeking) consist of only 10 items each, and the monotony avoidance (M) scale does not sample all of the four sensation factors (although it shows moderate correlations with General SS). I have found that some of the 10-item scales used for each of the SS factors in form V (Zuckerman, Eysenck, & Eysenck, 1978) do not have desirable levels of internal reliability, largely because of the short scale length. Inasmuch as many studies show one of the factors (Disinhibition) to be the sole correlate of specific biological variables (e.g., augmenting–reducing), I have felt compelled to develop an expanded version of this scale in my new form (VI). I believe that Schalling would find higher correlations with variables such as testosterone and MAO if she used longer scales of impulsivity and monotony avoidance.

The attempt to find specific items most highly related to MAO is an interesting demonstration of the possibility of developing psychological tests designed to maximize their relationships with crucial biological variables. Donnelly, Murphy, Waldman, Buchsbaum, and Coursey (1979) have attempted to find MMPI items correlating with MAO in college students. Unfortunately, different sets of items were found for males and females. It may be premature to use specific criteria such as MAO to develop our personality dimensions because there may not be a single biological phenomenon underlying a psychological trait. But such item analyses may be useful in suggesting what kinds of items should be used in measuring dimensions of personality. Interestingly, in Schalling et al.'s chapter the impulsivity types of items were most discriminating, whereas in the Donnelly et al. analysis sociability items were more prominent in correlating with MAO.

Schalling and her colleagues have been the first to study MAO levels in relation to impulsivity. As shown in Table 4.7, MAO correlated negatively with two trait measures of impulsivity in one sample but did not correlate significantly with the impulsivity measure used in the other sample (study 1). But in the study 1 samples, MAO did correlate significantly with their M measure of sensation seeking. They also used translations of our sensation seeking scale (form IV) and found a significant correlation only with the Disinhibition subscale (the correlations with the General scale were very slightly lower but just on the other side of significance). As can be seen in this table, all of the correlations are in the predicted direction, but even the significant ones are relatively low ($-.2$ to $-.3$). The problem here is partly due to the lack of high reliability in the scales and, in the case of the SS scales, by the problems of translation and difficulties in cross-cultural appropriateness of the items alluded to by Schalling et al.

The problem of weak relationships between biological variables like MAO and trait measures is one that plagues the field of biological psychiatry as well as personality study. In an ingenious survey of the findings relating low MAO levels to chronic schizophrenia, Buchsbaum and Rieder (1979) collected individual data from 14 controlled studies of platelet MAO activity in chronic schizophrenics. Ten of these studies reported that the schizophrenics were significantly lower than controls, two found a non-significant trend in that direction, and two found the mean value for schizophrenics to be higher. Only a small group of the schizophrenics (3%) lies below the range of the normals; most schizophrenics cluster in the lower half of the essentially normal distribution of the controls. When we eventually collect the results of all studies of high versus low sensation seekers and high versus low impulsives I would expect to find the same kind of result.

These kinds of findings suggest two possibilities. One is that there are different types of sensation seekers, impulsives, and schizophrenics, and inherited low level of MAO is a significant causal factor in only some of them. Other biological traits might produce the same effects. For instance, low MAO might be a determinant in some persons, whereas extreme variations in one or more of the monoamines regulated by MAO might be a determinant in others. The other causes might also be social factors, so that only low MAO persons raised by parents in a certain way, or exposed to peers of a certain type, may show the phenotypic manifestations of impulsivity, sensation seeking, or schizophrenia. But from either a biological, social, or interactional viewpoint, it seems unlikely that only one biological factor or one specific social factor would be involved in a personality disposition or a complex behavior disorder like schizophrenia. If low MAO were only one of a number of casual factors, then only the confluence of a certain number of factors would produce extremes of the personality disposition or behavior disorder. Such a situation would lead to the kind of inconsistent and weak relationships seen between MAO and impulsivity or sensation seeking. The answer lies in multivariate studies of many biological variables that might be involved in the traits. Unfortunately, studies like these are expensive and involve interdisciplinary collaboration in a medical setting. Increasing the number of variables increases the possibility of chance findings. The use of large samples of subjects and replications are even more important than they are with bivariate studies.

Thoughtful theory and models can reduce the number of variables to those of greatest relevance. In regard to MAO we must ask what biological variables are of closest relevance. Here the answer is obvious because MAO is a neuroregulator of three monoamines: dopamine, norepinephrine, and serotonin. Can we measure theses in living humans? We can, but only indirectly through measures of metabolites, such as MHPG, HVA, and 5-HIAA, or through levels of the amines somewhere other than in the brain, such as norepinephrine in the cerebrospinal fluid (CSF).

Schalling et al. report that such studies are under way in Sweden and preliminary results (always dangerous to report) show a negative relationship between the concentration of CSF HVA (a dopamine metabolite), CSF 5-HIAA (a serotonin metabolite), and monotony avoidance, and a negative relationship between CSF MHPG (a noradrenaline metabolite) and impulsivity.

A study has been completed at the National Institute of Mental Health in America that has found negative relationships between CSF norepinephrine and sensation seeking in both men and women. These results are discussed further in Chapter 7.

The further development of these theories that postulate neurochemical bases for psychophysiological, behavioral, and personality traits is not impossible. But we must persevere beyond the discouragement of occasional correlations that fall on the wrong side of arbitrary significance levels.

REFERENCES

Buchsbaum, M. S., & Rieder, R. O. Biological heterogeneity and psychiatric research. *Archives of General Psychiatry*, 1979, *36*, 1163–1169.

Buss, A. H., & Ploman, R. *A temperament theory of personality development*. New York: Wiley, 1975.

Coursey, R. D., Buchsbaum, M. S., & Murphy, D. L. Platelet MAO activity and evoked potentials in the identification of subjects biologically at risk for psychiatric disorders. *British Journal of Psychiatry*, 1979, *134*, 372–381.

Daitzman, R., & Zuckerman, M. Disinhibitory sensation seeking, personality and gonadal hormones. *Personality and Individual Differences*, 1980, *1*, 103–110.

Donnelly, E. F., Murphy, D. L., Waldman, I. N., Buchsbaum, M. S., & Coursey, R. D. Psychological characteristics corresponding to low *versus* high platelet monoamine oxidase activity. *Biological Psychiatry*, 1979, *14*, 375–383.

Redmond, D. E., Jr., Murphy, D. L., & Baulu, J. Platelet monoamine oxidase activity correlates with social affiliative and agonistic behaviors in normal rhesus monkeys. *Psychosomatic Medicine*, 1979, *41*, 87–100.

Zuckerman, M., Eysenck, S., & Eysenck, H. J. Sensation seeking in England and America: Cross-cultural, age and sex comparisons. *Journal of Consulting and Clinical Psychology*, 1978, *46*, 139–149.

5 The Chemistry of Positive Reinforcement

Larry Stein
Department of Pharmacology,
University of California at Irvine

THE OPERANT-RESPONDENT DISTINCTION

Behavior refers to those functions of the organism, acting as a whole, involving commerce with or adaptation to the environment. According to Skinner (1938), significant stimuli in the environment exert control over behavior by two distinctly different processes, depending on the temporal relationship of the stimulus and response (Table 5.1). In the case of respondent (reflex) processes, the controlling stimulus precedes the response. The

TABLE 5.1
Respondent and Operant Control of Behavior

Type of Control	*Controlling Stimulus*	*Effect on Behavior*
Respondent (reflex) *Classical*	Antecedent	Elicitation
Operant *Cond*	Consequent	Reinforcement

effect is to elicit a particular behavior as, for example, the taste of food elicits salivation. The second process has been termed operant to emphasize the fact that some behaviors operate on the environment to generate consequences. Here the controlling stimulus follows the response and, by operant reinforcement, increases the likelihood of future occurrences of that behavior. A typical example is the reinforcement of a pedal-press response by food.

Confidence in operant reinforcement as a fundamental behavior process would be increased if one could identify its biological substrate. The methods of physiology have served well for the identification of the neuronal substrates of reflexes. For example, to map reflex pathways one can systematically stimulate many brain points and chart those that elicit the reflex in question. How may the methods of physiology be adapted to map the brain systems that mediate operant reinforcement?

Consider the following behavioral sequence: A lever-press response delivers food, which then causes a rat to salivate. These events are diagramed in the upper part of Fig. 5.1. Note that the same stimulus (food) stands in operant relationship to an antecedent behavior (lever press) and in respondent relationship to a consequent behavior (salivation). Thus, more

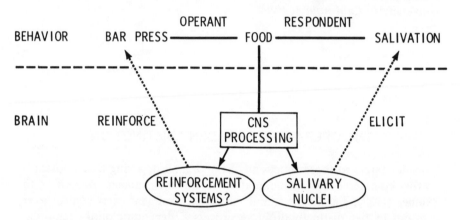

FIG. 5.1   The same food stimulus causes respondent elicitation of salivation and operant reinforcement of bar pressing. The two processes may be mediated by parallel brain events, as shown in the diagram below the broken line from Stein, Wise, & Belluzzi.

or less simultaneously, the same stimulus can exert operant and respondent control over different behaviors. The putative brain events that underlie these behavioral effects are diagrammed in the lower part of Fig. 5.1. After central nervous system (CNS) processing, food stimuli are shown to activate the salivary nuclei to elicit salivation and, by analogy, to activate "reinforcement systems" to reinforce bar pressing. How could one identify these hypothetical reinforcement systems? One approach would be to borrow the method of stimulation from physiology, but with an important change in order to adapt it for operant purposes. The change merely involves giving over operational control of the stimulator to the animal. Use of a Skinner box greatly simplifies the procedure. Each time the animal operates the bar, a specific brain region is stimulated via permanently in dwelling electrodes. Those probes, which generate high bar-press rates, are presumed to have activated the reinforcement system. It should be obvious to most readers that this is the famous self-stimulation experiment of Olds and Milner (1954).

CATECHOLAMINES AND REWARD

In the years following the discovery of self-stimulation, Olds and his collaborators prepared extensive maps of brain reinforcement regions (Olds, 1976). The original maps revealed a focus for self-stimulation in the hypothalamus with reward points extending along the medial forebrain bundle into limbic and olfactory forebrain. The discovery of self-stimulation in the hypothalamus was of particular interest because stimulation of this region also elicited various drive behaviors. Thus, eating, drinking, and mating could be obtained from the same hypothalamic electrodes that supported self-stimulation.

These observations suggested the possibility that reward neurons might be subdivided into distinctive subgroups. Each subgroup might mediate a particular drive-reward modality, and each might make use of a different neurotransmitter. To test the idea that reward neurons are chemically heterogeneous, self-stimulation behavior from a variety of hypothalamic probes was subjected to a pharmacological analysis. The assumption of neurochemical heterogeneity seemed to be quite wrong. Indeed, reward behavior maintained by all the probes shared a common pharmacology. In general, it appeared that self-stimulation was controlled by catecholamine neurotransmission (for a review, see Stein, 1978). Thus, drugs that release catecholamines rapidly from functional stores (e.g., amphetamine, α-methyl-m-tyrosine, or phenethylamine in combination with a monoamine oxidase inhibitor) facilitate self-stimulation. Conversely, drugs that deplete catecholamine stores (reserpine) block catecholamine receptors (chlorpromazine, haloperidol), inhibit catecholamine synthesis (α-methyl-p-tyrosine), or suppress self-stimulation. Pharmacological activation of acetylcholine or serotonin systems usually suppresses self-stimulation, and pharmacological blockade often facilitates the behavior; hence, it seems more likely that these systems act to antagonize rather than to promote reward. With the possible exception of the opioid peptides to be discussed later, the direct involvement of other neurotransmitters in self-stimulation remains to be demonstrated.

Even in the case of the catecholamine treatments, interpretation of drug effects on self-stimulation is difficult because many factors other than reward can affect response rates. Still, there were hints already in the earliest experiments (Stein, 1962; Stein & Ray, 1960) that amphetamine and chlorpromazine may act specially on reward thresholds. In one study (Stein, 1962), methamphetamine greatly augmented the very low self-stimulation rates maintained by subthreshold currents. Because methamphetamine's effect closely resembles that produced by a small increase in the brain-stimulation intensity, it was suggested that the drug effectively converts the subthreshold stimulus into a suprathreshold one by lowering the reward threshold. Inasmuch as a zero-intensity stimulus should not be so benefited, this idea was tested in a second experiment by reducing the current to zero at the time of drug administration. Consistent with the lowered threshold hypothesis, the rate-enhancing action of methamphetamine was now virtually abolished. In another approach (Stein & Ray, 1960), a current-resetting procedure was used to obtain rate-independent estimates of the self-stimulation threshold. Although the confounding effects of nonspecific stimulation or depression are largely excluded by this method, the results supported the suggestion that amphetamine lowers and chlorpromazine raises the threshold for brain-stimulation reward (Fig. 5.2).

Noradrenaline

Most catecholamine treatments exert similar effects on dopamine and noradrenaline; hence, it has been difficult to distinguish actions associated with the one catecholamine from those associated with another. Selective

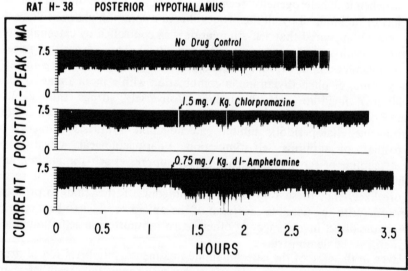

FIG. 5.2 Two-pedal "current-resetting" test for rate-independent estimation of brain-stimulation reinforcement thresholds. One pedal delivers brain stimulations that decrease stepwise in intensity with successive responses. When the reward threshold is reached, the rat operates the second pedal to reset the current (and the recording pen) to the top step. The jagged edge of the records gives, in sequence, the current intensities at which resets response is expedited by chlorpromazine and retarded by amphetamine. These uncharacteristic efforts cannot be attributed to nonspecific actions of chlorpromazine and amphetamine, and thus may be best interpreted as reflecting elevation and lowering, respectively, of the reward threshold. The ordinal markings indicate the 16 current levels available from Stein & Ray, 1960.

blockage of noradrenaline synthesis can be accomplished, however, by inhibiting dopamine-beta-hydroxylase, the enzyme that converts dopamine to noradrenaline. Central or systemic administration of the dopamine-beta-hydroxylase inhibitors disulfiramor diethyldithiocarbamate abolished self-stimulation and eliminated the rate-enhancing action of amphetamine (Wise & Stein, 1969). Intraventricular administration of 1-NE after dopamine-β-hydroxylase inhibition reinstated self-stimulation and restored the facilitative action of amphetamine; in control experiments, similar injections of d-NE, dopamine, and clonidine were ineffective. These observations have been confirmed in recent studies with two newer and supposedly more specific dopamine-beta-hydroxylase inhibitors, U-14,624 and fusaric acid (Wise, Belluzzi, & Stein, 1977). In agreement with earlier findings (Fuxe, Nystrom, Tovi, Smith, & Ogren, 1974; Lippa, Antelman, Fisher, & Canfield, 1973), a dependable behavioral suppression was not observed with a third dopamine-β-hydroxylase inhibitor, FLA-63. However, Franklin and Herberg (1975) found that FLA-63 suppresses self-stimulation if rats are pretreated with reserpine to deplete "reserve" pools of catecholamines; according to these workers, the action of FLA-63 may be short enough in duration so that, in the absence of reserpine, reserve pools of noradrenaline are sufficient to maintain self-stimulation until synthesis recovers.

Antabuse

Arousal Versus Reward. Because dopamine-beta-hydroxylase inhibitors leave brain dopamine levels unaffected (or even slightly increased) and because replenishment of depleted transmitter stores by intraventricularly administered noradrenaline produces rapid and almost complete behavioral recovery, the dopamine-beta-hydroxylase inhibitor experiments would seem to provide strong support for the conclusion that noradrenaline neurons are specifically involved in self-stimulation. In a widely cited paper, however, Roll (1970) has challenged this conclusion on the grounds that dopamine-beta-hydroxylase inhibitors may decrease self-stimulation merely by making animals drowsy. Although the suggestion may be valid, the experimental evidence offered in its support is weak. Noting that disulfiram induced long pauses in self-stimulation, the experimenter replaced the rats on the lever each time they quit responding and primed them with "free" stimulations. The disulfiram rates were then recalculated after eliminating the long intervals of no response; not surprisingly, it was now found that these rates were much higher. As extinction of self-stimulation induces a similar pattern of pausing (during which rats often go to sleep), the same experimental manipulations and statistical treatment could be used to support the conclusion that reduction of current intensity to zero does not affect reward value, but merely makes rats drowsy.

In another test of the sedation hypothesis, Rolls, Kelly, and Shaw (1974)

clonidine
anti-hypertensive, alpha stimulator

observed that disulfiram had relatively greater depressant effects on two presumed measures of arousal—spontaneous locomotor activity and spontaneous rearing—than it did on self-stimulation. Rolls et al. (1974) concluded that disulfiram's effects "on self-stimulation reward are relatively nonspecific [p. 736]." The validity of this conclusion obviously rests on the assumption that spontaneous locomotion and rearing are relatively independent of reward effects. It is known, however, that rats eagerly explore novel environments and even work for the opportunity to do so. It is also a fact that exploration extinguishes rapidly as novelty wears off and that the rats go to sleep unless the environment provides a fresh source of positive reinforcement or other significant stimulation. Thus, it is not inconceivable that disulfiram's depressant action on locomotor activity and rearing may reflect in part an accelerated depreciation of the rewarding effects of novel stimulation due to depletion of reward transmitter. Even the greater susceptibility of locomotion and rearing to the effects of the doapmine-beta-hydroxylase inhibitor, when compared to that of self-stimulation, is consistent with this suggestion. Direct activation of noradrenaline neurons during self-stimulation would release large amounts of transmitter (Stein & Wise, 1969), which would tend to counteract disulfiram's action until the noradrenaline stores by disulfiram could reasonably suppress exploration because noradrenaline neurons would be only weakly activated by the mild reward available in the activity tests. Some support for these ideas may be found in the Rolls et al. (1974) paper. An additional group of rats was allowed to self-stimulate continuously for 2 hours after disulfiram administration; presumably, this caused in these rats a more complete depletion of transmitter in the reward pathways stimulated. When compared to controls not so treated, the self-stimulators subsequently exhibited a significantly enhanced drug depression, not only in self-stimulation, but in the activity tests as well.

Proof of Reward: The Response-Contingency Requirement. Rewards may be defined as events, outcomes, or consequences that increase the probability of the behaviors they regularly follow. Rewards are efficacious only when the presentation of the rewarding event is made contingent on the occurrence of the response; noncontingent rewards fail to facilitate operant behavior. The contingency requirement is an absolute one, and it serves to distinguish the reward process from other facilitative actions on behavior. The contingency test should be applied, of course, in the verification of putative "reward" transmitters. Here it is necessary to show that behavior is facilitated only when the candidate transmitter is released on a response-contingent basis.

Evidence to indicate the noncontingent stimulation of noradrenaline receptors does not facilitate self-stimulation was found by Ritter (cited in

Stein, 1975). Centrally administered clonidine, a directly acting noradrenaline-receptor stimulant, did not reverse the suppression of self-stimulation by dopamine-β-hydroxylase inhibitors. Indeed, clonidine alone always suppressed self-stimulation, presumably because its chronic activation of noradrenaline receptors confused the contingency relationship between self-stimulation behavior and electrically induced noradrenaline release; a similar effect has been reported for systemically administered clonidine (Herberg, Stephens, & Franklin, 1976). Shaw and Rolls (1976) nicely confirmed that response-contingent activation of noradrenaline systems is required for behavioral facilitation. Three directly acting noradrenaline-receptor stimulants (clonidine, oxymetazoline, and nephazoline) failed to restore self-stimulation in disulfiram-treated rats, whereas three indirectly acting stimulants (amphetamine, methylphenidate, and phenylephrine), which enhance the release of noradrenaline from partially depleted stores, did counteract disulfiram. These findings were taken to support the original suggestion of Wise and Stein (1969) that the restorative effects of intraventricularly administered noradrenaline after disulfiram treatment are due to presynaptic uptake of the noradrenaline, which can then be released in response-contingent fashion by the electrical brain stimulation.

Two other arguments can be made for the notion that noradrenaline is important in self-stimulation because it mediates positive reinforcement. First, only response-contingent stimulation of noradrenaline pathways or of the relatively homogeneous noradrenaline cell concentrations in the locus coeruleus is behaviorally facilitative (Crow, Spear, & Arbuthnott, 1972; Ritter & Stein, 1973)—the self-stimulation experiment itself. Noncontingent brain stimulation, of course, does not maintain operant behavior. Second, there is evidence that noradrenaline generally plays a critical role in learning, not just in self-stimulation (Stein, Belluzzi, & Wise, 1975).

Anatomical Evidence Favoring Noradrenaline. The pharmacological observations fit nicely with the results of self-stimulation mapping studies on the one hand and histochemical maps of noradrenaline pathways on the other. The histochemical work presently demonstrates three major ascending noradrenaline fiber systems in the rat brain stem (Fuxe, Hokfelt, & Ungerstedt, 1970; Lindvall & Bjorklund, 1974; Ungerstedt, 1971). A dorsal pathway originates mainly in the principal locus coeruleus and innervates neocortex, cerebellum, hippocampus, and thalamus. A ventral pathway originates more heterogeneously and mainly from noradrenaline cell groups in the medulla oblongata and pons and innervates hypothalamus and ventral parts of the limbic system. And a newly discovered periventricular pathway originates in part from disseminated noradrenaline cell bodies in the central gray matter and innervates medial regions of thalamus and hypothalamus. All three noradrenaline systems may subserve self-stimulation (for a review, see Stein, 1978).

The possibility that evolution has selected the noradrenaline neuron for reward functions raises interesting questions about the neurochemical characteristics that suit it for this role and the anatomical organization that permits its fulfillment. It is also interesting to consider in what ways reward functions may be differentiated or specialized among the three systems. The innervation of neocortex, hippocampus, and cerebellum by the dorsal pathway and the capacity of neurons in this pathway for regeneration and new growth (Stenevi, Bjerre, Bjorklund, & Mobley, 1974), and hence for reorganization, suggest its involvement in associative thinking and learning (Crow, 1968; Kety, 1970). The innervation of hypothalamus and limbic system by the ventral pathway suggests involvement in motivation, mood, and neuroendocrine function (Olson & Fuxe, 1972). And the periventricular system's innervations of medial hypothalamus and mesencephalic central gray suggests, respectively, an involvement in feeding (Leibowitz, 1972) and interactions with pain and punishment systems (Mayer & Liebeskind, 1974).

Some Apparently Negative Findings.   Findings from a series of studies by Breese and Cooper and their colleagues (Breese & Cooper, 1976; Cooper, Cott, & Breese, 1974) seem to present a serious challenge to the conclusion that noradrenaline neurons are involved in self-stimulation; indeed, the results suggest that the important catecholamine may actually be dopamine. The catecholamine poison 6-hydroxydopamine was used in conjunction with other drugs to produce relatively selective and approximately equal depletions of either noradrenaline or dopamine. To reduce brain noradrenaline preferentially, 6-hydroxydopamine was administered intracisternally in three 25-ug doses 2 days apart; to reduce brain dopamine selectively, a single 200-ug intracisternal dose of 6-hydroxydopamine was administered after desipramine pretreatment (which prevents the uptake of the poison by noradrenaline neurons). Beginning 2 days after completion of the treatments, lateral hypothalamic self-stimulation was assessed in daily 15-minute tests. The dopamine-depleting treatment caused a sharp reduction in response rates for the first few days after injection; at 5 days, however, self-stimulation had largely recovered to predrug levels. In contrast, rats that had received multiple small injections of 6-hydroxydopamine to deplete noradrenaline displayed rates that did not differ significantly from control at any time (Fig. 5.3).

As it could be argued that the depletion of noradrenaline resulting from the multiple injections was not complete, Cooper and Breese used the dopamine-beta-hydroxylase inhibitor U-14,624 to induce additional depletion of brain noradrenaline. Despite further reduction of noradrenaline to 8% of normal, self-stimulation remained unaffected. On the other hand, a

DATA OF COOPER ET. AL. (1974)

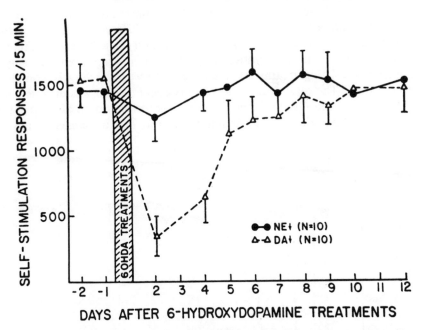

FIG. 5.3 Effect of noradrenaline or dopamine depletion on lateral hypothalamic self-stimulation. NE refers to rats treated intracisternally with three 25-mg doses of 6-hydroxydopamine (60 HDA) 48 hours apart to deplete brain NE. DA refers to rats that received desipramine (25 mg/kg, i.p.) 1 hour before single intracisternal injection on the same day. The daily 15-minute self-stimulation tests were interrupted for 60 HDA injections, but were resumed 2 days after completion of the treatments. N = number of rats Cooper et al., 1974.

moderate dose of the tyrosine hydroxylase inhibitor a-methyltyrosine effectively resuppressed the recovered response rates of the rats depleted of brain dopamine. Somewhat surprisingly, the same results were obtained for self-stimulation of the locus coeruleus (Cooper et al., 1974), a predominantly noradrenergic structure.

This work strongly suggests that dopamine systems may play an important or even essential role in hypothalamic and locus coeruleus self-stimulation. Dopamine's precise role, however, admittedly remains an open question; involvement in motivation or sensory-motor integration, for example, can be considered as likely as reward. Taken at face value, the data furthermore suggest that noradrenaline is not critical for self-stimulation, not even that of the locus coeruleus. Although it is only fair to point out that Breese and Cooper take pains to qualify this conclusion, the validity of their methods for assessment of the relative importance of dopamine and noradrenaline systems in self-stimulation must nevertheless be called into question. The treatments by which dopamine and noradrenaline were depleted differ in several ways. Perhaps most important was the difference in the duration of the treatments (1 vs. 5 days), a difference that allowed the noradrenaline-depleted rats a full 7 days of recovery time between the initial insult to the brain and testing (Fig. 5.4). Recovery from the single dopamine-depleting treatment, it may be recalled, was largely complete after 5 days. The total dose of 6-hydroxydopamine also was different for the two treatments (200 vs. 75 mg), and if peak concentration of toxin in the brain at any one time was an important factor, that difference would be

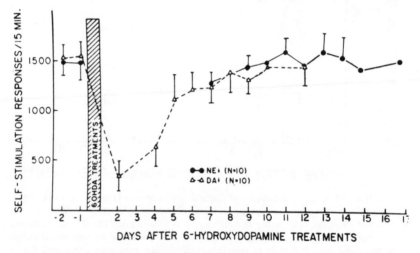

DAYS AFTER 6-HYDROXYDOPAMINE TREATMENTS

FIG. 5.4   Data of Cooper et al. (1974) after correction for treatment duration (compare with Figure 5.3). Abscissal values are replotted to show the number of days between the onset of treatments and testing on the theory that recovery processes are triggered by the initial insult to the brain.

very marked indeed. Use of a brief self-stimulation test (15 minutes) further mitigated the apparent efficacy of the noradrenaline treatments. Because it takes time to exhaust the transmitter pool after synthesis inhibition, testing could have been cut off before the effects of the dopamine-β-hydroxylase inhibitor were manifest. Even the route of administration of the toxin seems poorly chosen. Intracisternal injections may preferentially treat caudally located noradrenaline systems, but it is probably the rostrally located noradrenaline cells and terminals that have the most important role in self-stimulation. On the other hand, although the dopamine cells are also placed rostrally, they are compactly localized. In any case, the single large dose of toxin used to treat them would have had a wide effective distribution. In view of these differences, it would not seem sufficient merely to have matched the two treatments on the basis of whole brain catecholamine depletion.

Dopamine

Anatomy. The localization of positive electrodes in the dopamine cell groups of the substantia nigra (Routtenberg & Malsbury, 1969) and the region around the interpeduncular nucleus (Dresse, 1966) led Crow (1972, 1973) to suggest that there are dopamine neurons whose activation yields self-stimulation. Both nigrostriatal and mesolimbic dopamine systems are thought to be involved. Self-stimulation can be traced along the nigrostriatal pathway (Prado-Alcala, Kent, & Reid, 1975) and into the caudate nucleus (Phillips, Carter, & Fibiger, 1976); in the case of the mesolimbic system, the distribution of reward points coincides nicely with that of the dopamine terminals in nucleus accumbens and frontal cortex (Routtenberg & Sloan, 1972).

Pharmacology. Pharmacological evidence also tends to support the dopamine theory. Drugs that block dopamine receptors (pimozide, spiroperidol) or inhibit dopamine synthesis (a-methyl-p-tyrosine) suppress self-stimulation (Wauquier, 1976), whereas drugs that enhance dopamine release (amphetamine) facilitate self-stimulation. Noncontingent stimulation of dopamine receptors by apomorphine or other dopamine agonists should not facilitate self-stimulation, of course, if the rewarding effect of the brain stimulation were mediated by dopamine. Such experiments with apomorphine have yielded mixed results. Apomorphine was found in early studies not only to suppress self-stimulation (Liebman & Butcher, 1973; Wauquier, 1976) but also to enhance it (St. Laurent, Leclerc, Mitchell, & Millaressis, 1973; Wauquier & Niemegeers, 1973). Although suppressant effects continue to be reported, facilitative effects predominate in more recent work. Using a single, low dose of apomorphine (.2 mg/kg), Broekkamp and von Rossum (1974) observed consistent increases in response rate in some rats and consistent decreases in other, which were seemingly independent of electrode location. In many cases, apomorphine-induced facilitation was obtained even if the stimulating current was reduced to zero. Stinus, Thierry, and Cardo (1976) pretreated rats with a large dose of reserpine that drastically suppressed self-stimulation rates for more than 24 hours. Apomorphine (.25 mg/kg) completely reinstated the control rates of response. Using higher apomorphine doses (.3 and 1 mg/kg), Herberg et al. (1976) demonstrated the self-stimulation was powerfully enhanced with electrodes were placed in noradrenergic structures (locus coeruleus and perifornical hypothalamus) and suppressed when electrodes were placed in dopaminergic structures (substantia nigra and far-lateral hypothalamus). These findings were ingeniously interpreted by Herberg et al. (1976) "in terms of a hypothesis that DA and NA play complementary roles in self-stimulation and that both are essential; or, more specifically, that DA pathways, implicated in other motivational activities, contribute to a state of drive or arousal necessary for self-stimulation; while response-contingent noradrenergic activity (elicited by the electrodes directly, or indirectly via a transsynaptic route) mediates reinforcement [p. 575]."

Self-Administration.   Although it is likely that dopamine functions do involve motivational or drive aspects, there are no a priori reasons why dopamine systems cannot also participate in reward. Indeed, strong evidence in favor of the dopamine-reward hypothesis has been obtained from self-administration experiments in which animals are trained to pedal press for intravenous injections of drugs. Catecholamine-facilitating agents (e.g., amphetamines and cocaine) provide especially potent reinforcement for self-administration behavior, consistent with the hypothesis that positive reinforcement generally is mediated by catecholamine systems. The reinforcing properties of dopamine in particular are revealed even more directly by the demonstration that apomorphine, a dopamine-receptor stimulant, is avidly self-administered (Baxter, Gluckman, Stein, & Scerni, 1974; Davis & Smith, 1977). Action at the dopamine receptor is suggested by observation that apomorphine self-administration (unlike that of amphetamine or morphine) is unaffected by catecholamine depletion (Baxter, Gluckman, & Scerni, 1976; Davis, Smith, & Khalsa, 1975) but is blocked by the dopamine antagonist pimozide (Baxter et al., 1974). Because increases in dopamine-receptor activation are contingent on occurrences of the operant response in apomorphine self-administration, the behavioral facilitation may be taken to reflect a dopamine-reward effect.

Davis and Smith (1977) find a similar pattern of results with the a-NE agonist clonidine. Self-administration of this agent is unaffected by noradrenaline-synthesis inhibition but is blocked by the a-antagonist phenoxybenzamine.

Conclusions

Positive reinforcement of operant behavior is mediated by catecholamine systems in the brain. This idea, which has received critical scrutiny since its inception more than 15 years ago, continues to be supported by a consistent pattern of anatomical and pharmacological data from studies on brain self-stimulation and drug self-administration. In the absence of definitive evidence favoring one catecholamine over another, the original question of which catecholamine is the more important has given way to a more detailed inquiry into the precise roles of noradrenaline and dopamine systems. Abolition of self-stimulation by disruption of either the noradrenaline or the dopamine system suggests that these systems act jointly rather than separately and that the activity of both systems is required for the successful performance of operant behavior.

OPIOID PEPTIDES:
MEDIATORS OF DRIVE-REDUCTION REWARD?

Common observation provides support both for the view that reward can be identified with events that increase drive (incentives) and for the contrary view that it can be identified with events that reduce drive (satisfiers) (Table 5.2). Although events of either type may yield positive reinforcement, incentives increase the level of activity and excitement, whereas satisfiers cause relaxation and quiescence. Psychologists accordingly have formulated

TABLE 5.2
Pharmacological Evidence for Two Types of Reward

Reward Type	Drug of Abuse	Behavioral Effect	Neurochemical Substrate
Incentive	Cocaine or Amphetamine	Increases Drive and Arousal	Catecholamines
Satisfier	Morphine	Reduces Drive and Arousal	Opioid Peptides?

"drive-induction" theories of reward on the one hand and "drive-reduction" theories on the other. In a critical review of this work, Berlyne (1973) has concluded: "The persistence of these apparently opposite theoretical positions through the centuries certainly suggests that both have their elements of validity and that the ultimate answer will be found in some synthesis of them [p. 17]."

Pharmacological data also reveal that reward may be associated with increase or decrease in the level of arousal. Thus, agents that increase arousal (e.g., amphetamine) and those that decrease arousal (e.g., morphine) both are avidly self-administered by animals and humans. On the basis of this and other evidence, Belluzzi and Stein (1977) recently proposed that drive-inducing reward functions may be mediated by catecholamines and that drive-reducing reward functions may be mediated by enkephalin, or a related opioid peptide.

How may one test the hypothesis that endorphine or enkephalins are involved in reward function? First, by use of drug self-administration procedures, one may ask whether rats will work for enkephalin injections delivered directly into the ventricles of their own brains. Second, by use of brain stimulation procedures, one may ask whether electrical activation of enkephalin-rich brain regions will serve as a reward in self-stimulation experiments. And third, by use of appropriate brain-wave recordings, one may ask whether enkephalin injections can mimic the electrocortical changes known to be associated with natural rewards.

Enkephalin Self-Administration

Rats implanted with permanently indwelling intraventricular cannulas had continuous access during a single 66-hour test to one of the drug solutions shown in Fig. 5.5. Each lever-press response delivered 1 ml of fluid to the brain in .9 seconds. Each rat was tested once and had access to only one solution. No lever-press training was given; rats were merely placed in the Skinner box with food and water available for the 66-hour session. Rates of self-administration were significantly higher for the enkephalins and morphine (but not the structurally related tetrapeptide, Tyr-Gly-Gly-Phe) than for Ringer's solution (Fig. 5.5). The order of preference for the peptides when tested at either 1 or 10 mg per injection was leucine-enkephalin f methionine-enkephalin f Tyr-Gly-Gly-Phe. Massive doses of leucine-

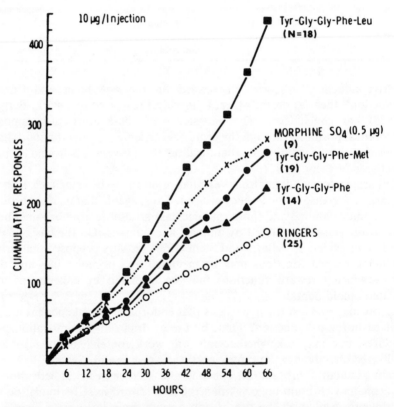

FIG. 5.5   Intraventricular self-administration of opiate peptides (10 mg per injection) and morphine (.5 mg per injection). Curves show mean number of self-injections cumulated at successive 6-hour intervals over the entire 66-hour test. Number of rats per group indicated in parentheses (after Belluzzi & Stein, 1977).

enkephalin in particular were taken by the best responders, despite the possibility of tissue damage or other adverse effects that might have been produced by passage of large volumes of fluids through the brain ventricles.

It was also observed that the 1-mg dose of both pentapeptides caused more rapid learning of self-administration behavior than the 10-mg dose, but the 10-mg dose generated a more sustained performance level. Thus, the 1-mg dose of leucine-enkephalin was self-administered at a higher rate than the 10-mg dose during the first 24 hours, but the 10-mg dose yielded a higher rate after prolonged exposure to the peptide. These results can be explained if tolerance develops to leucine-enkephalin's reinforcing action, as it does to morphine's. Prior to the development of tolerance, 1 mg per injection of the peptide provides satisfactory reinforcement, whereas 10 mg represents an overdose. After tolerance develops, the 10-mg dose is more nearly optimal, whereas 1 mg represents an underdose.

In related experiments, substance P was offered as a reward for self-administration behavior. In the case of this peptide, behavioral suppression rather than facilitation was regularly observed over a wide range of intraventricular doses. These results are generally consistent with the opposite pattern of biological effects typically displayed by opioid peptides and substance P (von Euler & Pernow, 1977) and further suggest a possible role for substance P in the mediation of behavioral punishment.

Self-Stimulation of Enkephalin-Rich Brain Sites

Avid self-administration of leucine-enkephalin supports the idea that opioid peptides may serve as reward transmitters. If this conjecture were true, reward should be produced not only by administration of exogenous enkephalin, but also by release of endogenous peptide following electrical activation of enkephalin-containing neurons in the brain. Behavioral (Stein, 1978; Stein, Wise, & Belluzzi, 1977) and immunohistochemical (Elde, Hokfelt, Johansson, & Terenius, 1976) observations may be consistent with this prediction. Sites that yield high rates of self-stimulation and those that contain dense networks of enkephalin-like immunoreactivity often overlap in precisely the same brain regions. According to our hypothesis, self-stimulation of these regions would depend at least in part on the electrically induced release of enkephalin and the consequent activation of opiate "reward" receptors. However, brain regions rich in enkephalin also contain high concentrations of catecholamines (Versteeg, Van Der Gugten, DeJong, & Palkovits, 1976), substances previously shown to be involved in self-stimulation (Stein et al., 1977). Hence, it is possible that the release of catecholamines rather than the release of enkephalins is responsible for the brain stimulation reward.

If self-stimulation depends on the activation of opiate receptors by electrically released enkephalin, then the behavior should be suppressed or extinguished following administration of an opiate receptor antagonist such as naloxone. On the other hand, if reward behavior depended only on the release of catecholamines, then naloxone should be ineffective and only catecholamine receptor blockers or synthesis inhibitors should suppress self-stimulation. The central gray region was selected for initial pharmacological testing because electrical stimulation of this site induces profound analgesia as well as high-rate self-stimulation (Mayer, Wolfe, Akil, Carder, & Liebeskind, 1971). Different doses of naloxone were administered at weekly intervals immediately before the behavioral test, and in further tests, the noradrenaline synthesis inhibitor diethyldithiocarbamate was administered a maximum of 1 hour before the test. Dose-related decreases in self-stimulation rates were obtained after administration of both agents. These results suggest that central gray self-stimulation depends on the activation of both enkephalin-containing and noradrenaline-containing neurons. Studies on intravenous self-administration of morphine similarly suggest that noradrenergic mechanisms are involved in opiate reinforcement (Davis et al., 1975; Pozuelo & Kerr, 1972).

The effects of naloxone on self-stimulation at a number of other rewarding brain sites have also been studied. The septal region is of particular interest because Hokfelt, Elde, Johansson, Terenius, and Stein (1977) find a well-defined group of enkephalin-immunoreactive cell bodies in this region. As in the case of central gray self-stimulation, naloxone and diethyldithiocarbamate treatments produced dose-related decreases in septal self-stimulation. Interestingly, of all self-stimulation sites tested so far, substantia nigra appears to be the most sensitive to naloxone suppression (Stein & Belluzzi, 1979).

A strong demonstration that self-stimulation may depend on enkephalin release would be the identification of new self-stimulation sites on the basis of enkephalin mapping. As the brain has been closely mapped for self-stimulation, demonstration of a new reward site would not be trivial. Most regions of thalamus do not support self-stimulation, and they also contain little enkephalin. However, one region of thalamus, the nucleus paratenialis, is reported by Elde et al. (1976) to yield a high enkephalin immunoreactivity. As predicted, five probes in or near the nucleus paratenialis in fact supported a respectable rate of self-stimulation, and the behavior was suppressed in a dose-related fashion by naloxone.

The globus pallidus yields profuse and intense enkephalin immunofluorescence, perhaps the most intense in the brain (Elde et al., 1976; Simantov, Kuhar, Uhl, & Snyder, 1977). To the best of our knowledge, self-stimulation has not yet been localized in the globus pallidus, hence, this structure provides an ideal test of the enkephalin-reward hypothesis. Eight probes in or near the globus pallidus yielded maximum self-stimulation rates of 1000 responses/hour or more (Fig. 5.6). Reward effects seem highly

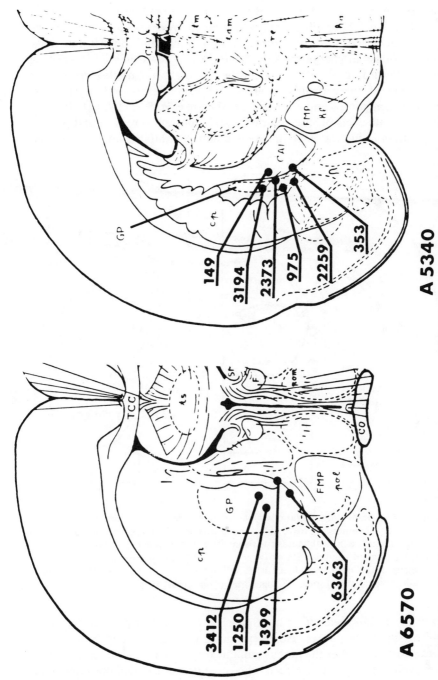

A 5340

A 6570

FIG. 5.6   Reward probes in or near the globus pallidus. Numbers indicate the maximum hourly self-stimulation rate obtained for each of the placements. Brain section drawings and stereotaxic levels after Konig and Klippel (1963) (from Stein & Belluzzi, in press).

localized in this region because two electrodes in the internal capsule (just medial to the globus pallidus) supported much lower response rates. It may be no coincidence that Keene (1975) has found single units in medical globus pallidus whose discharge rates are controlled by rewarding and punishing inputs. Rewarding stimulation of the medial forebrain bundle increased the firing rate of these pallidal neurons, whereas escape-eliciting midbrain reticular formation stimulation decreased them (Fig. 5.7). The pallidal units alone exhibited this precise contrasting relationship to reward and punishment (units in intralaminar thalamus uniquely exhibited an opposite pat-

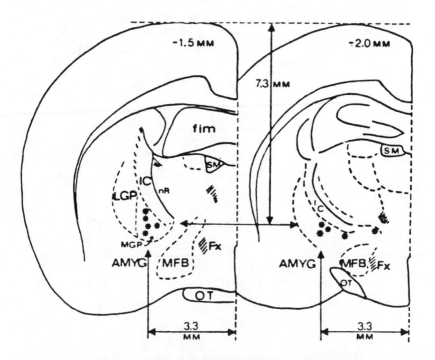

FIG. 5.7   Location of units (asterisks) in globus pallidus on which reward-evoked excitation and punishment-evoked inhibition converged. Compare locations of these "affect-coding" units with those of self-stimulation probes in Fig. 5.6. Abbreviations: fim, hippocampal fimbria; SM, stria medullaris; IC, internal capsule; LGP, lateral pallidum; MGP, medial pallidum; nR, n. reticularis; AMYC, amygdala; MFB, medial forebrain bundle; Fx, fornix; OT, optic tract (from Keene, 1975).

tern); most units were either unresponsive to reward or punishment or exhibited similar responses, either excitation or inhibition, to both inputs. Keene concluded that the globus pallidus may play a significant role in the neural coding of positive affect, whereas intralaminar thalamus may code negative affect.

Enkephalin and Electrocortical Pleasure Rhythms

Recent work from Leibeskind's laboratory (Frenk, Urca, & Liebeskind, in press; Urca, Frenk, Liebeskind, & Taylor, 1977) demonstrates that low doses of the enkephalins cause cortical spindle activity similar to that observed in satiated, drowsy animals in a comfortable and safe situation. Slow wave synchronous activity in the electroencephalogram was reliably evoked by intraventricular doses of leucine- and methionine-enkephalin as low as 1 to 10 ug (Fig. 5.8); as noted earlier, these same doses support avid self-administration behavior. Furthermore, Frenk et al. (1978) point out that an identical rhythmicity is widely reported to accompany "diverse rewarding events such as food or water consumption in deprived animals, vaginal probing, and electrical self-stimulation [p. 335]" (Fig. 5.9). These electrocortical phenomena accordingly have been termed "pleasure rhythms" by Myslobodsky (1976), who, in addition, speculates that these rhythms may be precursors for petit mal epilepsy.

These observations are consistent with the present hypothesis that enkephalin systems normally may mediate states of pleasure and reward. Furthermore, as Frenk et al. (1978) ingeniously suggest, in certain disease conditions (e.g., epilepsy), enkephalin-induced hypersynchrony may develop into actual seizures. Emotional disturbances are a frequent concomitant of epilepsy and often constitute part of the aura of the onset of the seizure. Extraordinary feelings of joy and satisfaction have been described during electrical stimulation of an enkephalin-rich area in the amygdala of epileptic and violence-prone patient (Mark, Ervin, & Sweet, 1972) and in the moments preceding the fits experienced by Feodor Dostoevsky (Yarmolinsky, 1934).

ROLES OF REWARD: SOME SPECULATIONS

In a review of brain reward mechanisms published shortly before his death, James Olds (1976) elegantly analyzed the role of rewards and drives in the problem of learned behavior:

> The key factors in the programming of mammal behaviors go under names like motivation, reward and learning. Subjects learn to do things, if they are rewarded for doing them; and if they are motivated to do them. There is, of course, a continuum from higher to lower motives. The lower end of the continuum is the one we have most in common with the laboratory rat. At this end there are four key factors. First there are drives, that is, special states created by alarming or dangerous deficits. Second there are incentive mechanisms, that is, reactions to promising stimuli which guide behavior even though deficits are not alarming. Third there are rewards, that is, targets that become objects of pursuit under either of the two kinds of motivating conditions, and which modify behavior repertoires a little or a lot when they are achieved (or when they are brought to bear as stimuli). Fourth, and finally, there are

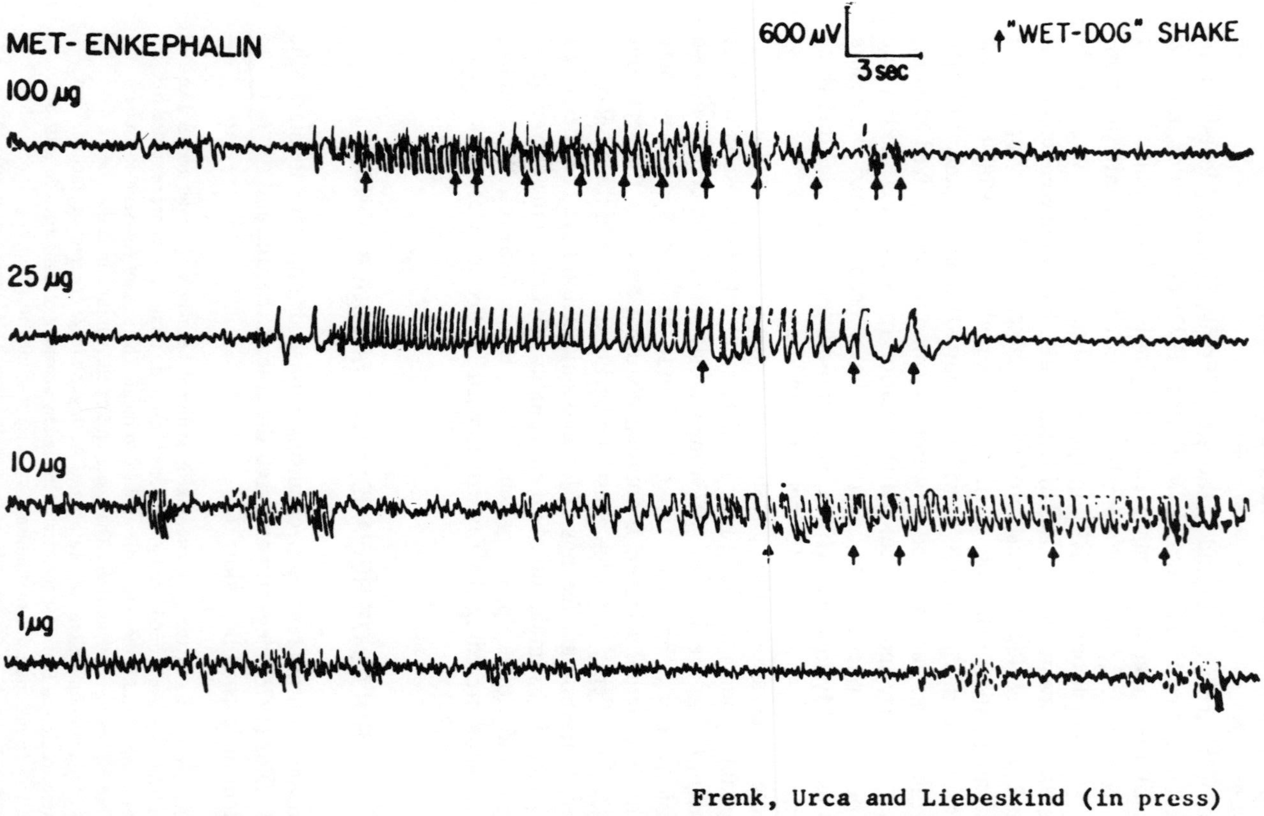

FIG. 5.8 Electrocortical spindles induced by intraventricularly administered methionine-enkephalin in four different rats. The electroencephalogram, recorded between frontal and occipital leads, starts 40 seconds after enkephalin injections (after Frenk et al., in press).

170

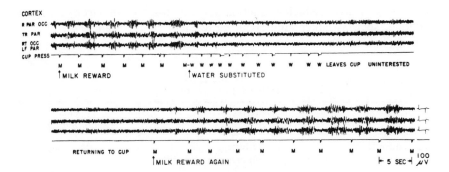

FIG. 5.9 Cortical spindles in the electroencephalogram of a trained, hungry cat regularly follow operant response and consumption of a milk-broth reward. When water is substituted for the milk reward, the spindles disappear and the EEG pattern exhibits only low voltage, high frequency activity. When milk again is made available, operant behavior is reinstated and the postreinforcement reward rhythms quickly reappear (from Clemente et al., 1964).

the learning mechanisms, that is, the set of built-in rules for modifying the repertoire with or without rewards.

Whichever way the behavior gets started it is "steered" by rewards. By steering I mean that the rewards shape the response repertoire, and in the long run this can be reflected in radically altered response probabilities. One way or another responses closer to rewards in a series get their probabilities elevated, and sensory signals close to rewards in a series are rendered attractive so that they become targets of pursuit. . .

Besides being steered, behavior is punctuated and eventually terminated by rewards. These functions are equally as important to the animal as the steering function, even if not as interesting to the psychologist. When the animal is suddenly given access to a quantity of food, this immediately halts the instrumental behavior whether it was sustained by an incentive or a more alarming condition. The searching and the working stop, and there is an end or pause in the urgent and driven look in the animal's behavior [pps. 1–2].

According to this analysis, rewards act in several ways to influence operant behavior—they motivate, steer, and eventually terminate the rewarded response. Expected rewards mobilize approach responses and generally increase the level of excitement and arousal. Following Crow (1973), we argue that these motivational or incentive functions may be mediated in large measure by dopamine neurons. Remembered rewards steer behavior by shaping the response repertoire and elevating the probabilities of previously rewarded responses. This planning or problem-solving function may be mediated at least in part by noradrenaline neurons, possibly via the feedback of "yes" signals to stimulus or response members of previously reinforced instrumental sequences. Obtained rewards bring the behavioral episode to a satisfying termination. We suggest that this gratifying or drive-reducing function may be subserved in part by an opioid peptide, such as enkephalin (Belluzzi & Stein, 1977; Stein & Belluzzi, in press) (Table 5.3).

TABLE 5.3
Different Roles of Reward

Role	Behavioral Effect	Putative Neurotransmitter
Incentive	Activate pursuit behavior	Dopamine
Reinforcement	Guide response selection via knowledge of response consequences	Noradrenaline
Gratification	Bring behavioral episode to satisfying termination	Enkephalin

REFERENCES

Baxter, B. L., Gluckman, M. I., & Scerni, R. A. Apomorphine self-injection is not affected by alpha-methylparatyrosine treatment: Support for dopaminergic reward. *Pharmacology Biochemistry & Behavior,* 1976, *4,* 611–612.

Baxter, B. L., Gluckman, M. L., Stein, L., & Scerni, R. A. Self-injection of apomorphine in the rat: Positive reinforcement by a dopamine receptor stimulant. *Pharmacology Biochemistry & Behavior,* 1974, *2,* 387–391.

Belluzzi, J. D., & Stein, L. Enkephalin may mediate euphoria and drive-reduction reward. *Nature,* 1977, *266,* 556–558.

Berlyne, D. E. The vicissitudes of apolopathematic and thelematoscopic pneumatology (or the hydrography of hedonism). In D. E. Berlyne, & K. B. Madsen (Eds.), *Pleasure, reward, preference.* New York: Academic Press, 1973.

Breese, G. R., & Cooper, B. R. Effects of catecholamine-depleting drugs and d-amphetamine on self-stimulation obtained from lateral hypothalamus and region of the locus coeruleus. In A. Wauquier & E. T. Rolls (Eds.), *Brain-stimulation reward.* Amsterdam: North-Holland, 1976.

Broekkamp, C. L. E., & Van Rossum, J. M. Effects of apomorphine on self-stimulation behavior. *Psychopharmacologia,* 1974, *34,* 71–80.

Clemente, C. D. Post-reinforcement EEG synchonization during alimentary behavior. *Electroencephalography and Clinical Neurophysiology,* 1964, *16,* 335–365.

Cooper, B. R., Cott, J. M., & Breese, G. R. Effects of catecholamine-depleting drugs and amphetamine on self-stimulation of brain following various 6-hydroxy-dopamine treatments. *Psychopharmacologia,* 1974, *36,* 235–248.

Crow, T. J. Catecholamine-containing neurones and electrical self-stimulation: 1. A review of some data. *Psychological Medicine,* 1972, *2,* 414–421.

Crow, T. J. Catecholamine-containing neurones and electrical self-stimulation: 2. A theoretical interpretation and some psychiatric implications. *Psychological Medicine,* 1973, *3,* 66–73.

Crow, T. J. Cortical synapses and reinforcement: A hypothesis. *Nature,* 1968, *219,* 736–737.

Crow, T. J., Spear, P. J., & Arbuthnott, G. W. Intracranial self-stimulation with electrodes in the region of the locus coeruleus. *Brain Research,* 1972, *36,* 275–287.

Davis, W. M., & Smith, S. G. Catecholaminergic mechanisms of reinforcement: Direct assessment by drug self-administration. *Life Sciences,* 1977, *20,* 483–492.

Davis, W. M., Smith, S. G., & Khalsa, J. H. Noradrenergic role in the self-administration of morphine or amphetamine. *Pharmacology Biochemistry & Behavior,* 1975, *3,* 477–484.

Dresse, A. Importance du systeme mesencephalo-telencephalique noradrenergique comme substratum anatomique du comportement d'autostimulation. *Life Sciences,* 1966, *5,* 1003–1014.

Elde, R., Hokfelt, T., Johansson, O., & Terenius, L. Immunohistochemical studies using antibodies to leucine-enkephalin initial observations on the nervous system of the rat. *Neuroscience,* 1976, *1,* 349–351.

Franklin, K. B. J., & Herberg, L. J. Self-stimulation and noradrenaline: Evidence that inhibition of synthesis abolishes responding only if the 'reserve' pool is dispersed first. *Brain Research,* 1975, *97,* 127–132.

Frenk, H., Urca, G., & Liebeskind, J. C. Epileptic properties of leucine- and methionine-enkephalin: Comparison with morphine and reversibility by naloxone. *Brain Research,* 1978, *147,* 327–337.

Fuxe, K., Hokfelt, T., & Ungerstedt, U. Morphological and functional aspects of central monoamine neurons. *International Review of Neurobiology,* 1970, *13,* 93–126.

Fuxe, K., Nystrom, M., Tovi, M., Smith, R., & Ogren, S.-O. Central cathecholamine neurons, behavior and neuroleptic drugs: An analysis to understand the involvement of catecholamines in schizophrenia. *Journal of Psychiatric Research,* 1974, *11,* 151–161.

Herberg, L. J., Stephens, D. N., & Franklin, K. B. J. Cathecholamines and self-stimulation: Evidence suggesting a reinforcing role for noradrenaline and a motivating role for dopamine. *Pharmacology Biochemistry & Behavior,* 1976, *4,* 575–582.

Hokfelt, T., Elde, R., Johansson, O., Terenius, L., & Stein, L. The distribution of enkephalin-immunoreactive cell bodies in the rat central nervous system. *Neuroscience Letters,* 1977, *5,* 25–31.

Keene, J. J. Reward-associated excitation and pain-associated inhibition lasting seconds in rat medial pallidal units. *Experimental Neurology,* 1975, *49,* 97–114.

Kety, S. S. The biogenic amines in the central nervous system: Their possible roles in arousal, emotion, and learning. In F. O. Schmitt (Ed.), *The neurosciences: Second study program.* New York: Rockefeller University Press, 1970.

Leibowitz, S. F. Central adrenergic receptors and the regulation of hunger and thirst. In I. J. Kopin (Ed.), *Neurotransmitters.* Baltimore: Williams & Wilkins, 1972.

Liebman, J. M., & Butcher, L. L. Effects on self-stimulation behavior of drugs influencing dopaminergic neurotransmission mechanisms. *Nauyn-Schmeidelberg's Archiv feur Experimentelle Pathologie und Pharmakologie,* 1973, *277,* 305–318.

Lindvall, O., & Bjorklund, A. The organization of the ascending catecholamine neurons systems in the rat brain as revealed by the glyoxylic acid fluorescence method. *Acta Physiologica Scandinavica,* 1974, Suppl. *412,* 1–48.

Lippa, A. S., Antelman, S. M., Fisher, A. E., & Canfield, D. R. Neurochemical mediation of reward. A significant role for dopamine. *Pharmacology Biochemistry & Behavior,* 1973, *1,* 23–25.

Mark, V. H., Ervin, F. R., & Sweet, W. H. Deep temporal lobe stimulation in man. In B. E. Eleftheriou (Ed.), *The neurobiology of the amygdala.* New York: Plenum Press, 1972.

Mayer, D. J., & Liebeskind, J. C. Pain reduction by focal electrical stimulation of the brain: An anatomical and behavioral analysis. *Brain Research,* 1974, *68,* 73–93.

Mayer, D. J., Wolfe, T. L., Akil, H., Carder, B., & Liebeskind, J. C. Analgesia from electrical stimulation in the brainstem of the rat. *Science,* 1971, *174,* 1351–1354.

Myslobodsky, M. *Petit mal epilepsy.* New York: Academic Press, 1976.

Olds, J. Reward and drive neurons: 1975. In A. Wauquier & E. T. Rolls (Eds.), *Brain-stimulation reward.* Amsterdam: North-Holland, 1976.

Olds, J., & Milner, P. Positive reinforcement produced by electrical stimulation of septal area and other regions. *Journal of Comparative and Physiological Psychology,* 1954, *47,* 419–427.

Olson, L., & Fuxe, K. Further mapping out of central noradrenaline neuron systems: Projections of the "subcoeruleus" area. *Brain Research,* 1972, *43,* 289–295.

Phillips, A. G., Carter, D. A., & Fibiger, H. C. Dopaminergic substrates of intracranial self-stimulation in the caudate-putamen. *Brain Research,* 1976, *104,* 221–232.

Pozuelo, J., & Kerr, F. W. L. Suppression of craving and other signs of dependence in morphine-addicted monkeys by administration of alpha-methyl- para-tyrosine. *Mayo Clinic Proceedings,* 1972, *47,* 621–628.

Prado-Alcala, R. A., Kent, E. W., & Reid, L. D. Intracranial self-stimulation effects along the route of the nigro-striatal bundle. *Brain Research,* 1975, *84,* 531–540.

Ritter, S., & Stein, L. Self-stimulation of noradrenergic cell group (A6) in locus coeruleus of rats. *Journal of Comparative and Physiological Psychology,* 1973, *85,* 443–452.

Roll, S. K. Intracranial self-stimulation and wakefulness: Effect of manipulating ambient brain catecholamines. *Science,* 1970, *168,* 1370–1372.

Rolls, E. T., Kelly, P. H., & Shaw, S. G. Noradrenaline, dopamine and brain-stimulation reward. *Pharmacology Biochemistry & Behavior,* 1974, *2,* 735–740.

Routtenberg, A., & Malsbury, C. Brainstem pathways of reward. *Journal of Comparative and Physiological Psychology,* 1969, *68,* 22–30.

Routtenberg, A., & Sloan, M. Self-stimulation in the frontal cortex of *Rattus norvegicus.* *Behavioral Biology,* 1972, *7,* 567–572.

Shaw, S. G., & Rolls, E. T. Is the release of noradrenaline necessary for self-stimulation of the brain? *Pharmacology Biochemistry & Behavior,* 1976, *4,* 375–379.

Simantov, R., Kuhar, M. J. Uhl, G. R., & Snyder, S. H. Opioid peptide enkephalin: Immunohistochemical mapping in rat central nervous system. *Proceedings of the National Academy of Science,* 1977, *74,* 2167–2171.

Skinner, B. F. *The behavior of organisms.* New York: Appleton-Century-Crofts, 1938.

Stein, L. Effects and interactions of imipramine, chlorpromazine, reserpine and amphetamine on self-stimulation: Possible neurophysiological basis of depression. In J. Wortis (Ed.), *Recent advances in biological psychiatry* (Vol. 4). New York: Plenum Press, 1962.

Stein, L. Norepinephrine reward pathways: Role in self-stimulation, memory consolidation and schizophrenia. In J. K. Cole, & T. B. Sonderegger (Eds.), *Nebraska Symposium on Motivation.* Lincoln: University of Nebraska Press, 1975.

Stein, L. Reward transmitters: Catecholamines and opioid peptides. In M. A. Lipton, A. DiMascio, & K. F. Killam (Eds.), *Psychopharmacology: A generation of progress.* New York: Raven Press, 1978.

Stein, L., & Belluzzi, J. D. Brain endorphins: Possible mediators of pleasurable states. In E. Usdin, W. E. Bunney, & N. S. Kline (Eds.), *Endorphins in mental health research.* New York: Oxford University Press, 1979.

Stein, L., Belluzzi, J. D., & Wise, C. D. Memory enhancement by central administration of norepinephrine. *Brain Research,* 1975, *84,* 329–335.

Stein, L., & Ray, O. S. Brain stimulation reward "thresholds" self-determined in rat. *Psychopharmacologia,* 1960, *1,* 251–256.

Stein, L., & Wise, C. D. Release of norepinephrine from hypothalamus and amygdala by rewarding medial forebrain bundle stimulation and amphetamine. *Journal of Comparative and Physiological Psychology,* 1969, *67,* 189–198.

Stein, L., Wise, C. D., & Belluzzi, J. D. Neuropharmacology of reward and punishment. In L. L. Iverson, S. D. Iverson, & S. H. Snyder (Eds.), *Handbook of psychopharmacology* (Vol. 8). New York: Plenum Press, 1977.

Stenevi, U., Bjerre, B., Bjorklund, A., & Mobley, W. Effects of localized intracerebral injections of nerve growth factor on the regenerative growth of lesioned central noradrenergic neurons. *Brain Research,* 1974, *69,* 217–234.

Stinus, L., Thierry, A. M., & Cardo, B. Pharmacological and biochemical studies of intracranial self-stimulation: Roles of dopaminergic and noradrenergic neuronal systems with electrodes either in area ventralis tegmenti or in lateral hypothalamus. In A. Wauquier & E. T. Rolls (Eds.), *Brain-stimulation reward.* Amsterdam: North-Holland, 1976.

St. Laurent, J., Leclerc, R. R., Mitchell, M. L., & Milliaressia, T. E. Effects of apomorphine on self-stimulation. *Pharmacology Biochemistry & Behavior,* 1973, 581–585.

Ungerstedt, U. Sterotaxic mapping of the monoamine pathways in the rat brain. *Acta Physiological Scandinavia,* 1971, *Suppl. 367, 82,* 1–48.

Urca, G., Frenk, H., Liebeskind, J. C., & Taylor, A. N. Morphine and enkephalin: Analgesic and epileptic properties. *Science,* 1977, *197,* 83–86.

Versteeg, D. H. G., Van Der Gugten, J., DeJong, W., & Palkovits, M. Regional concentrations of noradrenaline and dopamine in rat brain. *Brain Research,* 1976, *113,* 563–574.

von Euler, U. S., & Pernow, B. (Eds.). *Substance P.* New York: Raven Press, 1977.

Wauquier, A. The influence of psychoactive drugs on brain self-stimulation in rats: A review. In A. Wauquier & E. T. Rolls (Eds.), *Brain-stimulation reward.* Amsterdam: North-Holland, 1976.

Wauquier, A., & Neimegeers, C. J. E. Intracranial self-stimulation in rats as a function of various stimulus parameters. III. Influence of apomorphine on medial forebrain bundle stimulation with monopolar electrodes. *Psycho-pharmacologia,* 1973, *23,* 163–172.

Wise, C. D., Belluzzi, J. D., & Stein, L. Possible role of dopamine-β-hydroxylase in the regulation of norepinephrine biosynthesis in rat brain. *Pharmacology Biochemistry & Behavior,* 1977, *7,* 549–553.

Wise, C. D., & Stein, L. Facilitation of brain self-stimulation by central administration of norepinephrine. *Science,* 1969, *163,* 299–301.

Yarmolinsky, A. *Dostoevsky: a life.* New York: Harcourt Brace, 1934.

In the next chapter Gray presents a critique of Stein's theory, or that part of it which suggests that norepinephrine (NE) is a neurotransmitter in the reward system. For this reason, my critical comments at this point can be brief, and further relevant remarks can be reserved for the commentary following Gray's chapter.

The findings relating MAO to sensation seeking (Chapter 2) and impulsivity (Chapter 4) point toward some involvement of the monoamine systems in these traits because MAO is involved in the breakdown of these amines within the neurons that release them. Poschel and Ninteman (1966) have reported that MAO-inhibiting drugs enhance self-stimulation in some norepinephrine-containing areas, presumably by lowering MAO levels and allowing more NE to accumulate in the neurons. This would tie the MAO findings in humans to Stein's theory that NE availability in these neurons is necessary for, and directly related to, responding for brain stimulation reinforcement.

One of the criticisms of Stein's theory is that it rests mostly on self-stimulation studies. Are these a good model for sensation seeking? Other than the fact that these two share the same acronym (SS), what do the phenomena have in common? At the phenomenal level, sensation seeking involves the predilection to engage in activities that have a strong positive arousal effect for the sake of some kind of hedonistic reward, often intrinsic to the stimulation itself. Both sensation-seeking activities and brain stimulation represent challenges to the view of reinforcement as stimulus reduction and suggest the existence of a direct neurophysiological site for reward or pleasure effect. Although most humans do not have access to the technology of direct brain stimulation, they do engage in activities that produce the same effect chemically. Both stimulants, like amphetamine and cocaine, and brain stimulation release catecholamines from their neurons with euphoria-producing effects. Activity and stress also may release these bioamines. High sensation seekers may expose themselves to stress or danger to obtain these sensations produced by catecholamine release in the brain. Incidentally, our knowledge of what brain stimulation "feels like" stems from some unsystematic studies by Heath (1977), who has stimulated psychotic and epileptic patients and also recorded from the same sites during various activities. Stimulation of the septal region in humans has produced reports of intense pleasure. Recall of pleasant memories, marijuana, and sexual orgasm all produced high amplitude activity in the septum with the frequency of the particular activity varying with its subjective sensation of pleasure (slower for memories, faster for orgasm). Painful emotions have been correlated with changes in the hippocampus, amygdala, and connected sites.

But what is the evidence that self-stimulation is analogous to "natural reward" e.g., food) and is mediated by three bioamines: NE, dopamine, and endorphins? Stein has summarized much of this evidence in his chapter. A somewhat broader review of the field was written by Olds and Fobes (1981). Their conclusions are as follows:

1. The data support the view that the mammalian brain includes "a functional system that mediates motivational-reinforcing properties of behavior. [p. 564]."

2. "The sites are not homogeneously distributed in the brain, but instead are highly localized, though present at each brain level (p. 564)."

3. Evidence indicates a role of catecholamine systems (NE and dopamine) and endorphins in supporting self-stimulation behavior. However, they note that the use of drugs that change levels of neurotransmitters, or block receptor sites for them, have led to equivocal results. The drugs used have several behavioral effects, such as general suppression of activity level, that confuse the issue. Also the site of injection, the specific techniques, and the locus of injection all make results equivocal. Olds and Fobes (1981) conclude: "The problem is compounded by interdigitation of the pathways containing various transmitters and by the likelihood that various transmitters implicated in SS (self-stimulation) work as a system, in balance with one another rather than in isolation. Just as there may be any 'centers' for mediating feeding, there may not be one transmitter for mediating the rewarding effects [p. 565]."

Stein has not attempted to speculate on the application of his theory to individual differences in normal personality traits, although he (Stein &

Wise, 1971) has formulated a theory of schizophrenia on the assumption that the depletion of NE may result in the anhedonia (lack of capacity to feel pleasure) characteristic of this disorder. Other theories relate NE to depression and mania. In the simplest form, one such theory (Schildkraut, 1965) suggests that some depressions are due to depletion of NE and that mania is due to an excess of this neurotransmitter. The behavioral characteristics of manics represent an extreme of impulsive and sensation seeking behaviors. Furthermore, recovered manics are high on sensation seeking (Zuckerman & Neeb, 1979), which suggests some enduring difference in this trait.

If the status of these bioamines has this relationship to abnormal behavior, it is not too unreasonable to hypothesize that they may also regulate the dispositions characterizing normal personality variation. Applying Stein's roles of reward (see Table 5.3), the incentive role of dopamine might be involved in impulsivity and the restlessness that is characteristic of sensation seekers in a confined, nonstimulating situation (Zuckerman, Persky, Hopkins, Murtaugh, Basu, & Schilling, 1966) and embodied in the Boredom Susceptibility subscale of the SSS. The reinforcement value of noradrenaline might be related to the sensation seekers' greater expectations of positive rather than negative reinforcement and their low appraisal of risk in risky situations (Zuckerman, 1979). The gratification by enkephalin might be related to the excessive need for change in sensation seekers because of the rapid habituation and behavioral suppression mediated by endogenous opiates.

The aforementioned hypotheses would assume that sensation seekers would have abundant levels of these reward neurotransmitters in their nervous system and that they would have low levels of neuroregulators, such as MAO, that might reduce the transmitter levels. However some recent data, discussed in Chapter 7, have led us to a rethinking of this simple notion. If reward transmitters were abundant in the CNS of high sensation seekers, why would there be such a strong need to engage in unusual and dangerous activities or to seek novel and complex stimulation? More moderate stimulation would release NE from reward centers. Another possibility is that the high sensation seekers might have a relative deficit of these transmitters, so that more radical kinds of activities and stimulation might be necessary to release sufficient amounts of the transmitters to produce optimal hedonic effects. This new version of an optimal level of arousal theory, specific to catecholamine and endorphin systems, would predict negative relationships between sensation seeking and the neurotransmitters with a behavior-brain negative feedback system.

Stein's theory has served as a stimulant for this investigator, although Stein himself has refrained from extrapolation to the human level except in the area of psychopathology. The next author, Jeffrey Gray, has moved from the field of human personality, studied through psychophysiology, to the study of neurophysiology using rodents. His conceptualization of the role of the NE system has led to a direct confrontation with Stein's conception.

REFERENCES

Heath, R. G. Subcortical brain function correlates of psychopathology and epilepsy. In C. Gershon, & A. J. Friedhoff (Eds.). *Psychopathology and brain dysfunction.* New York: Raven Press, 1977.

Olds, M. E., & Fobes, J. F. The central bases of motivation: Intracranial self-stimulation studies. In M. R. Rosenzweig, & L. W. Porter (Eds.), *Annual review of psychology (Vol. 32).* Palo Alto, Cal.: Annual Review, 1981.

Poschel, B. P. H., & Ninteman, F. W. Hypothalamic self-stimulation: Its suppression by blockade of norepinephrine biosynthesis and reinstatement by metamphetamine. *Life Sciences,* 1966, *5,* 11–16.

Schildkraut, J. J. The catecholamine hypothesis of affective disorders: A review of supporting evidence. *American Journal of Psychiatry,* 1965, *122,* 509–522.

Stein, L., & Wise, C. D. Possible etiology of schizophrenia: Progressive damage to the noradrenergic reward system by 6-hydroxy-dopamine. *Science,* 1971, *171,* 1032–1036.

Zuckerman, M. Sensation seeking and risk taking. In C. E. Izard (Ed.), *Emotions in personality and psychopathology.* New York: Plenum Press, 1979.

Zuckerman, M., & Neeb, M. Sensation seeking and psychopathology. *Psychiatry Research,* 1979, *1,* 255–264.

Zuckerman, M., Persky, H., Hopkins, T. R., Murtaugh, T., Basu, G. K., & Schilling, M. Comparison of stress effects of perceptual and social isolation. *Archives of General Psychiatry,* 1966, *14,* 356–365.

6

Psychological and Physiological Relations Between Anxiety and Impulsivity

Jeffrey A. Gray
Susan Owen
Nicola Davis
Eleftheria Tsaltas
Department of Experimental Psychology,
University of Oxford

Because research in our laboratory is largely concerned with the biological basis of sensitivity to punishment and *non*reward, the contribution we are able to make to the topic of this volume—the biological basis of sensitivity to reward—is largely indirect and inferential. The possibility of drawing such inferences must rest upon an adequate theory of the relations among these three different kinds of reinforcement: reward, punishment, and nonreward. To these we need also to add a fourth kind: nonpunishment. Such a theory has been developed elsewhere (Gray, 1972a, 1975); here, we sketch only its main lines.

REINFORCEMENT AND EMOTION

The primitive terms of the theory are defined by the effects of presenting, terminating, or omitting a stimulus contingent upon the emission of an instrumental response (Fig. 6.1). If the contingent presentation of a stimulus increases the subsequent probability of emission of the response, the operation is one of reward; if such contingent presentation of a stimulus decreases the subsequent probability of response emission, the operation is one of punishment. Conversely, if the contingent termination or omission of a stimulus decreases the probability of emission of the response, the

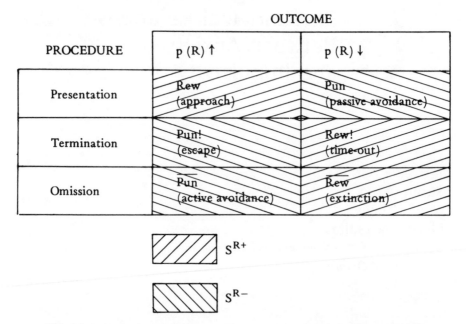

FIG. 6.1   The abbreviations and symbols are as defined by the intersection of row (procedure) and column (outcome). $p(R)\uparrow$: Outcome is an increase in the probability of the response on which the reinforcing event is made contingent. $p(R)\downarrow$: Outcome is a decrease in the probability of this response. Crosshatching indicates those procedures-plus-outcomes that define the stimulus as an S^{R+} or an S^{R-}, respectively. Phrases in parentheses refer to typical learning situations in which various reinforcing procedures are employed. *Rew:* reward; *Pun:* punishment; *!:* termination; —: omission.

operation is one of frustrative nonreward (Amsel, 1962); and if such termination or omission increases the probability of response emission, the operation is one of "relieving nonpunishment" (Gray, 1972a). The theory holds that reward and nonpunishment are functionally equivalent events; and that punishment and nonreward are similarly functionally equivalent, a proposition for which there is much empirical support (Gray, 1967, 1975; Wagner, 1966). It also holds that secondary or conditioned reinforcers can be set up by pairing initially neutral stimuli with a primary reinforcer (i.e., classical conditioning); that such secondary reinforcers acquire many of the properties of the primary reinforcer with which they are paired; but that, nonetheless, the mechanisms upon which such secondary reinforcers act are different from those upon which the primary reinforcers act (Gray, 1972c, 1975). This set of definitions and axioms leads to a classification of eight possible emotional states (i.e., states elicited in the brain or conceptual nervous system by reinforcers, whether primary or secondary) as set out by Gray (1972c, 1973).

However, the available evidence suggests that at the level of lower mammals (e.g., the rat) only three of these states need be taken into account: *Anxiety,* elicited by secondary punishing or nonrewarding ("frustrative") stimuli; *elation/relief,* elicited by secondary rewarding or nonpunishing stimuli; and *anger,* elicited by unconditioned punishing or nonrewarding stimuli (Gray, 1972c, 1973).

ANXIETY

Our research has been chiefly concerned with the biological (neural, hormonal, and genetic) mechanisms underlying the state of anxiety (Gray, 1978, 1979c). We have tried to deduce the *psychology* of anxiety from the behavioral effects of *anti*anxiety drugs (benzodiazepines, barbiturates, and alcohol; Gray, 1977) in animals, following the strategy poineered by Masserman (Masserman & Yum, 1946) and Miller (1951). In addition, we have tried to deduce the *physiology* of anxiety by studying the neural routes by which the antianxiety drugs exert their influence on behavior, a strategy also adopted with considerable success by Stein (e.g., Stein, Wise, & Berger, 1973). There have been many studies of the first kind, carried out in a variety of species by investigators in many different laboratories. Yet these permit a surprisingly simple summary of the behavioral effects of the antianxiety drugs (Gray, 1978, 1979c). This summary of the behavioral effects of the antianxiety drugs may be expressed in the form of a diagram (Fig. 6.2), which is at the same time a hypothesis (Gray, 1977). The hypothesis is that there exists in the brain a *behavioral inhibition system* (BIS) whose function is to receive information concerning the occurrence of any one of the adequate stimuli for anxiety (secondary punishing, or frustrative stimuli, or novel stimuli) and to operate the behavioral outputs listed to the right of Fig. 6.2 (because these are the behavioral reactions that are antagonized by the an-

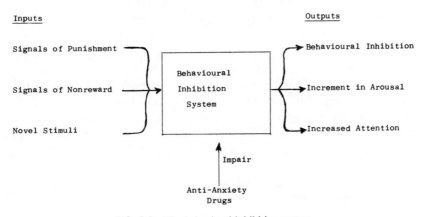

FIG. 6.2   The behavioral inhibition system.

tianxiety drugs). *Ex hypothesi,* the antianxiety drugs affect behavior by acting on the BIS, and anxiety consists in activity in the BIS. Identification of the neural mechanisms that mediate anxiety is therefore equivalent to discovering the structures constituting the BIS.

We turn to the physiology of the BIS later. There is first one more move of psychological theory construction of concern to us. This extends the theory to cover individual differences in susceptibility to anxiety. It is made in two steps. The first is an obvious one: It holds that anxious individuals are those who are particularly sensitive to the threat posed by secondary punishing or frustrative stimuli (i.e., to signals of punishment or nonreward). The second is more complex: It consists in situating the resulting theoretical dimension of Anxiety[1] in the general personality space defined by factor analytic studies of human individual differences. For this purpose, I have used Eysenck's two-dimensional space defined by Introversion–Extraversion (I–E) and Neuroticism (N) (e.g., Eysenck & Eysenck, 1969). As shown in Fig. 6.3, the dimension of Anxiety is conceived as running from Eysenck's stable extravert (low Anxiety) to his neurotic introvert (high Anxiety) quadrant (Gray, 1970a). This location is in good agreement with the empirical evidence from studies of personality both in the laboratory and in the psychiatric clinic (e.g., Eysenck, 1957). Note that the hypothesis shown in Fig. 6.3 is not concerned with the relations between Anxiety and Eysenck's dimensions merely at the descriptive level. It proposes that the lines of *causal* influence are not those postulated by Eysenck (I–E and N), but other dimensions rotated by approximately 45° from his (Anxiety and, as we shall now see, Impulsivity) (Gray, 1972b, 1973). (A more exact rotation probably leaves Anxiety somewhat closer to N than to I–E; see Gray, 1970a, in press.)

IMPULSIVITY AS SENSITIVITY TO SIGNALS OF REWARD

The model in Fig. 6.3 was first proposed (Gray, 1970a) principally as a theory of Anxiety. But a rotation of one of the Eysenkian axes requires rotation of the other if orthogonality is to be preserved. The second rotation produces a dimension running from Eysenck's stable introvert to his neurotic extravert quadrant. It was natural to suggest that, if Anxiety reflects sensitivity to signals of punishment and nonreward, this second dimension might correspond to sensitivity to signals of reward and non-

---

[1]The first letter of *anxiety* and similar terms is capitalized to indicate the trait, as distinct from the emotional state going by the same name.

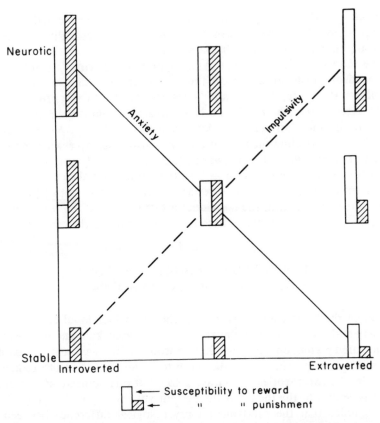

FIG. 6.3 Proposed relationships of (1) susceptibility to signals of reward and susceptibility to signals of punishment to (2) the dimensions of introversion–extraversion and neuroticism. The dimensions of anxiety and impulsivity (diagonals) represent the steepest rates of increase in susceptibility to signals of punishment and reward, respectively.

punishment. It was also proposed that high sensitivity to signals of reward, occurring *ex hypothesi* in neurotic extraverts, might underlie the trait of high Impulsivity found in such individuals (Eysenck & Eysenck, 1969) and related by Eysenck (e.g., 1964) to the antisocial behavior that his theory of psychopathy attributes to them. On this view, impulsive or antisocial behavior occurs in individuals who find the attractions of promised reward both strong in absolute terms and relatively stronger than the deterrent effects of threatened punishment. This is a simple hypothesis with a certain face validity; indeed, it corresponds to a widely held lay view of the character of antisocial individuals. But when it was proposed (Gray, 1970a), it had little direct evidence in its favor, and there has been little relevant research since that time. We hope that the present chapter succeeds in drawing the attention of research workers in the field of personality to what is, after all, an eminently researchable problem.

The model in Fig. 6.3 treats Anxiety and Impulsivity as primary and independent causal influences in the Eysenckian two-dimensional space; it follows, therefore, that I–E and N are derivatives of these primary influences. Accordingly, both I–E and N are treated within the theory as functions of the joint influence of Anxiety and Impulsivity. Neuroticism is conceived as reflecting the sum of the two sensitivities (to reward/nonpunishment and punishment/nonreward), that is, as overally emotionality. Introversion–extraversion is seen as resulting from the balance between the two sensitivities: If sensitivity to reward/nonpunishment outweighs that to punishment/nonreward, the individual is extraverted; in the converse case, the individual is introverted. These relations are made clear in Fig. 6.3.

EYSENCK'S AND GRAY'S THEORIES
OF CONDITIONING AND PERSONALITY

Although the basic framework of this theory of individual differences in Anxiety and Impulsivity remains recognizably Eysenckian and makes many of the same predictions, it is also in important respects a drastic revision of Eysenck's theory. This is not the place to detail the different predictions made by the two theories (see Gray, 1981), but one point at issue between them is central to the theme of the present volume. Eysenck's (e.g., 1967) theory holds that the fundamental psychological difference between introverts and extraverts is that introverts condition well but extraverts condition poorly irrespective of the nature of the reinforcement used for conditioning. According to Gray's (1970a) model, in contrast, introverts should condition better than extraverts when aversive reinforcers (punishment or nonreward) are used, but extraverts should condition better than introverts when appetitive reinforcers (reward or nonpunishment) are used.

Since 1970 there have been four studies relevant to this issue. Gupta and Nagpal (1978) used Taffel's (1955) technique of verbal conditioning with either reward (verbal approval) for correct responses or punishment (electric shock) for incorrect responses. They found that introverts conditioned better than extraverts under the latter condition, as predicted by both Eysenck and Gray; but in the former condition extraverts conditioned better than introverts, as predicted by Gray but not by Eysenck. Seunath (1975) studied pursuit rotor learning with either monetary reward or punishment by loud noise: Under the former conditions, extraverts learned better, under the latter, introverts learned better, again supporting Gray's theory. Also in support of this theory, Kantorowitz (1978) found sexual conditioning (penile tumescence to a slide of a nude female associated with orgasm) to be better in extraverts than introverts. In this study, it was also found that conditioned detumescence (to a slide associated with the postorgasmic state) was acquired better by introverts than extraverts. If one assumes that satiation has properties in common with nonreward, as suggested by animal studies of satiation of hunger and thirst (Morgan, 1974), this part of Kantorowitz's results is also in agreement with the model shown in Fig. 6.3. Finally, though more indirectly, Nicholson and Gray (1972) report evidence from a study of discrimination learning using operant conditioning techniques (lever-pressing) in children that subjects high on N and low on E are particularly sensitive to nonreward (in that they show a strong peak shift in the curve of stimulus generalization), whereas individuals with the converse personality characteristics are particularly sensitive to reward (in that they show strong generalized responding to stimuli that resemble the positive training stimulus). Thus, such evidence as exists on this important point all supports Gray's hypothesis rather than Eysenck's.

IMPULSIVITY: TWO FURTHER HYPOTHESES

As indicated, Gray (1970a) proposed that impulsive behavior would be greatest in neurotic extraverts because these individuals would be most sensitive to promised reward in absolute terms and also relatively more sensitive to promised reward than to threatened punishment. This proposal was a simple adoption, within the framework provided by the new theory, of Eysenck's (1964) hypothesis that neurotic extraverts are the most prone to impulsive and antisocial behavior. However, a deeper consideration of Fig. 6.3 shows that it is only one of two equally plausible hypotheses suggested by Gray's model. For one might deduce that the least impulsive individuals would be those in which fear of punishment is the strongest (i.e., highly anxious individuals); in that case, the most impulsive behavior would be seen in individuals lowest in Anxiety. But these are located, not in Eysenck's neurotic extravert quadrant, but in his *stable* extravert quadrant. To complicate matters still further, it now appears necessary to consider a third possible hypothesis.

This third hypothesis arises from the recent factor analytic work of Zuckerman and the Eysencks (Eysenck & Eysenck, 1977, 1978; Eysenck & Zuckerman, 1978) placing Sensation Seeking (Zuckerman, 1979, and this volume) and Impulsivity in the three-dimensional space defined by N, I-E, and Psychoticism (P) (Eysenck & Eysenck, 1976). This work shows that individuals who score highly on measures of Sensation Seeking or Impulsivity also tend to score highly on P. In an effort to fit this third Eysenckian dimension into the same kind of framework as that shown in Fig 6.3 for I-E and N, Gray (1973) suggested that individual differences in P might correspond to differences in sensitivity to unconditioned punishment and nonreward (as distinct from signals of these aversive events). On this view, high P scorers would be prone to the emotion of anger and to aggressive behavior in response to unconditioned punishment or nonreward (Gray, 1972c, 1973). This approach gives rise to the third hypothesis regarding Impulsivity, namely, impulsive individuals might be those who respond aggressively to unconditioned punishment/nonreward.

A more detailed consideration of the findings reported by Zuckerman and the Eysencks (Eysenck & Eysenck, 1977, 1978; Eysenck & Zuckerman, 1978; Zuckerman, 1979); suggests that these three hypotheses can perhaps be consolidated into two. Their findings indicate the existence of two kinds of impulsive individuals—one high on E and low on N, the other high on E and high on N, and both high on P. Eysenck and Eysenck (1978) have called the trait corresponding to the first kind of individual *Venturesomeness* and that corresponding to the second *Impulsiveness*. A very similar picture has emerged from studies of psychopathy. Hare and Cox (1978), in a review of such studies, distinguish between primary psychopathy (high E, low N) and secondary psychopathy (high E, high N). Thus, if we ignore for the moment the relation of impulsive behavior to P, these results suggest that both of the first two aforementioned hypotheses are correct: There are two kinds of impulsive individuals—one relatively fearless (in the stable extravert quadrant), the other impulsive in spite of normally high levels of anxiety (in the neurotic extravert quadrant). Furthermore, studies (Fowles, 1980; Hare, 1978) of primary psychopaths give direct support to the hypothesis that these individuals have a specific deficit in fear conditioning and passive avoidance learning, as first demonstrated by Lykken (1957). Note that, in line with the distinction between active and passive avoidance (the former mediated by the same processes that mediate reward learning, the latter mediated by the BIS; Gray, 1975), primary psychopaths are *not* deficient in active avoidance learning (Hare, 1978).

Following these lines of argument, it would therefore seem possible to fit both primary and secondary psychopaths (venturesome and impulsive individuals, in the Eysencks' terminology) reasonably comfortably into the model shown in Fig. 6.3. However, the relation of both Venturesomeness and Impulsiveness to P (Eysenck & Eysenck, 1978) complicates matters. In terms of the extended model proposed by Gray (1973), this finding suggests a connection between high sensitivity to reward relative to punishment (high extraversion) on the one hand, and aggressive responses to unconditioned punishment/nonreward on the other. Such a connection would appear as a further rotation of the diagonal axes of Fig. 6.3 so that the right-hand side of this figure tilts toward the high P pole of Eysenck's third dimension. Although suggested by the existing data, this solution to the problem is undesirable because it attributes a space that it is clearly more than two-dimensional (Eysenck & Eysenck, 1976) to only two causal influences. Conceivably, this situation has arisen because insufficient effort has been made to distinguish between impulsive behavior with an aggressive coloring and impulsive behavior of a less violent kind. This is an issue to which future research might fruitfully be directed.

THE NEUROLOGY OF ANXIETY

Let us now turn to the neurology of the emotional states and personality dimensions we have been considering. This is almost exclusively based on work in experimental animals, but Fowles (1980) has made the interesting suggestion, supported by an exhaustive review of the relevant data, that high sensitivity to signals of punishment is related in humans to good conditioning of skin-conductance responses, and that high sensitivity to signals of reward is related to good conditioning of cardiac responses. This suggestion tallies with the evidence (Hare, 1978) for good skin-conductance but poor cardiac conditioning in primary psychopaths. The evidence relating to the neurology of sensitivity to signals of reward and reactions to unconditioning punishment/nonreward is too incomplete for relevant useful conclusions to be drawn (though Stein might not agree with this view). What follows, therefore, is largely confined to the neurology of anxiety. This is only indirectly related to impulsive behavior (though for individuals in the stable extravert quadrant, the relation is a close one), but it nonetheless gives rise to a number of conclusions relevant to our theme.

Although the information currently available concerning the brain systems that respond to signals of punishment and nonreward is more extensive than similar data concerning those that respond to other reinforcing stimuli, the neurology of anxiety remains controversial. A number of different research groups have concerned themselves with the problem. Work in Stein's and Iversen's laboratories (e.g., Tye, Everitt, & Iversen, 1977; Wise, Berger, & Stein, 1973) has implicated the serotonergic pathways ascending from the raphe nuclei in the brain stem to innervate the forebrain. Research in Fuxe's, Redmond's, and our own laboratories (e.g., Gold, Redmond, & Kleber, 1979; Gray, Feldon, Rawlins, Owen, & McNaughton, 1978; Lidbrink, Corrodi, Fuxe, & Olson, 1973) has implicated the noradrenergic pathways that similarly ascend from the locus coeruleus in the brain stem to innervate the forebrain. Recent biochemical investigations, stemming from the discovery of a high affinity, specific receptor for the benzodiazepines in the brain (Möhler & Okada, 1977; Squires & Braestrup, 1977), have demonstrated a role for the inhibitory neurotransmitter GABA (γ-aminobutyric acid) (Guidotti, Toffano, & Costa, 1978). Our own experiments have suggested an important role for the septal area and hippocampus, which together constitute an integrated "septo-hippocampal system" (SHS; Gray et al., 1978). Finally, evidence from human subjects who have suffered accidental or deliberate injury to the prefrontal cortex has implicated this area (Gray, 1970a; Marks, 1969).

This variety of suggestions does not necessarily reflect a diversity of conflicting hypotheses. All the structures listed are extensively connected with each other. Thus, the SHS receives serotonergic fibers from the median raphe nucleus and noradrenergic fibers from the locus coeruleus, as well as a descending projection from the frontal cortex; in addition, there are important interconnections between the raphe nuclei and the locus coeruleus. As for GABA, it is located all over the brain, as is the benzodiazepine receptor, so that the problem is to determine which are the critical sites of action of this neurotransmitter with regard to anxiety (Gray, 1979a). Likely candidates are the GABAnergic terminals in the locus coeruleus, the septal area, and the hippocampus. In this way, it is possible to construct an overall model of the brain systems mediating anxiety that is consistent with the bulk of the evidence from behavioral, pharmacological, biochemical, and morphological studies. One such model is presented in a highly schematic form in Fig. 6.4.

Nonetheless, many issues remain in doubt. Two of the most controversial issues concern the exact functions exercised by the SHS (e.g., Elliott & Whelan, 1978; O'Keefe & Nadel, 1978; Olton, Becker, & Handelmann, 1979) and the dorsal ascending noradrenergic bundle (DANB), that is, the fiber bundle carrying efferents from the locus coeruleus to the forebrain, in-

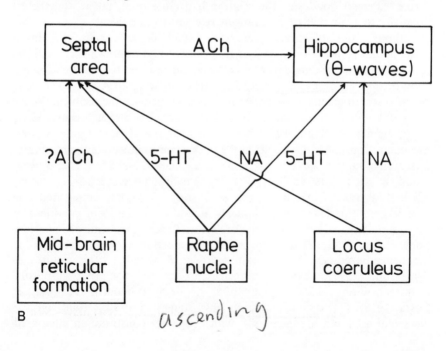

B

A   SEPTO-HIPPOCAMPAL SYSTEM.

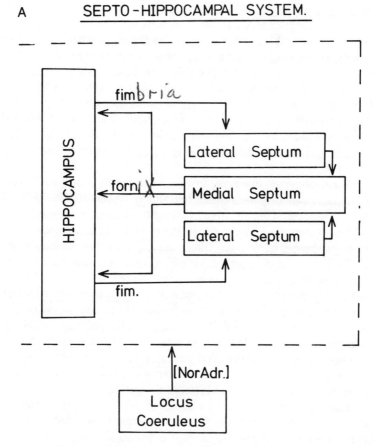

FIG. 6.4   The interrelations between structures that may mediate responses to signals of punishment and nonreward. *A*. Ascending serotonergic (5-HT), noradrenergic (NA), and cholinergic (ACh) projections to the septal area and hippocampus. *B*. Interconnections between septal area and hippocampus.

cluding the SHS (e.g., (Crow, 1973; Gray et at., 1978; Lidbrink et al., 1973; Mason, 1979; Stein et al., 1973). This is not the place to enter into the first of these controversies, but the second has an important bearing on the biological basis of reward seeking and impulsivity, and we can devote some attention to it.

The Dorsal Noradrenergic Bundle

The first hypothesis to gain wide currency in this controversy was advocated in slightly different forms by Stein (1969) in Philadelphia and Crow (1973) in London. The hypothesis states that norepinephrine (NE) plays a critical role in reward, reinforcement, and learning. This hypothesis has been adopted by Zuckerman (e.g., 1979) as part of his theory of the biological basis of sensation seeking; according to this theory, central noradrenergic mechanisms subserving reward are highly active in individuals high in the sensation seeking trait. Initially, the chief source of evidence supporting a role for Ne in reward processes came from studies of electrical self-stimulation of the brain in rats and other experimental animals. Further evidence was then provided by an experiment from Crow's laboratory (Anlezark, Crow, & Greenaway, 1973), since widely cited, in which electrolytic lesions of the locus coeruleus impaired running in an L-shaped runway for food reward in rats.

More recent evidence, however, from both self-stimulation and lesion experiments has weakened the reward hypothesis to the extent that it is no longer easily tenable. This negative evidence has come from experiments in which the neurotoxin 6-hydroxydopamine (6-OHDA) is used selectively to destroy only the noradrenergic fibers traveling to the forebrain in the DANB. Thus, Clavier, Fibiger, and Phillips (1976) showed that, even when self-stimulation was sustained by electrodes located in the cells of origin of the DANB, destruction of this fiber bundle by local injection of 6-OHDA failed to eliminate this behavior. This finding is, of course, incompatible with the view (which was the basis for the reward hypothesis of NE function) that self-stimulation depends on activation of these fibers. Similarly, there are now several reports that destruction of the DANB causes no impairment in a rat's capacity to learn and perform a rewarded response in the alley or in a Skinner box (e.g., Mason & Fibiger, 1979; Mason & Iversen, 1977). Thus, Anlezark et al.'s (1973) result must have been due to the destruction of tissue other than the noradrenergic fibers that travel in the DANB or to some other feature of their experiment.

Experiments in our laboratory have confirmed and extended these observations. Table 6.1 shows the pattern of biochemical change observed in the brains of our animals after injection of 6-OHDA into the DANB (Owen, Boarder, Gray, & Fillenz, 1982b). There is considerable loss of NE in the terminal areas exclusively innervated by the locus coeruleus (neocortex, hippocampus); in terminal areas innervated by both the DANB and the ventral noradrenergic bundle, which collects fibers from several brain-stem nuclei other than the locus coeruleus, the loss of NE is intermediate and compatible with the known distribution (Moore & Bloom, 1979) of noradrenergic fibers to these areas from the dorsal and ventral bundles (hypothalamus, septal area); and there is no significant loss of dopamine in the striatum nor of serotonin in the hippocampus. Thus, the experimental animals have sustained a substantial and selective destruction of the DANB. Yet, like Mason and Iversen (1977), we find no difficulty in training rats with this lesion to

TABLE 6.1
Effect of injection of 6-hydroxydopamine into the dorsal ascending
noradrenergic bundle on levels of noradrenaline in various brain regions.

	Wet weight in mg ± S.E.	Noradrenaline in ng/g ± S.E. (n)			
		Sham	Lesion	% depletion	P
Olf. lobes	70 ± 5	209 ± 38 (8)	10 ± 4 (8)	95	<0.001
Septum	23 ± 1	699 ± 90 (8)	330 ± 72 (8)	52	<0.01
Hippocampus	118 ± 3	368 ± 48 (8)	25 ± 17 (8)	93	<0.001
Cortex	250 ± 10	228 ± 40 (7)	31 ± 16 (8)	86	<0.001
Striatum	93 ± 4	273 ± 85 (8)	111 ± 44 (7)	49	n.s.
Amygdala	17 ± 1	510 ± 54 (7)	101 ± 26 (6)	80	<0.001
Hypothalamus	39 ± 4	1194 ± 89 (7)	765 ± 106 (6)	36	<0.01

[handwritten annotation: but can still train]

run down an alley for food reward (Owen et al., 1982b; e.g., Fig. 6.6). On Crow's (1973) version of the reward/reinforcement hypothesis, which stresses learning rather than performance, this might be because the task makes little demand on the animal's memorial processes (though it is, in fact, very similar to the task used by Anlezark et al., 1973). But, when we set the intertrial interval at 24 hours rather than the few minutes used in our first experiment, thus greatly increasing the role played by memory, the outcome was the same: There was no learning deficit in the lesioned animals.

In a third experiment, however, we were able to produce an apparent learning deficit in the lesioned rats and thereby throw some light on the conditions that may have given rise to the Anlezark et al. (1973) result. The latter investigators appear not to have handled their animals or habituated them to the alley before training them to run (Crow, personal communication). We therefore looked at the effects of destruction of the DANB (using 6-OHDA as before) on alley running in animals given no handling or habituation to the alley as compared to animals that underwent normal pretraining procedures. The results are shown in Fig. 6.5. It can be seen that the lesioned animals, which had no pretraining, ran more slowly than sham-operated animals treated in the same way, whereas there was no learning or performance deficit in lesioned but normally pretrained rats (Owen, Boarder, Gray & Fillenz, 1982a). Thus, the impairment in alley running observed by Anlezark et al. (1973) after electrolytic lesions of the locus coeruleus may have been due to their use of animals that were not pretrained. This is made more likely by the fact that other investigators (Crow, Longden, Smith, & Wendlandt, 1977; Fibiger, Roberts, & Price, 1975; Roberts, Price, & Fibiger, 1976) have failed to reproduce Anlezark et al.'s results even using the same lesion technique as these workers.

[handwritten annotation: pre training not learning deficit]

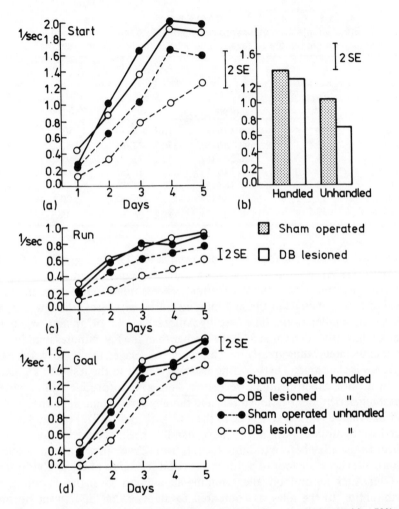

FIG. 6.5   Running speeds during training of handled and unhandled rats with a 70% lesion of the dorsal noradrenergic bundle (DB lesioned) or a sham operation. (a) Start section. (b) Start section data merged across days of acquisition. (c) Run section. (d) Goal section.

The Dorsal Noradrenergic Bundle and Nonreward

A possible defense against negative findings such as those by Mason and Iversen (1977); Fibiger et al. (1975), Roberts et al. (1976), and ourselves (Fig. 6.6) is to argue that the lesion was insufficiently extensive to produce positive results. Although the extent of the loss of forebrain NE (Table 6.1) makes such a defense implausible, it is not absurd. We have seen in our laboratory that the behavioral effects of a lesion that reduces forebrain NE by 75% may be quite slight, whereas a lesion that is more extensive (>90% depletion of NE) produces marked behavioral changes (Owen et al., 1982b). Conceivably, the lesions made in the experiments in which rewarded behavior was normal after 6-OHDA injection into the DANB were not big enough. The best way to counter this defense is to show other behavioral impairments in the same animals. This pattern of results has emerged clearly in our experiments. These were designed to test the hypothesis that the DANB is involved in reactions, not to reward, but to signals of nonreward or of punishment. Because they were also intended to allow a direct comparison between the effects of DANB lesions and the injection of antianxiety drugs, it is first necessary to describe the effects of the latter agents.

Our experiments have focused on the effects of partial reinforcement (PRF) schedules on behavior in the alley. Such a schedule delivers a reward for reaching the goal box, not on every trial as on a continuous reinforcement (CRF) schedule, but on a randomly chosen proportion (in our case, 50%) of trials. Compared to animals trained on a CRF schedule, PRF-trained animals differ in two ways: (1) during acquisition of the running response, they tend to run faster, especially late in training and in early sections of the alley (the "Goodrich–Haggard" or "partial reinforcement acquisition effect," PRAE); (2) subsequently, they show greater resistance to extinction (the extremely robust "partial reinforcement extinction effect," PREE). It can be predicted from the hypothesis that antianxiety drugs block the behavioral effects of signals of nonreward that these agents should eliminate both the PRAE and the PREE, in both cases by shifting the performance of PRF animals toward that of their CRF controls. Both these predictions have been supported (for a review, see Gray, 1977; also, Feldon, 1977; Feldon, Guillamon, Gray, De Wit, & McNaughton, 1979; Feldon and Gray, 1981). Blockade of the PREE by these drugs is due to their presence during training on a PRF schedule. Given during extinction alone, they increase resistance to extinction in both CRF- and PRF-trained rats (Feldon & Gray, 1981; Feldon et al., 1979) or in CRF-trained rats alone (Gray, 1969) and leave the PREE intact. When the drug is present throughout both training and extinction, the results reflect both these effects: CRF rats are more resistant to extinction (due to the presence of the drug during extinction), PRF rats may show reduced resistance to extinction or little overall change (balancing the effects of the drug during acquisition and extinction), and the PREE is attenuated or abolished (due to the presence of the drug during acquisition) (Feldon & Gray, 1981; Feldon et al., 1979).

From the hypothesis that the DANB forms part of the neural system that subserves anxiety, it follows that destruction of this fiber bundle should block responses to signals of nonreward in the same way as administration of an antianxiety drug. In an experiment on the effects of DANB lesions on the behavior of CRF and PRF groups in the alley, therefore, we should expect the following pattern of results (based on those observed in animals drugged throughout training and extinction): (1) the PRAE should be abolished owing to a reduction in running speed in the lesioned PRF animals with no change in running speed in the lesioned CRF animals; (2) resistance to extinction in the CRF group should be increased; (3) resistance to extinction in the PRF group should either be unchanged or reduced; (4) the PREE should be attenuated or abolished. To test these predictions we made use of training parameters similar to those that have been successful in demonstrating the effects of septal (Feldon & Gray, 1979b; Henke, 1974) and hippocampal (Rawlins, Feldon, & Gray, 1980) lesions in this situation: 50 acquisition trials with an intertrial interval of 3–4 minutes. Under these conditions, the PRAE was abolished by destruction of the DANB (Fig. 6.6), as was the PREE; Fig. 6.7; Owen et al. 1982b). Furthermore, the pattern of change was exactly as predicted by the nonreward hypothesis of DANB function. The loss of the PRAE was due to reduced running speeds in PRF animals, with no change in the CRF group; resistance to extinction was increased by the lesion in the CRF group; and it was decreased by the lesion in the PRF group. The fact that this total blockade of the effects of nonreward was observed in the same animals whose rewarded running performance (i.e., during acquisition on a CRF schedule) was unchanged by the lesion rules out the argument that this negative finding was due to an insufficiently extensive lesion.

The experiment whose results are shown in Fig. 6.6 was conducted with 50 training trials. Under these conditions, total septal (Henke, 1974), lateral septal (Feldon & Gray, 1979b), and total hippocampal (Rawlins et al., 1980) lesions have very similar effects to those of destruction of the DANB. This suggests that the critical projection of the DANB for the behavior under investigation is to the SHS. However, the DANB also projects extensively to the neocortex and the amygdala, among other structures. As a way of testing whether the SHS is the important target area of the DANB insofar as responses to nonreward are concerned, we have made two other comparisons between the effects of DANB destruction and those of damage to other forebrain regions to which the DANB projects.

First, we have investigated the effects of doubling the number of training trials in the PREE paradigm already described. For reasons presently unknown, this increase in the length of training restores the PREE in total septal (Henke, 1974) and lateral septal (Feldon & Gray, 1979b) animals. This also happens in the case of DANB lesions (Owen et al., 1982b). With 100 training trials, the PREE was not reduced from control levels, and resistance to extinction was unchanged in either CRF-trained animals (as in the case with lateral but not total septal lesions; Feldon & Gray, 1979b; Henke, 1974) or in PRF animals (as is the case with both total and lateral septal animals).

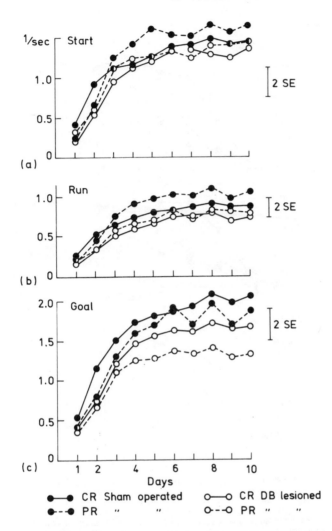

FIG. 6.6 Running speeds during training as a function of continuous (CR) or partial (PR) reinforcement in rats with a lesion of the dorsal noradrenergic bundle (DB lesioned) or a sham operation. (a) Start section. (b) Run section. (c) Goal section.

Second, we have investigated the double-runway frustration effect (FE) (Amsel & Roussel, 1952) in which running speed in the second of two consecutive alleys is found to be faster after nonreward than after reward in the middle goal box. It follows from the hypothesis that the antianxiety drugs affect responses only to signals of nonreward, not to nonreward itself, that the FE should *not* be affected by these agents (Gray, 1969). The evidence (Gray, 1977) clearly supports this prediction. If the SHS is part of the brain system that mediates anxiety, it can also be predicted that lesions to the sep-

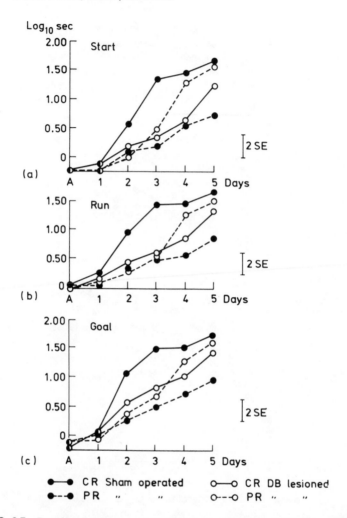

FIG. 6.7   Running time (Log$_{10}$ sec) in extinction as a function of continuous (CR) or partial (PR) reinforcement during training in rats with a lesion of the dorsal noradrenergic bundle (DB lesioned) or a sham operation. The point "A" marks the final day of acquisition. (a) Start section. (b) Run section. (c) Goal section.

tal area or hippocampus should not affect the FE. This prediction, too, is supported by the data (Henke, 1977; Mabry & Peeler, 1972; Swanson & Isaacson, 1969). Amygdaloid lesions, in contrast, eliminate the FE and leave the PREE observed in the same animals intact (Henke, 1977). Thus, if the DANB subserves anxiety and if it does so in virtue of its projection to the SHS rather than to the amygdala, its destruction should not alter the FE. This is the result that we have obtained in our experiments (Owen et al., 1982b). Furthermore, as in Henke's (1977) experiment with total septal le-

amygdala not involved

sions and Gray and Dudderidge's (1971) experiment with sodium amobarbital injections, the same animals that showed a normal FE were impaired in the PREE (confirming the results shown in Fig. 6.7) when they were subsequently extinguished in the first half of the double runway. This pattern of results is consistent with the hypothesis that the critical DANB projection is to the SHS. And, in conjunction with Henke's (1977) findings, it weakens the case that a critical role is played by the DANB projection to the amygdala, at least insofar as responses to nonreward or to signals of nonreward are concerned.

The hypothesis that the DANB projection of to the SHS, rather than the entire NE projection to the forebrain, mediates behavioral responses to signals of nonreward is potentially capable of reconciling the otherwise contradictory positions adopted by Stein (this volume) and the present authors. An important part of the evidence gathered by Stein's group in support of his position was derived from experiments in which NE and other substances were injected into the ventricles of animals performing various rewarded and/or punished responses (Wise et al., 1973). Provided we make the important assumption that the injected substances acted on the postsynaptic receptor (discussed later), their evidence is indeed consistent with the hypothesis that NE mediates reward processes, not responses to punishment or nonreward. For example, NE did not increase the suppression of punished behavior, as must be predicted from our hypothesis, but rather decreased it, a finding which is consistent with an increase in the approach (rewarded) component of the approach-avoidance conflict in which the animals found themselves. What is not clear, however, is which brain structures are affected by NE injected into the ventricles. The bulk of the noradrenergic innervation of the hippocampal formation is located in the hilus, some distance from the ventricles. It is likely, therefore, that intraventricular NE acts mainly on structures other than the SHS. Thus, it is possible that noradrenergic terminals in certain circumventricular structures play a role in mediating behavioral responses to reward, as postulated by Stein, whereas those in the SHS are concerned with nonreward and punishment.

But a second possible account[2] of the effects seen after ventricular injection of NE is that these are due to an action on presynaptic receptors. Favoring this interpretation is the fact that Wise et al.'s (1973) pharmacological experiments showed that the NE acted on an alpha-adrenergic, not a beta-adrenergic, receptor. And alpha receptors in the brain have usually been identified as presynaptic (Starke, 1979). Because the effect of an adrenergic agonist at a presynaptic receptor is to *decrease* (by homeostatic feedback) the output of the adrenergic neuron to the

define

[2]The arguments set out in this paragraph owe much to a discussion with Larry Stein during the original symposium in Philadelphia.

postsynaptic receptor (Langer, 1979), this account of Wise et al.'s (1973) findings would completely reverse the interpretation these authors placed upon them. The fact that intraventricular NE *decreased* the suppression of punished behavior would now be consistent with the hypothesis that forebrain NE mediates the effects of punishment for the decreased behavioral suppression would arise from reduced activity at postsynaptic receptors. If this interpretation of Wise et al.'s (1973) findings is correct, it should be possible to abolish the effects they observed by destroying the noradrenergic fibers on which the presynaptic alpha receptors are located (e.g., by injection of 6-OHDA in the DANB). If intraventircular NE acts presynaptically, animals treated in this way would no longer respond to it. However, if the action of the neurotransmitter is postsynaptic, intraventricular NE would continue to act as in the intact animal; indeed, it is possible that one might obtain a supranormal effect owing to the development of denervation supersensitivity.

It may be possible along one or another of these lines to reconcile the data supporting Stein's position and those supporting our own. Some resolution of this issue is certainly necessary. For we have recently extended our experiments to encompass the same kind of conflict behavior studied by Stein's group, and our results are, on the face of it, in flat contradiction to theirs.

The Dorsal Noradrenergic Bundle and Punishment

These experiments have been concerned with a phenomenon that is closely analogous to the PREE, namely, the "partial punishment effect" (PPE). Like the PREE, the PPE is demonstrated in the straight alley as a difference in running speed between two groups that receive different kinds of training. One group is given simple CRF training with food reward. The other, "partial punishment" (PP), group also receives food on every trial, but in addition it receives electric food shock in the goal box on a randomly chosen proportion of trials. The shock is initially of low intensity, but gradually it is increased to a moderately high level (in our experiments, .3–.35 mA). At the end of training both groups enter a test phase in which, on every trial, running into the goal box is followed by both food and the high intensity shock. As shown in Fig. 6.8, the PP group shows much more resistance to the punishing effects of shock (i.e., it runs down the alley much more rapidly) than the CRF group during the test phase: This phenomenon is the PPE (Davis, Brookes, Gray, & Rawlins, 1981).

We first studied the effects of an antianxiety drug, chlordiazepoxide *Libriu* (CDP) HCl 5 mg/kg, on the PPE (Davis et al., 1981). As shown in Fig. 6.8,

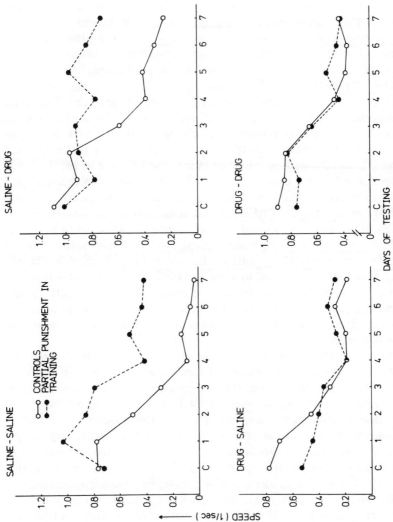

FIG. 6.8   Effect of 5mg/kg chlordiazepoxide ("Drug") given in acquisition only (Drug-Saline), test only (Saline-Drug), or both (Drug-Drug) on the increased resistance to punishment in the test phase produced by partial punishment during training. Controls were not punished during training. The point "C" on the abscissa marks the final day of training. Ordinate: speed in the goal section of the alley.

the effects of this drug are exactly what would be predicted from its known effects on the PREE (Feldon & Gray, 1981) if one simply assumes that signals of punishment are equivalent to signals of nonreward (Gray, 1967; Wagner, 1966). Given during acquisition only, CDP blocks the PPE by reducing resistance to punishment in the PP group during the test phase, without affecting resistance to punishment in the CRF group. Given during the test phase only, CDP increases resistance to punishment in both groups and leaves the PPE unaltered. If CDP is given during both acquisition and the test phase, a compromise between these effects is observed: Resistance to punishment is increased in the CRF group (due to the drug's presence during test); resistance to punishment is changed little in the PP group (the resultant of the opposing effects of the drug given in acquisition and test separately); and the PPE is abolished (due to the presence of the drug during acquisition). These effects are seen when one trial is run each day, but little change occurs when the interval between trials is short, as is also generally the case for the PREE (Feldon et al., 1979).

Given these results and the network of hypotheses set out in this chapter, it follows that animals with lesions to the DANB should behave like the group that received CDP in both acquisition and test. Preliminary results suggest that lesioned rats fail to show the PPE when one trial is run each day due to an increase in resistance to punishment in the CRF group. However, these rats suffered extensive nonspecific damage to brain tissue, so that no firm conclusions can yet be drawn. Further work is needed to clarify this result.

If this result were confirmed, it would seem to oppose two other reports. We have already commented on one of these (Wise et al., 1973) in which NE injected into the ventricles decreased the punishment-produced suppression of bar pressing. The second report is by Mason and Fibiger (1978), who found that DANB lesions had no effect on the acquisition of passive avoidance behavior. However, the behavioral paradigm used in their experiment (step-down passive avoidance) was one that is relatively insensitive to the effects of either antianxiety drugs (Gray, 1977) or lesions to the SHS (Gray, 1982). Using two more sensitive paradigms—the suppression of bar pressing by response-contingent foot shock (punishment) or by a stimulus associated with response-independent shock (on-the-baseline conditioned suppression)—we have observed a reliable release from suppression after DANB lesions in three separate experiments (Tsaltas & Gray, in preparation).

LEARNED PERSISTENCE

Until now, we have discussed the PREE and the PPE simply as examples of the behavioral effects of signals of nonreward and punishment, respectively. However, these two behavioral paradigms also have other implications for the theme of this volume. We have thus far considered impulsivity to be either excessive sensitivity to promised reward or excessive insensitivity to threatened punishment (or nonreward). If we apply these notions to an animal that has experienced partial reinforcement or partial punishment training, we may be inclined to regard it as "impulsive" because these training regimes bias behavior toward continued reward-seeking in spite of the threat of nonreward or punishment, respectively. This point of view is the more compelling, because there is good evidence that the effects of both training schedules spread far beyond the conditions in which training takes place, so that one may speak of a veritable "character formation." Thus, for example, training with a PRF schedule renders an animal also more resistant to punishment; training with a PP schedule renders it also more resistant to extinction; and similar training schedules give rise to increased resistance even to physiological stressors such as extreme cold (for a review, see Gray, Davis, Feldon, Owen, & Boarder, 1981).

There is, however, something undeniably strange about treating persistence in the face of intermittent punishment or nonreward (or "failure," as one might refer to the latter in more familiar human terms) as a sign of impulsivity: on the contrary, one would normally take it to be a sign of a trait ("steadfastness," perhaps), which is the reverse of impulsivity. Thus, there appears to be a major ambiguity in the concept of impulsivity, at least as it has been interpreted in this paper. It is possible that further psychometric research would help dispel this ambiguity. In this connection it is relevant that the older literature (e.g., Eysenck, 1947) attributes traits of persistence to the *introvert*. Assuming this to be the opposite of the extravert's impulsivity, such a trait might arise from the same kind of learning process as that which is provoked in experimental animals by PRF and PP schedules.

The latter point of view is consistent with the results of our experiments on the PREE. These show that the same brain mechanisms responsible for the immediate responses to repeated nonreward (extinction) are also responsible for the development of persistence in the face of intermittent nonreward (PREE). Thus, antianxiety drugs *both* increase resistance to extinction if given after CRF training *and* block the PREE if given during training on a PRF schedule (Feldon et al., 1979; Feldon & Gray, 1981). The same seems to be true for septal (Henke, 1974, 1977), hippocampal (Rawlins, Feldon, & Gray, 1980), and DANB lesions (Owen et al., 1982b). The only physiological treatments that have so far been found to separate these two kinds of effect are small, discretely localized lesions within the septal area. Lesions of the medial septal nuclei increase resistance to extinction without blocking the PREE, and lesions of the lateral septal nuclei block the PREE without increasing resistance to extinction (Feldon & Gray, 1979a, 1979b). The effects of antianxiety drugs on the PPE are also consis-

Behavior Inhibition System

tent with this view. If we apply these findings to the problem of individual differences, it is possible to argue that an animal which is particularly rapid to extinguish after CRF training (i.e., has a particularly reactive BIS) will also be particularly likely to develop added resistance to extinction on a PRF schedule (because this, too, is a function executed by the BIS). A similar argument can be used for the effects of punishment.

There is some evidence in favor of this proposition from studies of sex differences. Beatty and O'Briant (1973) and Guillamon (personal communication) have found that female rats (which are by many measures less fearful than males; Gray, 1971a, 1971b, 1979b) extinguish more slowly than males after CRF training, and Guillamon has also found that females show a smaller PREE. If this pattern holds at the human level, we would expect anxious individuals (neurotic introverts) to show excessive fear when they first encounter threat, but also to become particularly persistent under conditions of repeated threat (provided their behavior does not become totally inhibited early on in this sequence, a pattern which, clinically, might be manifest as a phobia). Such a combination of anxiety and persistence perhaps takes a pathological form in the obsessive-compulsive syndrome. This is a problem to which more psychometric attention might profitably be paid.

We have attempted to study the brain mechanisms involved in the development of resistance to extinction when an animal is trained on a PRF schedule. Our experiments have led to the model shown in Fig. 6.9 (Feldon & Gray, 1979a, 1979b; Gray et al., 1978; Rawlins et al., 1980). According to this model, signals of nonreward are received by neurons in the medial septal area (perhaps sent via the DANB from the locus coeruleus) and then

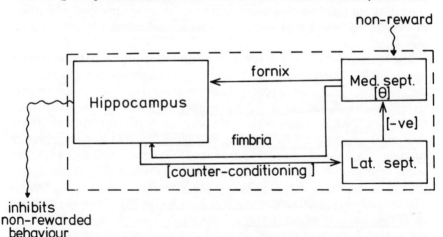

FIG. 6.9   A model for the role played by the septo-hippocampal system in the partial reinforcement extinction effect.

transmitted to the hippocampus by the same pathway that triggers the hippocampal theta rhythm (Rawlins, Feldon, & Gray, 1979; Stumpf, 1965). The hippocampus then has the task: (1) of inhibiting ongoing behavior; (2) of determining the right behavioral strategy under the new conditions. If the right strategy is to continue with the old behavior (as on a PRF schedule), the hippocampus sends a signal to the lateral septal nuclei to cancel the input it is receiving from the medial septal area. This model is able to account for much of the existing data, but it stands in need of much more extensive testing (for some particular problems, see Rawlins et al., 1980).

Responses to Novelty

One virtue of the model shown in Fig. 6.9 is that it enables a rapprochement to be made between experiments on nonreward and the PREE on the one hand and those concerned with novelty and habituation on the other. This possibility arises from the experiments of Vinogradova's group in Moscow (Vinogradova & Brazhnik, 1978). These workers have used single-unit recordings to study orienting reflexes and their habituation in the hippocampal formation of the rabbit. Their observations have led them to propose a model for habituation that is in important respects congruent with our model for partial reinforcement effects. In particular, the critical pathway on which Vinogradova thinks habituation depends is the hippocampal projection to the lateral septal nuclei (Fig. 6.9), which is also the central pathway for the development of the PREE in our model. This convergence of the two models is encouraging because, as pointed out earlier in this paper, one of the postulates of our psychological theory is that novelty, like nonreward, is one of the adequate stimuli for anxiety. Thus, these arguments and the data on which they rest suggest that the habituation of responses to novelty is psychologically similar to the increased resistance to extinction produced by a PRF schedule and physiologically dependent on the same brain mechanisms.

The Dorsal Noradrenergic Bundle and Novelty

Applying this hypothesis to the particular case of DANB lesions, we must predict that these will: (1) impair the immediate response to novelty; (2) impair habituation of responses to novelty. This approach to the behavioral functions of the DANB contrasts with that advocated by Mason (1978), who has proposed that the fundamental deficit produced by DANB lesions is a widening of the span of attention. The major difficulty in Mason's position is that the concept of "attention" is notoriously ill-defined, except within the context of particular theories. Thus, some of the explanations he has advanced for particular experimental findings have a disturbingly post hoc quality about them (e.g., his account of the failure to find increased resistance to extinction in DANB-lesioned animals exposed to repeated extinction of a response rewarded on CRF; Davis, 1979b; Gray, 1982; Mason, 1978). Furthermore, when he has allied his hypothesis to a well-defined theory of attention, as in his attempt (Mason, 1979) to account for the blockade of the PREE by DANB lesions in terms of Sutherland and Mackintosh's (1971) attentional account of this phenomenon, he has been unable to explain the detailed behavior observed (Davis, 1979b; Owen et al., 1982b).

Both hypotheses predict that habituation will take longer in DANB-lesioned rats. This prediction arises directly from our theory: Just as PRF training may be viewed as a way of reducing reactions to nonreward, so too is habituation training a way of reducing reactions to novelty; and just as DANB lesions block the effect of PRF training, so too should they block the effect of habituation. On Mason's hypothesis, the prediction about habituation is derived more loosely from the general notion of a widened span of attention (Mason & Iversen, 1978). The evidence supports the prediction: Mason (Mason & Fibiger, 1977; Mason, Roberts, & Fibiger, 1978) has reported that DANB-lesioned rats persist longer than control animals in exploring a novel object. Where the two hypotheses part company is in their treatment of the immediate response to novelty. As discussed earlier, our hypothesis clearly predicts that this will be weakened, but Mason's hypothesis is ambiguous at this point. If one argues that the increased span of attention increases the likelihood that the target stimulus will be attended to, a greater-than-normal response to novelty is predicted, but if one argues that the increased span of attention will result in the animal attending to stimuli other than the target, a weakened response will be observed. It is not clear how one could distinguish between these two possibilities. The data show both increased and decreased responses to novelty in DANB-lesioned animals; so the ambiguity of Mason's position is perhaps an advantage as well as a weakness.

An increased response to novelty was observed in DANB-lesioned animals by Fibiger et al. (1975) and by Roberts et al. (1976) in experiments in which novel stimuli were placed in an alley during performance of a learned running response. Our results (Fig. 6.5) in the experiment in which DANB-lesioned and intact rats were compared with and without pretraining before rewarded running in the alley may perhaps be interpreted in the same way. Impaired running was seen in the lesioned animals only when they were not given pretraining; this finding could be attributed to the interfering effects of responses to the novel alley and to the novel stimuli associated with handling. An alternative account of this finding might attribute it not to strong immediate responses to novelty but (in accordance with our theory) to excessive slowness to habituate in the lesioned animals. This would predict that the deficit seen in the lesioned animals would be absent on early training trials; as shown in Fig. 6.5, there was only a tendency for this to be the case. So these results, like those reported by Fibiger et al. (1975) and Roberts et al. (1976), are difficult to integrate into our theory, whereas they fit comfortably into Mason's.

Results more in line with our theory were obtained in an experiment specifically designed to test it. This made use of the rat's tendency to approach a novel stimulus in an otherwise familiar environment. The apparatus consists of a T-maze in which one arm is black and one white (counterbalanced as to side). The rat is first placed in the stem of the maze, with access to the arms barred by plexiglass partitions. It is left like this for 3 minutes and then removed. One arm is now changed so that both are either black or white, the partitions are removed, and the animal is replaced in the stem. About 75% of normal animals enter the changed arm, but this response is blocked by the antianxiety drug, sodium amobarbital, as shown by Ison, Glass, and Bohmer (1966) and confirmed in our laboratory (Table 6.2). This effect is consistent with the hypothesis that antianxiety drugs block responses to novelty. It also allows us to make the strong prediction that DANB lesions should have the same effect. As shown in Table 6.2, this is indeed what we observed (Owen et al., in preparation). Furthermore, injection of sodium amobarbital had no effect on the behavior of the lesioned animals; this observation is consistent with the hypothesis that the lesion removes a critical site of action of this drug. It is doubtful whether it is possible to predict this result from Mason's attentional hypothesis, but no doubt one can make sense of it after the event (the lesioned animal would be said to be so busy attending to other things that it failed to notice the alteration in the brightness of one arm of the maze).

Novelty and Impulsivity

Clearly, this is a problem that requires much more research, preferably using paradigms for which a well-articulated theory of attention offers definite predictions. For the moment, it seems possible to conclude only

TABLE 6.2
Effect of 20 mg/kg sodium amylobarbitone ("Amytal") on choice of changed arm in a T-maze in sham-operated rats or rats with a lesion of the dorsal noradrenergic bundle.

| | Number Choosing Changed Arm (out of 16) | | |
	No Drug	Saline	Amytal
Sham	13	12	9
Dorsal NA bundle	7	8	9

that DANB lesions impair habituation (Mason & Fibiger, 1977; Mason et al., 1978); in addition, they apparently alter the immediate response to novelty in a somewhat unpredictable manner. When the data are unreliable, theory is perhaps a better guide to reality; so let us brashly assume that our theory is correct on the second point as well as the first (i.e., that DANB lesions generally decrease the immediate response to novelty). What implications would these conclusions have for the nature of impulsivity?

Ex hypothesi DANB lesions reduce anxiety; that is, in terms of individual differences, they move an individual from the neurotic introvert quadrant of Eysenck's two-dimensional space to the stable extravert quadrant. Thus, we would predict that an impulsive individual occupying this quadrant (venturesome, as defined by Eysenck & Eysenck, 1978; a primary psychopath in some of the reports reviewed by Hare, 1978) would: (1) have weak responses to novelty; (2) be slow to habituate them. The literature on skin-conductance responses supports the first of these predictions when primary Psychopathy or Extraversion is the trait measured (Fowles, 1980; Hare, 1978), although not when Zuckerman's (1978) Sensation Seeking is the trait in question. As to the second, the literature relating habituation of orienting responses to E and N is very contradictory (e.g., Coles, Gale, & Kline, 1971; Mangan & O'Gorman, 1969; Sadler, Mefferd, & Houck, 1971; Stelmack, Bourgeois, Chian, & Pickard, 1979; Wrigglesworth & Smith, 1976). Some probable reasons for this confusion have been discussed by Koriat, Averill, and Malmstrom (1973). Many of them spring from the well-attested "law of initial values," that is, the fact that the rate of habituation is greater, the higher the amplitude of the intitial response (Koriat et al., 1973). This has usually been taken merely as an annoying impediment to easy measurement of habituation rate (as indeed it is). But, in the light of the arguments followed in this section, it may have a more fundamental significance because it is exactly along the lines we predict (high reactivity to novelty going along with rapid habituation). This speculation apart, the relevant literature offers little comfort for the prediction that stable extraverts should habituate slowly, and indeed, this proposition meets with direct contradiction from at least two studies (Mangan & O'Gorman, 1969; Sadler et al., 1971).

CONCLUSION

This chapter has followed a tortuous path through diverse areas of data and theory. We console ourselves with the thought that the state of the art in this truly multidisciplinary field does not yet permit many straight lines. In this final section, we recapitulate the main points of our arguments and the major unanswered questions to which these arguments lead.

In discussing impulsivity we have restricted ourselves to the conceptual framework provided by learning theory and a theory of the emotions (Gray, 1972c, 1973) derived from this. Within this framework we have distinguished four possible approaches to the concept of impulsivity.

First, this may be regarded as excessive sensitivity to stimuli associated with reward (or nonpunishment) coupled with relatively low sensitivity to stimuli associated with punishment (or nonreward). At the personality level (Gray, 1970a) this approach identifies the impulsive individual with an Eysenckian neurotic extravert. In support of this approach, there is evidence from psychometric research (Eysenck & Eysenck, 1977, 1978; Eysenck & Zuckerman, 1978) that some individuals who score high on questionnaire measures of impulsive behavior (those high on the trait designated *Impulsiveness* by these authors) also obtain high E and N scores. There is also evidence that extraverts, as compared to introverts, are more highly sensitive to reward (Gray & Nicholson, 1972; Gupta & Nagpal, 1978; Kantorowitz, 1978; Seunath, 1975).

Second, impulsivity may be regarded as excessive insensitivity to stimuli associated with punishment or nonreward. At the personality level, this approach identifies the impulsive individual with an Eysenckian stable extravert. In support of this approach, the psychometric experiments mentioned in this chapter have disclosed a second trait of impulsive behavior (designated *Venturesomeness* by Eysenck & Eysenck, 1978), which is strong in stable extraverts. It is possible that these individuals include in their number (though presumably as a minority) the primary psychopaths described by Hare and Cox (1978) (secondary psychopaths similarly form part of the neurotic-extravert impulsive group). Strong support for this approach comes from the evidence (Fowles, 1980; Hare, 1978) that primary psychopaths display a specific deficit in fear conditioning and passive avoidance learning.

Third, impulsivity may be treated as an excessive tendency toward aggressive behavior in response to unconditioned punishment or nonreward. It has been tentatively suggested (Gray, 1973) that this tendency underlies individual differences in Eysenck's P dimension. Eysenck and Eysenck (1978) report that both traits of impulsive behavior that they distinguish, Impulsiveness and Venturesomeness, are positively loaded on P. If this observation is reliable, it raises a twofold problem. It suggests a connection between high sensitivity to reward relative to punishment (extraversion) and aggressive responses to unconditioned punishment, a connection for which there is otherwise no obvious biological basis; correspondingly, in psychometric terms, it reduces a three-dimensional space to only two causal mechanisms by linking E and P. Future research should attempt to resolve impulsive traits into those with and without aggressive elements. If this proves to be impossible, the theory advocated in this chapter will require radical surgery.

A fourth and final approach to impulsivity is suggested by the evidence that very general traits of persistence can be developed in animals by training them on schedules in which appetitive and aversive events are unpredictably intermingled (for a review, see Gray et al., 1981). Such traits, if they exist in Man, would naturally be considered the obverse of impulsive behavior. There is evidence that the same brain mechanisms which mediate the initial response to signals of punishment/nonreward also mediate the development of persistence in the face of unpredictable punishment/nonreward (Gray et al., 1978, 1981). Arguments based on this evidence suggest that such persistence should be strongest in Eysenckian neurotic introverts. There is a small amount of data in favor of this deduction insofar as introversion is concerned (Eysenck, 1947), but much more research is required. If the deduction is correct, it is in line with the arguments based on the second approach to impulsivity outlined above. Thus, on both counts the neurotic introvert should be especially unlikely to display impulsive behavior.

This volume is concerned not merely with the psychological nature of impulsivity, but also with its physiological basis. In terms of the various approaches to impulsivity that have been described above, this amounts to a concern with the brain processes that mediate, respectively: (1) responses to stimuli associated with reward (including nonpunishment), (2) responses to stimuli associated with punishment or nonreward (including the development of persistence in the face of such stimuli), and (3) aggressive responses to unconditioned punishment or nonreward.

We have said nothing in this chapter about the first and last of these three processes. This is because we know of little relevant information to add to the treatment accorded these issues by Gray (1972c, 1973). Indeed, in the case of reward processes, in spite of—or perhaps because of—the enormous amount of research prompted by Olds' discovery of electrical self-stimulation of the brain (Wauquier & Rolls, 1976), the picture is now more ambiguous than ever before. For it has become clear that self-stimulation in a particular brain region is a very poor guide as to the functions exercised by that region; it certainly cannot be taken as an indication that these functions include the mediation of reward processes. Time and again it has been shown that destruction of a region that sustains self-stimulation does not lead to any impairment in learning for conventional rewards; instead, as is the case with the dorsal noradrenergic bundle considered in this paper, the most common consequence of such a lesion is that the resistance to extinction of conventionally rewarded behavior is increased. This happens, for example, after lesions to the septal area or frontal cortex (Gray, 1970a, 1970b), both of which sustain self-stimulation (Rolls, 1975; Wauquier & Rolls, 1976). In the case of the dorsal bundle, one possible reason for this pattern of results is that this structure may carry the information "reward expected" to the septo-hippocampal system, which uses it to process and organize responses to *non*reward. On this view, the same information might also be used by other terminal areas to which the locus coeruleus projects (e.g., the amygdala or the cerebellum) in the organization of responses to reward. Stimulation of other DANB terminals would antidromically excite the cell bodies in the locus coeruleus and then orthodromically excite this "reward" target area, giving rise to the self-stimulation phenomenon. But only in the reward target area itself would such self-stimulation be a good index of normal function, and there would be no way of telling from self-stimulation studies alone which the reward target area is.

Unable to contribute much directly to the physiology of reward, we have concentrated instead on the brain system that mediates responses to signals of nonreward and punishment. We have dealt in detail with only one part of this system: the dorsal ascending noradrenergic bundle. Stein has argued forcefully that this fiber tract mediates responses to reward, and Zuckerman has adopted this hypothesis in his theory of the biological basis of Sensation Seeking. We believe that Stein's hypothesis is wrong, and therefore that Zuckerman should look elsewhere for the biological basis of the personality traits he has described. We have reviewed some of the evidence, including that gathered in several unpublished experiments in our laboratory, which is incompatible with the reward hypothesis of the functions of the DANB and which indicates instead a role in response to signals of nonreward, and possibly to those of punishment. Our experiments show that destruction of the dorsal bundle not only reduces the response to nonreward when this event first occurs, but also the capacity to develop persistence or behavioral tolerance for this event. In addition, they suggest that the critical projection of the DANB for these effects is to the SHS, a system that has previously been implicated in these kinds of behavior (Gray et al., 1978).

If we apply these findings to the theme of this volume, we can infer that anxious (neurotic-introverted) individuals have a highly reactive SHS and/or DANB input to the SHS, giving rise both to strong reactions to threatened nonreward and the development of behavioral persistence after exposure to intermittent nonreward. The converse biological characteristics would then underlie the kind of impulsive behavior seen in the stable extravert (i.e., Venturesomeness, according to Eysenck and Eysenck, 1978).

A different view of the functions of the DANB has been advanced by Mason (Mason & Iversen, 1978), namely, that this is concerned with the focusing of attention on task-relevant stimuli. On this view, the consequences of damage to the DANB consist of a widening in the span of attention. Our own theory also predicts that destruction of the DANB will alter behavioral responses to novelty, because this is one of the stimuli that activate the BIS. Furthermore, Vinogradova's research on the way in which the SHS processes information about novelty/familiarity (Vinogradova &

Brazhnik, 1978) has generated a model for habituation of orienting reflexes that is congruent with our model (Gray et al., 1978) for the PREE, a phenomenon which may be viewed as the habituation of responses to signals of nonreward. It follows from both Mason's theory and ours that habituation should be slowed after DANB lesions, and there is evidence in support of this deduction (Mason & Fibiger, 1977; Mason et al., 1978). Our hypothesis also predicts that the immediate response to novelty should be weakened, whereas Mason's is ambiguous—as are the data—on this point. This is an area in which further experimental work is badly needed.

At the personality level, our theory predicts that stable extraverts should show weak responses to novelty, and this prediction is generally supported by the data (Fowles, 1980; Hare, 1978). It also predicts that stable extraverts should be slow to habituate. On this point there is a dearth of clearly established findings, but there is little sign that the prediction can be supported.

It is right that we should finish our chapter on this cautious note, for we are conscious that we have raised many more questions than we have answered. We hope that by posing these questions, we shall stimulate attempts to answer them, at both the animal and the human levels.

ACKNOWLEDGMENTS

The research reported in this paper is supported by the United Kingdom Medical Research Council.

REFERENCES

Amsel, A. Frustrative nonreward in partial reinforcement and discrimination learning: Some recent history and a theoretical extension. *Psychological Review,* 1962, *69,* 306–328.

Amsel, A., & Roussel, J. Motivational properties of frustration. I. Effects on a running response of the addition of frustration to the motivational complex. *Journal of Experimental Psychology,* 1952, *43,* 363–368.

Anlezark, G. M., Crow, T. J., & Greenaway, J. P. Impaired learning and decreased cortical norepinephrine after bilateral locus coeruleus lesions. *Science,* 1973, *181,* 682–684.

Beatty, W. W., & O'Briant, D. A. Sex differences in extinction of food-rewarded approach responses. *Bulletin of the Psychonomic Society,* 1973, *2,* 97–98.

Clavier, R. M., Fibiger, H. C. & Phillips, A. G. Evidence that self-stimulation of the region of the locus coeruleus in rats does not depend upon noradrenergic projections to telencephalon. *Brain Research,* 1976, *113,* 71–81.

Coles, M. G. H., Gale A., & Kline, P. Personality and habituation of the orienting reaction: Tonic and response measures of electrodermal activity. *Psychophysiology,* 1971, *8,* 54–63.

Crow, T. J. Catecholamine neurones and self-stimulation: 2. A theoretical interpretation and some psychiatric implications. *Psychological Medicine,* 1973, *3,* 66–73.

Crow, T. J., Longden, A., Smith, A., & Wendlandt, S. Pontine tegmental lesions, monoamine neurones and varieties of learning. *Behavioral Biology,* 1977, *20,* 184–196.

Davis, N. M. Attentional hypothesis in question. *Trends in Neuroscience,* 1979, *2,* 170–171.(a)

Davis, N. M. *The role of serotonergic and other mechanisms in behavioural responses to punishment.* Unpublished doctoral dissertation, Oxford University, 1979.(b)

Davis, N. M., Brookes, S., Gray, J. A., & Rawlins, J. N. P. Chlordiazepoxide and resistance to punishment. *Quarterly Journal of Experiment Psychology,* 1981, *33B,* 227–239.

Elliott, K., & Whelan, J. (Eds.). *Functions of the septo-hippocampal system* (CIBA Foundation Symposium 58, new series). Amsterdam: Elsevier, 1978.

Eysenck, H. J. *Dimensions of personality.* New York: Praeger, 1947.

Eysenck, H. J. *The dynamics of anxiety and hysteria.* New York: Praeger, 1957.

Eysenck, H. J. *Crime and personality.* Boston: Houghton Mifflin, 1964.

Eysenck, H. J. *The biological basis of personality.* Springfield, Ill.: Thomas, 1967.

Eysenck, H. J., & Eysenck, S. B. G. *The structure and measurement of personality.* London: Routledge & Kegan Paul, 1969.

Eysenck, H. J., & Eysenck, S. B. G. *Psychoticism as a dimension of personality.* London: Hodder & Stoughton, 1976.

Eysenck, S. B. G., & Eysenck, H. J. The place of impulsiveness in a dimensional system of personality description. *British Journal of Social and Clinical Psychology,* 1977, *16,* 57–68.

Eysenck, S. B. G., & Eysenck, H. J. Impulsiveness and venturesomeness: Their position in a dimensional system of personality description. *Psychological Reports,* 1978, *43,* 1247–1255.

Eysenck, S. B. G., & Zuckerman, M. The relationship between sensation-seeking and Eysenck's dimensions of personality. *British Journal of Psychology,* 1978, *69,* 483–487.

Feldon, J. *The effects of anti-anxiety drugs and selective lesions of the septo-hippocampal system on behavioural responses to non-reward and punishment.* Unpublished doctoral dissertation, Oxford University, 1977.

Feldon, J., & Gray, J. A. Effects of medial and lateral septal lesions on the partial reinforcement extinction effect at one trial a day. *Quarterly Journal of Experimental Psychology,* 1979, *31,* 653–674.(a)

Feldon, J., & Gray, J. A. Effects of medial and lateral lesions on the partial reinforcement extinction effect at short inter-trial intervals. *Quarterly Journal of Experimental Psychology,* 1979, *31,* 675–690.(b)

Feldon, J., & Gray, J. A. The partial reinforcement extinction effect after treatment with chloridazepoxide. *Psychopharmacology,* 1981, *73,* 269–275.

Feldon, J., Guillamon, A., Gray, J. A., De Wit, H., & McNaughton, N. Sodim amylobarbitone and responses to nonreward. *Quarterly Journal of Experimental Psychology,* 1979, *31,* 19–50.

Fibiger, J. C., Roberts, D. C. S., & Price, M. T. C. On the role of telecephalic noradrenaline in learning and memory. In G. Jonsson, T. Malmfors, C. Sachs, (Eds.), *Chemical tools in catecholamine research.* Amsterdam: North-Holland, 1975.

Fowles, D. The three arousal model: Implications of Gray's two-factor learning theory for heart rate, electrodermal activity and psychopathy. *Psychophysiology,* 1980, *17,* 87–104.

Gold, M. S., Redmond, D. E., & Kleber, H. D. Noradrenergic hyperactivity in opiate withdrawal supported by clonidine reversal of opiate withdrawal. *American Journal of Psychiatry,* 1979, *136(1),* 100–101.

Gray, J. A. Disappointment and drugs in the rat. *Advancement of Science,* 1967, *23,* 595–605.

Gray, J. A. Sodium amobarbital and effects of frustrative non-reward. *Journal of Comparative and Physiological Psychology,* 1969, *69,* 55–64.

Gray, J. A. The psychophysiological basis of introversion-extraversion. *Behavioral Research and Therapy,* 1970, *8,* 249–266.(a)

Gray, J. A. Sodium amobarbital, the hippocampal theta rhythm and the partial reinforcement extinction effect. *Psychological Review,* 1970, *77,* 465–480.(b)

Gray, J. A. *The psychology of fear and stress.* New York: McGraw-Hill, 1971.(a)

Gray, J. A. Sex differences in emotional behaviour in mammals including man: Endocrine bases. *Acta Psychologica,* 1971, *35,* 29–46.(b)

Gray, J. A. Learning theory, the conceptual nervous system and personality. In V. D. Nebylitsyn & J. A. Gray (Eds.), *Biological bases of individual behavior.* New York: Academic Press, 1972.(a)

Gray, J. A. The psychophysiological basis of introversion–extraversion: A modification of Eysenck's theory. In V. D. Nebylitsyn & J. A. Gray (Eds.), *Biological bases of individual behaviour.* New York: Academic Press, 1972.(b)

Gray, J. A. The structure of the emotions and the limbic system. In R. Porter, & J. Knight (Eds.), *Physiology, emotion and psychosomatic illness.* Amsterdam: Associated Scientific Publishers, 1972.(c)

Gray, J. A. Causal theories of personality and how to test them. In J. R. Royce (Ed.), *Multivariate analysis and psychological theory.* London: Academic Press, 1973.

Gray, J. A. *Elements of a two-process theory of learning.* London: Academic Press, 1975.

Gray, J. A. Drug effects on fear and frustration: Possible limbic site of action of minor tranquilizers. In L. L. Iversen, S. D. Iversen, & S. H. Snyder (Eds.), *Handbook of psychopharmacology* (Vol. 8). New York: Plenum Press, 1977.

Gray, J. A. The 1977 Myers Lecture: The neuropsychology of anxiety. *British Journal of Psychology,* 1978, *69,* 417–434.

Gray, J. A. Editorial. Anxiety and the brain: Not by neurochemistry alone. *Psychological Medicine,* 1979, *9,* 605–609.(a)

Gray, J. A. Emotionality in male and female rodents: A reply to Archer. *British Journal of Psychology,* 1979, *70,* 425–440.(b)

Gray, J. A. A neuropsychological theory of anxiety. In C. E. Izard (Ed.), *Emotions and psychopathology.* New York: Plenum Press, 1979.(c)

Gray, J. A. A critique of Eysenck's theory of personality. In H. J. Eysenck (Ed.), *A model for personality.* Berlin: Springer-Verlag, 1981.

Gray, J. A. *The neuropsychology of anxiety: An enquiry into the functions of the septo-hippocampal system.* Oxford: Oxford University Press, 1982.

Gray, J. A., Davis, N. M., Feldon, J., Owen, S., & Boarder, M. Stress tolerance: Possible neural mechanisms. In M. Christie, & P. Mellet, (Eds.), *Foundation of psychosomatics* Vol. 1, Behavioural approaches. London: Wiley, 1981.

Gray, J. A., & Dudderidge, H. Sodium amylobarbitone, the partial reinforcement extinction effect and the frustration effect in the double runway. *Neuropharmacology,* 1971, *10,* 217–222.

Gray, J. A., Feldon, J., Rawlins, J. N. P., Owen, S., & McNaughton, N. The role of the septo-hippocampal system and its noradrenergic afferents in behavioural responses to nonreward. In J. Whelan, & K. Elliott (Eds.), *Functions of the septo-hippocampal system* (Ciba Foundation Symposium No. 58, new series). Amsterdam: Elsevier, 1978.

Guidotti, A., Toffano, G., & Costa, E. An endogenous protein modulates the affinity of GABA and benzodiazapine receptors in rat brain. *Nature,* 1978, *275,* 553–555.

Gupta, B. S., & Nagpal, M. Impulsivity/sociability and reinforcement in verbal operant conditioning. *British Journal of Psychology,* 1978, *69,* 203–206.

Hare, R. D. Electrodermal and cardiovascular correlates of psychopathy. In R. D. Hare & D. Schalling (Eds.), *Psychopathic behaviour: Approaches to research.* Chichester: Wiley, 1978.

Hare, R. D., & Cox D. N. Clinical and empirical conception of psychopathy, and the selection of subjects for research. In R. D. Hare & D. Schalling (Eds.), *Psychopathic behaviour: Approaches to research.* Chichester: Wiley, 1978.

Henke, P. G. Persistence of runaway performance after septal lesions in rats. *Journal of Comparative and Physiological Psychology,* 1974, *86,* 760–767.

Henke, P. G. Dissociation of the frustration effect and the partial reinforcement extinction effect after limbic lesions in rats. *Journal of Comparative and Physiological Psychology,* 1977, *91,* 1032–1038.

Ison, J. R., Glass, D. H., & Bohmer, H. M. Effects of sodium amytal on the approach to stimulus change. *Proceedings of the American Psychological Association,* 1966, *2,* 5–6.

Kantorowitz, D. A. Personality and conditioning of tumescence and detumescence. *Behaviour Research and Therapy,* 1978, *16,* 117–123.

Koriat, A., Averill, J. R., & Malmstrom, E. J. Individual differences in habituation: Some methodological and conceptual issues. *Journal of Research in Personality,* 1973, *7,* 88–101.

Langer, S. Presynaptic adrenoceptors and regulation of release. In D. M. Paton (Ed.), *The release of catecholamines from adrenergic neurons.* New York: Pergamon, 1979.

Lidbrink, P., Corrodi, H., Fuxe, K., & Olson, L. The effects of benzodiazepines, meprobamate and barbiturates on central monoamine neurones. In S. Garattini, E. Mussini, & L. O. Randall (Eds.), *The benzodiazepines.* New York: Raven Press, 1973.

Lykken, D. T. A study of anxiety in the sociopathic personality. *Journal of Abnormal and Social Psychology,* 1957, *55,* 6–10.

Mabry, P. D., & Peeler, D. F. Effects of septal lesions on response to frustrative nonreward. *Physiology and Behavior,* 1972, *8,* 909–913.

Mangan, G. L., & O'Gorman, J. G. Initial amplitude and rate of habituation of orienting reaction in relation to extraversion and neuroticism. *Journal of Experimental Research in Personality,* 1969, *3,* 275–282.

Marks, I. M. *Fears and phobias.* London: Heinemann, 1969.

Mason, S. T. Parameters of the dorsal bundle extinction effect: Previous extinction experience. *Pharmacology, Biochemistry and Behavior,* 1978, *8,* 655–659.

Mason, S. T. Noradrenaline and behaviour. *Trends in Neuroscience,* 1979, *2,* 82–84.

Mason, S. T., & Fibiger, H. C. Altered exploratory behaviour after 6-OHDA lesions to the dorsal noradrenergic bundle. *Nature,* 1977, *269,* 704–705.

Mason, S. T., & Fibiger, H. C. 6-hydroxydopamine lesion of the dorsal noradrenergic bundle alters extinction of passive avoidance. *Brain Research,* 1978, *152,* 209–214.

Mason, S. T., & Fibiger, H. C. Neurochemical basis of the dorsal bundle extinction effect. *Pharmacology, Biochemistry and Behavior,* 1979, *10,* 373–380.

Mason, S. T., & Iversen, S. D. Effects of selective forebrain noradrenaline loss on behavioural inhibition in the rat. *Journal of Comparative and Physiological Psychology,* 1977, *91,* 165–173.

Mason, S. T., & Iversen, S. D. Reward, attention and the dorsal noradrenergic bundle. *Brain Research,* 1978, *150,* 135–148.

Mason, S. T., Roberts, D. C. S., & Fibiger, H. C. Noradrenaline and neophobia. *Physiology and Behavior,* 1978, *21,* 353–361.

Masserman, J. H., & Yum, K. S. An analysis of the influence of alcohol on experimental neurones in cats. *Psychosomatic Medicine,* 1946, *8,* 36–52.

Miller, N. E. Learnable drives and rewards. In S. S., Stevens (Ed.), *Handbook of experimental psychology.* New York: Wiley, 1951.

Möhler, H., & Okada, T. Benzodiazepine receptor: Demonstration in the central nervous system. *Science,* 1977, *198,* 849–851.

Moore, R. Y., & Bloom, F. Central catecholamine neuron systems: Anatomy and physiology of the norepinephrine and epinephrine systems. *Annual Review of Neuroscience,* 1979, *2,* 113–167.

Morgan, M. J. Resistance to satiation. *Animal Behaviour,* 1974, *22,* 449–466.

Nicholson, J. N., & Gray, J. A. Peak shift, behavioural contrast and stimulus generalization as related to personality and development in children. *British Journal of Psychology,* 1972, *63,* 47–68.

O'Keefe, J., & Nadel, L. *The hippocampus as a cognitive map.* New York: Oxford University Press, 1978.

Olton, D. S., Becker, J. T., & Handelmann, G. E. Hippocampus, space and memory. *Behavioral & Brain Sciences,* 1979, *2,* 313–322.

Owen, S., Boarder, M., Gray, J. A., & Fillenz, M. Lesions of the dorsal noradrenergic bundle and rewarded running: The role of pretraining. *Behavioural Brain Reseach,* 1982, *5,* 3–9.(a)

Owen, S., Boarder, M., Gray, J. A., & Fillenz, M. Acquisition and extinction of continuously and partially reinforced running in rats with lesions of the dorsal noradrenergic bundle. *Behavioural Brain Research,* 1982, *5,* 11–41.(b)

Rawlins, J. N. P., Feldon, J., & Gray, J. A. Septo-hippocampal connections and the hippocampal theta rhythm. *Experimental Brain Research,* 1979, *37,* 49–63.

Rawlins, J. N. P., Feldon, J., & Gray, J. A. The effects of hippocampectomy and of fimbria section upon the partial reinforcement extinction effect in rats. *Experimental Brain Research,* 1980, *38,* 273–283.

Roberts, D. C. S., Price, M. T. C., & Fibiger, H. C. The dorsal tegmental noradrenergic projection: Analysis of its role in maze learning. *Journal of Comparative and Physiological Psychology,* 1976, *90,* 363–372.

Rolls, E. T. *The brain and reward.* New York: Pergamon Press, 1975.

Sadler, T. G., Mefferd, R. B., & Houck, R. L. The interaction of extraversion and neuroticism in orienting response habituation. *Psychophysiology,* 1971, *8,* 312–318.

Seunath, O. M. Personality, reinforcement and learning. *Perceptual and Motor Skills,* 1975, *41,* 459–463.

Squires, C., & Braestrup, R. F. Benzodiazepine receptors in rat brain. *Nature,* 1977, *266,* 732–734.

Starke, K. Presynaptic regulation of release in the central nervous system. In D. M. Paton (Ed.), *The release of catecholamines from adrenergic neurons.* New York: Pergamon, 1979.

Stein, L. Chemistry of purposive behaviour. In J. Tapp (Ed.), *Reinforcement and behaviour.* London: Academic Press, 1969.

Stein, L., Wise, C. D., & Berger, B. D. Anti-anxiety action of benzodiazepines: Decrease in activity of serotonin neurons in the punishment system. In S. Garattini, E. Mussini & L. O. Randall (Eds.) *The benzodiazepines.* New York: Raven Press, 1973.

Stelmack, R. M., Bourgeois, R. P., Chian, J. Y. C., & Pickard, C. W. Extraversion and the orienting reaction: Habituation rate to visual stimuli. *Journal of Research in Personality,* 1979, *13,* 49–58.

Stumpf, C. Drug action on the electrical activity of the hippocampus. *International Review of Neurobiology,* 1965, *8,* 77–138.

Sutherland, N. S., & Mackintosh, N. J. *Mechanisms of animal discrimination learning.* London: Academic Press, 1971.

Swanson, A. M., & Isaacson, R. L. Hippocampal lesions and the frustration effect in rats. *Journal of Comparative and Physiological Psychology,* 1969, *68,* 562–567.

Taffel, C. Anxiety and the conditioning of verbal behaviour. *Journal of Abnormal and Social Psychology,* 1955, *51,* 496–501.

Tye, N. C., Everitt, B. J., & Iversen, S. D. 5-hydroxytryptamine and punishment. *Nature,* 1977, *268,* 741–742.

Vinogradova, O. S., & Brazhnik, E. S. Neuronal aspects of septo-hippocampal relations. In K. Elliott & J. Whelan (Eds.), *Functions of the septo-hippocampal system* (Ciba Foundations Symposium, No. 58, new series). Amsterdam: Elsevier, 1978.

Wagner, A. R. Frustration and punishment. In R. M. Haber (Ed.), *Current research on motivation.* New York: Holt, Rinehart & Winston, 1966.

Wauquier, A., & Rolls, E. T. (Eds.) *Brain stimulation and reward.* Amsterdam: North-Holland, 1976.

Wise, C. D., Berger, B. D., & Stein, L. Evidence of noradrenergic reward receptors and serotonergic punishment receptors in the rat brain. *Biological Psychiatry,* 1973, *6,* 3–21.

Wrigglesworth, M. J., & Smith, B. D. Habituation and dishabituation of the elctrodermal orienting reflex in relation to extraversion and neuroticism. *Journal of Research in Personality,* 1976, *10,* 437–445.

Zuckerman, M. Sensation seeking and psychopathy. In R. D. Hare & D. Schalling (Eds.), *Psychopathic behaviour: Approaches to research.* Chichester: Wiley, 1978.

Zuckerman, M. Sensation seeking and risk taking. In C. E. Izard (Ed.), *Emotions in personality and psychopathology.* New York: Plenum Press, 1979.

Most personality theorists who have attempted to develop a psychobiological model for personality recognize that comparative studies are essential. If we are to understand human differences in terms of underlying biological systems, we must recognize that such systems have evolved over long periods of time and can be identified in nonhuman species as well as in humans. Furthermore, critical biological experiments must, by necessity, be performed on species other than humans. But theorists have differed in their strategy for identifying the common biological systems and their behavioral correlates across species. Some, like Eysenck, Barratt, Schalling, and myself, have preferred to work primarily at the human level, drawing from the work of others in the neurophysiological study of nonhuman animals where such work has seemed relevant. We have identified what we feel to be basic dimensions of personality through questionnaire, behavioral, and psychophysiological studies of humans. Others, most prominently Stein, have attempted to define major mechanisms of behavior from nonhuman species. Gray is a two-front theorist, working from the human level down and from the nonhuman level up. This is an exemplary strategy, and there are few psychologists with the Renaissance breadth of expertise to bridge the evolutionary gap. The general learning theories of the 1930s–1940s attempted to do this, but interest in such broad theories has waned. Gray has continued this attempt at broad theoretical synthesis and has published his own learning theory (Gray, 1975), which is equally applicable to humans and rats.

But the danger in this approach is similar to that of starting a railroad from two widely separated points in space: the tracks may not meet at the

same point in the middle. As an example, Gray points out that his definitions and axioms lead to a classification of eight possible emotional states,
but evidence from lower mammals (e.g., the rat) suggests that only three of
these states need be considered: anxiety, elation/relief, and anger. Studies
of basic human emotions have usually revealed a somewhat longer list
(Izard, 1977). Although some of the additional emotions may really represent blends of the neurophysiologically defined basic three or may be
limited to expressive functions, it is conceivable that the restricted view
from the behavior of the rat omits some crucial human dimensions.

Gray's (1964) earlier theory represented an attempt to integrate the
Pavlovian idea of "strength of the nervous system" and Western notions of
an optimal level of arousal as bases for individual differences in personality
(e.g., Eysenck, 1967; Zuckerman, 1969; Zuckerman, Kolin, Price, & Zoob,
1964). In the 1970s, Gray (1971, 1972) began to elaborate a new theory
based on the developments in neurophysiology that identified primary
reward and punishment areas in the limbic system (Olds & Olds, 1965).
These areas are also thought to mediate basic emotional reactions
associated with reward and punishment. Initially, Gray relied on Eysenck's
three basic dimensions of personality in an attempt to develop an isomor-
phic representation in the real nervous system. But later he (Gray, 1973)
concluded that the personality dimensions that directly paralleled the neurophysiological structure were at a 45° angle in factor-space to Eysenck's extraversion and neuroticism dimensions. (See Gray, 1982, for his most recent
critique of Eysenck's theory.) These dimensions of anxiety and impulsivity
are described in this chapter.

In this new formulation, introversion-extraversion represents the relative
strengths of the reward and punishment arousal sensitivities, and
neuroticism reflects general emotionality or arousability of either system.
Impulsivity represents the maximal contrast in favor of the reward relative
to the punishment susceptibility, and anxiety represents the reverse contrast.

The conclusion that anxious persons are more susceptible to signals of
punishment seems to be in accord with clinical observation as well as experimentation with such persons. But the conclusion that impulsives are
more susceptible to reward is less immediately obvious. Descriptions of
psychopaths, who represent the clinical extreme of impulsivity, stress their
lack of positive affective arousal as well as negative affective arousal. If
anything, they would be more like the stable extravert in Fig. 6.3, with weak
emotional responses in general but a predominance of reward-related emotions over punishment-related emotions. Gray does speak of two types of
psychopaths: (1) the primary psychopath, high on E and venturesomeness
(Eysenck's term for sensation seeking) and low on N; (2) the secondary
psychopath, high on E and narrow impulsivity *and* high on N. Studies by

Emmons and Webb (1974) and Blackburn (1978) show that the primary psychopath is high on sensation seeking, particularly that of the disinhibition variety. Apart from samples of psychopaths, sensation seeking is not correlated with the anxiety of neuroticism dimension at all, but it does correlate positively with both Eysenck's P and E dimensions. In terms of Gray's theory, this would mean that sensation seekers are those with a relatively greater susceptibility to reward, relative to punishment, and strong tendencies toward anger and aggression (P). Studies of sensation seeking do show a kind of positive affect associated with SS state (Zuckerman, 1979, 1980), but aggression trait correlates low with sensation seeking, and the correlation is largely limited to the Disinhibition scale.

Gray's theory is like Stein's at the behavioral level in that both theories suggest that reward and nonpunishment are functionally equivalent, and punishment and nonreward are also equivalent. Gray's theory stresses the states elicited by conditioned stimuli associated with punishing/nonrewarding events (anxiety) and stimuli associated with rewarding/nonpunishing events (elation/relief), whereas Stein's makes little distinction between primary and secondary reinforcement or conditioned and unconditioned stimuli. But apart from this, a fundamental disagreement has emerged about which neurotransmitters mediate the neural circuits involved in reward and punishment. As we saw in Chapter 5, Stein believes that the reward system is served by the catecholamine neurotransmitters, norepinephrine (NE) and dopamine, and that the punishment system is mediated by serotonin. Although not committing himself on the neurotransmitter of the reward system, Gray has marshaled a considerable amount of experimental evidence to support his contention that NE is the transmitter that serves the behavioral-inhibition system rather than the reward system and is therefore associated with the trait of anxiety or fearfulness.

One of the reasons for arranging the symposium from which this book grew was to bring the two theorists together to see if some resolution, or at least a clarification of differences, could be effected. Because my theory of sensation seeking involved Stein's catecholamine hypothesis of the biology of reward, I had hoped to see a resolution. Sparks flew, and some differences were clarified, but neither protagonist backed far from his position.

Although this volume is not primarily concerned with anxiety, it is clear that an understanding of the central mechanisms of this state and trait is crucial in understanding the states and traits of impulsivity and sensation seeking. Though most agree that anxiety and impulsivity/sensation seeking are orthogonal traits, it is acknowledged that the two states interact in a wide variety of conflict situations.

Gray has tried to deduce the mechanisms underlying the state of anxiety from the behavioral effects of the antianxiety drugs, among which he includes the benzodiazepines, barbituates, and alcohol. His hypothesis is that these drugs disinhibit anxiety-inhibited behavior through the behavioral inhibition system (BIS). NE is assumed to be one of the neurotransmitters of this system. The neurochemical mechanisms of action of these drugs is unclear. Although the barbiturates and benzodiazepines decrease turnover rates of dopamine and serotonin, and block stress-induced norepinephrine turnover, the mechanism for this is not clear. The action of the benzodiazepines seems to involve the serotonergic system more than the catecholamine systems (Raese, 1977). Gray does not disagree with Stein about the role of ascending serotonergic pathways in the anxiety system but maintains that the ascending noradrenergic pathways are also involved in this system.

In Chapter 5, Stein presented evidence of the crucial role of NE in maintaining brain self-stimulation. Gray, using a different methodology, finds that partial destruction of the dorsal noradrenergic bundle (DANB) has no effect upon the rat's capacity to learn to perform responses for natural rewards, such as food, in a running alley or a Skinner box. The question of the appropriateness of self-stimulation as a measure of reward motivation is raised in regard to Stein's views. Olds and Fobes (1981) have discussed this issue in their review of self-stimulation studies. Many of the same operations that increase or reduce hunger or thirst drives, and thereby increase or reduce responding for relevant reward reinforcements, also increase or reduce self-stimulation in hypothalamic brain sites. Olds and Fobes (1981) conclude:

> The findings are clearly indicative of some overlap between homeostatic mechanisms in the hypothalamus and SS reward mechanisms. However the view of a reward mechanism owing its properties to activities of hypothalamic homeostatic mechanisms may no longer be tenable and would in any event appear to be incomplete. Such an account says nothing about sites outside the hypothalamus that support SS [p. 534].

One can conceive of a central reward mechanism interlocked with more specific reward circuits but capable of being activated by signals associated with primary rewards or stimuli produced by the rewards themselves such as tastes, odors, sights, and sounds that may constitute unconditioned reward. Novelty itself, in the form of any stimuli of moderate intensity, may activate reward centers instead of just anxiety centers as suggested by Gray.

Another line of evidence that Gray presents concerns the sensitivity of the partial reinforcement effects to destruction of the DANB system on the assumption that this system mediates anxiety (nonreward) rather than reward. By making the partially reinforced animals less sensitive to signals of nonreinforcement, antianxiety drugs or destruction of the DANB should eliminate or reduce the difference between continuously and partially reinforced animals. Results confirming these hypotheses are presented by Gray.

The interpretation of these results depends on assumptions made about the basis for the partial reinforcement effect. If one were to assume, for instance, that the effect depended on a reward expectancy generated by the irregularity of reinforcement during training, then the influence of the destruction of DANB could be attributed to a decrease in strength of the reward rather than the anxiety mechanism.

More directly relevant to the reward versus anxiety controversy concerning NE are studies of the effects of NE and serotonin on behavior inhibited by association with punishment. Stein (1981 this volume), has presented a number of studies showing that norepinephrine injected into the ventricles enhances or restores responding for self-stimulation reward and increases the rate of punished responses. But Gray questions these results and suggests that intraventricular NE may be acting on structures other than the septo-hippocampal system (SHS) and that it is these structures that mediate reward, whereas the SHS norepinephrine mediates nonreward and punishment. An alternative hypothesis offered by Gray is that ventricular injection of NE acts on presynaptic rather than postsynaptic receptors. Such action would tend to *decrease* the release of NE homeostatically and therefore the output of the transmitter to the postsynaptic receptor. This would mean that reduced NE produced by injection of NE into the ventricles produced the decreased suppression of punished behavior actually seen in Stein's experiments. It is difficult to see why reduction of a transmitter for punishment-relative stimuli would enhance or restore reward-related responding. But this is still an interesting hypothesis, which suggests the possibility of an inverse relationship between ventricular NE and NE in the neurons. Many studies of humans, mostly patients, have used either cerebrospinal fluid NE or the NE metabolite 3-methoxy-4-hydroxy phenylglycol (MHPG) to make estimates of neuronal levels of NE. One such study of normals is presented in Chapter 7. This study found positive relationships between cerebrospinal fluid (CSF) NE and MHPG in CSF and plasma.

Stein (1981) has presented his most recent arguments for the idea that the benzodiazepines relieve punishment-induced inhibition primarily through reducing serotonin activity not NE activity. Specifically, he states: "Tranquilizers may exert their anxiety-reducing effects at least in part by a reduction of central serotonin activity" and their (high-dose) depressant effects at least in part by reduction in central norepinephrine activity" [p. 203].

Studies of conflict, which pit milk reward against shock punishment for response, show that release of punished behavior is produced only by benzodiazepines and related tranquilizers and not by phenothiazines and butyrophenones, which have a stronger central catecholamine blocking effect than the tranquilizers. Specific NE antagonists also failed to release punishment-suppressed behavior. In fact, one such antagonist of NE strongly suppressed both punished *and* nonpunished behaviors showing the involvement of NE in general activity. It is this reduction in activity that may lead to the misconception that the antipsychotic drugs are also antianxiety drugs. There is a difference between the selective effect on inhibited or agitated behavior of the antianxiety drugs and the general behavior-dampening effect of other types of drugs.

In contrast to the effect of NE antagonists, Stein (1981) reports that serotonin antagonists do counteract the suppressive effects of punishment. Furthermore, building up serotonin in the brain through infusion of a precursor and an inhibitor of monoamine oxidase (thereby reducing deamination) caused suppression of food-rewarded behavior. These results suggest that serotonin may inhibit reward-related activity as well as facilitate punishment-related activity. Gray might argue, as he did concerning NE infusion studies, that intraventricular administration actually reduces rather than increases the neuronal availability of serotonin through action on presynaptic rather than postsynaptic receptors.

Both Stein's and Gray's theories deal more with responses to stimuli or situations that have been associated with reward or punishment than with responses to novel stimuli or new situations. Gray's (1976) theory suggests that the response to novelty is mediated by the anxiety mechanism located in the DANB. The first response to novelty is the *orienting reflex* (OR), a behavioral inhibition with orientation of receptors toward the stimulus and a pattern of physiological arousal simliar in some respects, but not in others, to fear arousal. The differences in response patterns constitute the difference between what are called orienting reflexes (ORs) and *defensive reflexes* (DRs elicited by very intense or noxious stimuli). I have presented evidence in Chapter 2 that the OR is associated with high sensation seeking trait and is inhibited by state anxiety in normals (Neary & Zuckerman, 1976). Anxiety neurotics also show weak initial OR's and slow habituation of the OR (Lader & Wing, 1966). More recent evidence using heart rate (Orlebeke & Feij, 1979; Ridgeway & Hare, 1981) shows that high sensation seekers of the disinhibitory type show strong ORs, whereas low disinhibitors show weak ORs or strong DRs (and/or possibly startle responses) to stimuli of moderately strong intensity. The initial OR to a novel stimulus represents a state of heightened alertness or interest pending further appraisal of the stimulus. The adaptive value of the OR is to facilitate information processing, and it is reduced by states of anxiety. Defensive and startle reflexes are amplified by anxiety.

Depending on subsequent appraisal of the stimulus, the organism may engage in exploration, approaching the stimulus, or entering the situation. Sensation seekers and impulsives are defined as individuals who are more prone to explore novel situations and activities rather than to withdraw from them, even when there is some appraisal of risk. Studies of open-field behavior in rodents (discussed in Chapter 2) reveal two relatively independent factors in the open-field situation: exploration and emotionality (fearfulness). It is the interaction between these factors and the systems that underlie them that determines the behavior in the situation. Gray (1971) also suggested that more than fear is involved in open-field behavior. If, as Stein postulates, dopamine and NE mediate exploration and disinhibition and serotonin (5-HT) is the substrate of the punishment-inhibition system, then high levels of dopamine and NE and low levels of 5-HT should produce maximal exploratory behavior, whereas the opposite state of balance should produce inhibition and emotionality in the open field.

The studies of Ellison (1977), discussed briefly in Chapter 2, are quite relevant to these questions because he selectively depleted NE, serotonin (5-HT), or both in rats and observed their reactions in the familiar environment of a rat colony and in a novel environment (i.e., the open-field arena). The responses of the animals in the familiar environment support Stein's model and mine because the low serotonin-high norepinephrine (low 5-HT-high NE) animals (Ellison assumes that by depleting one amine the other is elevated) in the familiar environment are "aroused and exploratory," spending less time in burrows and more time in activity wheels, and are more prone to approach humans than are controls. The low NE-high 5-HT animals are described as "driveless and withdrawn," tending to stay in their burrows, inactive, and the last to come for feeding.

But the behavioral effects of the two kinds of monoamine depletion are quite different in the open-field situation and in the familiar environment. The usually active and exploratory low 5-HT–high NE animals now act "frightened and paranoid," with decreased locomotion, increased rearing (a typical OR in rodents), and a tendency to stay near the walls. The usually withdrawn and inactive low NE–high 5-HT rats act "fearless and nonvigilant" in the open field, locomoting more and hiding less than controls, and often entering the center of the field.

But what of the doubly depleted low NE–low 5-HT animals? These animals were the most helpless in the open field, neither locomoting nor rearing, but remaining huddled near the walls. Ellison concluded that depletion of NE and 5-HT produced reactions in rats that resembled the depression seen in some humans taking the drug reserpine, which also depletes both monoamines.

Unfortunately, these data do not resolve the Stein–Gray controversy, although the extension of findings to more natural situations is interesting. The behavior in familiar environments tends to support Stein's theory, but the behavior in the novel situation of the open field supports Gray's theory. The effects of double depletion suggest an interaction between the two monoamine systems. If we can infer to the opposite extreme of the depletion experiment, a rat high on NE *and* 5-HT would be extremely exploratory in both familiar and nonfamiliar situations. Ellison (1978, personal communication) guesses that such an animal would be "supremely confident and alert." He also speculates that both neurotransmitters are active in response to mild stress. The high norepinephrine animal is primarily conceived of as aroused, and therefore active, in its familiar environment but overaroused in the novel environment or beyond an optimal level of arousal. Ellison (1978, personal communication) agrees that sensation seeking state is correlated with NE release but suggests an interesting counterhypothesis for the trait: ". . . it is individuals with chronically *low* NE who must engage in excessive stimulus seeking (in order to increase their own NE levels)." This challenging hypothesis must be seriously considered in view of recent findings on humans presented in the next chapter.

The pioneering work of Gray represents the most ambitious attempt at a synthesis of human personality data and the neurophysiology of behavior as studied in rats. The Stein–Gray controversy should stimulate further research on the role of norepinephrine in reward and punishment. It is to be hoped that Gray will devote more attention now to the pharmacology of impulsivity and reward.

The conventional approach is to develop hypotheses from correlational data in humans and then to test these in more precisely controlled experiments in animals. But the inconsistencies of the results from the extensive experimental efforts of Stein and Gray suggest that we must move in both directions. Inasmuch as the ultimate goal of the work with rodents is to understand the biology of humans, we must turn back to our species for some answers to the questions raised by the experimental animal work. The earlier chapters have described the attempts to measure sensation seeking, impulsivity, and anxiety as human traits. Metabolites of the monoamines and their neuroregulators are obtainable from cerebrospinal fluid, blood, and urine. Although the relationships of these peripherally obtained measures to the central biochemical levels is mostly unknown, we must begin the work of testing personality-bioamine relationships in humans using the best methods now available. Almost everyone agrees that in living systems we must look at more than one variable at a time in order to make sense of the data. In the next chapter, such a multivariate personality-biochemical study on normal humans is described. This is the first study of such breadth in both psychological and biochemical realms. Let us see what answers we can find to the questions raised so far.

REFERENCES

Blackburn, R. Electrodermal and cardiovascular correlates of psychopathy. In R. D. Hare, & D. Schalling (Eds.), *Psychopathic behavior: Approaches to research.* New York: Wiley, 1978.

Ellison, G.D. Animal models of psychopathology: The low norepinephrine and low-serotonin rat. *American Psychologist,* 1977, *32,* 1036–1045.

Emmons, T. D., & Webb, W. W. Subjective correlates of emotional responsivity and stimulation seeking in psychopaths, normals, and acting-out neurotics. *Journal of Consulting and Clinical Psychology,* 1974, *42,* 620–625.

Eysenck, H. J. *The biological basis of personality.* Springfield, Ill.: Thomas, 1967.

Gray, J. A. Strength of the nervous system and levels of arousal: A reinterpretation. In J. A. Gray (Ed.), *Pavlov's typology.* New York: Macmillan, 1964.

Gray, J. A. *The psychology of fear and stress.* New York: McGraw-Hill, 1971.

Gray, J. A. The psychophysiological nature of introversion–extraversion: A modification of Eysenck's theory. In V. D. Nebylitsyn, & J. A. Gray (Eds.), *Biological bases of individual behavior.* New York: Academic Press, 1972.

Gray, J. A. Causal theories of personality and how to test them. In J. R. Royce (Ed.), *Multivariate analysis and psychological theory.* New York: Academic Press, 1973.

Gray, J. A. *Elements of a two-process theory of learning.* New York: Academic Press, 1975.

Gray, J. A. The neuropsychology of anxiety. In I. G. Sarason, & C. D. Speilberger (Eds.), *Stress and anxiety* (Vol. 3). Washington, D.C.: Hemisphere, 1976.

Gray, J. A. *The neuropsychology of anxiety: An enquiry into the functions of the septohippocampal system.* New York: Oxford University Press, 1982.

Izard, C. *Human emotions.* New York: Plenum Press, 1977.

Lader, M. H., & Wing, L. *Physiological measures, sedative drugs and morbid anxiety* (Maudsley Monograph No. 14). London: Oxford University Press, 1966.

Neary, R. S., & Zuckerman, M. Sensation seeking, trait and state anxiety, and the electrodermal orienting reflex. *Psychophysiology,* 1976, *13,* 205–211.

Olds, J., & Olds, M. E. Drives, rewards and the brain. In F. Baron (Ed.), *New directions in psychology.* New York: Holt, Rinehart, & Winston, 1965.

Olds, M. E., & Fobes, J. L. The central issues of motivation: Intracranial self-stimulation studies. In *Annual review of psychology* (vol. 32). Palo Alto, Cal.: Annual Reviews, 1981.

Orlebeke, J. F., & Feij, J. A. The orienting reflex as a personality correlate. In H. D. Kimmel, E. H. van Olst, & J. F. Orlebeke (Eds.), *The orienting reflex in humans.* Hillsdale, N.J.: Lawrence Erlbaum Associates, 1979.

Raese, J. Sedative hypnotics: Biological mechanisms. In J. D. Barchas, B. A. Berger, R. D. Ciaranello, & G. R. Elliot (Eds.), *Psychopharmacology: From theory to practice.* New York Oxford University Press, 1977.

Ridgeway, D., & Hare, R. D. Sensation seeking and psychophysiological responses to auditory stimulation. *Psychophysiology,* 1981, *6,* 613–618.

Stein, L. Behavioral pharmacology of benzodiazepines. In D. F. Klein, & J. G. Rabkin (Eds.), *Anxiety: New research and concepts.* New York: Raven Press, 1981.

Zuckerman, M. Theoretical formulations: I. In J. P. Zubek (Ed.), *Sensory deprivation: Fifteen years of research.* New York: Appleton-Century-Crofts, 1969.

Zuckerman, M. Sensation seeking: Beyond the optimal level of arousal. Hillsdale, N.J.: Erlbaum, 1979.

Zuckerman, M. To risk or not to risk: Predicting behavior from negative and positive emotional states. In K. R. Blankstein, P. Pliner, & J. Polivy (Eds.), *Assessment and modification of emotional behavior.* New York: Plenum Press, 1980.

Zuckerman, M., Kolin, E. A., Price, L., & Zoob, I. Development of a sensation seeking scale. *Journal of Consulting Psychology,* 1964, *28,* 477–482.

7

A Correlational Test in Humans of the Biological Models of Sensation Seeking, Impulsivity, and Anxiety

Marvin Zuckerman
Department of Psychology
University of Delaware

James C. Ballenger
Department of Behavioral
* Medicine and Psychiatry*
University of Virginia
School of Medicine

David C. Jimerson
Laboratory of Clinical Science
National Institute of
* Mental Health*

Dennis L. Murphy
Clinical Neuropharmacology
* Branch*
National Institute of
* Mental Health*

Robert M. Post
Biological Psychiatry Branch
National Institute of
* Mental Health*

The two preceding chapters presented biochemical theories of the role of neurotransmitters in the central nervous system in the traits of sensation seeking, impulsivity, and anxiety. Zuckerman's theory of sensation seeking (Chapter 2) and Schalling's theory (Chapter 4) have also implicated the monoamine systems in sensation seeking and impulsivity, with Zuckerman's theory being based on Stein's model and Schalling's on Gray's model. Schalling and Zuckerman worked with humans, whereas Stein and Gray approached the problem primarily through pharmacological, experimental studies of rats.

In Chapter 2 Zuckerman proposed an approach that might integrate the data obtained from human and nonhuman species, and Gray (1973) has also offered a plan for comparative studies. But until recently the biochemical studies of human personality dimensions have dealt primarily with neuroregulators, such as monoamine oxidase (MAO) and dopamine-beta hydroxylase (DBH), that regulate the monoamine neurotransmitter systems rather than the neurotransmitters and their metabolites. The neuro-regulators can only provide hints about the role of the bioamines in personality. Although implicating the three monoamine systems, they tell us little about the direction of the relationships or causation. These difficulties in interpreting the results of correlational studies are not to be minimized, but without direct access to the brains of living humans we cannot perform the kinds of experiments in which we directly vary the neurochemistry of the brain. Such studies are performed regularly on abnormal populations of humans who are given psychotropic drugs. Unfortunately, these studies confound the current clinical abnormalities with the personality character-istics that predated them. There have been few studies of the neurotransmit-ters and their metabolites in normal population, and these have focused on a narrow range of biochemical variables. Because the significance of any one of the biochemical measures has not been fully defined, it is useful at this stage to study the full range of measurable neurotransmitters and their metabolites and enzymes. It is to be hoped that this will contribute to the enhanced understanding of the biochemical bases of personality and the functional relationships between the biochemical variables.

The first such study has been recently completed at the National Institute of Mental Health (NIMH) in Bethesda, Maryland (Ballenger, Post, & Goodwin, in press). The study is limited in some respects, such as the number of subjects involved and the heterogeneity of the sample in regard to sex and age, but the results should be of interest to everyone in this field. Other papers based on various aspects of these data have been presented at meetings, published, or are being submitted for publication (Ballenger et al., in press; Ballenger, Post, Jimerson, Lake, Lerner, Bunney, & Goodwin, 1981; Post, Ballenger, Jimerson, & Bunney, submitted 1982; Zuckerman, 1981, 1982).

For the benefit of those readers new to the field of neurotransmitter neurochemistry, we first present a review of the known relationships be-tween the neurotransmitters of interest, their metabolites, and the enzymes that regulate them. Figure 7.1 portrays some of these relationships. The figure is highly schematic, omitting many of the intervening steps in the pro-duction and metabolism of the bioamines.

Central dopamine is acted upon by MAO, and other enzymes not shown, to reduce it to homovanillic acid (HVA). In the norepinephrine (NE) neurons, dopamine is converted to NE by the enzyme dopamine-beta-hydroxylase (DBH). NE is degraded by MAO and catecho-O-methyltrans-ferase (COMT) to 3-methoxy-4-hydroxyphenylglycol (MHPG) in the brain, although VMA is the major metabolite of peripheral NE in man. Serotonin

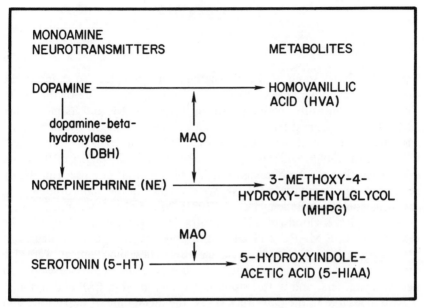

FIG. 7.1   Monoamine neurotransmitters, enzymes, and metabolites.

(5-hydroxytryptamine or 5-HT) is deaminated by MAO to 5-hydroxyin-doleacetic acid (5-HIAA).

The diagram shows why the MAO-sensation seeking relationships found in humans (Chapter 2) implicate at least some of the monoamine systems in the trait. However, it is not possible to make interpretations regarding the neurotransmitters from MAO alone. Even if the assumption is correct that platelet MAO is related to central MAO activity, MAO might be directly or inversely, or not related at all to the levels of the neurotransmitters that it deaminates. If it is related to the levels of the monoamines it might be related to one, two, or all of them. We must go beyond the MAO findings to neurotransmitters themselves, or at least their metabolites like MHPG, HVA, and 5-HIAA, that might have a more direct relationship to the activity of the three systems.

We do not want to underestimate the problems in appraising the activities of these systems in the brain from peripherally obtained samples in humans. However, a vast body of literature on psychopharmacology (Lipton, DiMascio, & Killam, 1978; Wood, 1982, in press) in human clinical populations and nonhuman species supports the validity and importance of using "downstream" measures in the cerebrospinal fluid (CSF) and the peripheral blood as reflectors of biochemical events in the brain.

THE RESEARCH

Biochemical Measures

Figure 7.2 shows some of the alternatives for attempting to estimate the turnover of the bioamines and their regulators from outside of the brain. These are the measures actually used in this study. NE and its metabolite MHPG were measured from the CSF. The locus coeruleus, which projects rostrally into the forebrain, also has tracts leading down to the spinal cord. CSF NE probably provides us with the best measure of activity of the brain NE system that can be obtained outside of the brain because it probably reflects levels of activity in the NE system which in the main originates in the locus coeruleus (Ballenger et al., 1981; Post, Lake, Jimerson, Bunney, Wood, Ziegler, & Goodwin, 1978). Central NE activity is also thought to be reflected in CSF MHPG and DBH and presumably to a lesser degree in plasma and urinary MHPG and plasma DBH. These biochemicals were also measured in the study. Calcium is involved in the release of all neurotransmitters, and in this study it was measured in CSF and serum.

Also measured in the CSF were HVA, the metabolite of dopamine, and 5-HIAA, the metabolite of serotonin. MAO was assayed from blood platelets, and amine oxidase (AO) was measured from the plasma. The urinary measure of MHPG was based on urine collections taken on 2 different days; the two measures were averaged. The platelet MAO and plasma

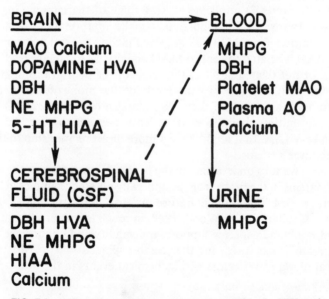

FIG. 7.2   CSF, plasma, and urinary measures used in the NIH study.

AO were also based on the average of two samples. Except for these measures, all of the other variables were measured from a single sample so that they might have been affected by the state of the subjects at the time they were drawn, possibly reflecting the arousal produced by the drawing of blood or the even more stressful lumbar puncture. In anticipation of this problem of interpretation, a state measure of anxiety, as well as trait measures, was used. The Multiple Affect Adjective Check List (MAACL) (Zuckerman & Lubin, 1965) state anxiety scale was given on the morning of the lumbar puncture, shortly before this procedure. The trait version of the same scale, as well as other trait scales, was given 2 weeks before the lumbar puncture. The specific methods used to measure the biochemical variables are described in Jimerson, Markey, Oliver, & Kopin (1981).

Psychological Trait Measures

The psychological tests used included: the Minnesota Multiphasic Personality Inventory (MMPI) (Hathaway & McKinley, 1951), form IV of the Sensation Seeking Scale (SSSIV) (Zuckerman, 1971), the Eysenck Personality Questionnaire (EPQ) (Eysenck & Eysenck, 1975), and the trait version of the MAACL. From the MMPI were selected the scales most likely to assess the traits of *impulsivity* (Psychopathic Deviate, Pd, and Hypomania, Ma), *anxiety* (Depression, D, and Psychasthenia, Pt), and extraversion (Social Introversion, Si). The MAACL provided a third measure of trait anxiety. The trait version of this scale contains the same adjectives as the state version, but the trait form asks the subjects to describe how they "generally" feel, whereas the state version asks how they feel "now." The General scale of the SSS was used because it has been the one most consistently related to MAO in previous studies and is the best overall measure of the trait in form IV.

Although other biochemical psychological measures were used, this analysis was limited to the measures most directly related to the monoamine systems, and to the trait and state measures of the three psychological dimensions of interest in this volume: sensation seeking, impulsivity, and anxiety. Introversion-extraversion was also examined for its relationship to biochemical measures because of its centrality as a dimension of personality. This limitation of the scope of the analysis to the most theoretically relevant variables is one guard against the dangers of post hoc interpretation of what might be chance findings. Other safeguards within the analyses will be described later.

Subjects

Forty-three male and female subjects volunteered to take the psychological tests, have a spinal lumbar puncture done to collect cerebrospinal fluid

(CSF), and donate specimens of blood and urine for analysis. Twenty-four of the subjects were in their second month as paid inpatient volunteers, and nineteen were brought in to stay at the NIH Clinical Center 1 day prior to the lumbar puncture (although the psychological trait tests were given to all subjects 2 weeks before the lumbar puncture). The mean age of the volunteers was 33 ± 14.3 years with a range of 19 to 64 years. Twenty-six subjects were male and seventeen were female. Actual numbers varied for different comparisons because of missing data on some subjects.

All volunteers were interviewed for 1 to 2 hours by a psychiatrist (JCB) using a semistructured interview to determine if they had any medical or psychiatric illness. The interview was evaluated using the Research Diagnostic Criteria (RDC) of Spitzer, Endicott, and Robins (1978). Volunteers were excluded if they met the criteria for any diagnosis at the time of the study. In terms of their history, one volunteer met the RDC criteria for "Alcoholism" 20 years prior to the study, and seven had minor or episodic minor depressions from 6 months to 20 years prior to the study.

Procedures

Because diet or activity could affect some of the biochemical measures, all subjects were on a low monoamine diet for 14 days prior to the blood tests and lumbar puncture. The lumbar puncture was performed after 9 hours of bed rest and fasting. The bed rest provided the control for activity for all subjects prior to the lumbar puncture. The 19 volunteer subjects who lived outside until the day before the lumbar puncture and the 24 who lived in the hospital for 4 to 6 weeks prior to the lumbar puncture did not differ significantly on any of the measured variables.

Statistical Analyses

The basic statistic used was bivariate correlations of the biochemical and psychological variables of interest. Partial correlations were derived from these, controlling for the variables of age, height, and weight. The variable of sex was controlled by examining the correlations for males and females separately as well as for the total group. Consistency between sexes in the magnitude and direction of the correlations was expected, although the low N's for the subgroups might preclude reaching the level of significance ($p < .10$). This sex comparison also provided some replication within the study and a control for chance that might be operating in producing some significant correlations.

Although the data could have been analyzed by multivariate methods (e.g., cannonical correlation), such methods require larger N's, and using them with smaller samples often yields dubious results of uncertain stability.

A two-tailed test of significance was used for the correlations. The .10 level of significance was used rather than the more conservative .05 level because of the exploratory nature of this study.

Results

Relationships among the biochemical variables. The correlations between the CSF and plasma measures indicated a high degree of relationship between measures of the same variable from both sources (Jimerson et al., 1981). CSF-MHPG correlated .74 with plasma total MHPG, and CSF DBH correlated .71 with plasma-DBH. Furthermore, both CSF and plasma MHPG correlated significantly with CSF-NE: .48 for CSF-MHPG and .53 for plasma MHPG. CSF DBH and plasma DBH also correlated positively with CSF-NE ($r = .36$ for CSF DBH, $r = .49$ for plasma DBH). CSF-DBH correlated significantly ($r = .49$) with CSF-MHPG, but plasma DBH did *not* correlate with plasma MHPG ($r = .10$). CSF calcium correlated significantly ($r = .48$) with serum calcium.

These data are consistent with findings that stimulation of the locus coeruleus in rats produces correlated increase in both lumbar CSF *and* plasma MHPG (Crawley, Roth, & Maas, 1979). The high correlation between CSF and plasma MHPG (Jimerson et al., 1981) and between CSF and plasma DBH may be produced in part by the common sources from brain. Data suggest that 20–60% ($\approx 30\%$) of urinary (and plasma) MHPG derive from brain (Blombery, Kopin, Gordon, Markey, & Ebert, 1980; Kopin, Gordon, Jimerson, & Polinsky, submitted, 1982). Alternately, central and peripheral NE systems may be intrinsically related and their neuronal and metabolic activity may be linked together. This interpretation is supported by the finding that CSF and plasma NE are also correlated (Ziegler, Lake, Wood, Brooks, & Ebert, 1977).

If CSF-NE is the most direct available measure of activity of the brain NE system, then the enzyme DBH and metabolite MHPG measured in CSF and plasma, which show moderate correlations with CSF-NE, have some validity as indices of central NE release and metabolism, at least in healthy, drug-free, normal subjects. Urinary MHPG correlated with plasma MHPG ($r = .50$) but not with CSF-NE or MHPG. Since urinary MHPG is derived from blood and is two steps removed from the brain, this finding is expected. Also relevant are data showing that CSF MHPG is 90% free while urinary MHPG is 90% conjugated. CSF 5-HIAA and HVA correlated very highly ($r = .79$), possibly reflecting the influence of a common metabolic acid transport system. These metabolites of serotonin (5-HIAA) and dopamine (HVA) also correlated significantly with CSF MHPG but not with CSF-NE or plasma MHPG.

Since platelet MAO has been considered as an indirect index of brain

MAO, and brain MAO is involved in the breakdown of dopamine, NE, and serotonin to their metabolites, we might expect some relationship between platelet MAO and these metabolites. In fact, platelet MAO correlated negatively with CSF HVA ($-.34$) and 5-HIAA ($-.31$) and positively with plasma MHPG ($r = .33$). Though all of these correlations are significant ($p < .05$), they are low, possibly because they are attenuated by the unknown and perhaps low degree of relationship between platelet and brain MAO.

Relationships among the psychological variables.   Table 7.1 shows the correlations among the psychological traits and state. The General Sensation Seeking Scale (SSS) and the Pd and Ma scales of the MMPI (presumed measures of impulsivity) were significantly intercorrelated, but the magnitudes of the correlations (.34 to .41) indicate that these are not alternate measures of the same construct but rather are assessing related constructs. The MMPI D and Pt (presumed measures of dysphoria or anxiety) were highly correlated ($r = .66$), but neither correlated very highly with the MAACL measure of trait anxiety. The MAACL trait and state measures correlated .31 ($p < .10$), which is a typical level of trait-state correlation (Zuckerman, 1976). The EPQ E and MMPI Si scales were significantly correlated ($r = -.40$), but the Si also correlated as highly or more highly with measures of trait anxiety. The MMPI Si, therefore, measures neurotic-introversion in contrast to the E scale, which measures an introversion–extraversion dimension that is orthogonal to neuroticism and anxiety.

Correlations between biochemical and psychological trait and state measures.   Of the 132 partial correlations between biochemical and psychological variables, 22 were significant. As approximately 13 correlations might have been expected by chance, the results suggest that something more than chance is operating. Furthermore, the patterning of correlations suggests systematic relationships between related variables rather than random ones. The significant partial correlations can be presented in groups of common variables for sake of exposition.

Table 7.2 presents the three significant partial correlations involving the SSS. Sensation seeking was the only psychological variable significantly related to CSF-NE ($r_p = -.49$). Figure 7.3 shows the scatterplot of the original data. The negative correlations were significant for males and females separately as well as for the total group.

The partial correlation between the SSS and plasma DBH was also significant ($r_p = -.60$) as were the original correlations for the total group and the males and females analyzed separately. Sensation seeking did not correlate significantly with platelet MAO ($r_p = -.17$), although one of the

TABLE 7.1
Correlations[a] Among Psychological Scales

	Ma[b]	Pd[b]	D	Pt[b]	MAACL A-t	MAACL A-s	Si	E	N	P
Sensation Seeking (SSS)	41**	38**	-23	15	06	-05	-04	-22	-01	19
Hypomania (Ma)		34**	13	27	-23	03	-28	12	16	41**
Psychopathic Deviate (Pd)			07	26	-21	00	-29	03	10	06
Depression (D)				66**	27	11	46**	-07	33*	33*
Psychasthenia (Pt)					17	03	38**	-13	23	13
Anxiety Trait (A-t)						31*	41**	-16	45**	11
Anxiety State (A-s)							18	06	56**	03
Social Introversion (Si)								-40*	33*	19
EPQ – Extraversion (E)									13	-01
Neuroticism (N)										17
Psychoticism (P)										

[a] decimals omitted
[b] K corrected
* p < .05
** p < .01

TABLE 7.2

Correlations* between the Sensation Seeking Scale (SSS) and CSF
Norepinephrine (NE), Plasma Dopamine-Beta-Hydroxylase (DBH)
and Plasma Amine Oxidase (AO)

	Total Group		Males	Females
SSS vs	r_p	r	r	r
CSF-NE	-49^c	-51^c	-40^a	-72^b
P1-DBH	-60^b	-44^a	-60^a	-72^a
P1-AO	-33^a	-38^b	25	-75^c

* decimals omitted
$^a p < .10$
$^b p < .05$
$^c p < .01$

subscales, Thrill and Adventure Seeking (not shown here), did so ($r_p = -.30$, $p < .10$). The General SSS, used in our analyses, correlated with plasma AO in the initial correlation ($r_p = -.38$, $p < .05$) and in the partial correlation ($r_p = -.32$, $p < .10$). However, the correlation was only significant in the females and was actually positive in sign in the males.

Table 7.3 shows the correlations between anxiety trait and state measures

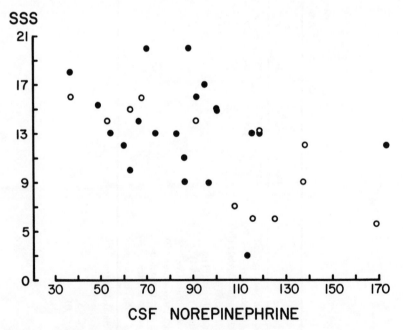

FIG. 7.3   Scatter plot for the correlation of CSF norepinephrine and sensation seeking. Black circles for males, open circles for females.

and biochemical variables, some of which are reported elsewhere (Ballenger et al., 1981; Ballenger, Post, Jimerson, Lake, Lerner, Bunney, & Goodwin, et al., submitted, 1982). Three of the four anxiety trait measures correlated *negatively* with plasma MHPG; two of them (D and Pt) correlated significantly in both males and females as well as in the total group. The partial correlation between Pt and CSF MHPG was also significant for the total group, but the original correlation was not significant in either the total group or the males and females separately. The MAACL anxiety state (A-s) measure correlated *positively* and significantly with CSF MHPG in the total group, but the correlation was significant in males and insignificantly and negative in direction in the females. None of the partial correlations between CSF NE and anxiety variables were significant.

Table 7.3 also shows an interesting group of correlations between the MAACL anxiety trait and state measures and both CSF and plasma DBH. The correlations are *negative* for the trait measure and *positive* for the state measure. Anxiety trait (A-t) correlated negatively with CSF-DBH in males and females separately as well as in the total group. The significance of the A-t versus plasma DBH correlation was limited to the total group, although the direction of the correlation was the same in both male and female groups. Neither of the A-s correlations with CSF or plasma DBH was significant in the separate sex groups.

Table 7.3 shows two additional significant partial correlations: one be-

TABLE 7.3
Correlations* between Anxiety Trait and State and Neuroticism (N)
Measures and CSF (C) Plasma (P) MHPG, DBH, 5-HIAA, and Platelet MAO

		Total Group		Males	Females
		r_p	r	r	r
N	vs P-MHPG	-44[a]	-50[b]	-38[a]	-84[c]
D	vs P-MHPG	-51[b]	-45[a]	-53[a]	-67[a]
Pt	vs P-MHPG	-57[b]	-49[b]	-55[b]	-74[a]
Pt	vs C-MHPG	-30[a]	-26	-25	-27
A-t	vs P-MHPG	-36[a]	-42[b]	-36	-53
A-s	vs C-MHPG	42[b]	30[a]	50[b]	-27
A-t	vs C-DBH	-48[b]	-50[c]	-43[a]	-62[a]
A-t	vs P-DBH	-42[a]	-45[a]	-19	-53
A-s	vs C-DBH	45[b]	25	36	-02
A-s	vs P-DBH	51[b]	31	73[c]	17
Pt	vs C-HIAA	36[b]	25	24	33
D	vs Pl-MAO	37[b]	24	46[b]	22

* decimals omitted
[a] $p < .10$
[b] $p < .05$
[c] $p < .01$

tween Pt and the serotonin metabolite 5-HIAA; and another between D and platelet MAO. Both correlations were positive. The original correlations were not significant for the total group or for both of the sexes, although the magnitudes of the correlations were similar for both sexes.

CSF calcium correlated positively with extraversion (EPQ E) and negatively with introversion (MMPI Si), although only the latter correlations was consistent in both sexes (Table 7.4). CSF calcium also correlated negatively with measures of neuroticism and dysphoria (N, D, Pt). The same correlational tendencies are seen for serum calcium with N and Pt.

DISCUSSION

If we restrict the discussion to the partial correlations that were significant before partialing in the total group *and* in both sexes *and* those that survived the partial correlation control for age, height, and weight in the total group, we are left with three groups of findings that are unlikely to be due to chance.

Sensation Seeking

Sensation seeking is *negatively* related to both CSF NE and plasma DBH. Because the theory (Zuckerman, 1979) predicted that sensation seeking trait is related to the reactivity of the NE and dopamine systems, finding a relationship with a measure of one of them is gratifying, particularly because CSF-NE is probably the one most likely to be directly related to the activity of the locus coeruleus and possibly the whole NE system

TABLE 7.4
Correlations* between Extraversion-Introversion, Neuroticism (N)
and CSF (C) and Serum (S) Calcium (Ca)

		Total Group		Males	Females
		r_p	r	r	r
EPQ E	vs C-Ca	36^b	30^a	42^a	18
MMPI Si	vs C-Ca	-47^b	-48^c	-53^c	-48
EPQ N	vs C-Ca	-32^a	-36^b	-09	-67^c
EPQ N	vs S-Ca	-31^a	-30^a	-05	-41
MMPI D	vs C-Ca	-48^c	-40^b	-57^c	-16
MMPI Pt	vs C-Ca	-33^a	-21	-35	04
MMPI Pt	vs S-Ca	-40^b	-27	-34	-25

* decimals omitted
[a] $p < .10$
[b] $p < .05$
[c] $p < .01$

in the brain. However, the direction of the relationship was a surprise because the theory predicted a positive rather than a negative relationship. Some preliminary results (Buchsbaum, Goodwin, & Muscettola, 1981) showing a positive correlation between urinary MHPG and the SSS in a small sample of 10 normal controls during both stress and nonstress periods also suggested such a positive relationship. This finding was not replicated in the present study; sensation seeking was not correlated with the MHPG metabolite in CSF, plasma, or urine. Although the present study also failed to replicate the relations between platelet MAO and the General SSS, it did find the relationship between plasma AO and the SSS found in the same prior studies.

But let us consider alternate explanations for the finding of a negative relationship between sensation seeking and CSF NE. Although this may be a chance finding, the magnitude and significance of the correlation, as well as the fact that it is significant in both males and females, argue against this interpretation. The negative correlation of the SSS with DBH also argues against the accidental nature of the SSS NE correlation. DBH is the enzyme that converts dopamine to NE and therefore would be expected to vary directly with NE. Also DBH is "packaged" in the same vesicles with NE in the neuron and is therefore released together with NE. In actual fact, plasma DBH correlated .49 with CSF-NE in this study, although surprisingly the CSF DBH correlation with NE was lower ($r = .23$), perhaps because CSF DBH reflects both NE release and a stable genetically determined level of DBH (Ballenger et al., 1981; Ballenger et al., submitted, 1982). The correlation between SSS and plasma DBH ($r = -.44$) is actually a replication of a significant one ($r = -.47$) found by Umberkoman-Wiita, Vogel, and Wiita (1981) between the same two variables.

Assuming these correlations are not chance, a second possibility is that the NE measured from CSF reflects the effect of the anxiety arousal produced by the immediate anticipation of the lumbar puncture on the activity of the NE system. CSF NE has been observed to be reactive to changes from depression to mania (Post, Lake, Jimerson, Bunney, Wood, Ziegler, & Goodwin, 1978) and with exercise. (Post, Ballenger, & Goodwin, 1980). A previous finding (Buchsbaum et al., 1981) involving urinary MHPG found it to be equally correlated with the SSS during a stress procedure and a rest period. But more to the point, there was no correlation between the SSS and either trait or state anxiety and no correlation between NE and trait or state anxiety in the present study. Thus, there is no evidence that anxiety state at the time of the lumbar puncture influenced the resultant value of CSF NE itself or its relationship to sensation seeking.

A third explanation is one that would require a change in the conception of the role of the NE system in sensation seeking and perhaps a revision of the optimal level theory. We could postulate that high sensation seekers seek stimulation in risky activities and use stimulant drugs because they have *low* levels of NE or a low rate of turnover. Also, low level of DBH would mean less dopamine converted to NE. Because stress and activity have been shown to release NE in animals and humans, in some circumstances temporarily depleting the supplies in the neuron, the sensation seeker may engage in risky activities as a means of "jogging" a depleted or sluggish system. This would still assume that the release of NE is intrinsically rewarding, whatever the first stimulus for release. Alternatively, the high sensation seeker might be more inclined to use drugs such as amphetamine and cocaine which release NE and dopamine from the neurons because of a basic deficit in the activity of these catecholamine systems.

None of the three explanations for the results is entirely satisfactory, but the third is not immediately refutable by the data of this study. Deficit or optimal level theories are slippery creatures, difficult to prove or disprove. Caution would argue that the other explanations be explored further. The possibility of the negative relationship between NE and sensation seeking being due to chance is the easiest to test by replication with larger normal samples. The question of whether CSF NE is primarily a biological trait or state can be assessed through reliability studies and genetic-twin studies, although the lumbar-puncture procedure makes it very difficult to study volunteers with repeated measurements and to obtain sufficient numbers of twins for biometrical-genetical analyses. It is unfortunate that sensation seeking is not related to the plasma or urinary MHPG measures. It is much easier to obtain samples from blood or urine than from cerebrospinal fluid in order to do experiments requiring repeated measurements.

Perhaps we should turn again to other animals for our answers. In the comments on Gray et al.'s Chapter 6 by Zuckerman, the first formulation of a norepinephrine-depletion hypothesis for sensation seeking by Ellison (personal communication, 1978) was cited. His hypothesis was based on the behavior of NE-depleted rats in the open-field situation. The problem might be addressed by a thorough study of the characteristics of the bioamines in the brains of exploratory and nonexploratory rats using the open-field reactions as a model for sensation seeking. But it is not clear that this is an appropriate model because NE-depleted rats behaved so differently in their natural habitats than in the open field.

Impulsivity

The correlational studies between the traits of sensation seeking and impulsivity in humans show that these are related, but not synonymous, dimensions of personality. Despite some common biological correlates (e.g., augmenting–reducing of the cortical evoked potential), it is conceivable that the two traits have different kinds of biochemical substrates. In the present study, there were no findings relating MMPI measures of impulsivity to the bioamines, enzymes, and metabolites studied. However, the measures used were not designed primarily as measures of impulsivity. Perhaps future studies using direct measures of impulsivity, such as those devised by the Eysencks, Schalling, and Barratt, may reveal more positive findings. It will also be useful to analyze the more narrow components of the broad impulsivity trait because these may have different kinds of biochemical substrates.

Extraversion

CSF calcium shows a positive correlation with extraversion and a negative correlation with introversion and anxiety. Studies have shown that calcium in the CSF is negatively related to behavioral activation and neuronal excitability (Carman, Wyatt, Smith, Post, & Ballenger, in press; Jimerson, Post, Carman, van Kammen, Wood, Goodwin, & Bunney, 1979). Lowering calcium levels in the brains of animals makes them more behaviorally hyperactive and susceptible to seizures. Conversely, raising calcium levels reduces activity and neuronal excitability. Regulation of CSF calcium levels within a normal range is not well understood. Moreover, the behavioral consequences of experimentally altered calcium levels involved larger fluctuations than those involved in this study. If we extrapolate from these animal studies, the positive correlation between calcium and extraversion provides chemical data that tends to support Eysenck's (1967) theory that introverts are more aroused and arousable (with lower levels of stimulation) than extraverts. However, the relationship also involves the neuroticism-anxiety dimension. The individuals scoring high on anxiety-neuroticism scales in the sample had the lowest calcium levels. This supports Gray's (1973) assertion that the basic arousability dimension is on the diagonal of Eysenck's factor scheme running from stable extraversion to neurotic introversion.

Anxiety

The original title for this book did not include *anxiety*. However, the submitted chapters made it clear that the anxiety trait must be considered in interpreting impulsive or sensation seeking behavior. The Stein–Gray controversy over the function of the NE system emphasized the need to consider the biochemical substrate of anxiety as well as sensation seeking and impulsivity. We did not find a relationship between trait anxiety and the CSF NE measure, but fairly strong and consistent relationships were found between both the NE metabolite MHPG in the plasma and the enzyme DBH in the CSF and anxiety *trait*. These results are in the wrong direction for Gray (1973) and Redmond's (1977) theories (Chapter 6) since MHPG and DBH measures were negatively related to anxiety trait while these theories would predict a positive relationship. The positive correlations between anxiety *state* and CSF-MHPG and CSF and plasma DBH measures are more supportive of the theories but would limit them to a description of the state of anxiety. Absence of a positive correlation between state anxiety and plasma MHPG in this study needs further evaluation in experimental studies since Sweeney, Maas, and Heninger (1978), Uhde, Post, Siever, and Buchsbaum (1981), and Wyatt, Portnoy, Kupfer, Snyder, and Engleman (1971) have all reported positive relationships between state anxiety and *peripheral* measures of catecholamine release and turnover. Moreover, given the high positive correlation between MHPG levels in CSF and plasma MHPG in these volunteers, one might expect similar relationships to the measure of state anxiety. Since plasma MHPG values are heavily influenced by such peripheral factors as autonomic arousal, and the conversion of MHPG to VMA (Blombery et al., 1980), these peripheral events may influence the correlation with measures of trait anxiety. Recent work shows that peripheral MHPG production (as reflected in plasma MHPG) contributes to CSF levels of the metabolite (Kopin et al., submitted 1982). In future studies, it will be important to adjust CSF MHPG values for interindividual variations in plasma MHPG prior to further data analysis.

If we were to accept the differential trait and state results, we would have to conclude that the DBH NE system may be involved in the behavior patterns that characterize the anxiety trait, but that the system also shows more transient changes associated with environmental stress (Ballenger et al., 1982). Anxious persons could be characterized by unusually low levels of NE turnover in non-aroused conditions, but would respond to stress with unusually high rates of production, release, and conversion of NE to MHPG. There is some precedent for this interpretation. Sweeney and Maas (1979) report that depressed patients with lower baseline urinary MHPG levels were the ones whose MHPG levels increased most under stressful conditions. The dopamine and serotonin metabolites HVA and 5-HIAA showed minimal relationships with psychological variables. The evidence for and against brain contribution to the metabolites HVA, 5-HIAA, and MHPG in CSF are discussed by Post et al., (1978). One significant relationship between Pt and 5-HIAA, the metabolite of serotonin, is supportive of Stein's (1978) theory that serotonin is the primary neurochemical mediator of anxiety. But this one was only significant after partialing and not significant in the separate sex groups. Similarly, the positive correlation between the D scale and platelet MAO is of questionable reliability.

SUMMARY

This study, the first of its kind, has obvious limitations and must be regarded as exploratory. However, the results are encouraging in several respects. The strong relationships between CSF NE, MHPG, DBH, and plasma MHPG and DBH may suggest that the activity in central and peripheral NE systems are correlated. In the case of MHPG, the contribution of peripheral sources to CSF levels will have to be evaluated in future studies.

The fact that any relationships are found between psychological traits and these indicators of NE activity is impressive considering the number of intervening steps between the biochemistry of the CNS and imperfect trait measurements. Although chance may play a role in some of these findings, many of them are replicated across the sex groups in this study or in prior studies. There are limitations to the interpretations from correlational studies making it important to pursue a comparative approach as outlined in Zuckerman's Chapter 2. Additional insights will come from semiexperimental studies of drug treatment in clinical groups.

The study results have raised some interesting challenges to preexisting theories of sensation seeking and anxiety traits. These theories had suggest that both traits were related positively to the tonic activity of the central NE system. They were not incompatible because the traits of sensation seeking and anxiety or neuroticism are not correlated at the phenomenal level (Zuckerman, 1979). The results show negative rather than positive correlations between both traits and indicators of activity of the NE system, although sensation seeking and anxiety are related to different indicators: sensation seeking to CSF NE and anxiety to plasma MHPG. A new optimal level of arousal hypothesis is suggested for sensation seeking making the arousal of a central NE system the focus of behavioral risk-taking tendencies seen in sensation seekers.

The finding of positive correlations between DBH and state anxiety and negative correlations with trait anxiety are intriguing, particularly because in other studies low DBH basal levels have been associated with psychopathology (Major, Lerner, Goodwin, Ballenger, Brown, & Lovenberg, 1980). These findings are consistent with the literature showing that stress activates the central NE system. It is this literature that led to the hypothesis that the NE system mediates the trait of anxiety. However, the different direction of trait and state relationships with the DBH measures suggest that the activity of this system may represent an effect rather than a cause of anxiety. Under nonthreatening conditions (e.g., ingesting cocaine or amphetamine), activation of the system may be rewarding. Under threatening conditions of the type that increase anxiety, the activation of the NE system may be an adaptive response to override the paralyzing effects of the behavioral-inhibition system. Clearly, if we are to progress in our understanding of the biochemistry of anxiety we must use nonthreatening and positive arousal stimuli as well as negative stress. Studies by Levi (1969) have shown that peripheral NE may be increased by watching erotic films as well as anxiety-provoking films. Could this be the case for central NE as well? In fact, the central NE system may respond to novel stimuli or to stimuli associated with reward or punishment, and serve as a central amplifying system (Bloom, 1982). Aston-Jones and Bloom (1981) have shown that the NE containing locus coeruleus (LC) neurons respond to mild, non-noxious stimuli of many sensory modalities. Responses of these neurons habituate with repeated presentation of the stimulus. Response magnitudes depend on the level of cortical arousal as indicated by the EEG. Spontaneous activity of the LC neurons varied directly with stages of sleep. Clearly these results indicate that the NE system acts as an arousal system sensitive to salient or novel external stimuli.

The results of the study reported in this chapter remind us of the imperfect measures of brain neurochemistry presently available for studies in humans. Plasma and urinary measures of the catecholamines and their metabolites are heavily influenced by rates of peripheral release, metabolism, and excretion. Lumbar CSF levels may be significantly influenced by local events in the spinal cord as well as brain, and are affected by input from peripheral sources. Development of new noninvasive measures (such as neurochemically selective emission tomography) may further clarify present preliminary observations.

REFERENCES

Aston-Jones, G., & Bloom, F. Norepinephrine-containing locus coeruleus neurons in behaving rats exhibit pronounced responses to non-noxious environmental stimuli. *The Journal of Neuroscience,* 1981, *1,* 887–900.

Ballenger, J. C., Post, R. M., & Goodwin, F. K. Neurochemistry of cerebrospinal fluid in normal individuals: Relationship between biological and psychological variables. In J. H. Wood (Ed.), *The neurobiology of cerebrospinal fluid,* Vol. II. New York: Plenum, in press.

Ballenger, J. C., Post, R. M., Jimerson, D. C., Lake, C. R., Lerner, P., Bunney, W. E., Jr., & Goodwin, F. K. Cerebrospinal fluid (CSF) noradrenergic correlations with anxiety in normals. *Scientific Proceedings of the American Psychiatric Association,* 1981, *134,* 235–236.

Ballenger, J. C., Post, R. M., Jimerson, D. C., Lake, C. R., Lerner, P., Bunney, W. E., Jr., & Goodwin, F. K. Cereborspinal fluid (CSF) noradrenergic correlations with anxiety in normals. Manuscript submitted, 1982.

Blombery, P. A., Kopin, I. J., Gordon, E. K., Markey, S. P., & Ebert, M. H. Conversion of MHPG to Vanillymandelic Acid. *Archives of General Psychiatry,* 1980, *37,* 1095–1098.

Bloom, F. E. Brain regulates responsiveness to environment. Paper presented in symposium "The Science of the Brain" at meeting of the American Psychiatric Association, Toronto, Canada, March, 1982.

Buchsbaum, M. S., Goodwin, F. K., & Muscettola, G. Urinary MHPG, stress response, personality factors, and somatosensory evoked potentials in normal subjects and patients with affective disorders. *Neuropsychobiology,* 1981, *7,* 212–224.

Carman, J. C., Wyatt, E. S., Smith, W., Post, R. M., & Ballenger, J. C. Calcium and calcitonin in biopolar affective disorder. In R. M. Post, & J. C. Ballenger (Eds.) *The neurobiology of the mood disorders.* Baltimore, Md.: Williams & Wilkins, in press.

Crawley, J. N., Roth, R. H., & Maas, J. W. Locus coeruleus stimulation increases noradrenergic metabolite levels in rat spinal cord. *Brain Research,* 1979, *166,* 180–184.

Ellison, G. D. Personal communication, 1978.

Eysenck, H. J. The biological basis of personality. Springfield, Ill.: Thomas, 1967.

Eysenck, S. B. G., & Eysenck, H. J. *Manual of the Eysenck Personality Questionnaire.* London: Hodder & Stoughton, 1975.

Gray, J. A. Causal theories of personality and how to test them. In J. R. Royce (Ed.), *Multivariate analysis and psychological theory.* New York: Academic Press, 1973.

Hathaway, S. R., & McKinley, J. C. *The Minnesota Multiphasic Personality Inventory manual* (rev. ed.). New York: Psychological Corp., 1951.

Jimerson, D. C., Ballenger, J. C., Lake, C. R., Post, R. M., Goodwin, F. K., & Kopin, I. J. Plasma and CSF MHPG in normals. *Psychopharmacology Bulletin,* 1981, *17,* 86–87.

Jimerson, D. C., Markey, S. P., Oliver, J. A., & Kopin, I. J. Simultaneous measurement of plasma 4-hydroxy-3-methoxyphenethylene glycol and 3, 4-dihydroxyphenethylene glycol by gas chromatography mass spectrometry. *Biomedical Mass Spectrometry,* 1981, *8,* 256–259.

Jimerson, D. C., Post, R. M., Carman, J. C., van Kammen, D. P., Wood, J. H., Goodwin, F. K., & Bunney, W. E., Jr. CSF Calcium: Clinical correlates in affective illness and schizophrenia. *Biological Psychiatry,* 1979, *14,* 37–51.

Kopin, I. J., Gordon, E. K., Jimerson, D. C., & Polinsky, R. S. Relationship of plasma and cerebrospinal fluid levels of 3-methoxy-4-hydroxyphenlglycol (MHPG): Their value as indices of noradrenergic activity. Submitted for publication, 1982.

Levi, L. Sympatho-adrenomedullary activity, diuresis, and emotional reactions during visual sexual stimulation in human females and males. *Psychosomatic Medicine,* 1969, *31,* 251–268.

Lipton, M. A., DiMascio, A., & Killam, K. F. *Psychopharmacology: A generation of progress.* New York: Raven Press, 1978.

Major, L. K., Lerner, P., Goodwin, F. K., Ballenger, J. C., Brown, G. L., & Lovenberg, W. Dopamine-beta-hydroxylase in cerebrospinal fluid: Relationship to personality measures. *Archives of General Psychiatry,* 1980, *37,* 308–310.

Murphy, D. L., Belmaker, R. H., Buchsbaum, M. S., Martin, N. F., Ciaranello, R., & Wyatt, R. J. Biogenic amine related enzymes and personality variations in normals. *Psychological Medicine,* 1977, *7,* 149–157.

Post, R. M., Ballenger, J. C., & Goodwin, F. K. Cerebrospinal fluid studies of neurotransmitter function in manic and depressive illness. In J. H. Wood (Ed.) *Neurobiology of cerebrospinal fluid.* Vol. I. New York: Plenum Press, 1980.

Post, R. M., Ballenger, J. C., Jimerson, D. C., & Bunney, W. E., Jr. Plasma MHPG is inversely correlated with depression, hypochondriasis, and psychasthenia scores on the MMPI in normal subjects. Manuscript submitted for publication, 1982.

Post, R. M. Lake, J. R., Jimerson, D. C. Bunney, W. E. Jr., Wood, J. M., Ziegler, M. G., & Goodwin, F. K. Cerebrospinal fluid norepinephrine in affective illness. *American Journal of Psychiatry,* 1978, *135,* 907–912.

Redmond, D. E., Jr. Alterations in the function of the locus coeruleus: A possible model for studies of anxiety. In I. Hanin, & E. Usdin (Eds.), *Animal models in psychiatry and neurology*. New York: Pergamon, 1977.

Schooler, C., Zahn, T. P., Murphy, D. L., & Buchsbaum, M. S. Psychological correlates of monoamine oxidase in normals. *Journal of Nervous and Mental Diseases*, 1978, *166*, 177–186.

Spitzer, R. L., Endicott, J., & Robins, E. Research diagnostic criteria: Rationale and reliability. *Archives of General Psychiatry*, 1978, *35*, 773–782.

Stein, L. Reward transmitters: Catecholamines and opioid peptides. In M. A. Lipton, A. DiMascio, & K. F. Killam (Eds.), *Psychopharmacology: A generation of progress*. New York: Raven Press, 1978.

Sweeney, D. R., & Maas, J. W. Stress and noradrenergic function in depression. In R. A. Depue (Ed.), *The psychophysiology of the depressive disorders*. New York: Academic Press, 1979.

Sweeney, D. R., Maas, J. W., & Heninger, G. R. State anxiety, physical activity, and urinary 3-methoxy-4-hydroxyphenlethylene glycol excretion. *Archives of General Psychiatry*, 1978, *35*, 1418–1473.

Uhde, T. W., Post, R. M., Siever, L., & Buchsbaum, M. S. Effects of clonidine on psychophysical pain. *Scientific Proceedings of the American Psychiatric Association*, 1981, *134*, 155, Abstract.

Umberkoman–Wiita, B., Vogel, W. H., & Wiita, P. J. Some biochemical and behavioral (sensation seeking) correlates in healthy adults. *Research Communications in Psychology, Psychiatry, and Behavior*, 1981, *6*, 303–316.

Wood, J. H. (Ed.) *Neurobiology of cerebrospinal fluid*. (Vols. I & II). New York: Plenum Press, Vol. I, 1982, Vol. II, in press.

Wyatt, R. J., Portnoy, B., Kupfer, D. J., Snyder, F., & Engleman, K. Resting plasma catecholamine concentrations in patients with depression and anxiety. *Archives of General Psychiatry*, 1971, *24*, 65–70.

Ziegler, M. G., Lake, C. R., Wood, J. H., Brooks, B. R., & Ebert, M. H. Relationship between norepinephrine in blood and cerebrospinal fluid in the presence of a blood-cerebrospinal fluid barrier for norepinephrine. *Journal of Neurochemistry*, 1977, *28*, 677–679.

Zuckerman, M. Dimensions of sensation seeking. *Journal of Consulting and Clinical Psychology*, 1971, *36*, 45–52.

Zuckerman, M. General and situation-specific traits and states: New approaches to the assessment of anxiety and other constructs. In M. Zuckerman, & C. D. Spielberger (Eds.), *Emotions and anxiety: New concepts, methods and applications*. Hillsdale, N.J.: Lawrence Erlbaum Associates, 1976.

Zuckerman, M. *Sensation seeking: Beyond the optimal level of arousal*. Hillsdale, N.J.: Lawrence Erlbaum Associates, 1979.

Zuckerman, M. The biological bases of sensation seeking. Paper presented at the meeting of the American Psychological Association, Los Angeles, August, 1981.

Zuckerman, M. The biochemistry of Eysenck's dimensions of personality and sensation seeking. Paper presented at the meeting of the American Psychological Association, August 1982.

Zuckerman, M., & Lubin, B. *Manual for the Multiple Affect Adjective Check List*. San Diego, Ca.: Educational and Industrial Testing Service, 1965.

8 A Summing Up with Special Sensitivity to the Signals of Reward in Future Research

Marvin Zuckerman
University of Delaware

The time has come to integrate the findings and theories in the preceding seven chapters. This is no mean feat, if it is possible at all, but perhaps there are enough communalities in the ground covered by each author to look for similarities and differences across areas.

Implicit in all approaches is that the traits called extraversion, sensation seeking, and impulsivity share some common phenomenal manifestations, some biological correlates, and perhaps some common biological determinism. Neuroticism or anxiety trait is assumed to form another dimension independent of the three aforementioned traits. There is evidence that these two dimensions interact in certain phenomenal expressions such as the behavior of rodents in the open field and the behavior of humans in novel situations. The two dimensions may relate to biological traits in opposite ways, with one relating positively and the other negatively to the trait in questions. But apart from convergence we must also look for divergence of findings and theoretical explanations. It is the latter that may furnish the best basis for devising new studies to test the proposed models.

GENETICS

In the first chapter, Eysenck presented data showing the genetic contributions to impulsivity and sensation-seeking scales and made an attempt to integrate these findings within a hierarchical model that conceives of impulsivity and sensation seeking as components of three supertraits.: extraversion (E), neuroticism (N), and psychoticism (P). The attempt at synthesis was not entirely successful, as Martin, Eaves, and Fulker (1979) have noted:

> However, the fundamental hypothesis we set out to test, that covariation between impulsiveness and sensation seeking variables would be largely explicable in terms of the E factor, has received only limited support. The P and L [L = the Lie score regarded as another dimension by the authors] factors seem equally important, but it is also apparent that the attempt to fit these variables within the straightjacket of P, E, N, and L, is far from satisfactory [p. 206].

The difficulty is not surprising because the traits of sensation seeking and impulsivity do not relate to one or the other superfactors, as implicit in a simple hierarchical model, but correlate with one, two, or even three of them. To complicate matters further the different subfactors in impulsivity and sensation seeking are related to different combinations of the superfactors. Further research utilizing factor analyses or cannonical correlation of both biological and personality trait measures might help clarify the problems in the structural organization of personality. If such studies were performed on large samples of identical and fraternal twins, the results would be immensely more valuable in defining the basic dimensions of temperament *and* personality.

Until we do such studies, we must look at the results of separate studies involving only one or two of the personality dimensions of interest. Table 8.1 summarizes, in a very simplified overview, the convergencies and divergencies in the relationship found between biological and personality variables.

TABLE 8.1
Summary[a] of Results Relating Biological to Psychological Traits

	Sensation Seeking	Extraversion	Impulsivity	Anxiety Trait/Neuroticism
EEG Arousal	0	−	−	+
Orienting Reflex	+	−	−	−
Augmenting of AEP	+	0	+	0
Monoamine Oxidase	−	−	−	0
CSF NE	−	0	0	0
Plasma MHPG	0	0	0	−
Plasma DBH	−	0	0	−
CSF Calcium	0	+	0	−
Testosterone	+	+	+	−
Heritability (% Genetic)	58	42	M 40 F 37	49
Heritability (corrected)	69	57	M 57 F 60	65

[a] + = positive relationship, - = negative relationship, 0 = no relationship

Comparisons of Heritability

Studies done on twins from the same population using the Jinks and Fulker (1970) method of biometric analyses have yielded the proportions of narrow heritability shown in Table 8.1. Also shown are the heritabilities corrected for the unreliability of the trait measures. The uncorrected heritabilities range from 37% for impulsivity (in females) to 58% for sensation seeking. Heritabilities corrected for unreliability range from 57% for extraversion and impulsivity (in males) to 69% for sensation seeking. It seems safe to conclude that heredity contributes somewhere between one half and two thirds of the variance for all of the traits of interest.

Tonic Arousal

Tonic levels of arousal have been assessed by EEG alpha indices, evoked cortical potentials, the contingent negative variation (CNV), and autonomic measures taken in base-line conditions, such as skin conductance, fluctuations in spontaneous skin-conductance responses, heart rate, and others. Methods dependent on behavioral reactions (e.g., critical flicker fusion and conditioning) have also been used, although these indirect measures of physiological arousal are more questionable. Because in most theories *cortical arousal* is meant when the term *arousal* is used, EEG or CNV measures would be most appropriate for assessing arousal.

Eysenck's (1967) theory proposed that intoverts should be more aroused than extraverts under resting, nonstimulated conditions. In a recent review of the evidence on this hypothesis, Stelmack (1981b) concludes: "the demonstration of higher levels of cortical activity for introverts using EEG measures of arousal remains equivocal [p. 42]." But Stelmack adds: "Nevertheless, one must concede that the general direction of the results of these inquiries is towards higher levels of cortical activity for introverts under conditions intermediate, between semi-somnolence and stressful [pp. 42–43]." Gale (1981) arrives at a similar conclusion after a critical and exhaustive review of EEG studies of extraversion-introversion.

With sensation seeking the results are less equivocal. No differences between high and low sensation seekers during base-line, resting conditions have been found for EEG or skin-conductance measures of arousal. The only differences in tonic arousal have been found in the cardiovascular system. Ridgeway and Hare (1981) found a higher heart rate and Carrol, Zuckerman, and Vogel (1982) found higher systolic blood pressure in low sensation seekers than in highs. For both variables the high sensation seekers' cardiovascular activity was relatively normal, whereas the lows showed high arousal patterns for what should have been base-line conditions.

Based on his studies, Barratt (Chapter 3) concludes that impulsives are underaroused relative to nonimpulsives. I am not entirely convinced by the data he uses to support this assertion, but the assertion would be congruent with the preponderance of evidence on EEG and skin-conductance measures that shows psychopaths to be underaroused, particularly during prolonged monotonous sessions (Hare, 1975).

Tonic arousal is, by definition, difficult to assess. If the subjects are awake, they are in some kind of situation. Even if the external stimulation is invariant, the subject's own expectations and other internal mental activities may affect the psychophysiological recordings. Initially, the level of anxiety in response to a novel situation may affect introverts, low sensation seekers, and nonimpulsives more than their opposite personality types. As the situation is prolonged and the novelty wears off, the extraverts, high sensation seekers, and impulsives may disregard instructions about trying to stay awake and alert and drift into drowsy or even sleep states, thus lowering measured arousal. These kinds of differences in response to an experimental situation, as affected by the experimental conditions, procedures, and instructions, may account for the inconsistencies in the findings on extraversion and psychopathy.

The findings on clinical levels of anxiety trait are fairly clear in showing high tonic levels of arousal in anxious patients measured by cortical or autonomic indices (Lader, 1975). Findings relating arousal measures to anxiety as a measured trait in normal populations are more equivocal (Hodges, 1976). Hodges points out many of the methodological problems in the area as well as the oversimplification of the generalized "arousal" construct as applied to both cortical and many kinds of unrelated peripheral autonomic measures. It is only in extreme anxiety *states* that we can expect to find signs of arousal in *all* response systems. Clinically anxious patients are much more likely than high anxiety trait normals to be in such states when tested in the strange surroundings of a psychophysiology laboratory.

AROUSABILITY: ORIENTING REFLEX
AND EVOKED POTENTIALS

Orienting Reflex (OR)

Stelmack (1979, 1981a), in his reviews of the literature relating the magnitude of the electrodermal OR to extraversion, concludes that there is a relationship: Introverts show stronger ORs and take longer to habituate the OR. However, these conclusions tend to be true only when the auditory stimuli are in a moderate range of intensity (75–90 db) or the visual or auditory stimuli are interesting enough to be mildly arousing. The finding of significant personality effects in response to the intermediately arousing situations or stimuli is similar to the EEG findings.

Inasmuch as we would expect high sensation seekers to respond more like extraverts and lows more like introverts, it was surprising to find that just the opposite was true in regard to the amplitude of the OR to novel visual or auditory stimuli (Neary & Zuckerman, 1976). High sensation seekers showed greater initial electrodermal ORs to novel stimuli than did lows. Similar findings have emerged using heart-rate deceleration as an OR measure (see Chapter 2).

Recently, Stelmack (1981a) correlated electrodermal ORs with extraversion and sensation seeking in the same group of subjects. In response to slides of words, but not pictures, extraversion correlated negatively and sensation seeking (particularly the Experience Seeking type) correlated positively with the amplitude of the OR to the first stimulus presentation. As is usually the case the correlations were low, but the different kind of responses to the same stimulus reinforces the conclusion from previous studies that there is something different in the psychophysiology of extraversion and sensation seeking.

As Barratt and Schalling do not provide data relating their impulsivity dimensions to the OR, we must again turn to studies of psychopaths to assess this dimension. Hare (1978) reports that, although psychopaths are hyporesponsive on the electrodermal OR to intense or aversive stimuli, they respond normally to tones in the more moderate range (e.g., 80 db). However, after range corrections were applied, it was found that psychopaths gave significantly smaller responses to *novel* tones of moderate intensity than did nonpsychopathic prison inmates.

Lader (1979) states that electrodermal measures show high arousal in anxious patients prior to and between stimulus presentations, but the actual OR to the initial stimulus is weaker than that of controls. The anxious patients, however, take longer to habituate the OR, as do normal subjects made anxious by experimental manipulations. Neary and Zuckerman (1976) found that trait anxiety in normals was unrelated to electrodermal OR magnitude, but state anxiety, measured just prior to the experiment, was related to OR. Those subjects in a high state of anxiety gave weaker initial ORs than did calmer subjects. These results are consistent with those of Lader (1975) with clinical anxiety patients.

Average Evoked Potential (AEP)

Earlier reports of negative relationships between extraversion and the amplitude of the AEP to a single stimulus intensity were not confirmed by later studies. Particularly important here was the study by Rust (1975), which used a variety of stimulus intensities with negative results. However,

Stelmack, Achorn, and Mechaud (1977) have reported that introverts do have greater amplitude AEPs than extraverts at two levels of stimulus intensity when low rather than high frequency tones are used. It is not clear why the frequency of tones should interact with the personality variable, but Stelmack (1981b) points out that interindividual variability of the AEP is greater at low than at high frequencies.

More theoretically relevant is the interaction between stimulus intensity and extraversion, which would be predictable from Eysenck's (1967, 1981) optimal level of arousal theory of extraversion. The study by Zuckerman, Murtaugh, and Siegel (1974) showed a significant interaction between the Disinhibition subscale of the SSS and the stimulus intensity affecting the amplitude of the visual AEP. High disinhibitors showed augmenting of AEP response with increases in stimulus intensity. Low disinhibitors showed little augmenting at low to midrange intensities and a definite reduction of response at the highest intensity. Eysenck (1981) cites this study as evidence for such an interaction for extraversion, which he equates with high disinhibition. It is true that the Disinhibition scale usually correlates significantly with the E scale, and it is the SS scale that shows the highest correlations with E, but the median correlation in 12 studies was only .31 (Zuckerman, 1979). More to the point, in the Zuckerman et al. (1974) study the E scale from the EPI did not correlate with the slope measure of augmenting–reducing, therefore it must be concluded that augmenting is related to disinhibition, or possibly impulsive-extraversion, but not to the broader trait of extraversion.

Disinhibition represents the socially impulsive type of sensation seeking, and it is not surprising that positive results relating augmenting of the visual AEP to impulsivity are reported by Barratt in Chapter 3. This provides an important convergence for the traits of sensation seeking and impulsivity. The CNV has not been studied in relation to sensation seeking, but Barratt reports that high impulsives were very underresponsive (compared to lows) on the CNV in response to simple geometric figures. But slides of nude females presented to male impulsives did elicit responses as great as those of lows. This study again shows the relevance of the stimulus dimension to the construct of arousal and the essential interaction between stimulus and personality dimensions. It is meaningless to say that extraverts or impulsives are less aroused or less arousable than introverts or nonimpulsives unless the stimulus is specified. Studies tend to show that the "action-oriented" personality type is less aroused by uninteresting, low intensity stimuli but equally or more aroused by interesting, novel, or high intensity stimuli.

Augmenting of the AEP has shown little relationship to anxiety trait, and the relationship that exists with depression (Coursey, Buchsbaum, & Frankel, 1975), is a negative one. Depressives, on the MMPI scale, tend to be reducers rather than augmenters, and unipolar depressive patients tend to be reducers.

BIOCHEMISTRY

Monoamine Oxidase

Low monoamine oxidase levels have been found to be related to all of the variables of interest except anxiety. Recent studies by Gattaz and Beckman (1981) and Demisch, Georgi, Patzke, Demish, and Bochnick (1982) have shown negative correlations between platelet MAO and extraversion in schizophrenic and normal populations. MAO constitutes the only biological correlate common to the three traits: sensation seeking, extraversion, and impulsivity. The common behavioral factor involved in all of these traits related to MAO is social activity or sociability. In humans and in monkeys, low platelet MAO is associated with high levels of social activity, and high MAO activity correlates with low sociability. In males of both species, more agonistic behavior is associated with low MAO levels (e.g., criminal behavior and illegal drug use in the low MAO types in humans; aggression and sexual activity in the low MAO types in monkeys).

Haier, Buchsbaum, Murphy, Gottesman, and Coursey (1980) have conceptualized the relationship between the social sensation seeking produced by low MAO levels, and the sensory protection (or lack of it) produced by the augmenting–reducing characteristics of the brain. Persons with either low MAO and augmenting or high MAO and reducing are unbalanced in sensation-seeking drive and the protective characteristics of the nervous system. Low MAO-augmenting types are likely to become overaroused, and high-MAO-reducing types are liable to be underaroused and withdrawn. As noted previously, the augmenting pattern is found in sensation seekers and impulsives but not necessarily in stable extraverts. As both sensation seekers and impulsives tend to have low MAO levels, this would put many of them in the unstable quadrant of Haier et al.'s system, which is characterized by overarousal.

How might high sensation seekers who are augmenters cope with this overarousal by their own activities? One answer might be to alter arousal through the use of alcohol and other depressant drugs. Murtaugh (1979) classified drug users into those with a predominant history of using physiological depressants (e.g., opiates and barbiturates) and those predominantly using stimulants (e.g., amphetamine and cocaine). The former depressant drug users were primarily augmenters, and the former stimulant users were mostly reducers on the VEP.

Norepinephrine and Its Metabolites

As noted in the last chapter, only sensation seeking was related to CSF-NE in the NIMH study. Extraversion and the MMPI measures of impulsivity were not related to the monoamine metabolites. However, a measure of aggressiveness (Buss–Durkee Assaultive Scale) and variety of heterosexual partners both related positively to plasma MHPG, which was negatively related to anxiety trait measures. Trait anxiety was also negatively related to CSF and plasma DBH, whereas state anxiety correlated positively with these variables. The NE system seems to be involved in sensation seeking and anxiety but not in social extraversion.

CSF Calcium

CSF calcium was not related to sensation seeking but was related positively to extraversion and negatively to neuroticism and social introversion (a neurotic type). The main dimension defined by CSF calcium runs from stable extraversion to neurotic introversion. This may represent an arousal dimension, with neurotic introverts being overarousable and stable extraverts being hypoarousable.

Testosterone

In the study by Daitzman and Zuckerman (1980) testosterone was positively correlated with sensation seeking, extraversion, activity, sociability, variety of heterosexual experience, and self-acceptance. Measures of neurotic introversion, anxiety, and feminine interests (all subjects were males) all correlated negatively with testosterone. The same dimension running from stable extraversion to neurotic introversion that characterizes the relation of CSF calcium to psychological traits also characterizes the testosterone relationships. Sociability was a more prominent correlate of testosterone than impulsivity, although the SSS Disinhibition scale that correlates with testosterone contains impulsivity types of items. Sociability and sexuality were traits correlated with low MAO levels, and they characterize high testosterone males as well. Gonadal hormones may activate the CNS through the inhibition of MAO (Broverman, Klaiber, Kobyaski, & Vogel, 1968).

COMMUNALITIES AND DIFFERENCES

Looking at Table 8.1 it is apparent that the personality variables of interest in this volume share some common biological correlates but differ on others. The most common correlates of the action-oriented variables (i.e., extraversion, sensation seeking, and impulsivity) are levels of MAO and testosterone. Although this might suggest a common pattern in the monoamine systems regulated by MAO, no such pattern emerged in the NIH study. Only sensation seeking and anxiety, or introverted neuroticism, showed relationships with indicators of activity in the noradrenergic system. However, the book cannot be closed on possible roles for dopamine and serotonin because these were less adequately measured in the NIH study where only CSF metabolites of these systems were used.

The concept of generalized arousal, as measured by tonic EEG activity, seems to be applicable to extraversion, impulsivity, and anxiety but not to sensation seeking. The findings relating extraversion to CSF calcium are consistent with the idea that neurotic or anxious introverts are basically more aroused at the level of the neuron. The greater capacity of impulsive sensation seekers (disinhibitors) to respond to high levels of stimulation, as indicated by the well-replicated findings on augmenting of the averaged evoked potential, represents a specific type of arousability that requires less explanation than the inhibitory reducing tendency seen in controlled low sensation seekers. One of the challenges for neurophysiologists is to define the neurophysiological mechanisms that depress cortical activity when stimulation becomes excessive. The work of Lukas and Siegel (1977) represents a beginning in this line of investigation, although this work left many unanswered questions as to the locus of the augmenting–reducing phenomenon.

More is known about the neural mechanisms for the orienting and defensive reflexes (Pribram & McGuiness, 1975; Sokolov, 1960) that show a divergence in the findings for sensation seeking and impulsive extraversion. Gray's chapter raises significant questions regarding the neuropharmacology of ORs and DRs. The answer to these questions may help solve the problem of whether the OR should be regarded as a component of an anxiety system or a sensation-seeking system.

A PARTING EDITORIAL

Would it be more profitable to work our way up from the biological level to the more complex human trait level via the more precisely controlled comparative studies? This approach might lead to a redefinition of basic dimensions of human personality, aligning them more closely with biological traits. Or is it more practical to work down from the human level, with all the imprecision of correlational studies? Is it more important to be able to generalize from rats to people or from people to rats? Although my own preference would be for the latter option ("man [and woman, of course] is the measure of all things"), a bridge is needed regardless of which bank we start from. It would be fine if our bridges meet in midstream, but this does not seem likely at present.

We must all return to our laboratories and, if there are any funds left, begin to build with at least one eye on the activity going on at the opposite bank. The current scarcity of funding is one reason that it is important to develop testable models, even if such models are based on less than optimal quantities and consistencies of data. "We have no money therefore we shall have to think." If the data relating sensation seeking to MAO, for instance, had not suggested a model involving the monoamines, there would have been little reason to include the Sensation Seeking Scale in the recent NIMH study (Chapter 7). The behavioral correlates of MAO and augmenting–reducing in humans and other species (Zuckerman, Buchsbaum, & Murphy, 1980) confirm that these variables are of great importance in our efforts to understand the biological bases of personality.

It is already apparent that the idea of one neurotransmitter, or neural tract, for each personality trait is highly oversimplified. Parsimony dictates that we start with such simple models and discard them when they fail to adequately describe data that more complex models can handle. But in order to move to higher levels of complexity we must overcome our natural aversion to multivariate studies. In the many studies of specific neurotoxins on behavior it is rare for the investigator to study the effects on more than one other neurotransmitter, and it is even rarer to attempt to see how a covarying neurotransmitter might interact with the target one in producing the behavioral results.

Investigators in our area are often criticized for the sin of "reductionism." I do not believe our goal is the substitution of biological for social explanation in the sense that an early, primitive behaviorism attempted to reduce mind (which we now call "cognitive processes") to behavior. We are not attempting to create a new phrenology based on "bumps" *in* the brain. Rather, our aim is to place our science of mind and behavior back into the biological context from which it emerged almost a century ago. We are in a much better position to do so today that we were then.

REFERENCES

Broverman, D. M., Klaiber, E. L., Kobyaski, Y., & Vogel, W. Roles of activation and inhibition in sex differences in cognitive abilities. *Psychological Review,* 1968, *75,* 23–50.

Carrol, E. N, Zuckerman, M., & Vogel, W. H. A test of the optimal level of arousal theory of sensation seeking. *Journal of Pesonality and Social Psychology,* 1982, *42,* 572–575.

Coursey, R. D., Buchsbaum, M. S., & Frankel, B. L. Personality measures and evoked responses in chronic insomniacs. *Journal of Abnormal Psychology,* 1975, *84,* 239–249.

Daitzman, R., & Zuckerman, M. Disinhibitory sensation seeking and gonadal hormones. *Personality and Individual Differences,* 1980, *1,* 103–110.

Demisch, L., Georgi, K., Patzke, B., Demisch, K., & Bochnik, H. J. *Correlation of platelet MAO activity with introversion: A study on a German rural population. Psychiatry Research,* 1982, *6,* 303–311.

Eysenck, H. J. *The biological basis of personality.* Springfield, Ill.: Thomas, 1967.

Eysenck, H. J. General features of the model. In H. J. Eysenck (Ed.), *A model for personality*. New York: Springer-Verlag, 1981.

Gale, A. EEG studies of extraversion-introversion: What's the next step? In R. Lynn (Ed.) Dimensions of personality: Papers in honour of H. J. Eysenck. New York: Pergamon, 1981.

Gattaz, W. F., & Beckmann, H. Platelet MAO activity and personality characteristics: A study in schizophrenic patients and normal individuals. *Acta Psychiatrica Scandinavica,* 1981, *63,* 479-485.

Haier, R. J., Buchsbaum, M. S., Murphy, D. L., Gottesman, I. T., & Coursey, R. D. Psychiatric vulnerability, monoamine oxidase and the average evoked potential. *Archives of General Psychiatry,* 1980, *37,* 340-345.

Hare, R. D. Psychophysiological studies of psychopathy. In D. C. Fowles (Ed.), *Clinical Applications of psychophysiology.* New York: Columbia University Press, 1975.

Hodges, W. F. The psychophysiology of anxiety. In M. Zuckerman, & C. D. Spielberger (Eds.), *Emotions and anxiety: New concepts, methods and applications.* Hillsdale, N.J.: Lawrence Erlbaum Associates, 1976.

Jinks, J. L., & Fulker, D. W. Comparison of the biometrical genetical, MAVA, and the classical approaches to the analysis of human behavior. *Psychological Bulletin,* 1970, *73,* 311-349.

Lader, M. The psychophysiology of anxious and depressed patients. In D. C. Fowles (Ed.), *Clinical applications of psychophysiology.* New York: Columbia University Press, 1975.

Lader, M. The orienting reflex in anxiety and schizophrenia. In H. D. Kimmel, E. H. van Olst, & J. F. Orlebeke (Eds.), *The orienting reflex in humans.* Hillsdale, N.J.: Lawrence Erlbaum Associates, 1979.

Lukas, J. H., & Siegel, J. Cortical mechanisms that augment or reduce evoked potentials in cats. *Science,* 1977, *196,* 73-75.

Martin, N. G., Eaves, L. J., & Fulker, D. W. The genetical relationship of impulsiveness and sensation seeking to Eysenck's personality dimensions. *Acta Genet Med Gemellol,* 1979, *28,* 197-210.

Murtaugh, T. L. *Neurophysiological factors in the choice of abused substances.* Unpublished doctoral dissertation, University of Delaware, 1979.

Neary, R. S., & Zuckerman, M. Sensation seeking, trait and state anxiety, and the electrodermal orienting reflex. *Psychophysiology,* 1976, *13,* 205-211.

Pribram, K. H., & McGuiness, D. Arousal, activation, and effort in the control of attention. *Psychological Review,* 1975, *82,* 116-149.

Ridgeway, D., & Hare, R. D. Sensation seeking and psychophysiological responses to auditory stimulation. *Psychophysiology,* 1981, *18,* 613-618.

Rust, J. Cortical evoked potential, personality, and intelligence. *Journal of Comparative and Physiological Psychology,* 1975, *89,* 1220-1226.

Sokolov, E. N. Neuronal models and the orienting reflex. In M. A. Brazier (Ed.), *The central nervous system and behavior.* New York: Macy, 1960.

Stelmack, R. M. Extraversion, orienting reaction, habituation rate, and sensitivity to visual stimuli. In H. D. Kimmel, E. H. van Olst, J. F. Orlebeke (Eds.), *The orienting reflex in humans.* Hillsdale, N.J.: Lawrence Erlbaum Associates, 1979.

Stelmack, R. M. The biological basis of introversion-extraversion: Psychophysiological evidence. Paper presented at the meeting of the American Psychological Association, Los Angeles, August 1981.(a)

Stelmack, R. M. The psychophysiology of extraversion and neuroticism. In H. J. Eysenck (Ed.), *A model for personality.* New York: Springer-Verlag, 1981.(b)

Stelmack, R. M., Achorn, E., & Mechaud, A. Extraversion and individual differences in auditory evoked response. *Psychophysiology,* 1977, *14,* 368-374.

Zuckerman, M. *Sensation seeking: Beyond the optimal level of arousal.* Hillsdale, N.J.: Lawrence Erlbaum Associates, 1979.

Zuckerman, M., Buchsbaum, M. S., & Murphy, D. L. Sensation seeking and its biological correlates. *Psychological Bulletin,* 1980, *88,* 187–214.

Zuckerman, M., Murtaugh, T. M., & Siegel, J. Sensation seeking and cortical augmenting-reducing. *Psychophysiology,* 1974, *11,* 535–542.

Author Index

Subject Index